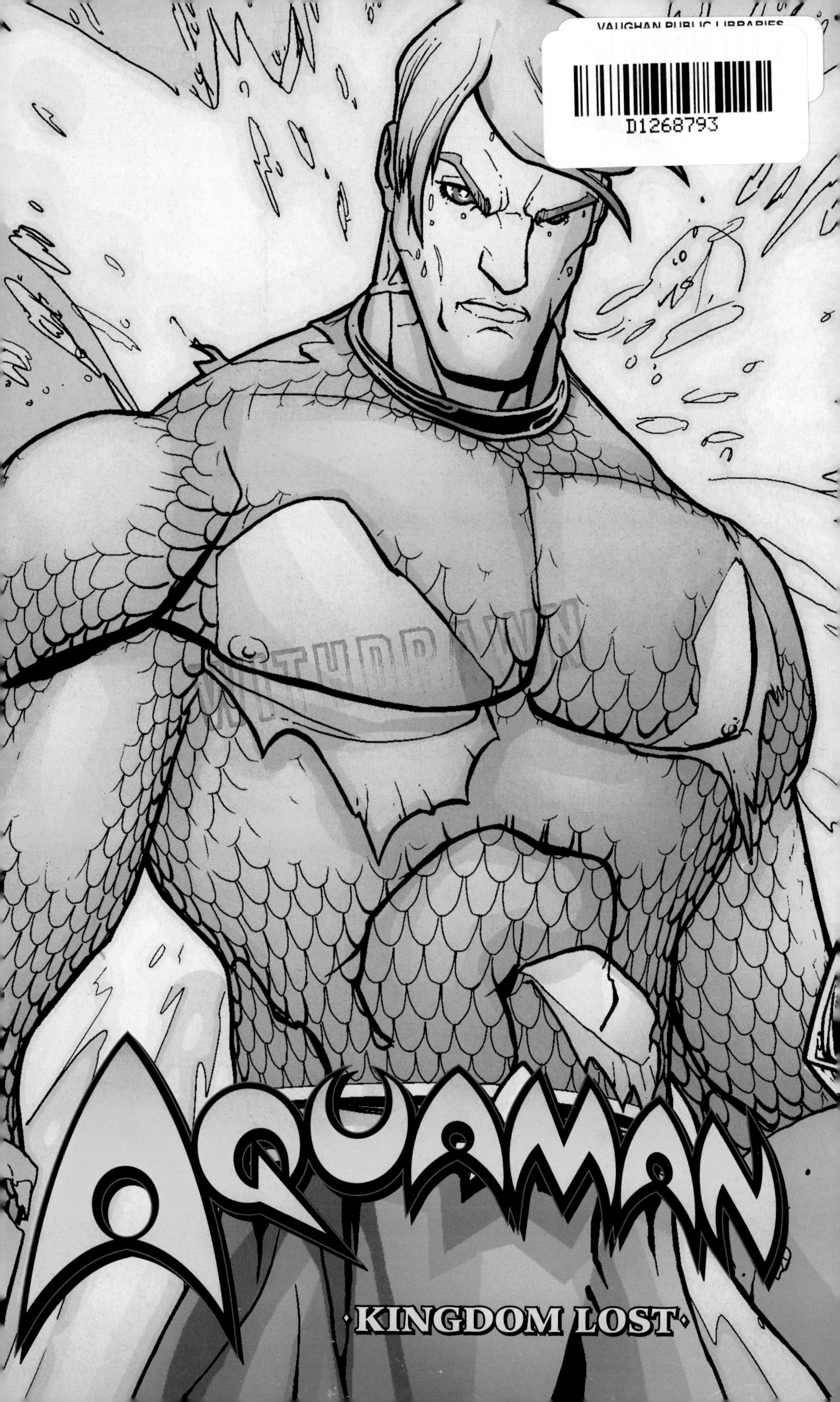
AQUAMAN
·KINGDOM LOST·

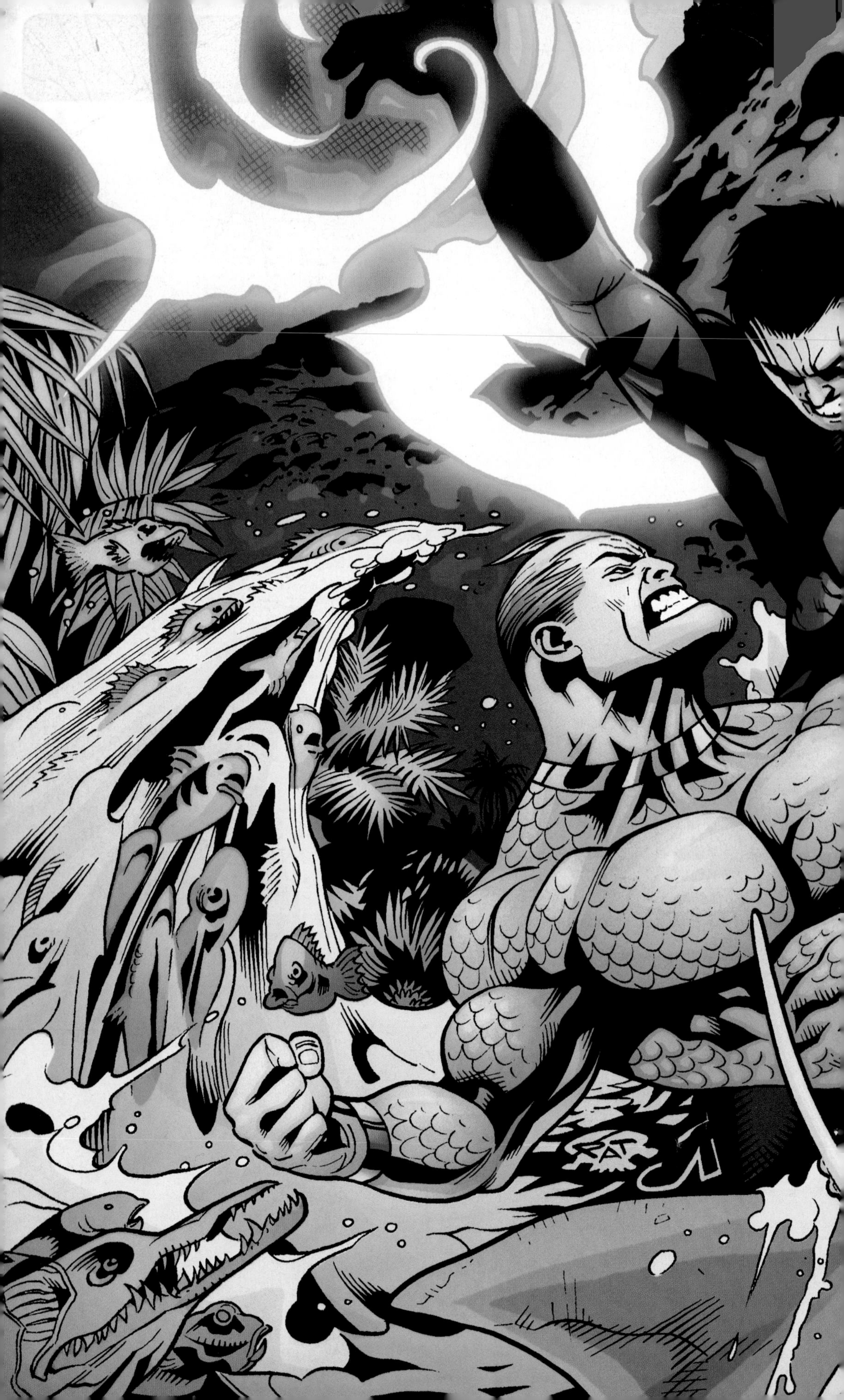

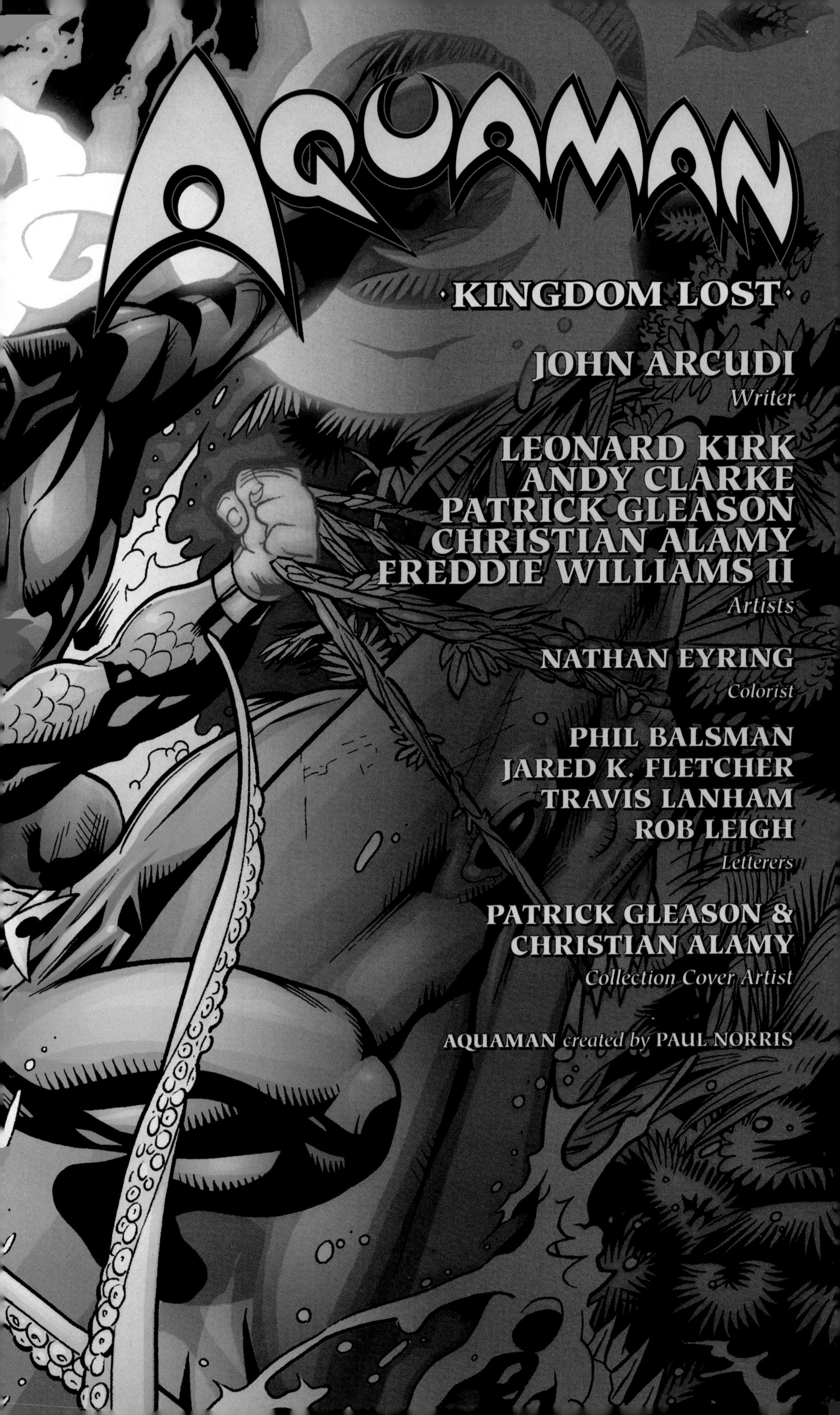

AQUAMAN

·KINGDOM LOST·

JOHN ARCUDI
Writer

LEONARD KIRK
ANDY CLARKE
PATRICK GLEASON
CHRISTIAN ALAMY
FREDDIE WILLIAMS II
Artists

NATHAN EYRING
Colorist

PHIL BALSMAN
JARED K. FLETCHER
TRAVIS LANHAM
ROB LEIGH
Letterers

PATRICK GLEASON &
CHRISTIAN ALAMY
Collection Cover Artist

AQUAMAN *created by* **PAUL NORRIS**

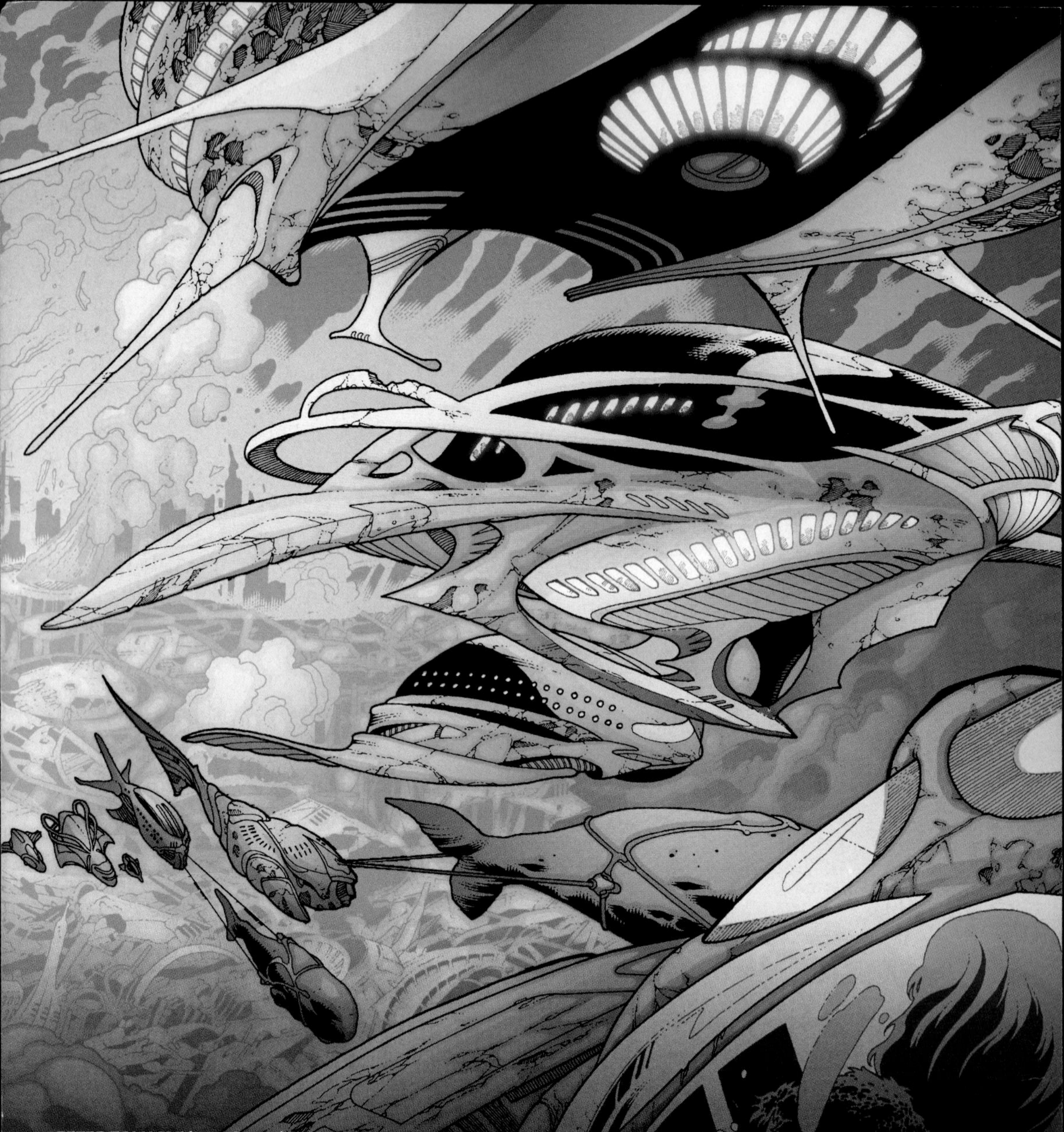

PETER TOMASI Editor – Original Series
MICHAEL SIGLAIN Associate Editor – Original Series
HARVEY RICHARDS Assistant Editor – Original Series
JEB WOODARD Group Editor – Collected Editions
STEVE COOK Design Director – Books
CURTIS KING JR Publication Design

BOB HARRAS Senior VP – Editor-in-Chief, DC Comics

DIANE NELSON President
DAN DiDIO Publisher
JIM LEE Publisher
GEOFF JOHNS President & Chief Creative Officer
AMIT DESAI Executive VP – Business & Marketing Strategy, Direct to Consumer & Global Franchise Management
SAM ADES Senior VP – Direct to Consumer
BOBBIE CHASE VP – Talent Development
MARK CHIARELLO Senior VP – Art, Design & Collected Editions
JOHN CUNNINGHAM Senior VP – Sales & Trade Marketing
ANNE DePIES Senior VP – Business Strategy, Finance & Administration
DON FALLETTI VP – Manufacturing Operations
LAWRENCE GANEM VP – Editorial Administration & Talent Relations
ALISON GILL Senior VP – Manufacturing & Operations
HANK KANALZ Senior VP – Editorial Strategy & Administration
JAY KOGAN VP – Legal Affairs
THOMAS LOFTUS VP – Business Affairs
JACK MAHAN VP – Business Affairs
NICK J. NAPOLITANO VP – Manufacturing Administration
EDDIE SCANNELL VP – Consumer Marketing
COURTNEY SIMMONS Senior VP – Publicity & Communications
JIM (SKI) SOKOLOWSKI VP – Comic Book Specialty Sales & Trade Marketing
NANCY SPEARS VP – Mass, Book, Digital Sales & Trade Marketing

AQUAMAN: KINGDOM LOST

DC Comics, 2900 West Alameda Ave., Burbank, CA 91505
Printed by Vanguard Graphics, LLC, Ithaca, NY, USA. 6/23/17. First Printing.
ISBN: 978-1-4012-7129-9

Library of Congress Cataloging-in-Publication Data is available.

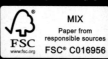

MIX
Paper from responsible sources
FSC® C016956

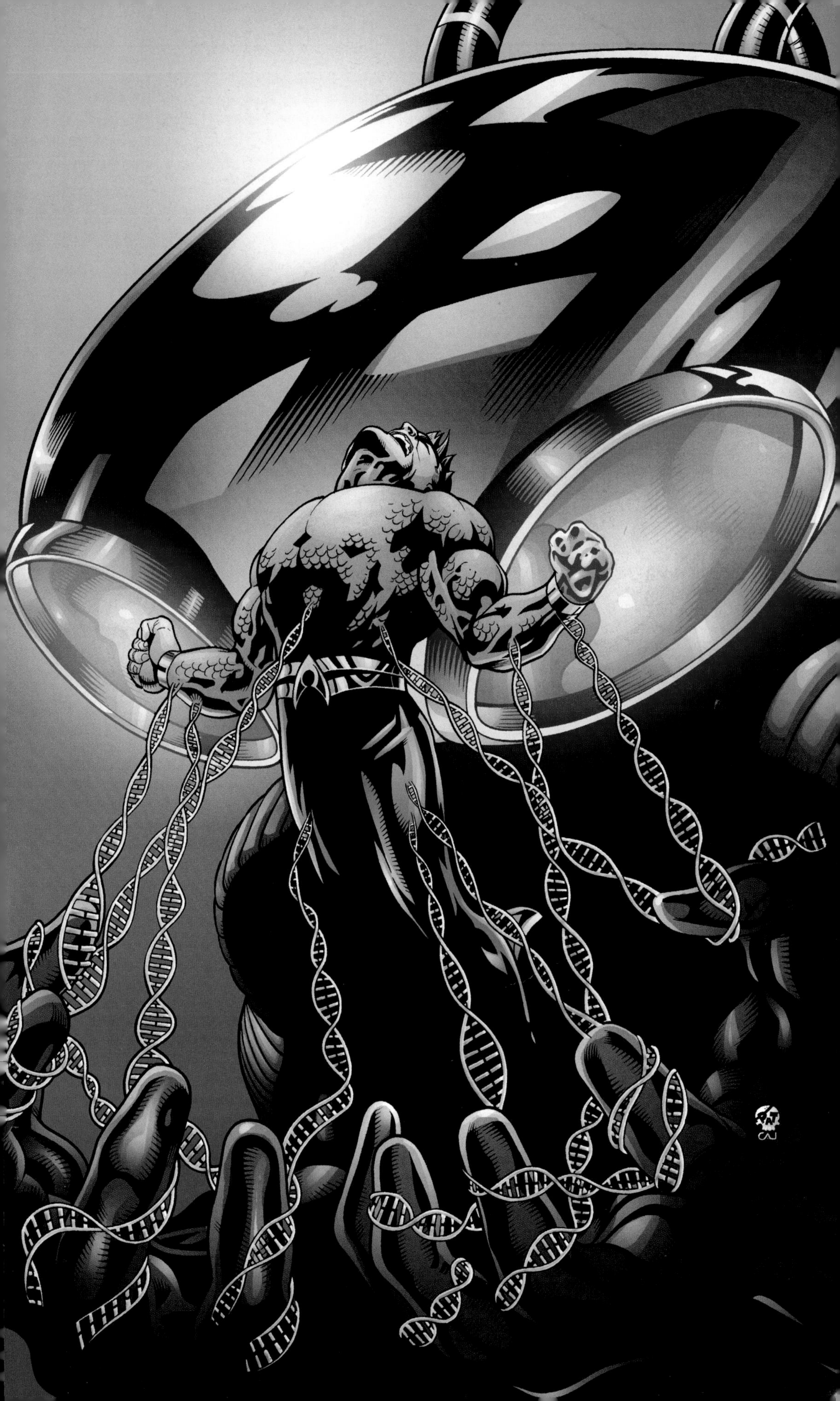

THE SHADE OF THINGS TO COME

JOHN ARCUDI
Writer

PATRICK GLEASON
Penciller

CHRISTIAN ALAMY
Inker

NATHAN EYRING
Colorist

PHIL BALSMAN
Letterer

**PATRICK GLEASON,
CHRISTIAN ALAMY &
NATHAN EYRING**
Cover

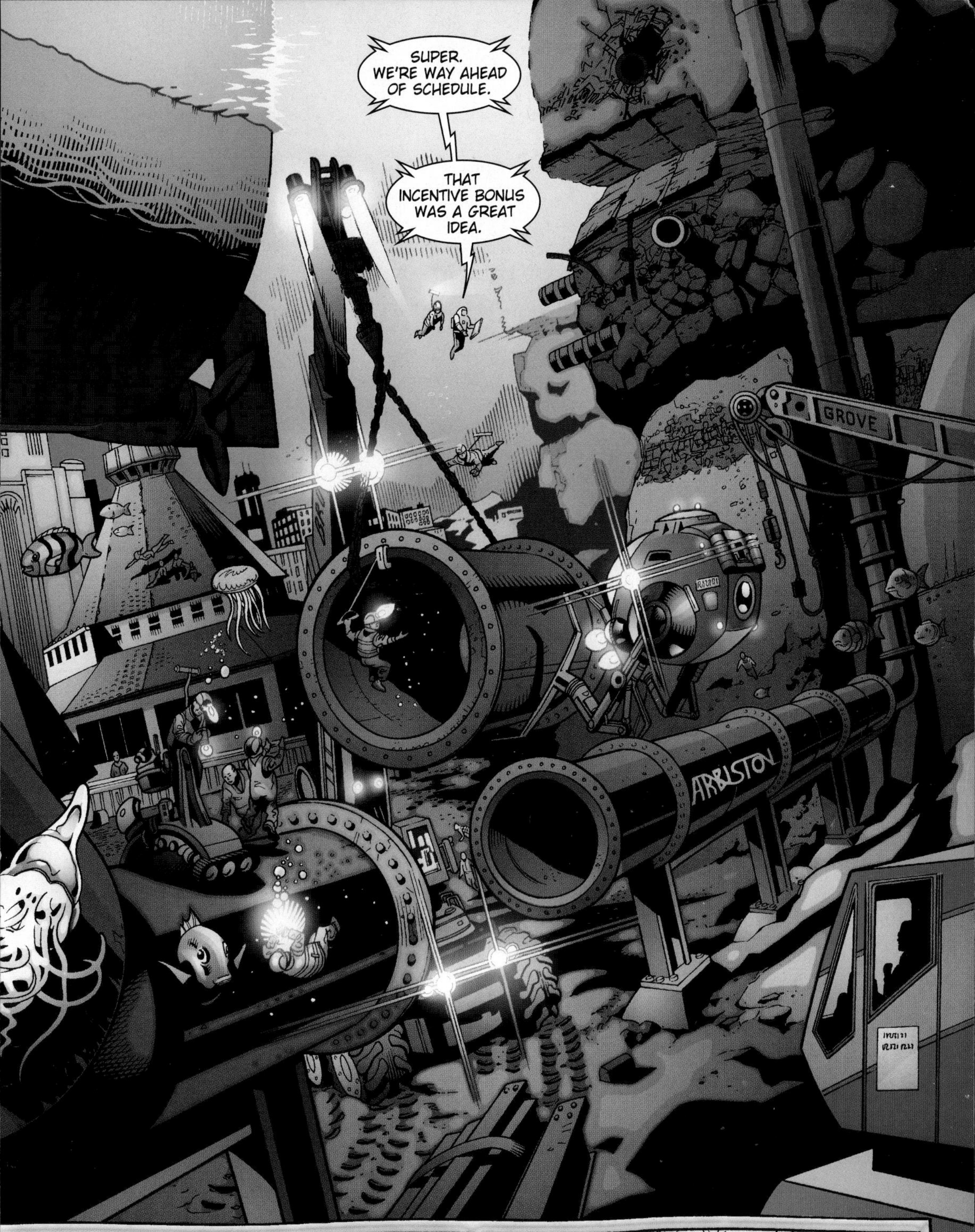
SUPER. WE'RE WAY AHEAD OF SCHEDULE.
THAT INCENTIVE BONUS WAS A GREAT IDEA.
GROVE
ARBISTON

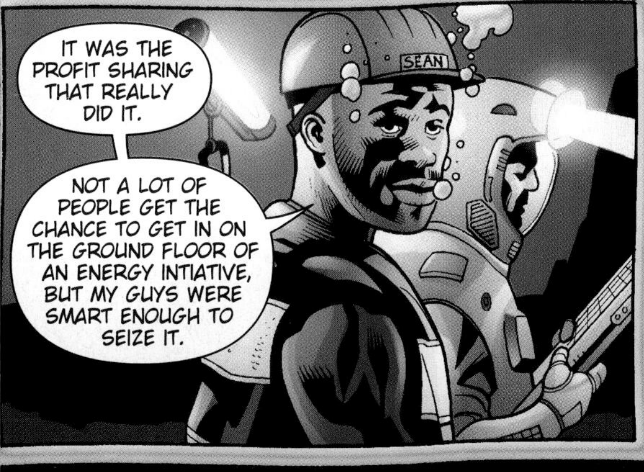
IT WAS THE PROFIT SHARING THAT REALLY DID IT.
NOT A LOT OF PEOPLE GET THE CHANCE TO GET IN ON THE GROUND FLOOR OF AN ENERGY INTIATIVE, BUT MY GUYS WERE SMART ENOUGH TO SEIZE IT.
SEAN

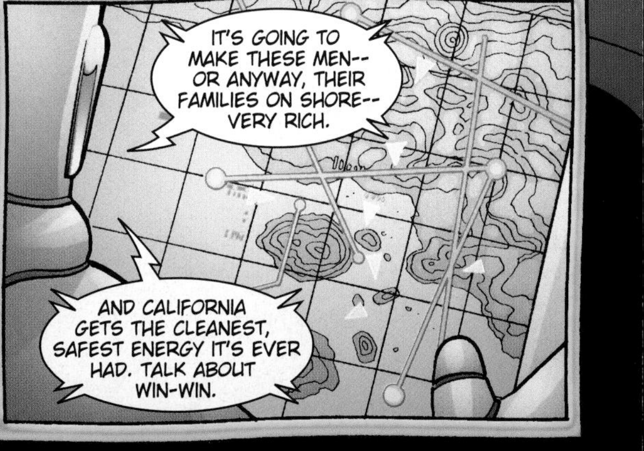
IT'S GOING TO MAKE THESE MEN-- OR ANYWAY, THEIR FAMILIES ON SHORE-- VERY RICH.
AND CALIFORNIA GETS THE CLEANEST, SAFEST ENERGY IT'S EVER HAD. TALK ABOUT WIN-WIN.

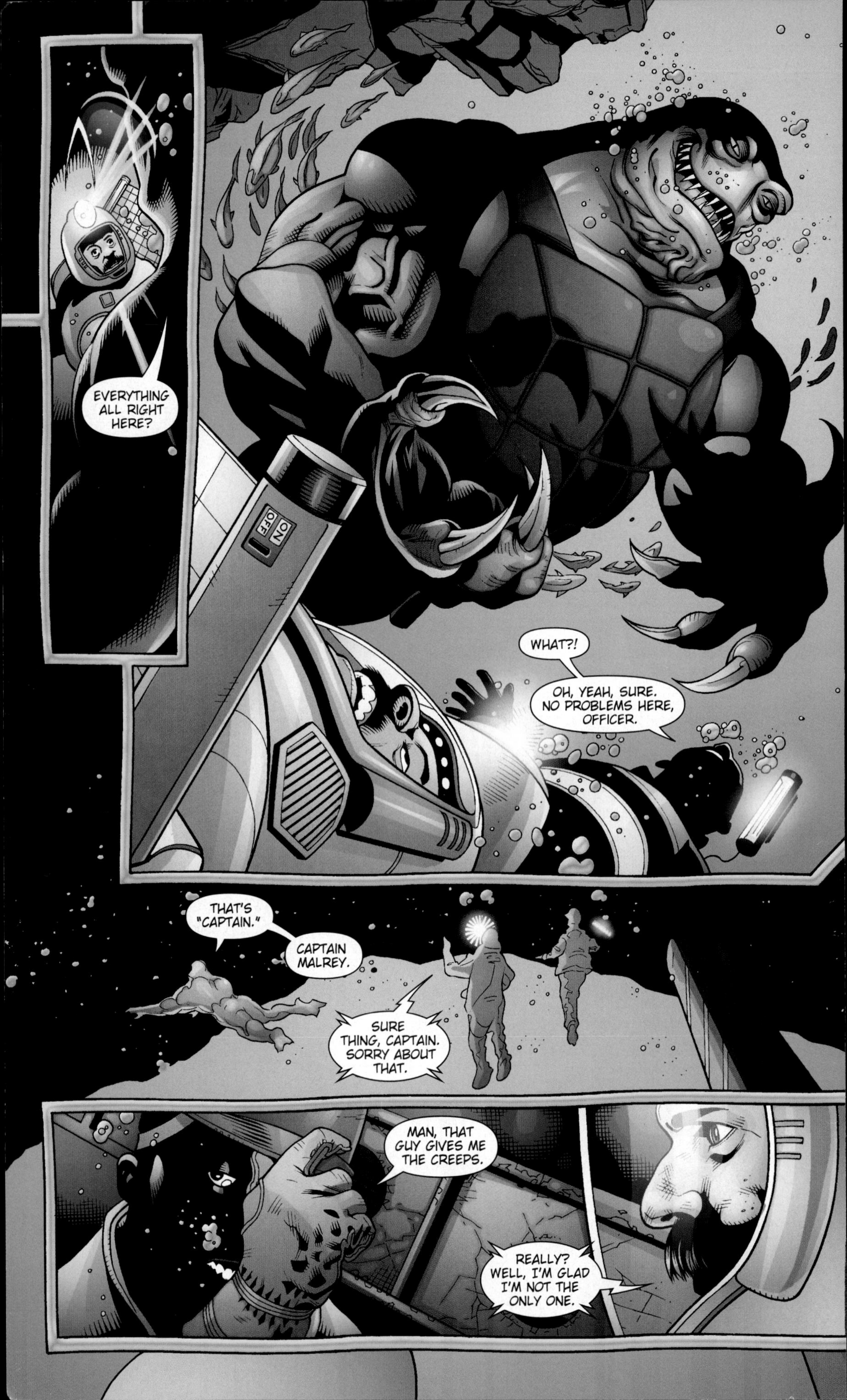
EVERYTHING ALL RIGHT HERE?
ON OFF
WHAT?!
OH, YEAH, SURE. NO PROBLEMS HERE, OFFICER.
THAT'S "CAPTAIN."
CAPTAIN MALREY.
SURE THING, CAPTAIN. SORRY ABOUT THAT.
MAN, THAT GUY GIVES ME THE CREEPS.
REALLY? WELL, I'M GLAD I'M NOT THE ONLY ONE.

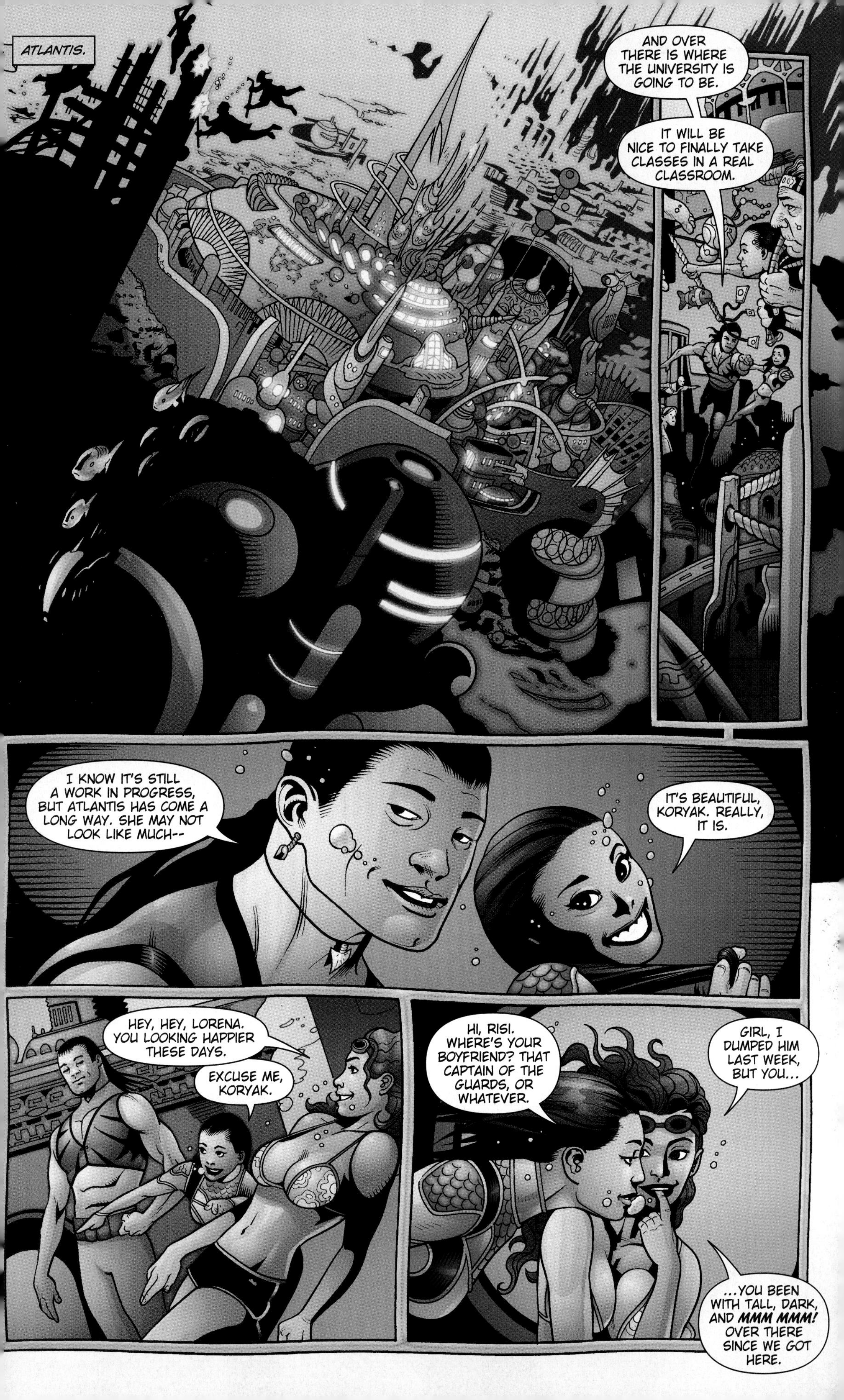
ATLANTIS.
AND OVER THERE IS WHERE THE UNIVERSITY IS GOING TO BE.
IT WILL BE NICE TO FINALLY TAKE CLASSES IN A REAL CLASSROOM.
I KNOW IT'S STILL A WORK IN PROGRESS, BUT ATLANTIS HAS COME A LONG WAY. SHE MAY NOT LOOK LIKE MUCH--
IT'S BEAUTIFUL, KORYAK. REALLY, IT IS.
HEY, HEY, LORENA. YOU LOOKING HAPPIER THESE DAYS.
EXCUSE ME, KORYAK.
HI, RISI. WHERE'S YOUR BOYFRIEND? THAT CAPTAIN OF THE GUARDS, OR WHATEVER.
GIRL, I DUMPED HIM LAST WEEK, BUT YOU...
...YOU BEEN WITH TALL, DARK, AND MMM MMM! OVER THERE SINCE WE GOT HERE.

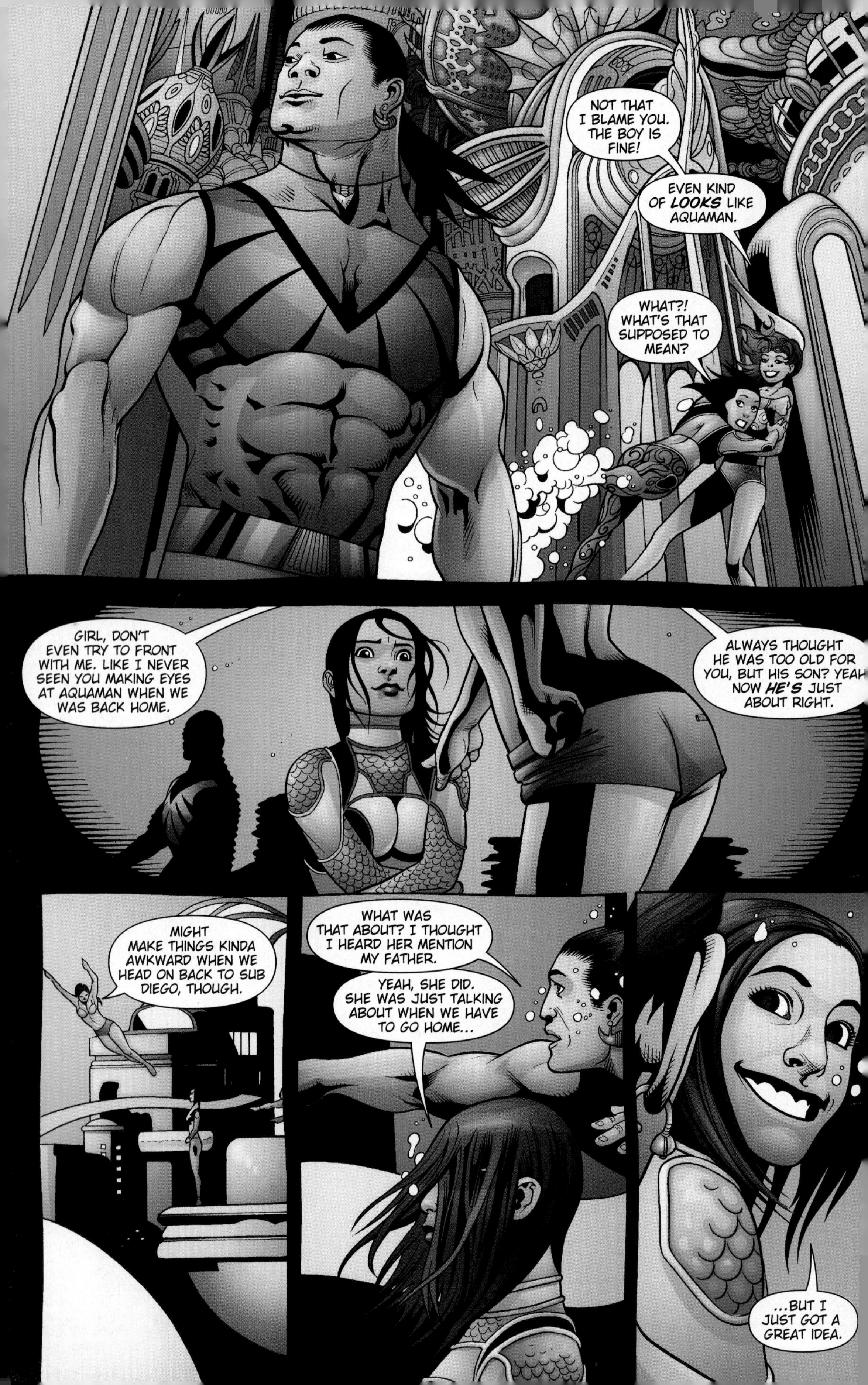
NOT THAT I BLAME YOU. THE BOY IS FINE!
EVEN KIND OF LOOKS LIKE AQUAMAN.
WHAT?! WHAT'S THAT SUPPOSED TO MEAN?
GIRL, DON'T EVEN TRY TO FRONT WITH ME. LIKE I NEVER SEEN YOU MAKING EYES AT AQUAMAN WHEN WE WAS BACK HOME.
ALWAYS THOUGHT HE WAS TOO OLD FOR YOU, BUT HIS SON? YEAH NOW HE'S JUST ABOUT RIGHT.
MIGHT MAKE THINGS KINDA AWKWARD WHEN WE HEAD ON BACK TO SUB DIEGO, THOUGH.
WHAT WAS THAT ABOUT? I THOUGHT I HEARD HER MENTION MY FATHER.
YEAH, SHE DID. SHE WAS JUST TALKING ABOUT WHEN WE HAVE TO GO HOME...
...BUT I JUST GOT A GREAT IDEA.

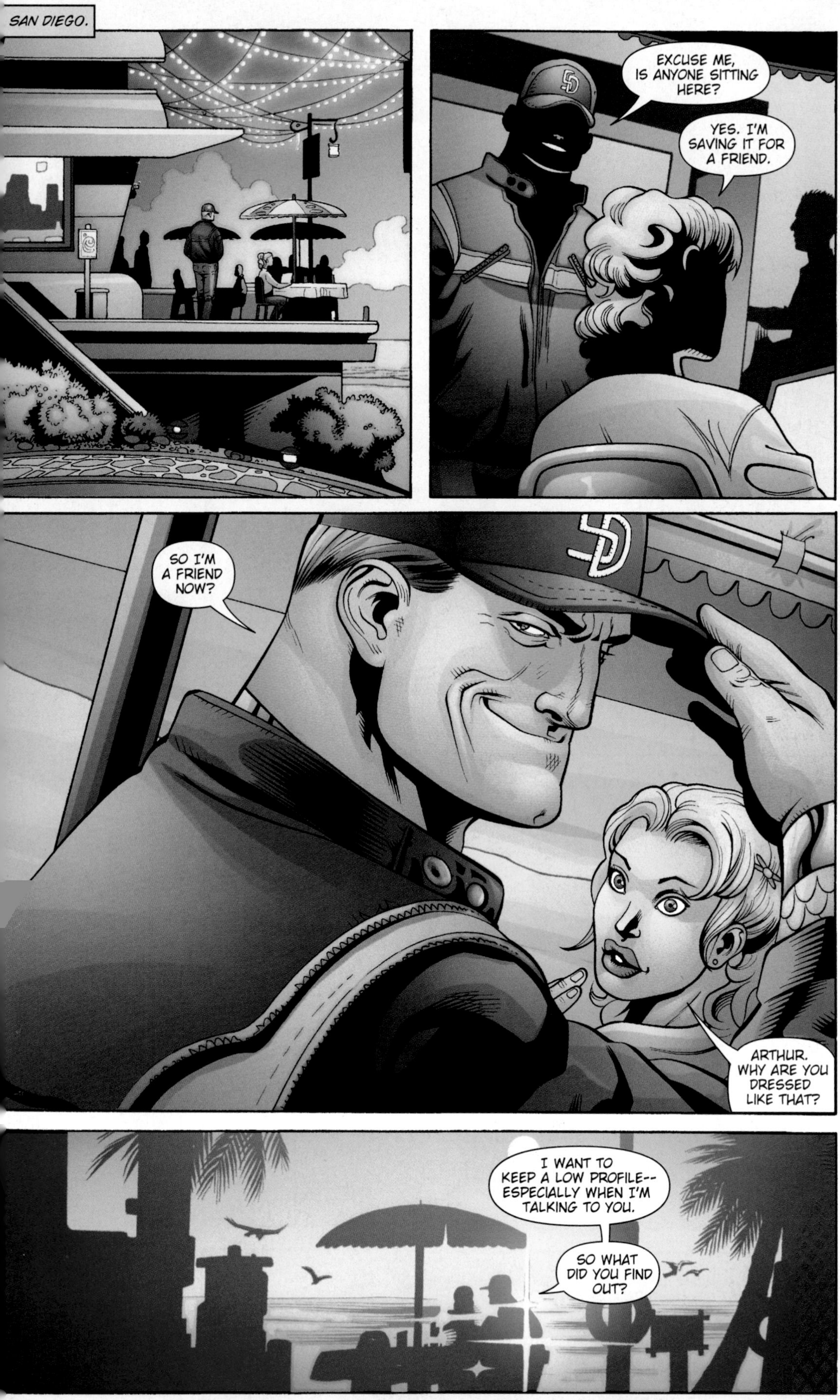
SAN DIEGO.
EXCUSE ME, IS ANYONE SITTING HERE?
YES. I'M SAVING IT FOR A FRIEND.
SO I'M A FRIEND NOW?
ARTHUR. WHY ARE YOU DRESSED LIKE THAT?
I WANT TO KEEP A LOW PROFILE-- ESPECIALLY WHEN I'M TALKING TO YOU.
SO WHAT DID YOU FIND OUT?

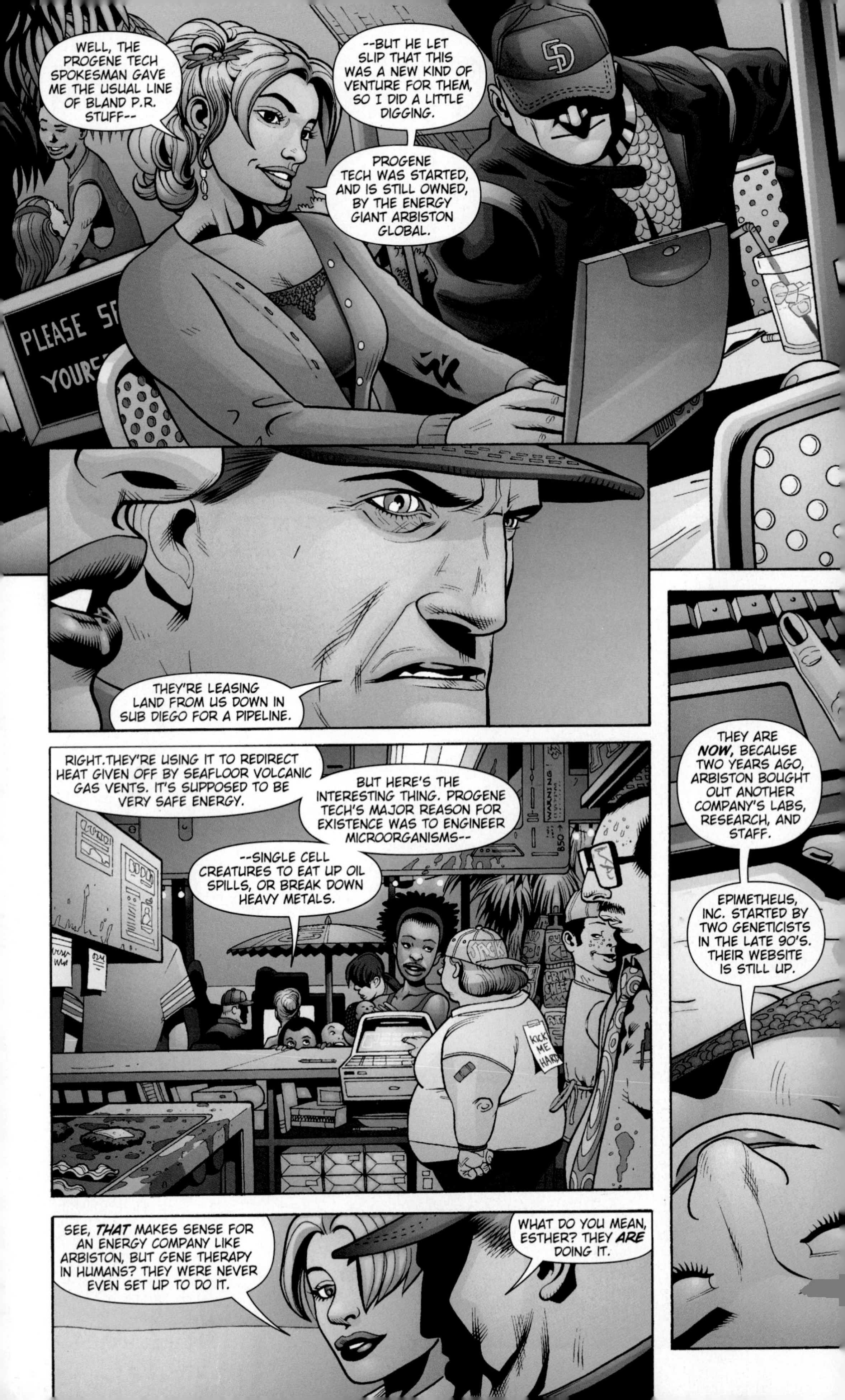
WELL, THE PROGENE TECH SPOKESMAN GAVE ME THE USUAL LINE OF BLAND P.R. STUFF--
--BUT HE LET SLIP THAT THIS WAS A NEW KIND OF VENTURE FOR THEM, SO I DID A LITTLE DIGGING.
PROGENE TECH WAS STARTED, AND IS STILL OWNED, BY THE ENERGY GIANT ARBISTON GLOBAL.
PLEASE SE
YOURS
THEY'RE LEASING LAND FROM US DOWN IN SUB DIEGO FOR A PIPELINE.
RIGHT. THEY'RE USING IT TO REDIRECT HEAT GIVEN OFF BY SEAFLOOR VOLCANIC GAS VENTS. IT'S SUPPOSED TO BE VERY SAFE ENERGY.
BUT HERE'S THE INTERESTING THING. PROGENE TECH'S MAJOR REASON FOR EXISTENCE WAS TO ENGINEER MICROORGANISMS--
--SINGLE CELL CREATURES TO EAT UP OIL SPILLS, OR BREAK DOWN HEAVY METALS.
WARNING
JACK
KICK ME HARD
THEY ARE ***NOW***, BECAUSE TWO YEARS AGO, ARBISTON BOUGHT OUT ANOTHER COMPANY'S LABS, RESEARCH, AND STAFF.
EPIMETHEUS, INC. STARTED BY TWO GENETICISTS IN THE LATE 90'S. THEIR WEBSITE IS STILL UP.
SEE, ***THAT*** MAKES SENSE FOR AN ENERGY COMPANY LIKE ARBISTON, BUT GENE THERAPY IN HUMANS? THEY WERE NEVER EVEN SET UP TO DO IT.
WHAT DO YOU MEAN, ESTHER? THEY ***ARE*** DOING IT.

TWO YEARS AGO? WHY THEN? WHY NOT--

--AFTER SUB DIEGO SANK? GOOD QUESTION.

OF COURSE IT MIGHT BE A TOTAL COINCIDENCE THAT ARBISTON BOUGHT UP AN ESSENTIALLY MEDICAL--

WAIT. WAIT. HOLD ON.

EPIMETHEUS INC.
THE FUTURE OF GENETIC ENGINEERING IS HERE TODAY
CO-FOUNDERS THOMAS BLOOME & ANTON GEIST

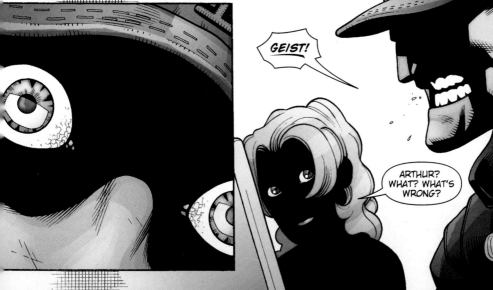

GEIST!

ARTHUR? WHAT? WHAT'S WRONG?

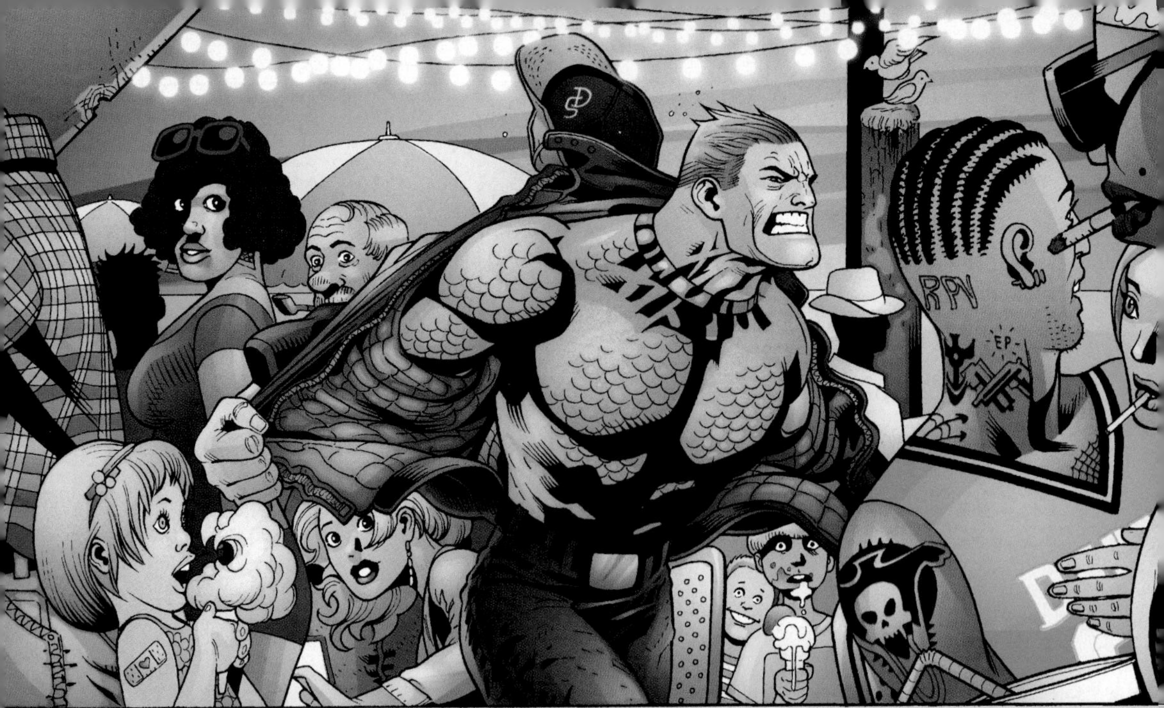

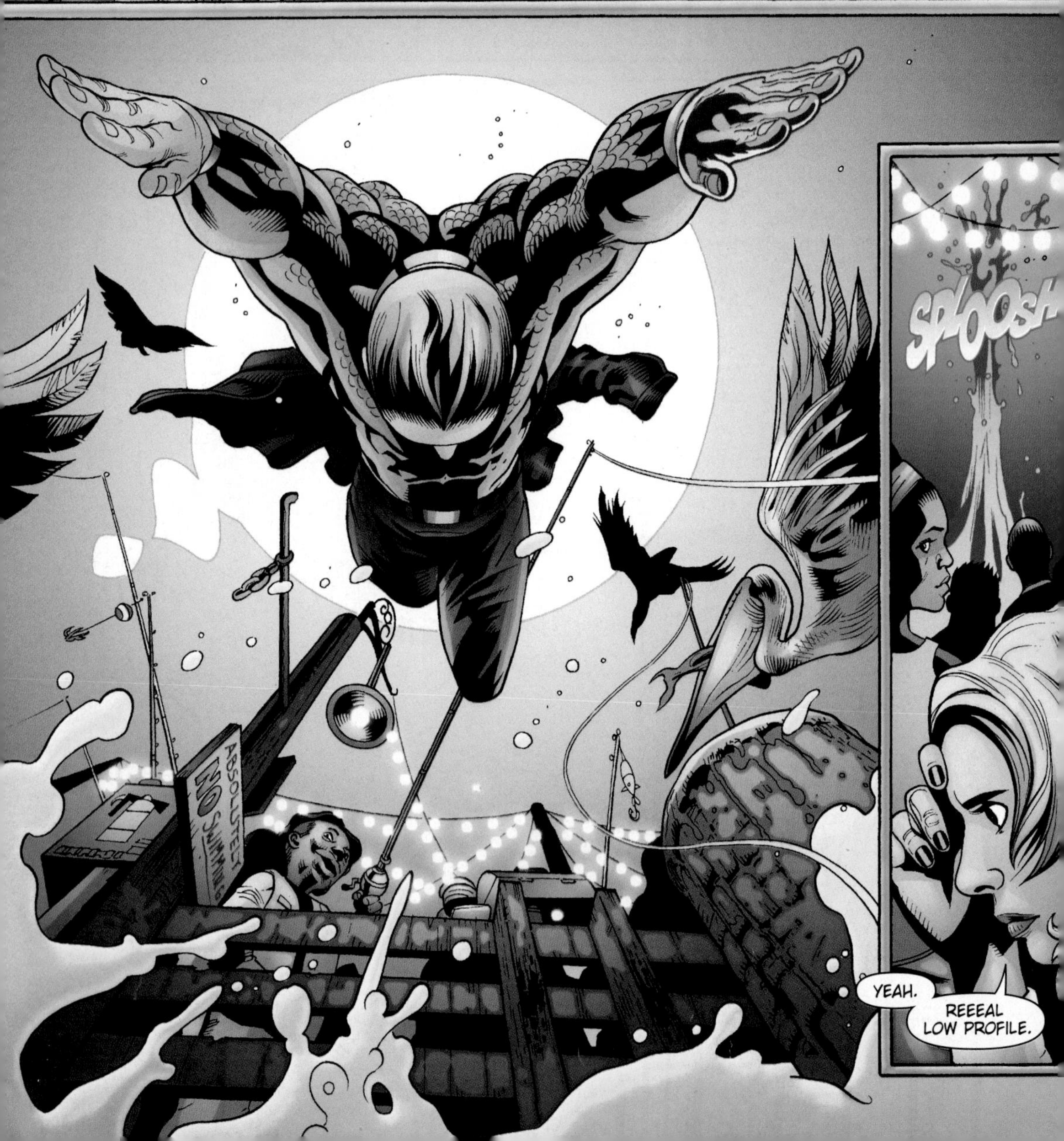
YEAH.
REEEAL LOW PROFILE.

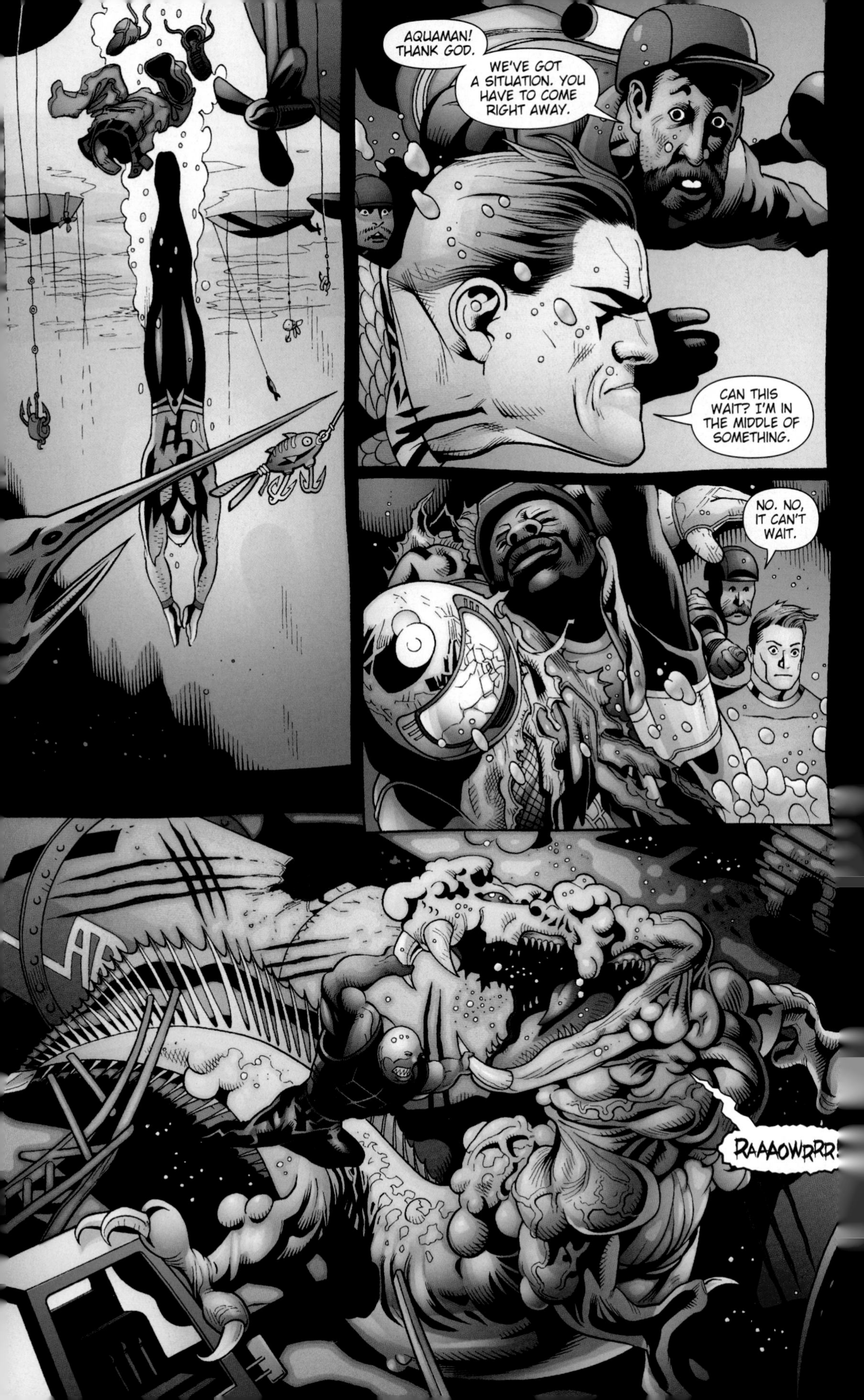
AQUAMAN! THANK GOD.
WE'VE GOT A SITUATION. YOU HAVE TO COME RIGHT AWAY.
CAN THIS WAIT? I'M IN THE MIDDLE OF SOMETHING.
NO. NO, IT CAN'T WAIT.
RAAAOWRRR!

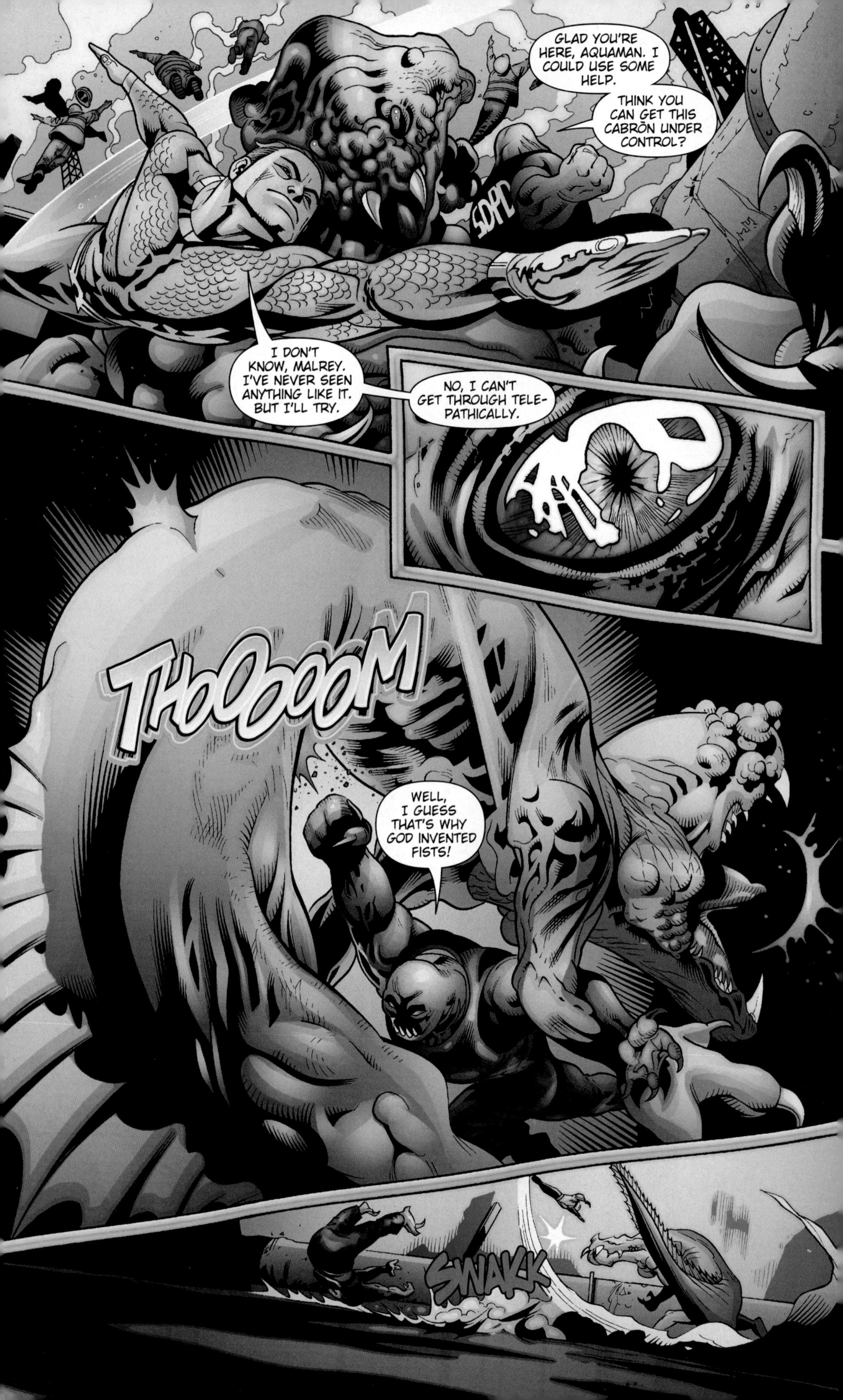
GLAD YOU'RE HERE, AQUAMAN. I COULD USE SOME HELP.
THINK YOU CAN GET THIS CABRÓN UNDER CONTROL?
SDPD
I DON'T KNOW, MALREY. I'VE NEVER SEEN ANYTHING LIKE IT. BUT I'LL TRY.
NO, I CAN'T GET THROUGH TELE-PATHICALLY.
THOOOOOM
WELL, I GUESS THAT'S WHY GOD INVENTED FISTS!
SWAKK

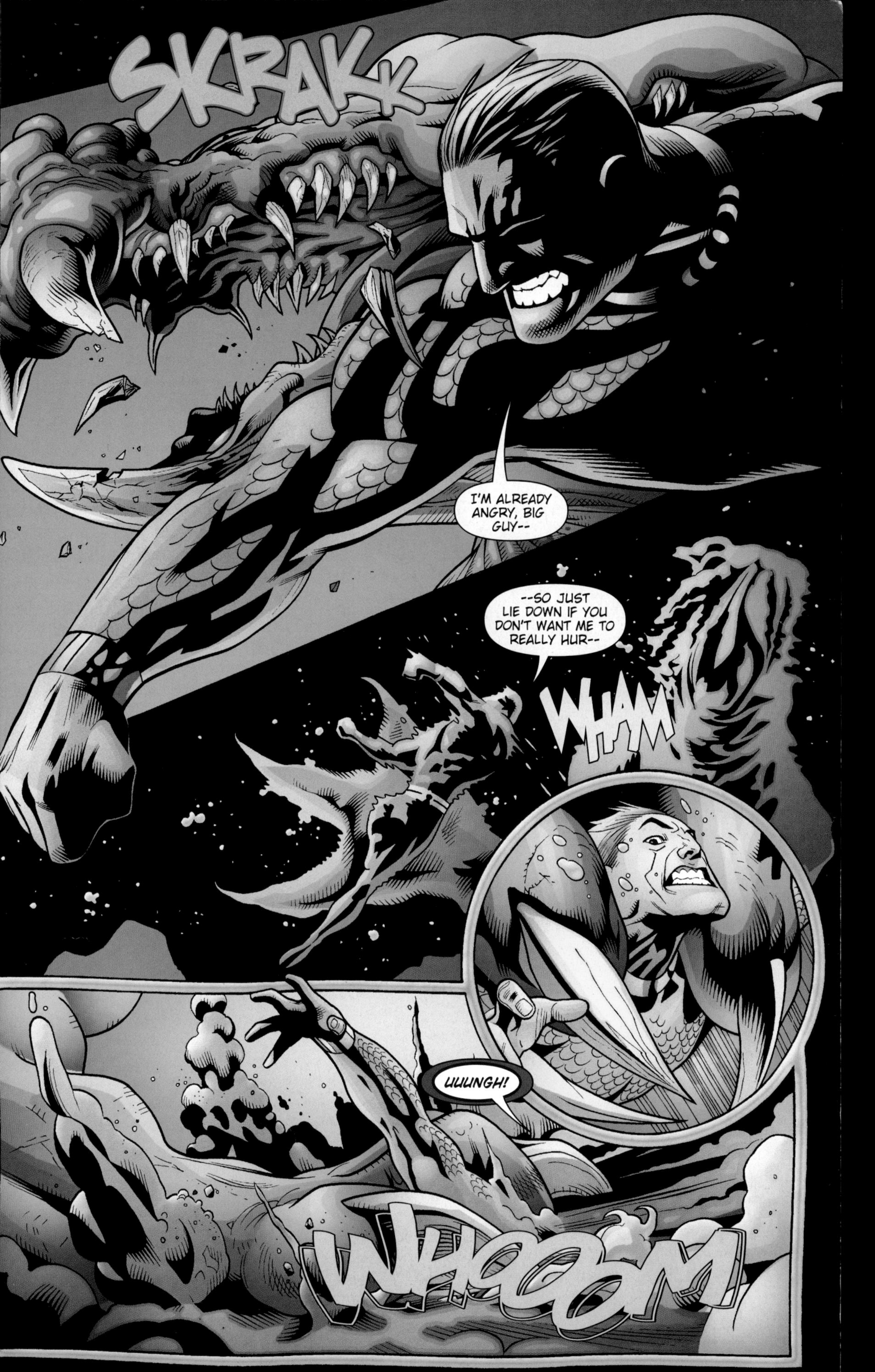
SKRAKK
I'M ALREADY ANGRY, BIG GUY--
--SO JUST LIE DOWN IF YOU DON'T WANT ME TO REALLY HUR--
WHAM
UUUNGH!
WHOOOM

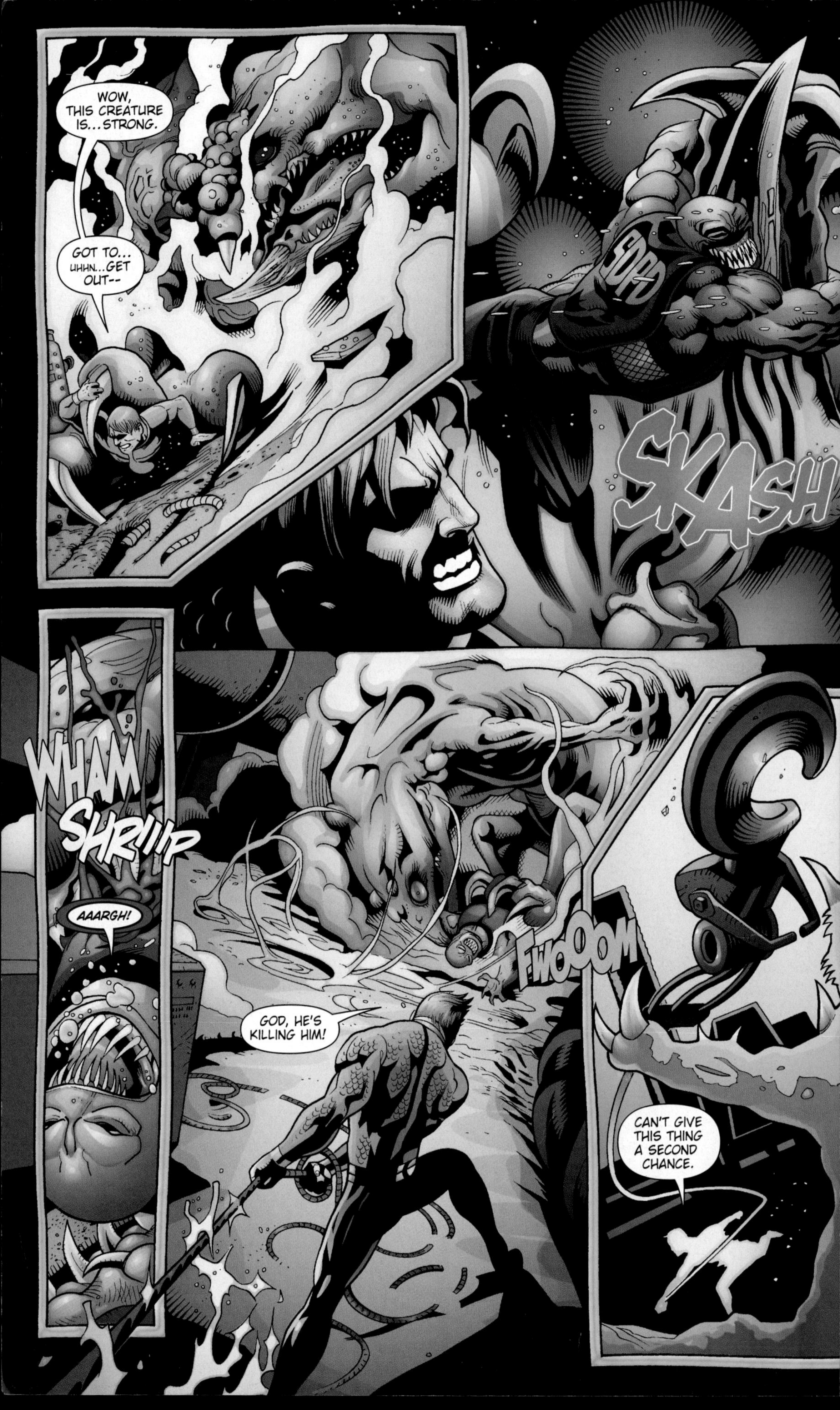

WOW, THIS CREATURE IS...STRONG.
GOT TO... UHHN...GET OUT--
SKASH
WHAM
SHRIIIP
AAARGH!
FWOOOM
GOD, HE'S KILLING HIM!
CAN'T GIVE THIS THING A SECOND CHANCE.

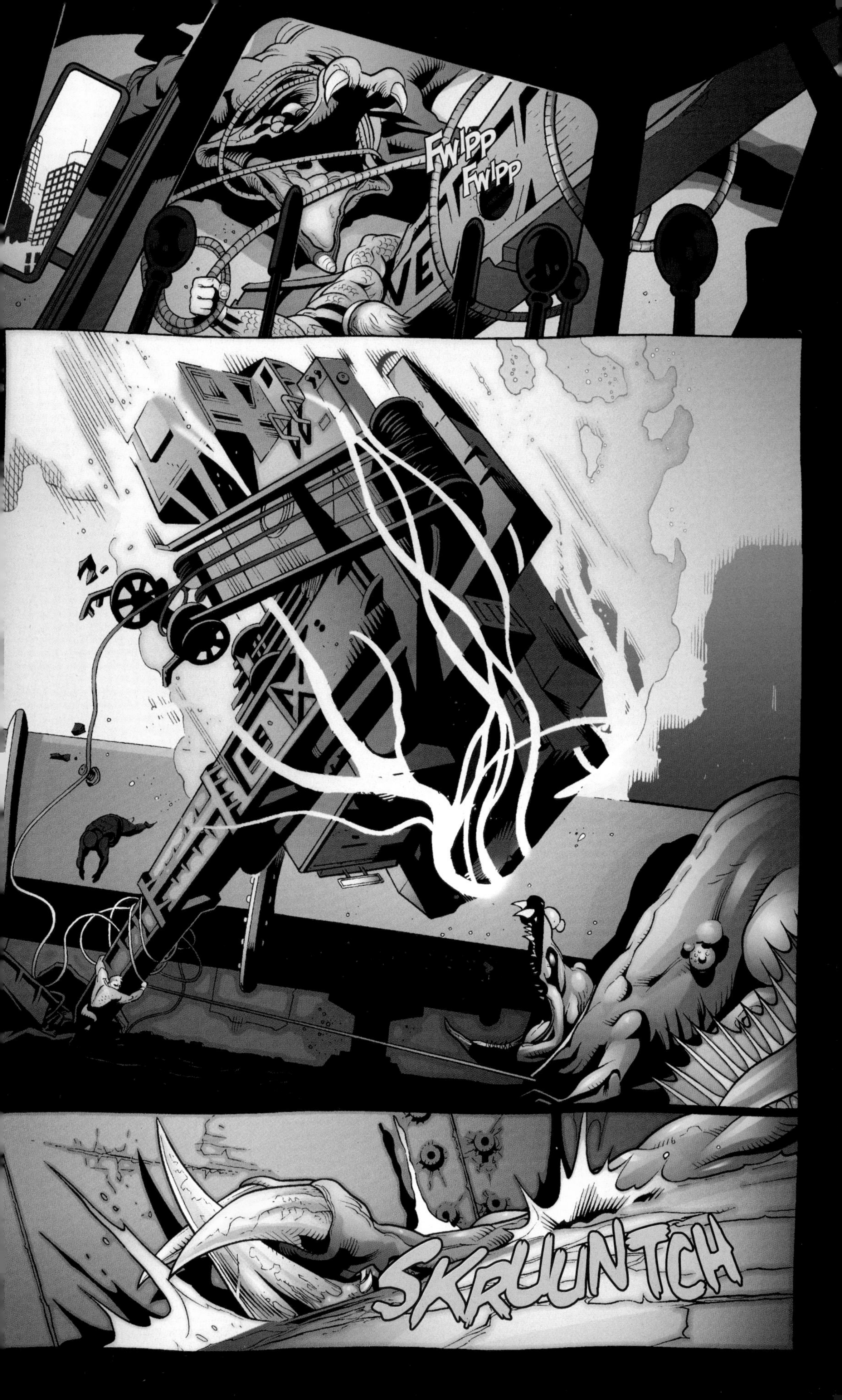
FWIPP
FWIPP
SKRUUNTCH

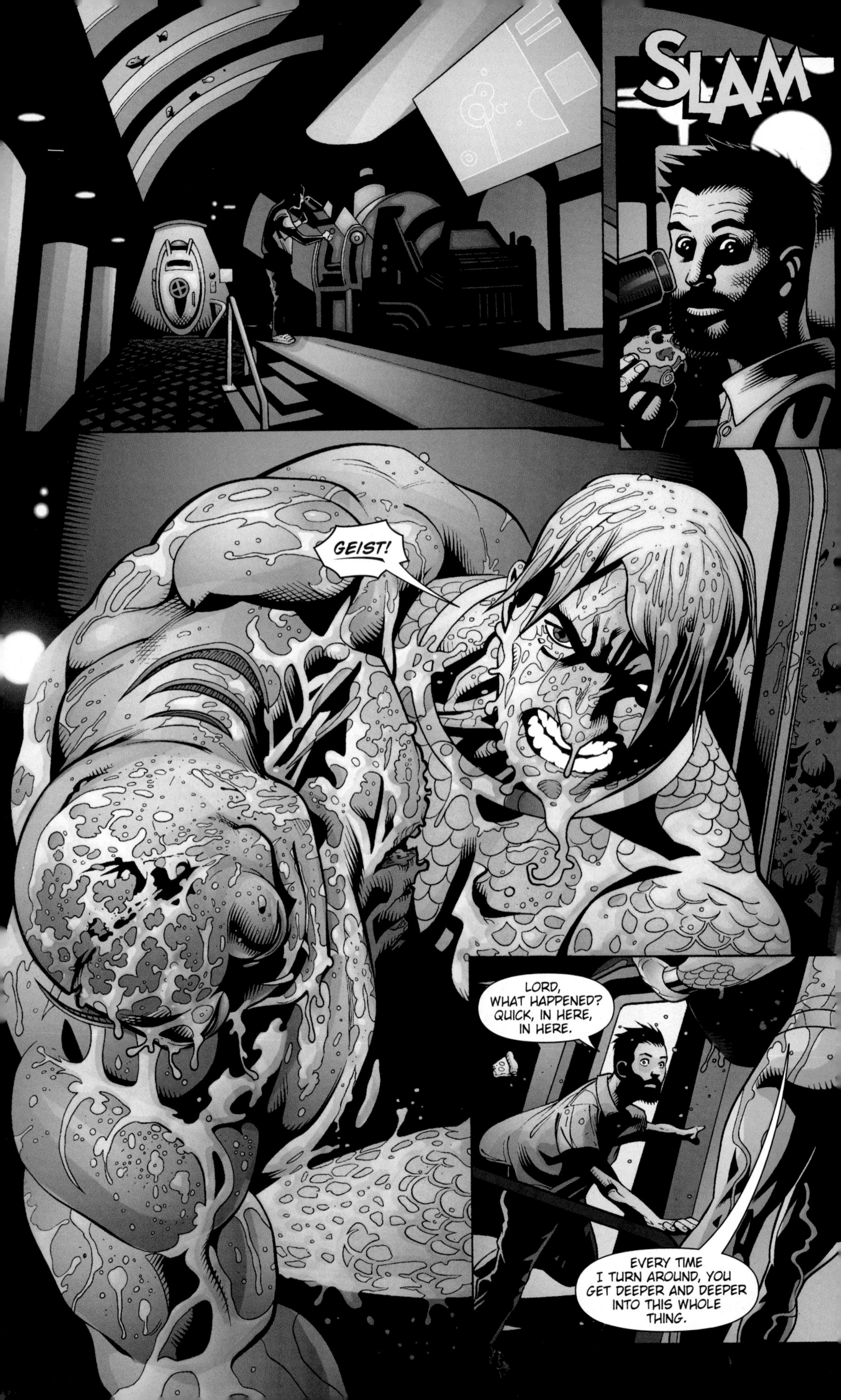
SLAM
GEIST!
LORD, WHAT HAPPENED? QUICK, IN HERE, IN HERE.
EVERY TIME I TURN AROUND, YOU GET DEEPER AND DEEPER INTO THIS WHOLE THING.

YOU'RE NOT MAKING ANY SENSE. I THINK YOU MIGHT BE IN SHOCK, ARTHUR.

YOU NEVER TOLD ME ABOUT EPIMETHEUS GENETICS, OR THAT ARBISTON BOUGHT YOU OUT.

UNN...

WHAT? WHY SHOULD I? ARBISTON BOUGHT EPIMETHEUS AFTER I LEFT THE COMPANY. I DIDN'T MAKE A DIME.

THAT'S NOT THE PROBLEM, GEIST. ARBISTON OWNS PROGENE TECH. THE COMPANY WITH THE PATENT ON MY DNA.

I DIDN'T KNOW THAT.

LOOK, YOU'RE GOING TO HAVE TO LEAVE. I NEED TO STERILIZE THIS TANK.

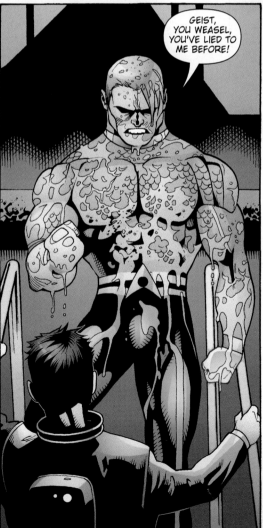

GEIST, YOU WEASEL, YOU'VE LIED TO ME BEFORE!

I CAN EITHER SIT HERE AND TALK WITH YOU, OR I CAN SAVE THIS MAN'S LIFE!

NOW WHICH IS IT GOING TO BE?

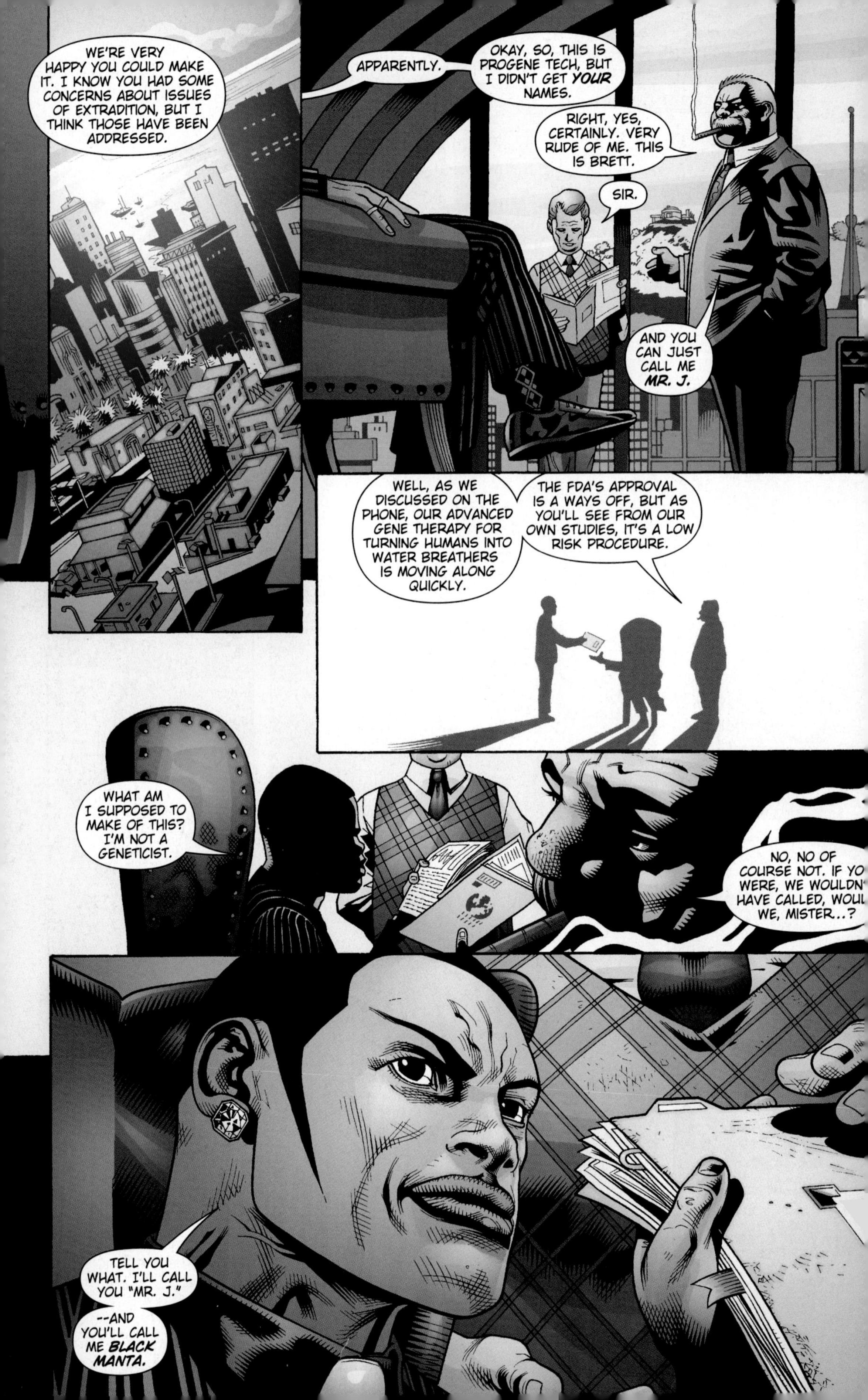
WE'RE VERY HAPPY YOU COULD MAKE IT. I KNOW YOU HAD SOME CONCERNS ABOUT ISSUES OF EXTRADITION, BUT I THINK THOSE HAVE BEEN ADDRESSED.
APPARENTLY.
OKAY, SO, THIS IS PROGENE TECH, BUT I DIDN'T GET *YOUR* NAMES.
RIGHT, YES, CERTAINLY. VERY RUDE OF ME. THIS IS BRETT.
SIR.
AND YOU CAN JUST CALL ME *MR. J.*
WELL, AS WE DISCUSSED ON THE PHONE, OUR ADVANCED GENE THERAPY FOR TURNING HUMANS INTO WATER BREATHERS IS MOVING ALONG QUICKLY.
THE FDA'S APPROVAL IS A WAYS OFF, BUT AS YOU'LL SEE FROM OUR OWN STUDIES, IT'S A LOW RISK PROCEDURE.
WHAT AM I SUPPOSED TO MAKE OF THIS? I'M NOT A GENETICIST.
NO, NO OF COURSE NOT. IF YO WERE, WE WOULDN HAVE CALLED, WOUL WE, MISTER...?
TELL YOU WHAT. I'LL CALL YOU "MR. J."
--AND YOU'LL CALL ME *BLACK MANTA.*

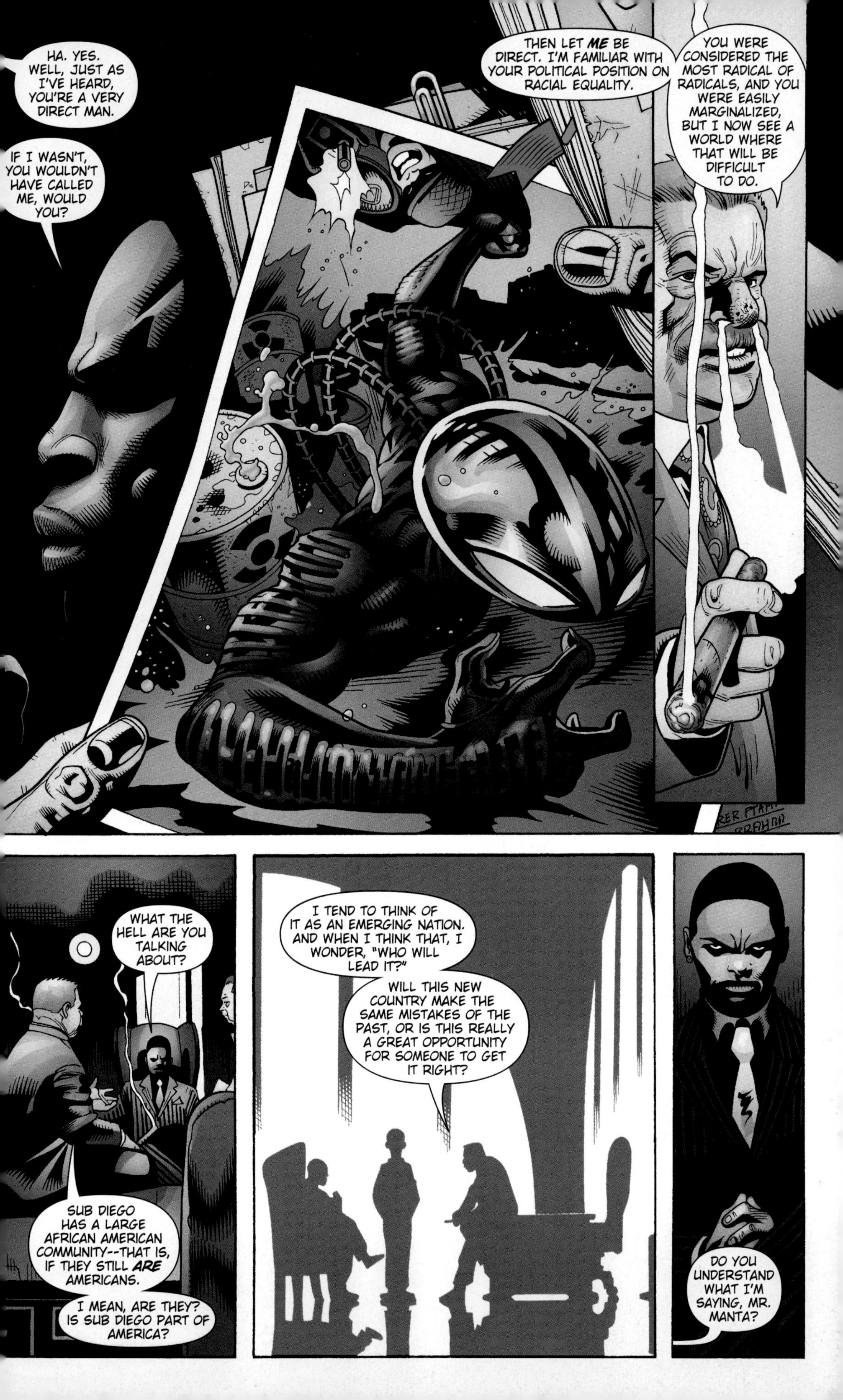
HA. YES. WELL, JUST AS I'VE HEARD, YOU'RE A VERY DIRECT MAN.
IF I WASN'T, YOU WOULDN'T HAVE CALLED ME, WOULD YOU?
THEN LET *ME* BE DIRECT. I'M FAMILIAR WITH YOUR POLITICAL POSITION ON RACIAL EQUALITY.
YOU WERE CONSIDERED THE MOST RADICAL OF RADICALS, AND YOU WERE EASILY MARGINALIZED, BUT I NOW SEE A WORLD WHERE THAT WILL BE DIFFICULT TO DO.
WHAT THE HELL ARE YOU TALKING ABOUT?
SUB DIEGO HAS A LARGE AFRICAN AMERICAN COMMUNITY--THAT IS, IF THEY STILL *ARE* AMERICANS.
I MEAN, ARE THEY? IS SUB DIEGO PART OF AMERICA?
I TEND TO THINK OF IT AS AN EMERGING NATION. AND WHEN I THINK THAT, I WONDER, "WHO WILL LEAD IT?"
WILL THIS NEW COUNTRY MAKE THE SAME MISTAKES OF THE PAST, OR IS THIS REALLY A GREAT OPPORTUNITY FOR SOMEONE TO GET IT RIGHT?
DO YOU UNDERSTAND WHAT I'M SAYING, MR. MANTA?

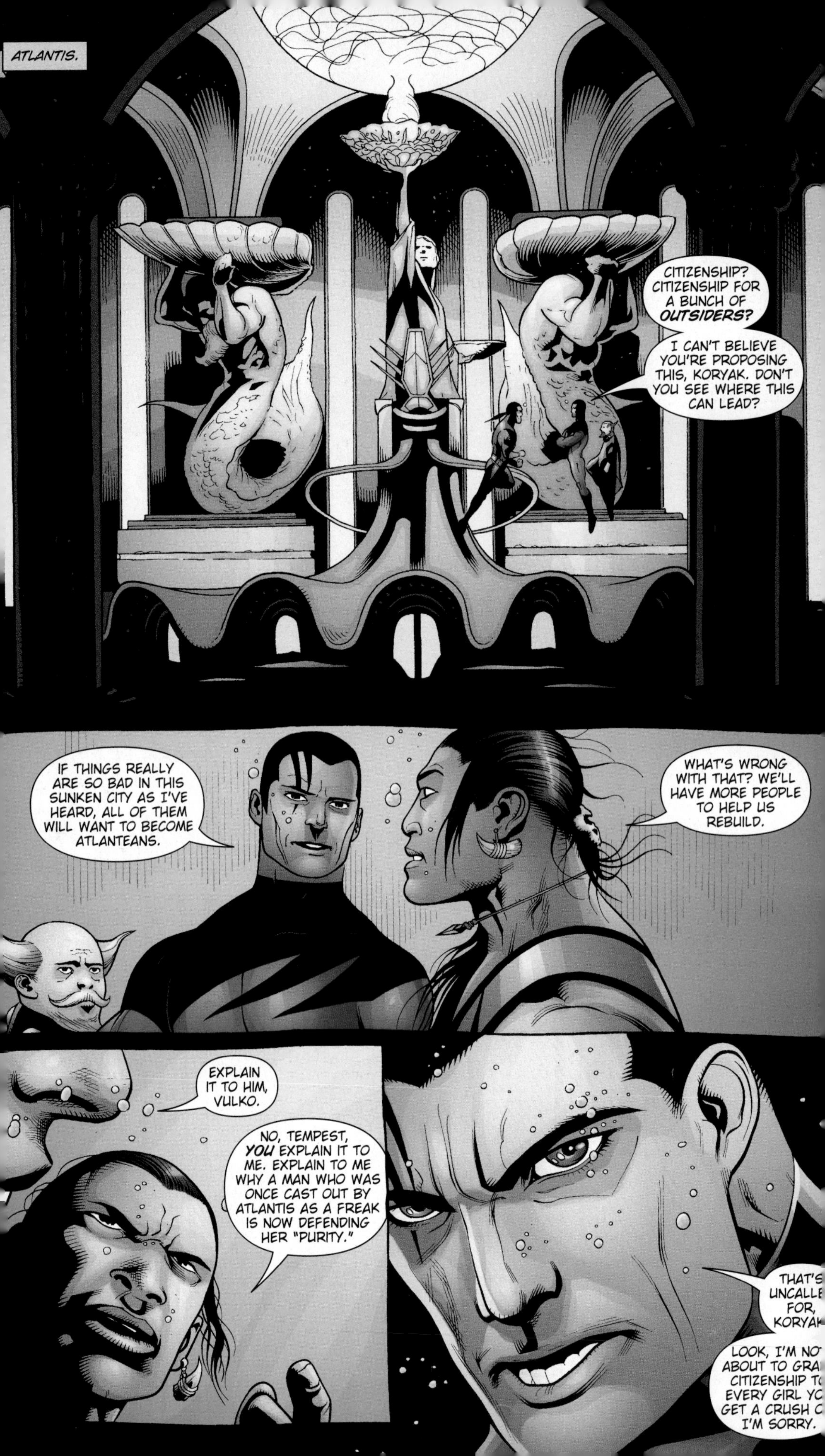
ATLANTIS.
CITIZENSHIP? CITIZENSHIP FOR A BUNCH OF OUTSIDERS?
I CAN'T BELIEVE YOU'RE PROPOSING THIS, KORYAK. DON'T YOU SEE WHERE THIS CAN LEAD?
IF THINGS REALLY ARE SO BAD IN THIS SUNKEN CITY AS I'VE HEARD, ALL OF THEM WILL WANT TO BECOME ATLANTEANS.
WHAT'S WRONG WITH THAT? WE'LL HAVE MORE PEOPLE TO HELP US REBUILD.
EXPLAIN IT TO HIM, VULKO.
NO, TEMPEST, YOU EXPLAIN IT TO ME. EXPLAIN TO ME WHY A MAN WHO WAS ONCE CAST OUT BY ATLANTIS AS A FREAK IS NOW DEFENDING HER "PURITY."
THAT'S UNCALLE FOR, KORYAK
LOOK, I'M NO ABOUT TO GRA CITIZENSHIP T EVERY GIRL YO GET A CRUSH C I'M SORRY.

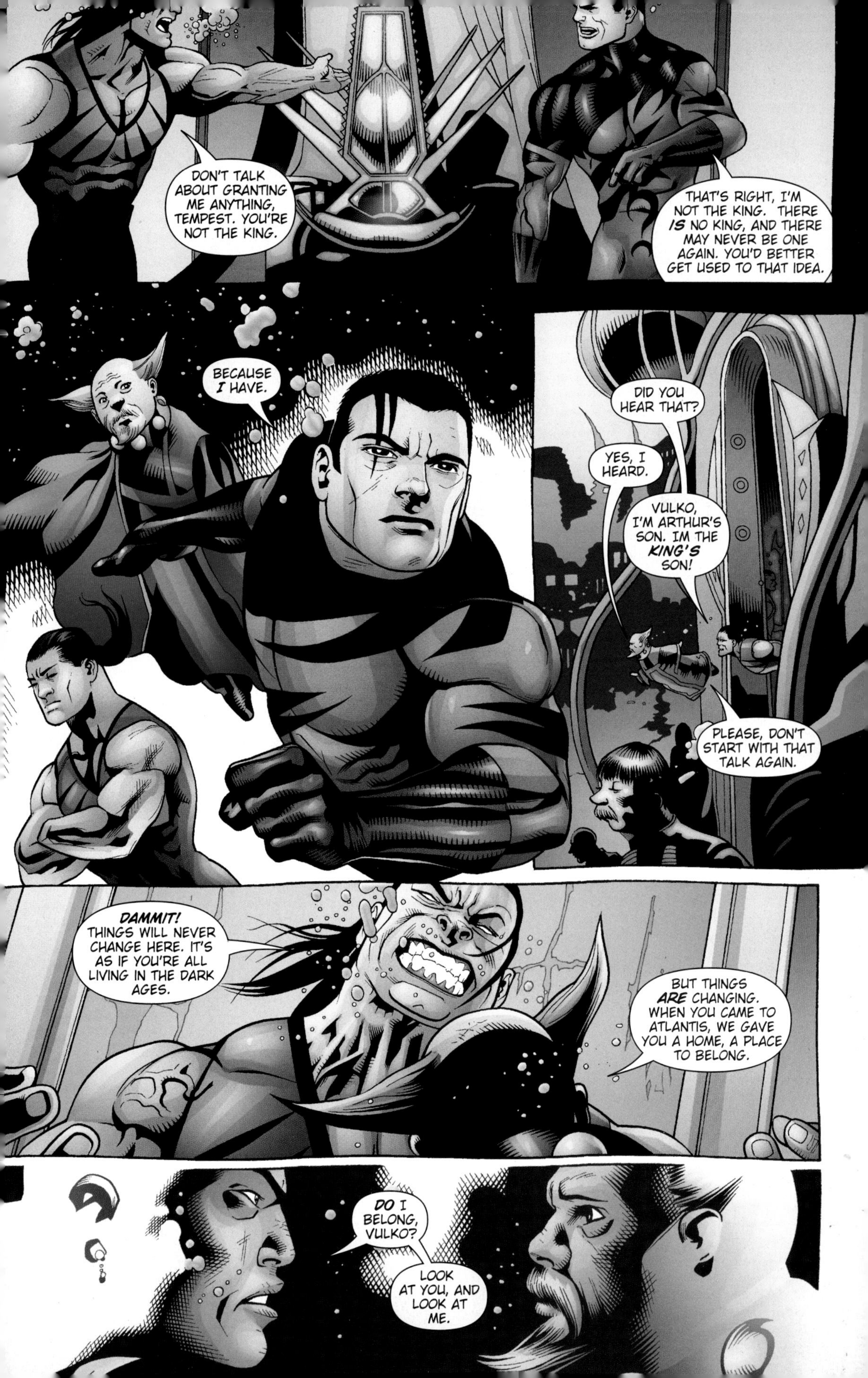
DON'T TALK ABOUT GRANTING ME ANYTHING, TEMPEST. YOU'RE NOT THE KING.
THAT'S RIGHT, I'M NOT THE KING. THERE *IS* NO KING, AND THERE MAY NEVER BE ONE AGAIN. YOU'D BETTER GET USED TO THAT IDEA.
BECAUSE *I* HAVE.
DID YOU HEAR THAT?
YES, I HEARD.
VULKO, I'M ARTHUR'S SON. IM THE *KING'S* SON!
PLEASE, DON'T START WITH THAT TALK AGAIN.
DAMMIT! THINGS WILL NEVER CHANGE HERE. IT'S AS IF YOU'RE ALL LIVING IN THE DARK AGES.
BUT THINGS *ARE* CHANGING. WHEN YOU CAME TO ATLANTIS, WE GAVE YOU A HOME, A PLACE TO BELONG.
DO I BELONG, VULKO?
LOOK AT YOU, AND LOOK AT ME.

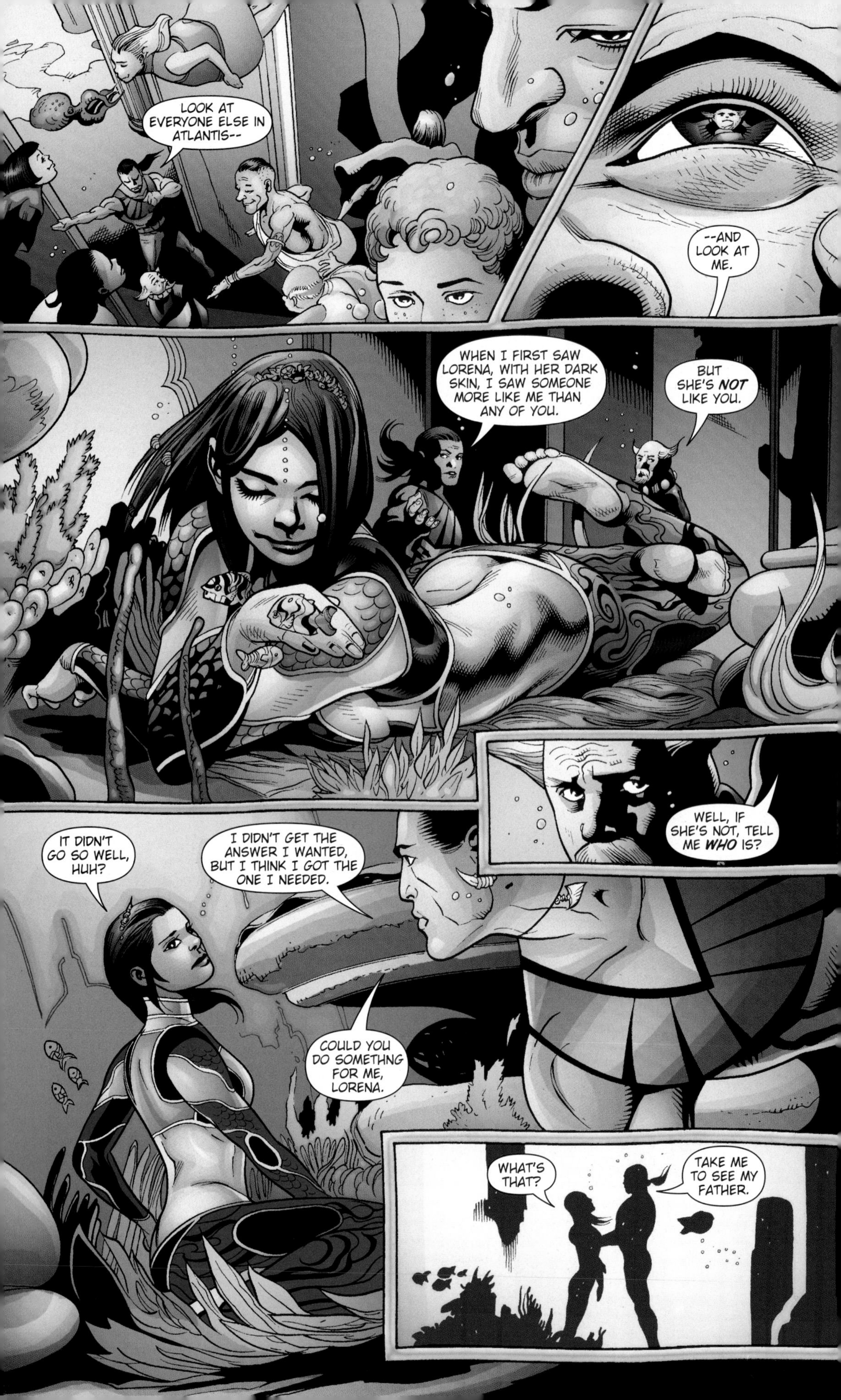
LOOK AT EVERYONE ELSE IN ATLANTIS--
--AND LOOK AT ME.
WHEN I FIRST SAW LORENA, WITH HER DARK SKIN, I SAW SOMEONE MORE LIKE ME THAN ANY OF YOU.
BUT SHE'S NOT LIKE YOU.
WELL, IF SHE'S NOT, TELL ME WHO IS?
IT DIDN'T GO SO WELL, HUH?
I DIDN'T GET THE ANSWER I WANTED, BUT I THINK I GOT THE ONE I NEEDED.
COULD YOU DO SOMETHNG FOR ME, LORENA.
WHAT'S THAT?
TAKE ME TO SEE MY FATHER.

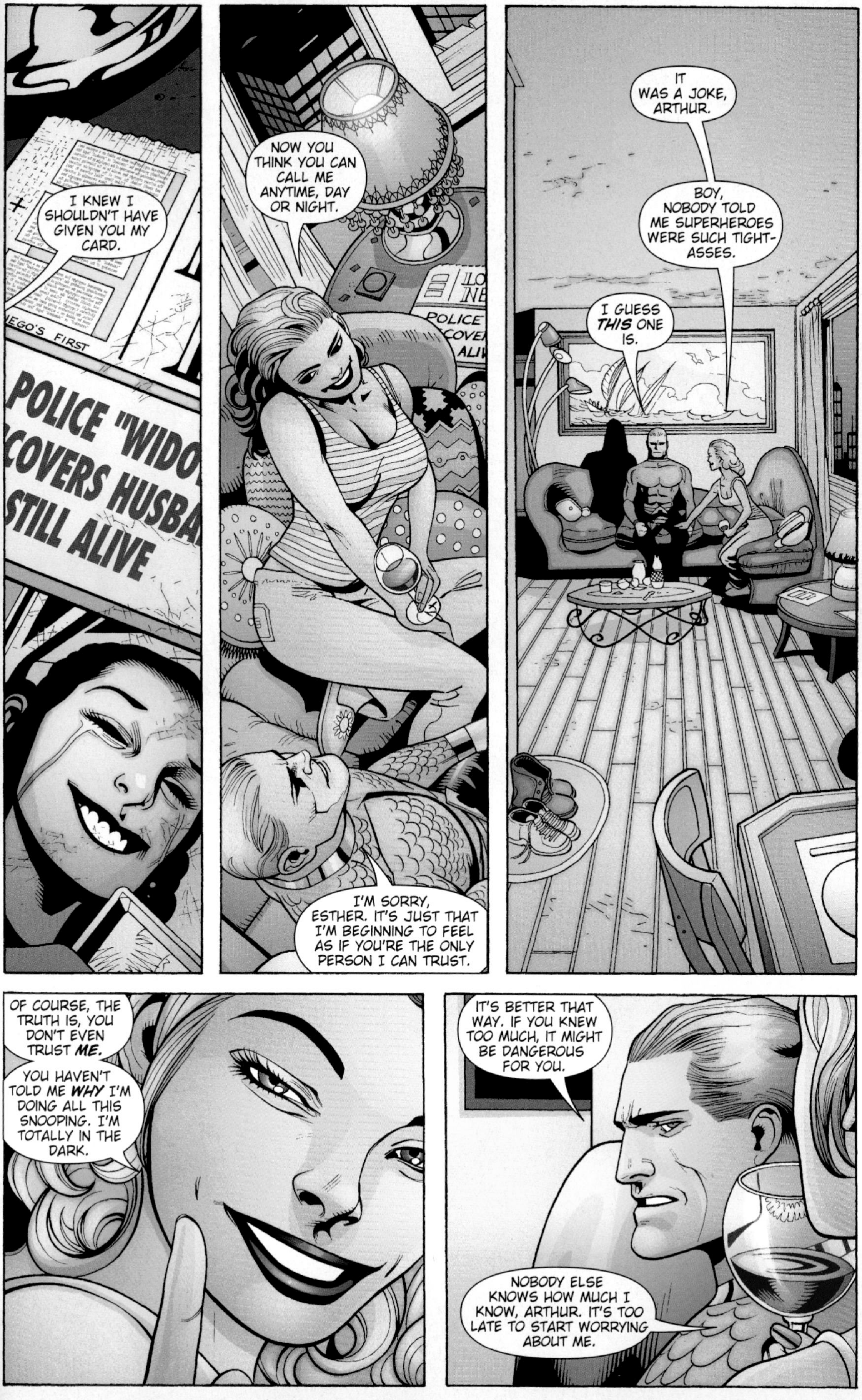

I KNEW I SHOULDN'T HAVE GIVEN YOU MY CARD.
POLICE "WIDO
COVERS HUSBA
STILL ALIVE
NOW YOU THINK YOU CAN CALL ME ANYTIME, DAY OR NIGHT.
POLICE
I'M SORRY, ESTHER. IT'S JUST THAT I'M BEGINNING TO FEEL AS IF YOU'RE THE ONLY PERSON I CAN TRUST.
IT WAS A JOKE, ARTHUR.
BOY, NOBODY TOLD ME SUPERHEROES WERE SUCH TIGHT-ASSES.
I GUESS THIS ONE IS.
OF COURSE, THE TRUTH IS, YOU DON'T EVEN TRUST ME.
YOU HAVEN'T TOLD ME WHY I'M DOING ALL THIS SNOOPING. I'M TOTALLY IN THE DARK.
IT'S BETTER THAT WAY. IF YOU KNEW TOO MUCH, IT MIGHT BE DANGEROUS FOR YOU.
NOBODY ELSE KNOWS HOW MUCH I KNOW, ARTHUR. IT'S TOO LATE TO START WORRYING ABOUT ME.

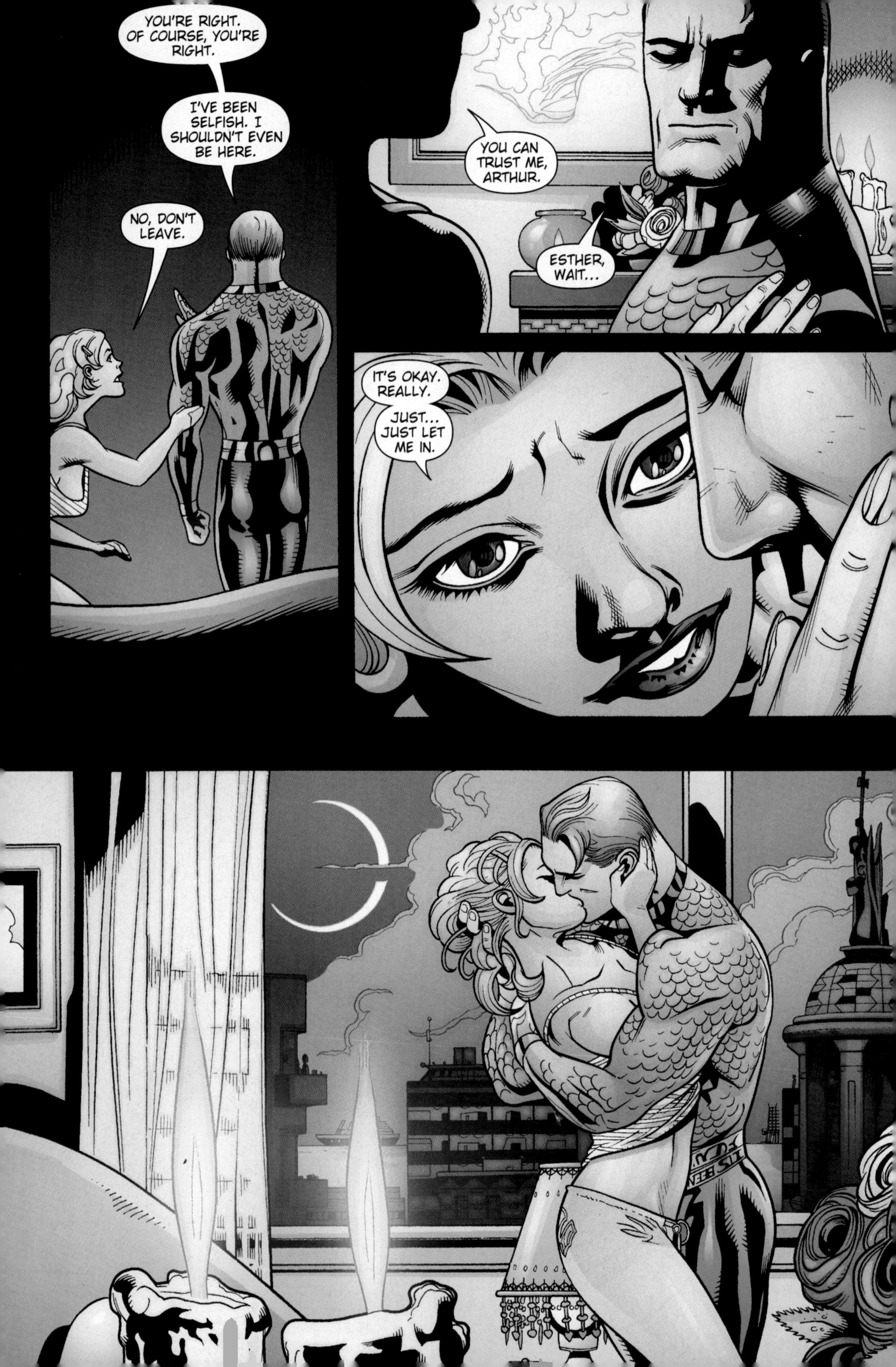
YOU'RE RIGHT. OF COURSE, YOU'RE RIGHT.
I'VE BEEN SELFISH. I SHOULDN'T EVEN BE HERE.
NO, DON'T LEAVE.
YOU CAN TRUST ME, ARTHUR.
ESTHER, WAIT...
IT'S OKAY. REALLY.
JUST... JUST LET ME IN.

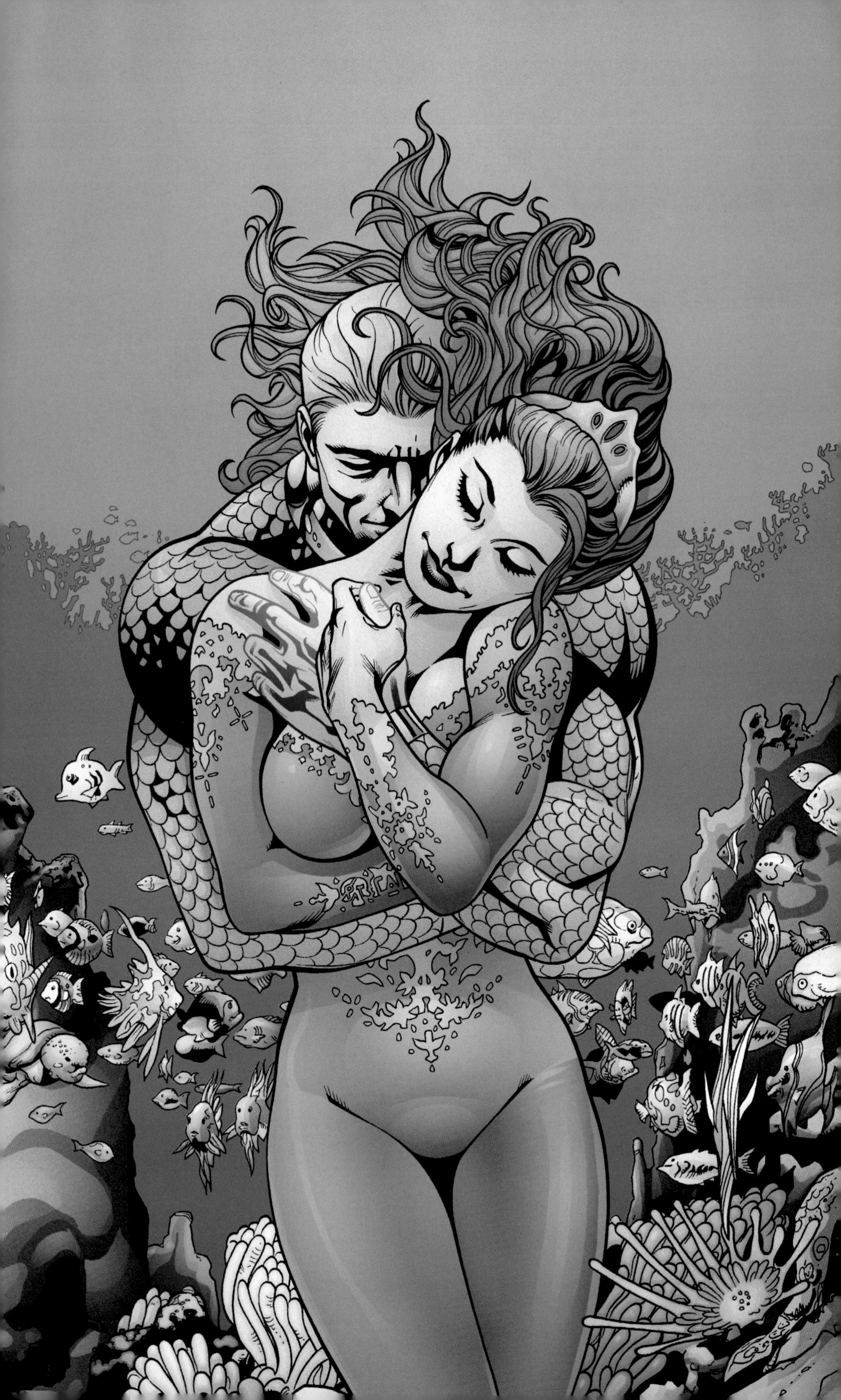

WHAT THE PAST REMEMBERS

JOHN ARCUDI
Writer

LEONARD KIRK
Layouts

ANDY CLARKE
Finishes

NATHAN EYRING
Colorist

JARED K. FLETCHER
Letterer

**PATRICK GLEASON &
CHRISTIAN ALAMY**
Cover

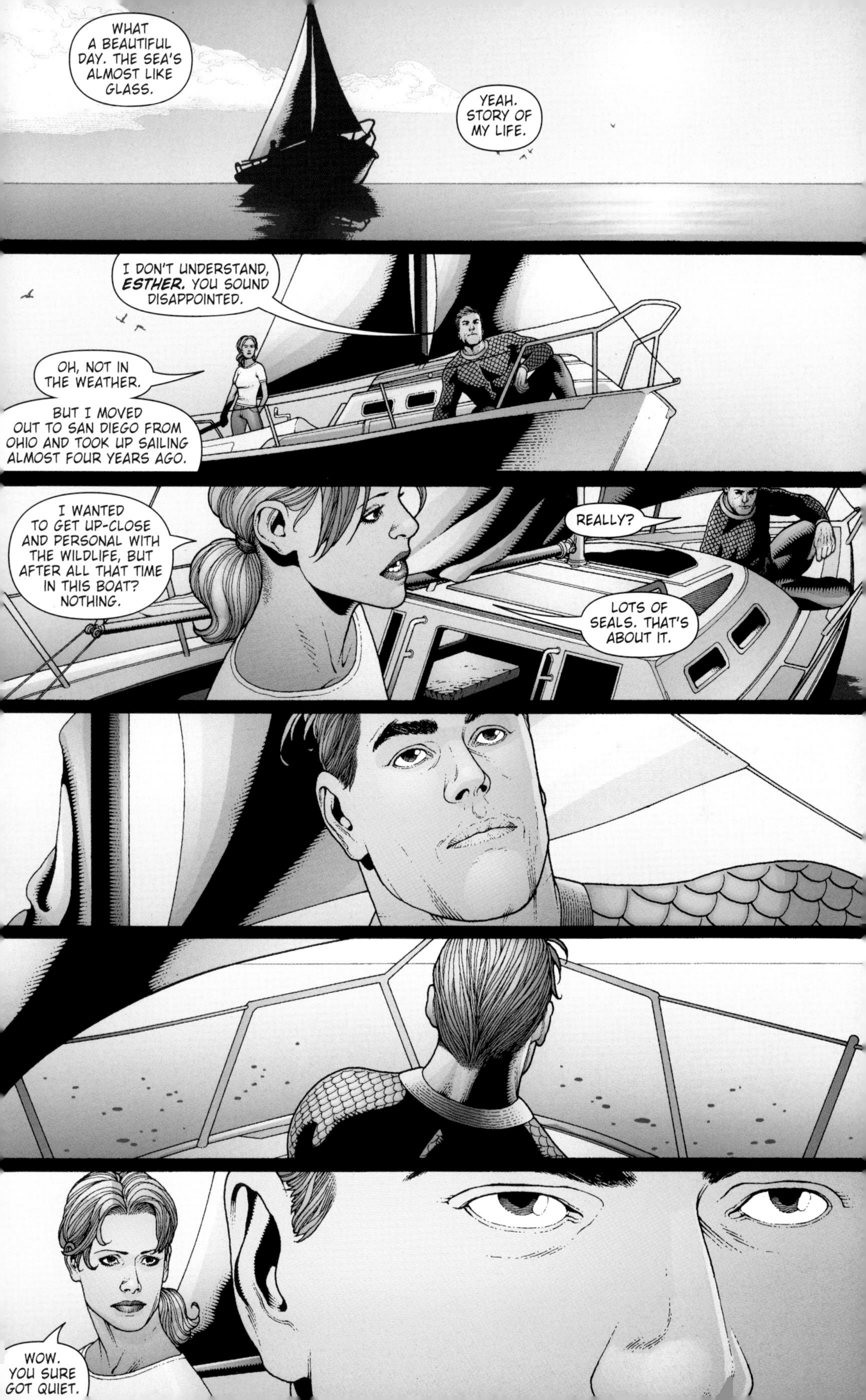
WHAT A BEAUTIFUL DAY. THE SEA'S ALMOST LIKE GLASS.
YEAH. STORY OF MY LIFE.
I DON'T UNDERSTAND, **ESTHER.** YOU SOUND DISAPPOINTED.
OH, NOT IN THE WEATHER.
BUT I MOVED OUT TO SAN DIEGO FROM OHIO AND TOOK UP SAILING ALMOST FOUR YEARS AGO.
I WANTED TO GET UP-CLOSE AND PERSONAL WITH THE WILDLIFE, BUT AFTER ALL THAT TIME IN THIS BOAT? NOTHING.
REALLY?
LOTS OF SEALS. THAT'S ABOUT IT.
WOW. YOU SURE GOT QUIET.

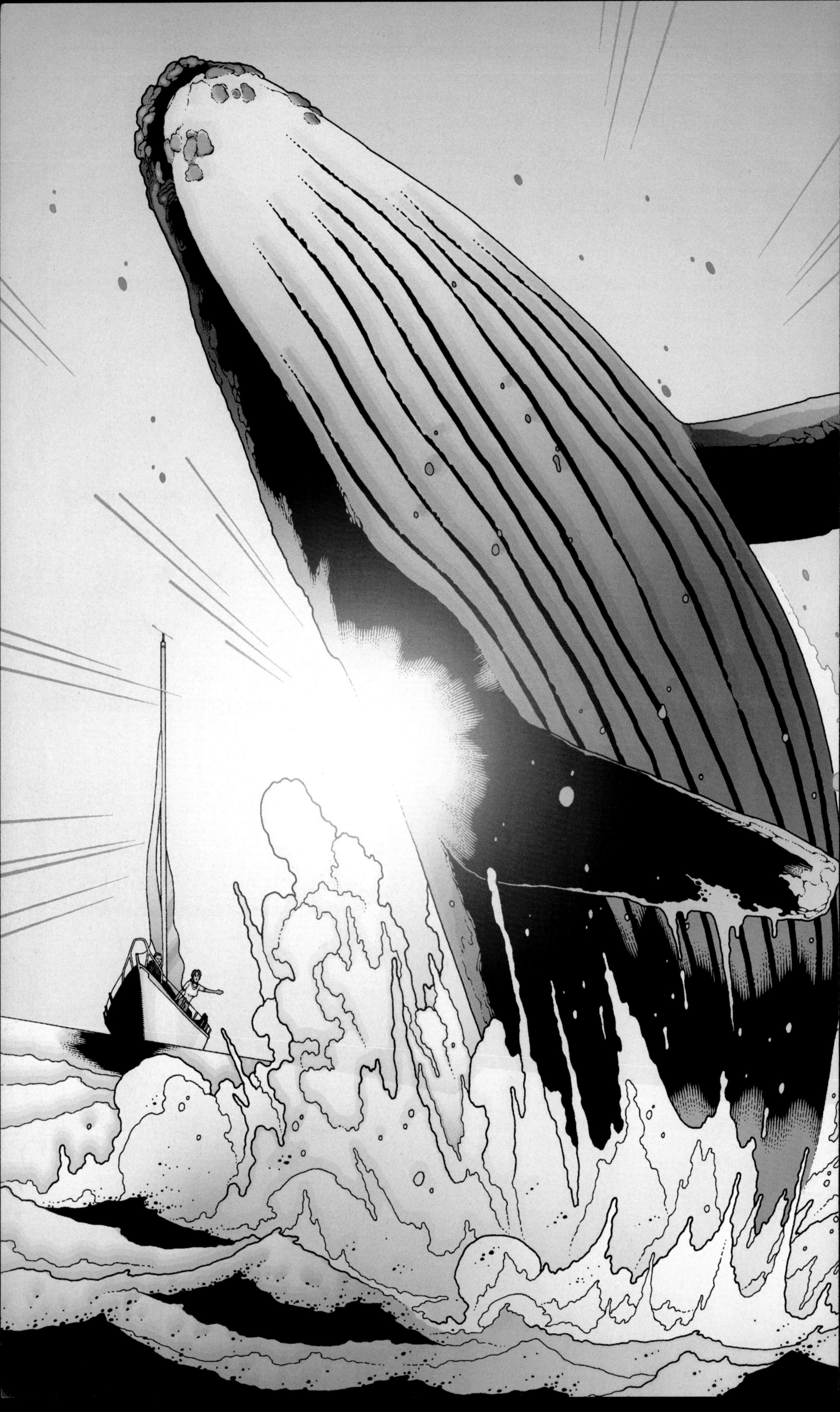

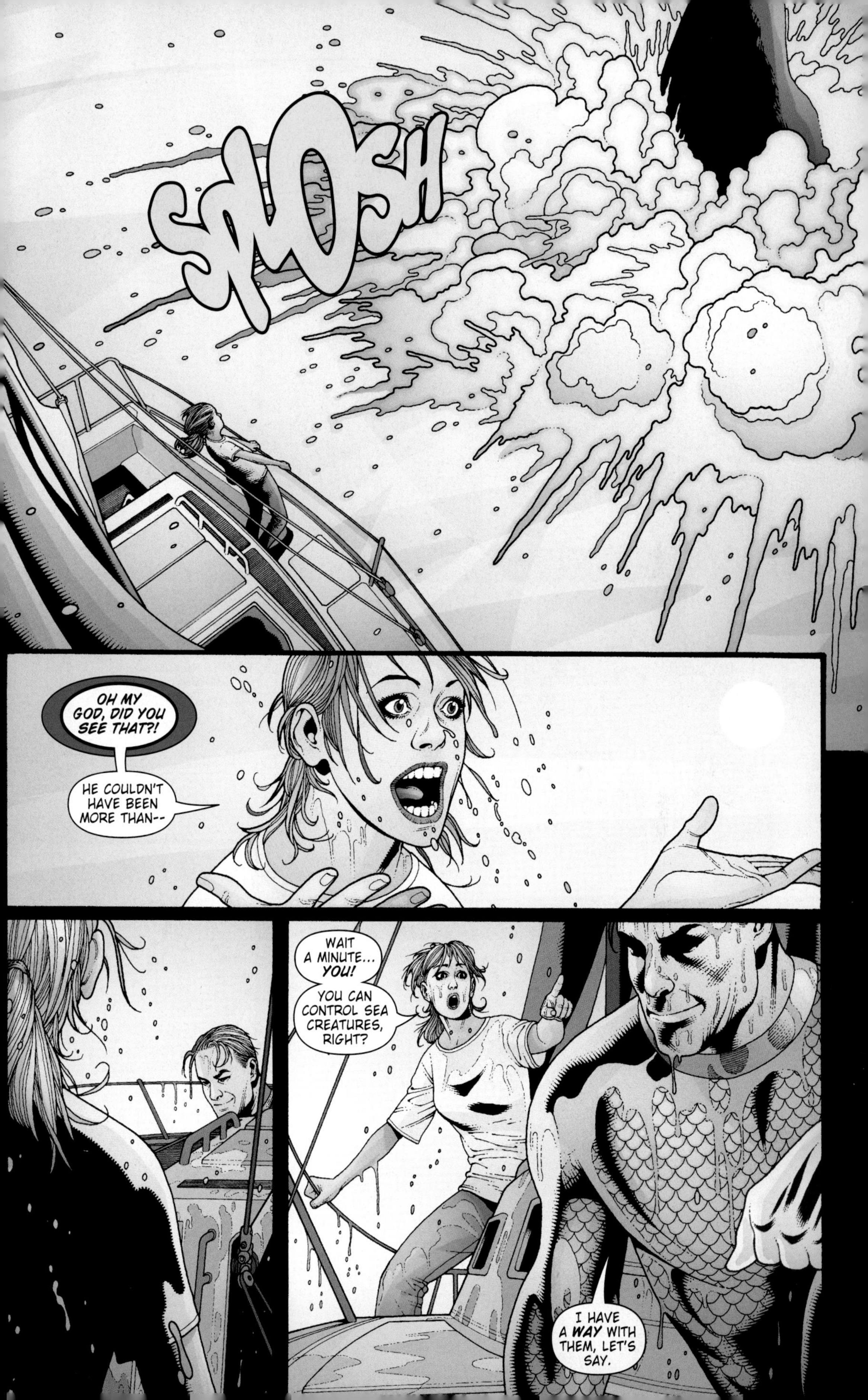
SPLOOSH
OH MY GOD, DID YOU SEE THAT?!
HE COULDN'T HAVE BEEN MORE THAN--
WAIT A MINUTE... YOU!
YOU CAN CONTROL SEA CREATURES, RIGHT?
I HAVE A WAY WITH THEM, LET'S SAY.

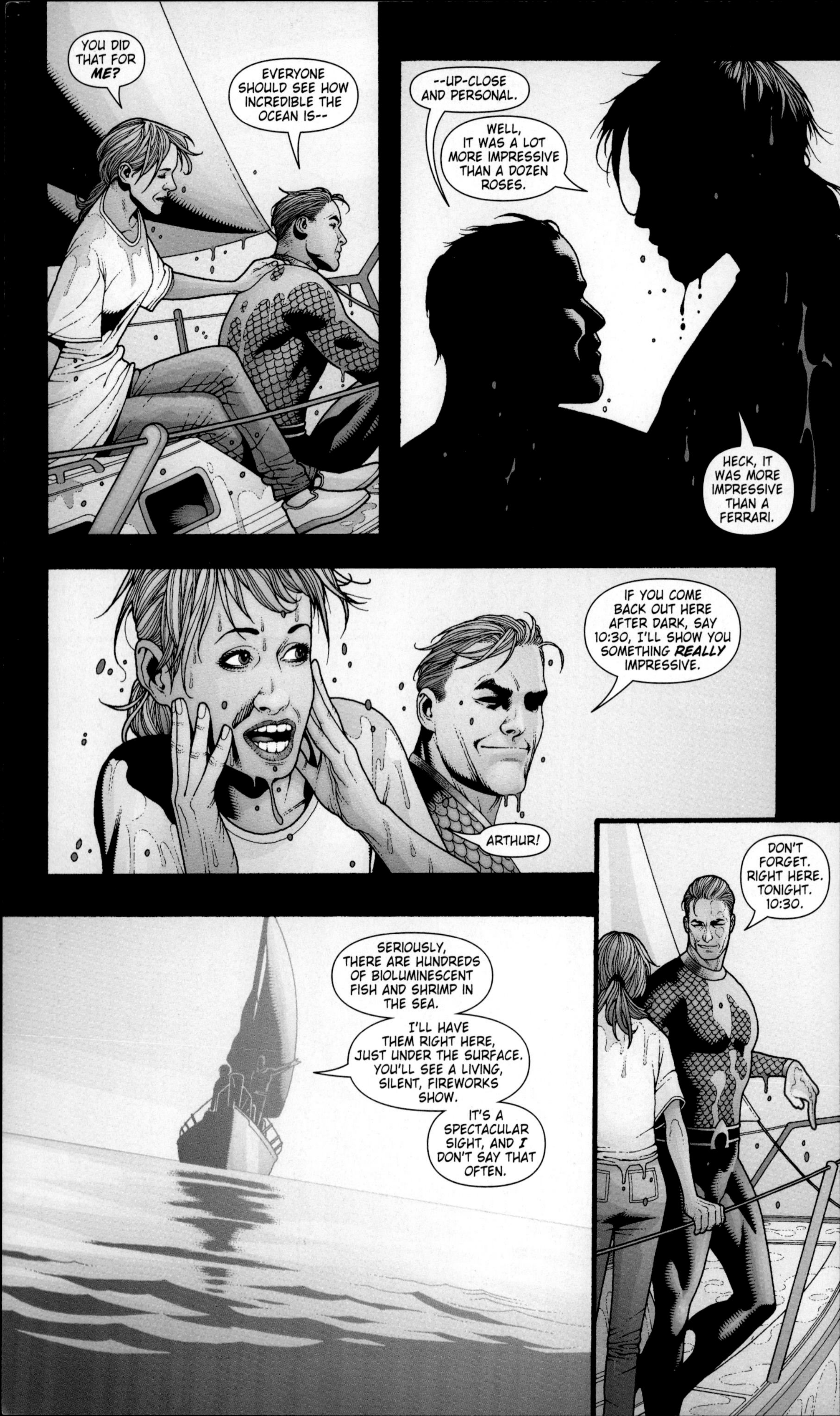

YOU DID THAT FOR ME?
EVERYONE SHOULD SEE HOW INCREDIBLE THE OCEAN IS--
--UP-CLOSE AND PERSONAL.
WELL, IT WAS A LOT MORE IMPRESSIVE THAN A DOZEN ROSES.
HECK, IT WAS MORE IMPRESSIVE THAN A FERRARI.
IF YOU COME BACK OUT HERE AFTER DARK, SAY 10:30, I'LL SHOW YOU SOMETHING REALLY IMPRESSIVE.
ARTHUR!
SERIOUSLY, THERE ARE HUNDREDS OF BIOLUMINESCENT FISH AND SHRIMP IN THE SEA.
I'LL HAVE THEM RIGHT HERE, JUST UNDER THE SURFACE. YOU'LL SEE A LIVING, SILENT, FIREWORKS SHOW.
IT'S A SPECTACULAR SIGHT, AND I DON'T SAY THAT OFTEN.
DON'T FORGET. RIGHT HERE. TONIGHT. 10:30.

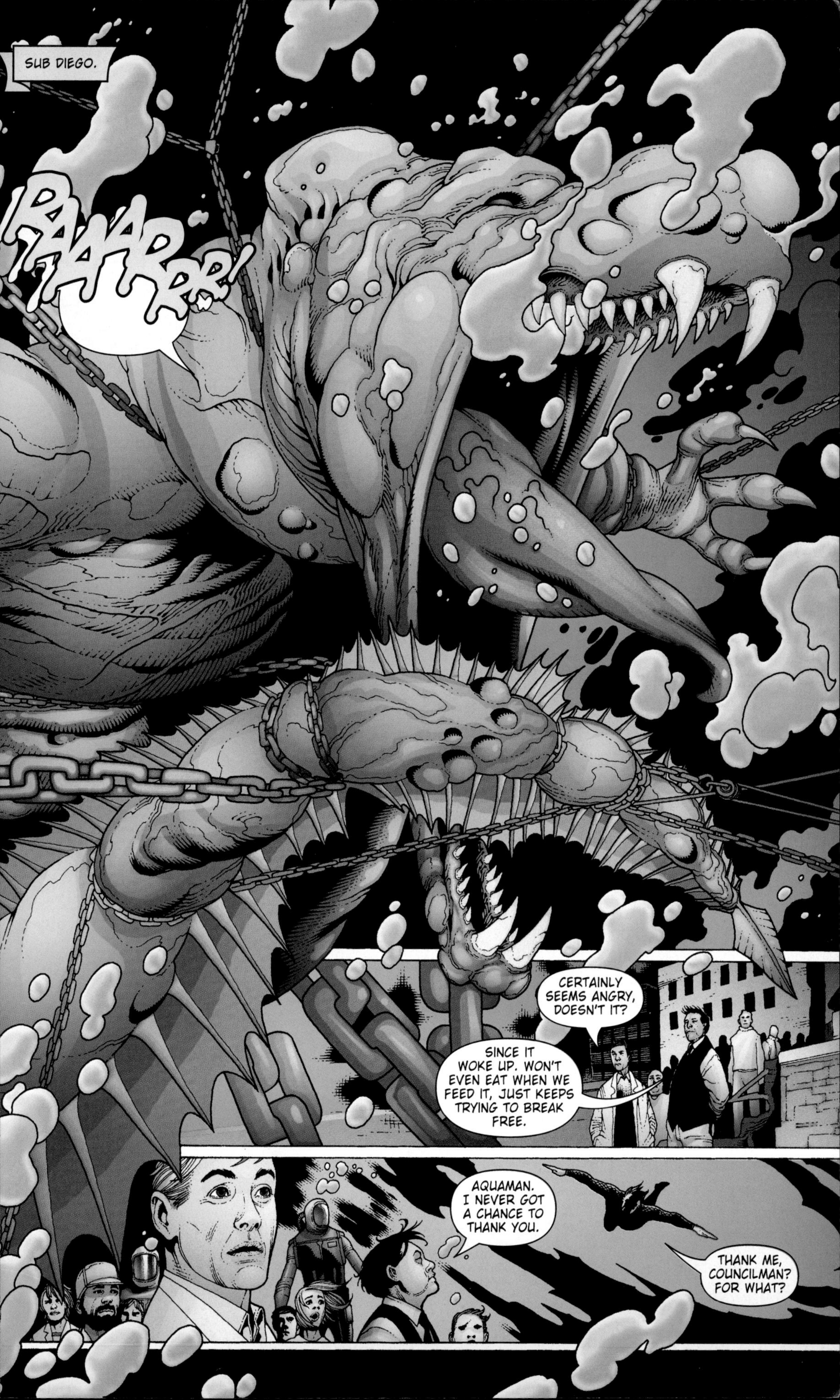
SUB DIEGO.
RAAARRR!
CERTAINLY SEEMS ANGRY, DOESN'T IT?
SINCE IT WOKE UP. WON'T EVEN EAT WHEN WE FEED IT, JUST KEEPS TRYING TO BREAK FREE.
AQUAMAN. I NEVER GOT A CHANCE TO THANK YOU.
THANK ME, COUNCILMAN? FOR WHAT?

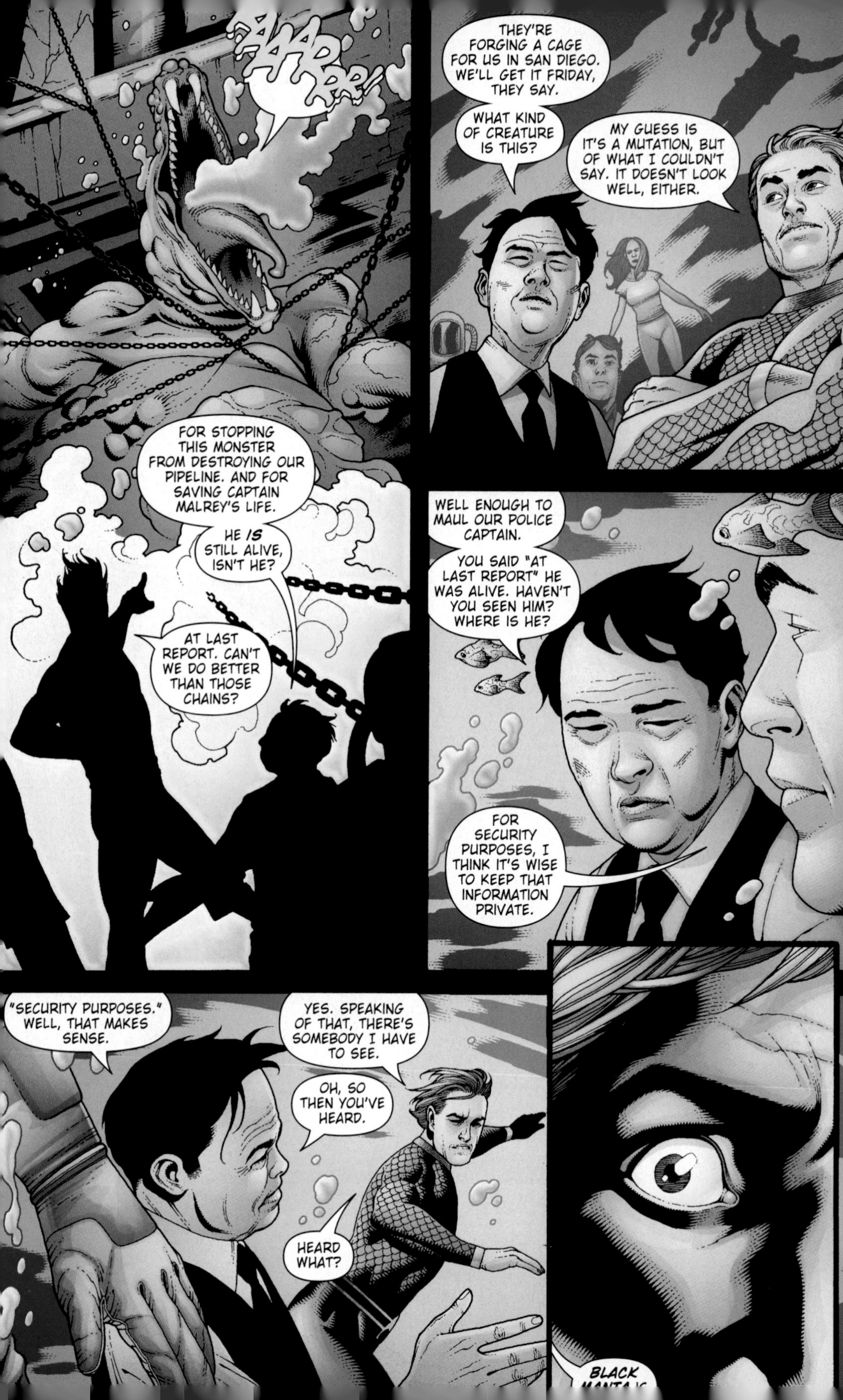

FOR STOPPING THIS MONSTER FROM DESTROYING OUR PIPELINE. AND FOR SAVING CAPTAIN MALREY'S LIFE.
HE *IS* STILL ALIVE, ISN'T HE?
AT LAST REPORT. CAN'T WE DO BETTER THAN THOSE CHAINS?
THEY'RE FORGING A CAGE FOR US IN SAN DIEGO. WE'LL GET IT FRIDAY, THEY SAY.
WHAT KIND OF CREATURE IS THIS?
MY GUESS IS IT'S A MUTATION, BUT OF WHAT I COULDN'T SAY. IT DOESN'T LOOK WELL, EITHER.
WELL ENOUGH TO MAUL OUR POLICE CAPTAIN.
YOU SAID "AT LAST REPORT" HE WAS ALIVE. HAVEN'T YOU SEEN HIM? WHERE IS HE?
FOR SECURITY PURPOSES, I THINK IT'S WISE TO KEEP THAT INFORMATION PRIVATE.
"SECURITY PURPOSES." WELL, THAT MAKES SENSE.
YES. SPEAKING OF THAT, THERE'S SOMEBODY I HAVE TO SEE.
OH, SO THEN YOU'VE HEARD.
HEARD WHAT?
BLACK

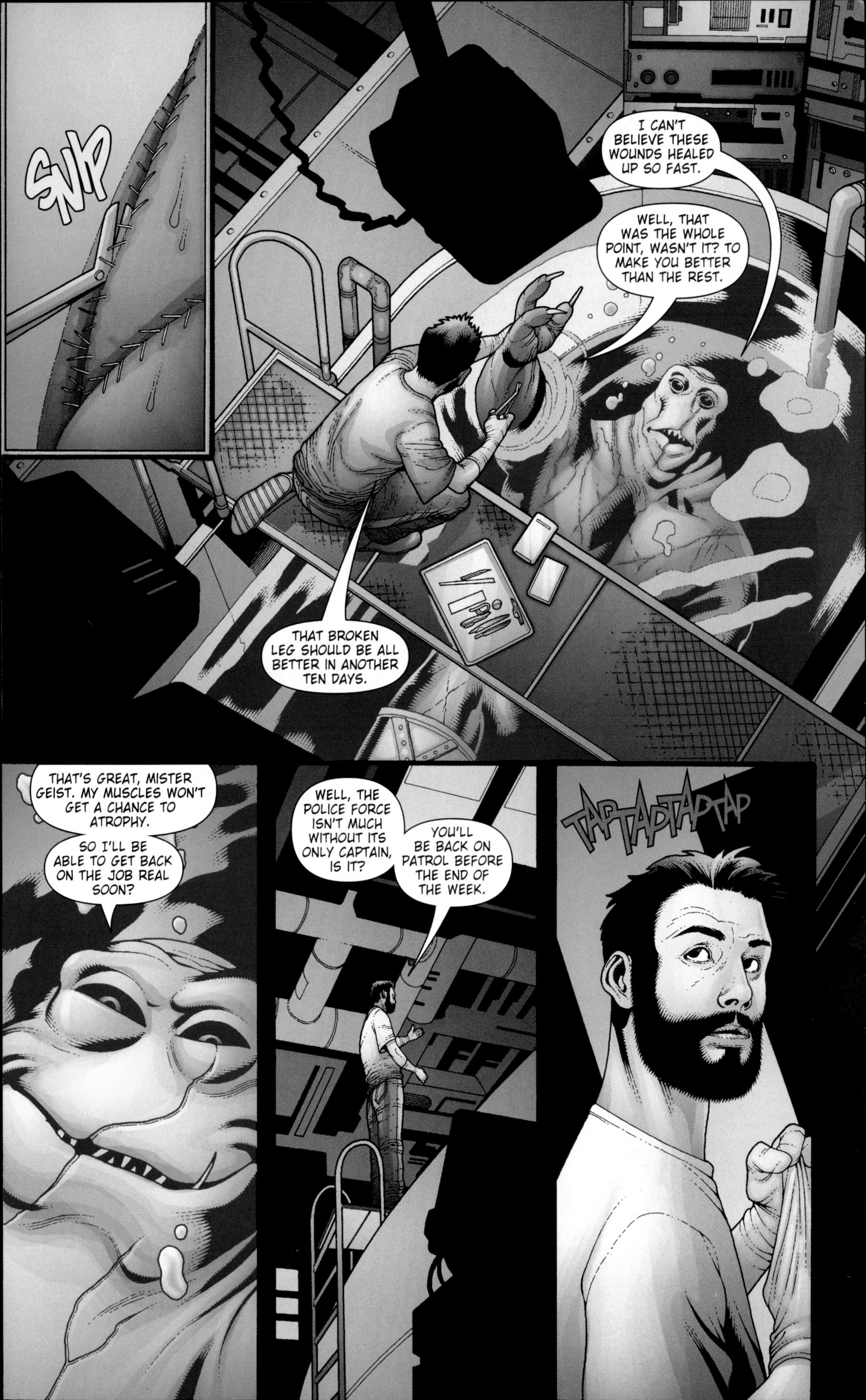
SNIP
I CAN'T BELIEVE THESE WOUNDS HEALED UP SO FAST.
WELL, THAT WAS THE WHOLE POINT, WASN'T IT? TO MAKE YOU BETTER THAN THE REST.
THAT BROKEN LEG SHOULD BE ALL BETTER IN ANOTHER TEN DAYS.
THAT'S GREAT, MISTER GEIST. MY MUSCLES WON'T GET A CHANCE TO ATROPHY.
SO I'LL BE ABLE TO GET BACK ON THE JOB REAL SOON?
WELL, THE POLICE FORCE ISN'T MUCH WITHOUT ITS ONLY CAPTAIN, IS IT?
YOU'LL BE BACK ON PATROL BEFORE THE END OF THE WEEK.
TAPTAPTAPTAP

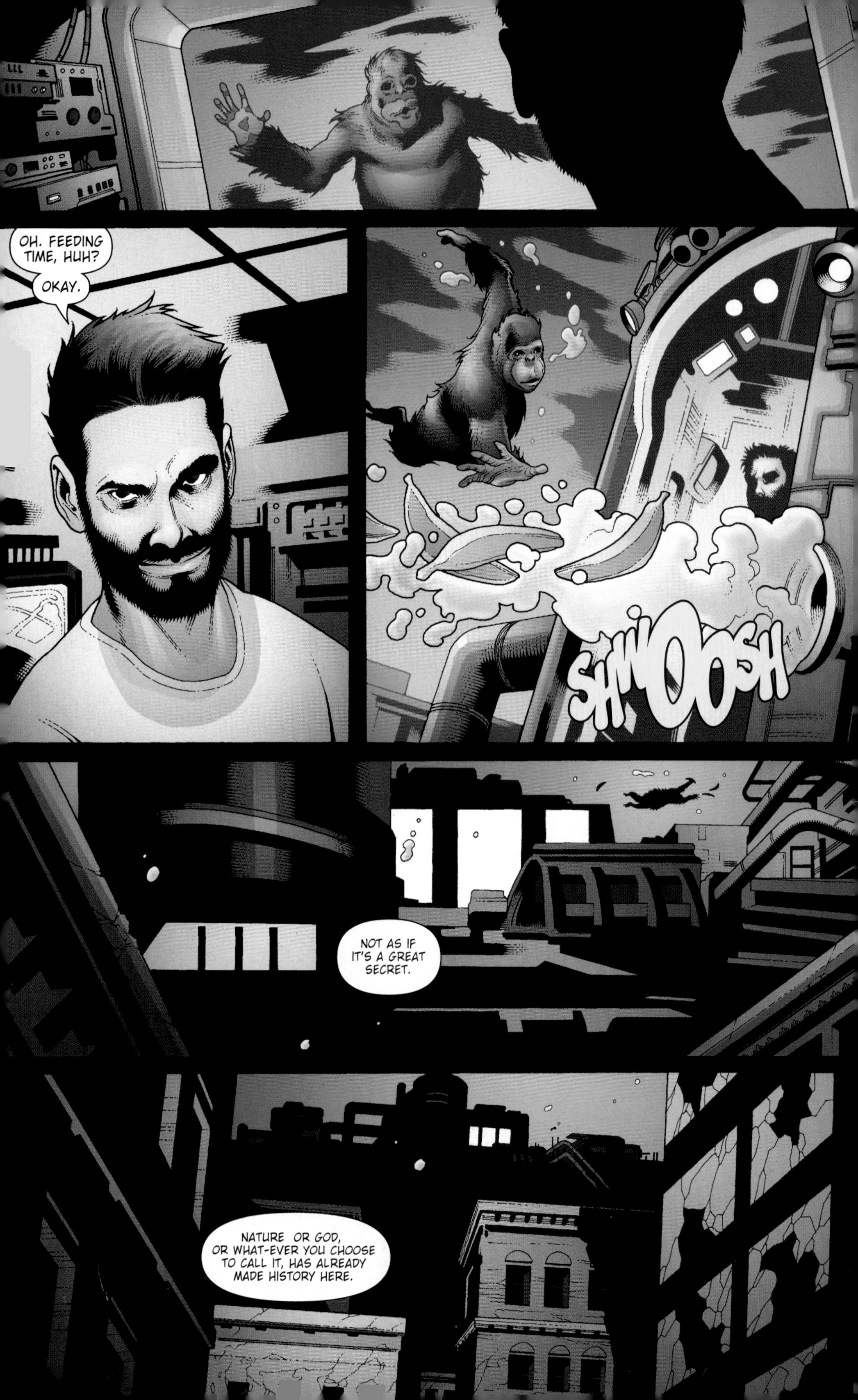
OH. FEEDING TIME, HUH?
OKAY.
SHWOOSH
NOT AS IF IT'S A GREAT SECRET.
NATURE OR GOD, OR WHAT-EVER YOU CHOOSE TO CALL IT, HAS ALREADY MADE HISTORY HERE.

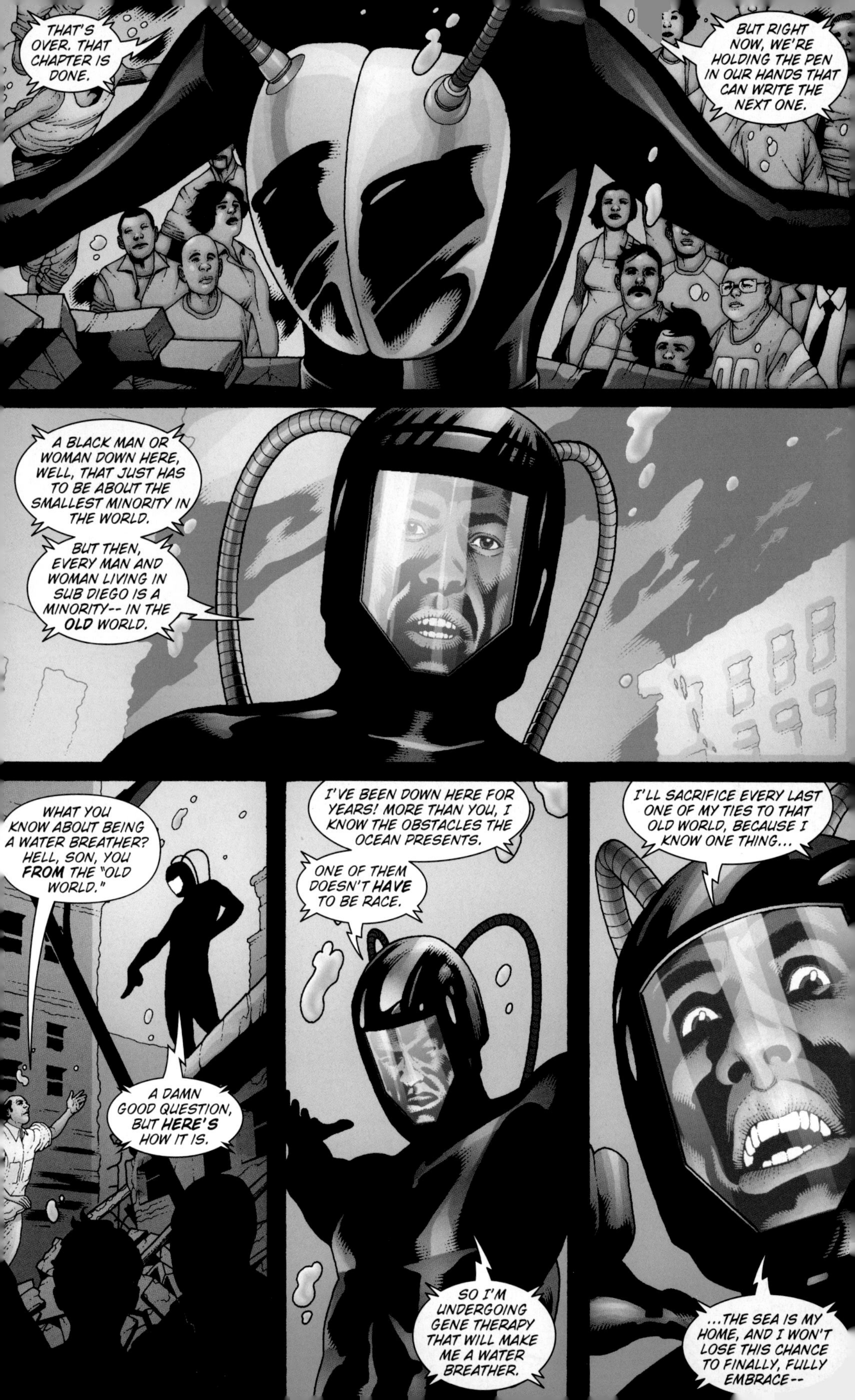
THAT'S OVER. THAT CHAPTER IS DONE.
BUT RIGHT NOW, WE'RE HOLDING THE PEN IN OUR HANDS THAT CAN WRITE THE NEXT ONE.
A BLACK MAN OR WOMAN DOWN HERE, WELL, THAT JUST HAS TO BE ABOUT THE SMALLEST MINORITY IN THE WORLD.
BUT THEN, EVERY MAN AND WOMAN LIVING IN SUB DIEGO IS A MINORITY-- IN THE OLD WORLD.
WHAT YOU KNOW ABOUT BEING A WATER BREATHER? HELL, SON, YOU FROM THE "OLD WORLD."
A DAMN GOOD QUESTION, BUT HERE'S HOW IT IS.
I'VE BEEN DOWN HERE FOR YEARS! MORE THAN YOU, I KNOW THE OBSTACLES THE OCEAN PRESENTS.
ONE OF THEM DOESN'T HAVE TO BE RACE.
SO I'M UNDERGOING GENE THERAPY THAT WILL MAKE ME A WATER BREATHER.
I'LL SACRIFICE EVERY LAST ONE OF MY TIES TO THAT OLD WORLD, BECAUSE I KNOW ONE THING...
...THE SEA IS MY HOME, AND I WON'T LOSE THIS CHANCE TO FINALLY, FULLY EMBRACE--

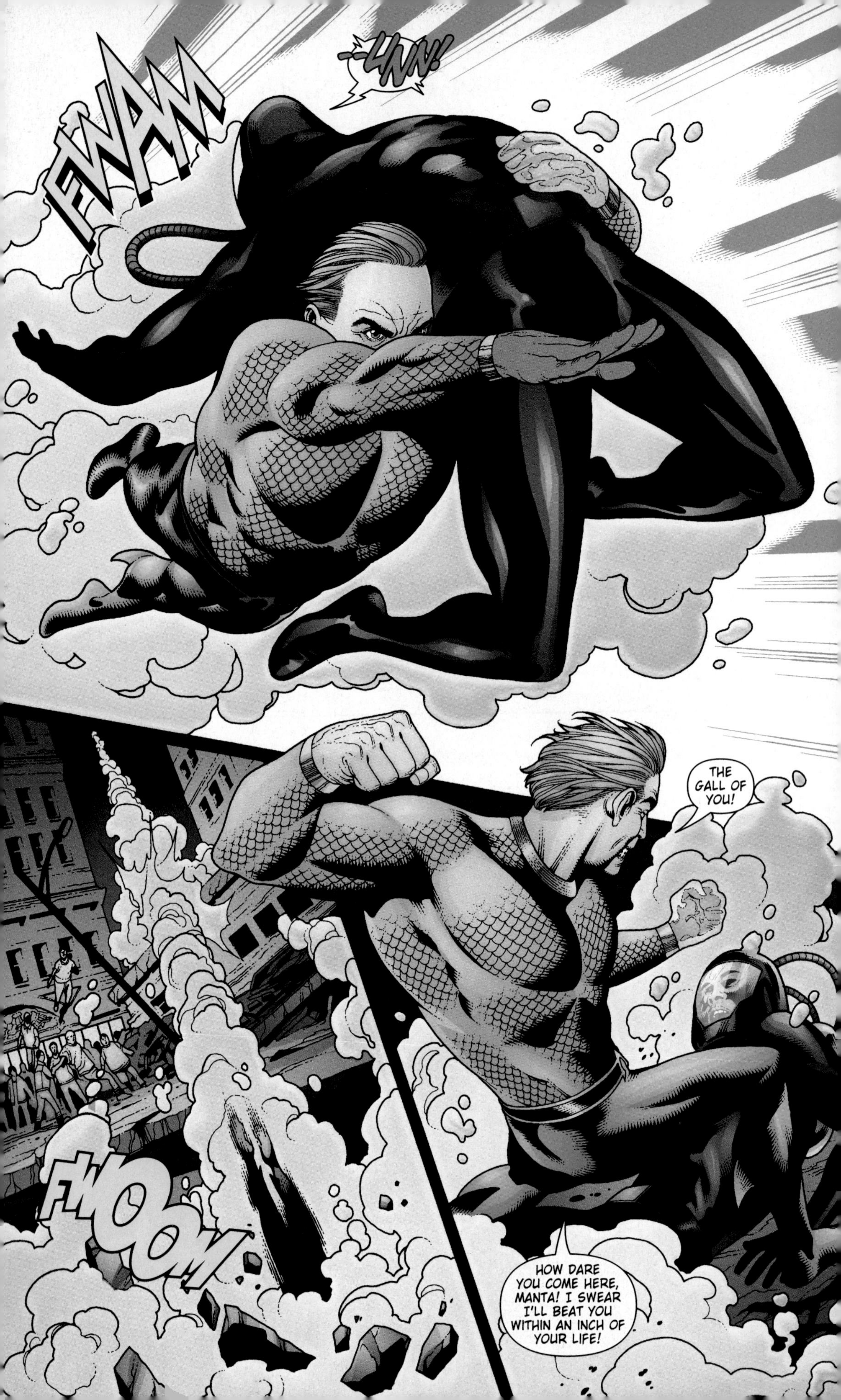
FWAM
-UNN!
THE GALL OF YOU!
FWOOM
HOW DARE YOU COME HERE, MANTA! I SWEAR I'LL BEAT YOU WITHIN AN INCH OF YOUR LIFE!

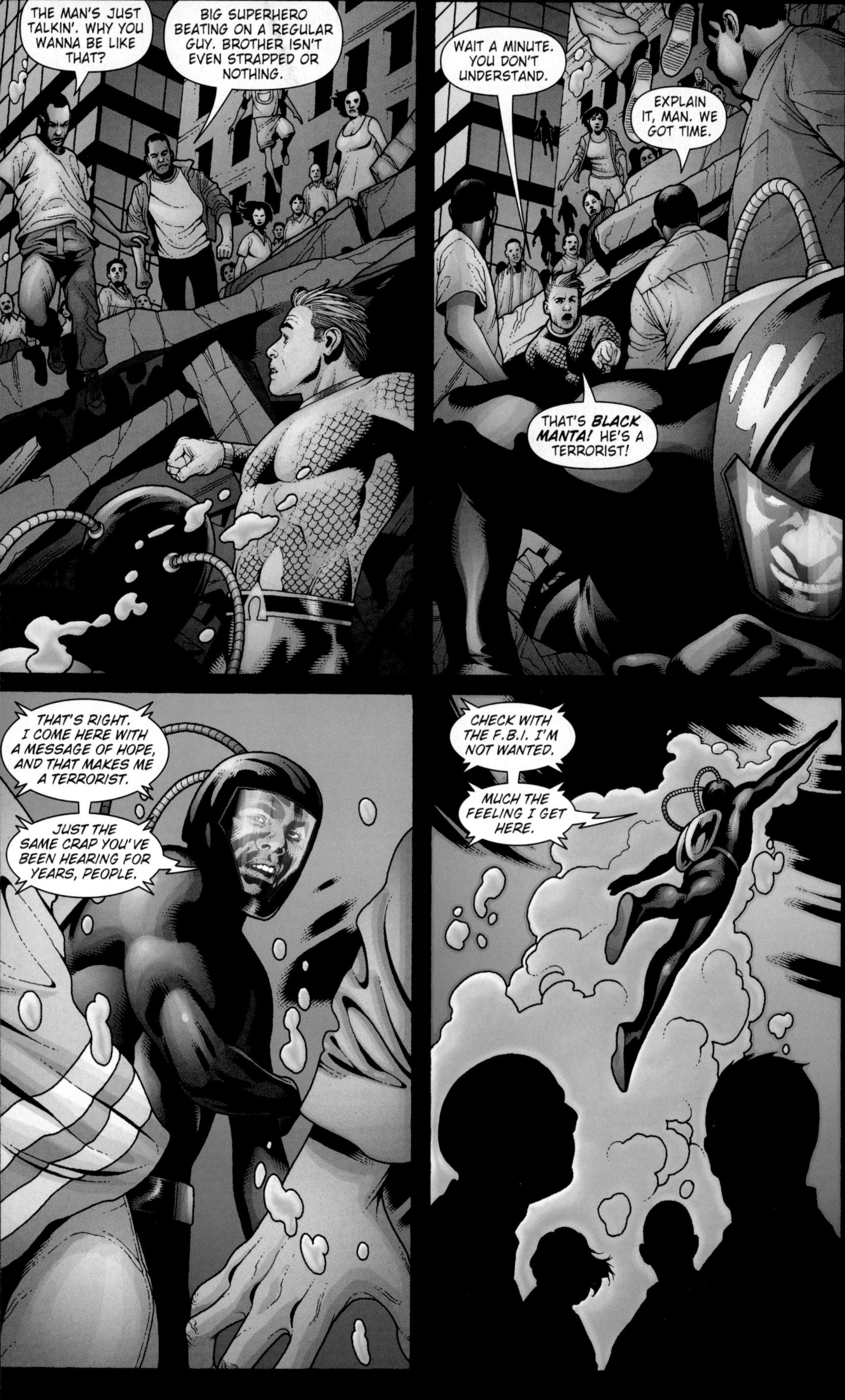
THE MAN'S JUST TALKIN'. WHY YOU WANNA BE LIKE THAT?
BIG SUPERHERO BEATING ON A REGULAR GUY. BROTHER ISN'T EVEN STRAPPED OR NOTHING.
WAIT A MINUTE. YOU DON'T UNDERSTAND.
EXPLAIN IT, MAN. WE GOT TIME.
THAT'S BLACK MANTA! HE'S A TERRORIST!
THAT'S RIGHT. I COME HERE WITH A MESSAGE OF HOPE, AND THAT MAKES ME A TERRORIST.
JUST THE SAME CRAP YOU'VE BEEN HEARING FOR YEARS, PEOPLE.
CHECK WITH THE F.B.I. I'M NOT WANTED.
MUCH THE FEELING I GET HERE.

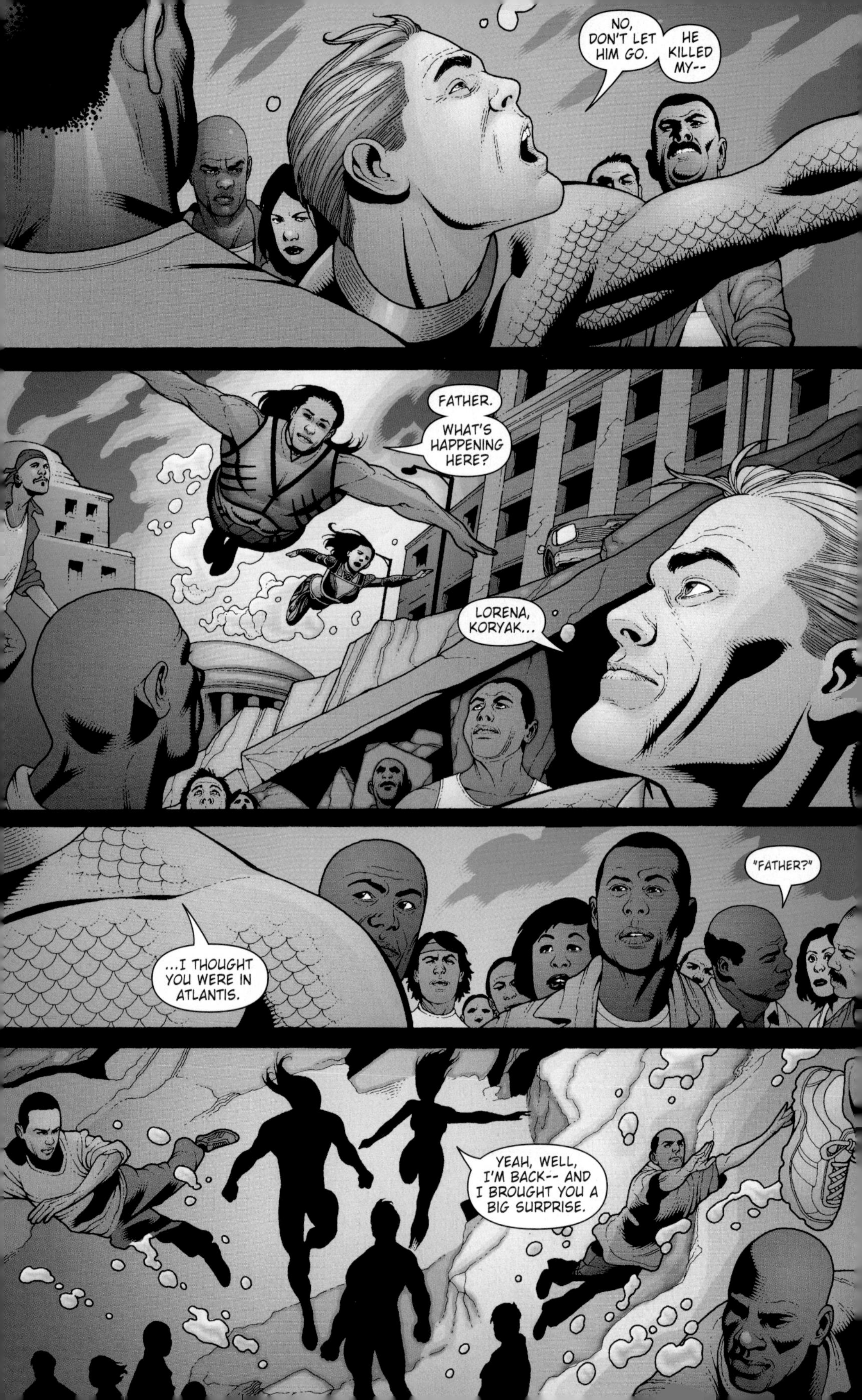
NO, DON'T LET HIM GO.
HE KILLED MY--
FATHER.
WHAT'S HAPPENING HERE?
LORENA, KORYAK...
...I THOUGHT YOU WERE IN ATLANTIS.
"FATHER?"
YEAH, WELL, I'M BACK-- AND I BROUGHT YOU A BIG SURPRISE.

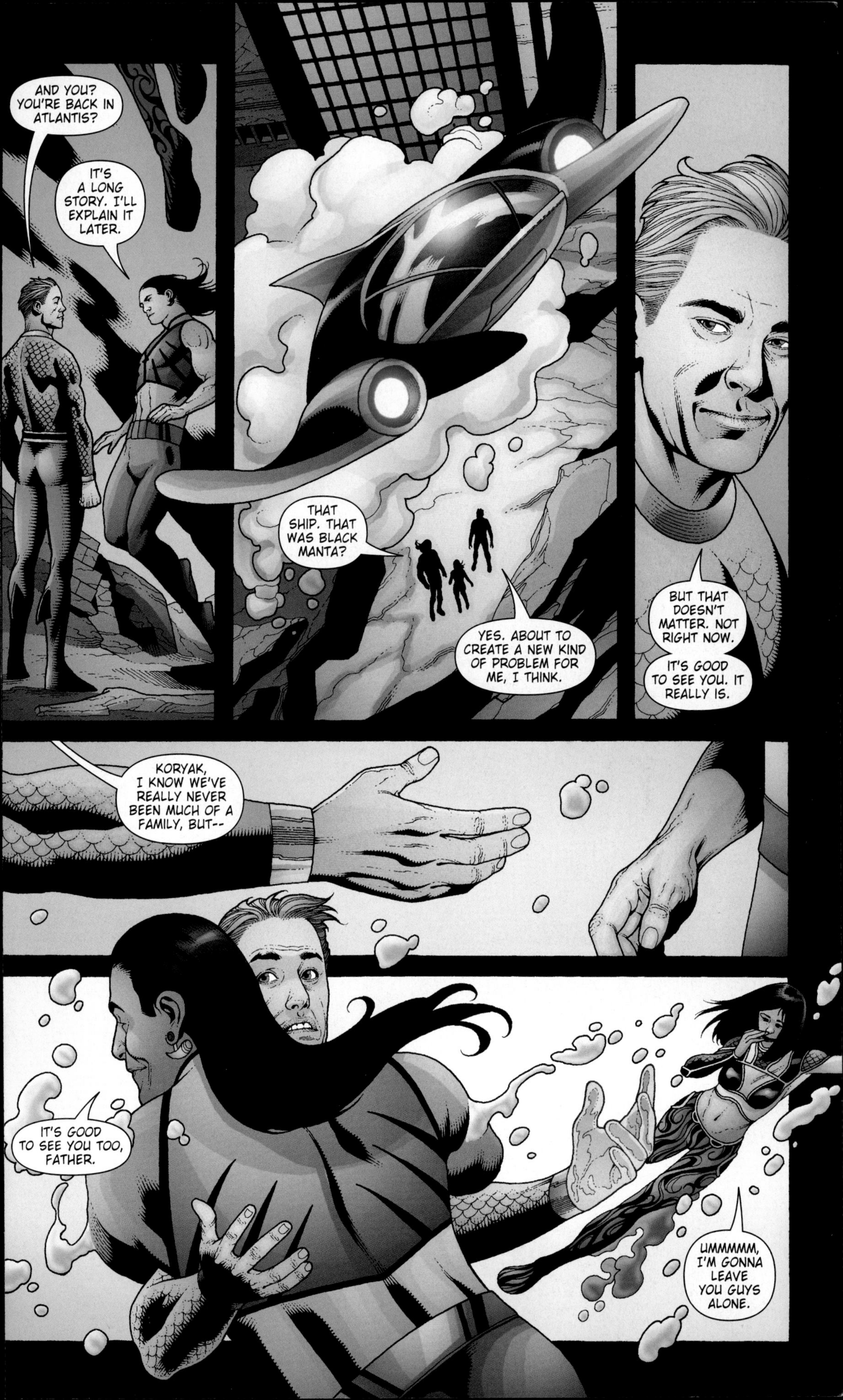
AND YOU? YOU'RE BACK IN ATLANTIS?
IT'S A LONG STORY. I'LL EXPLAIN IT LATER.
THAT SHIP. THAT WAS BLACK MANTA?
YES. ABOUT TO CREATE A NEW KIND OF PROBLEM FOR ME, I THINK.
BUT THAT DOESN'T MATTER. NOT RIGHT NOW.
IT'S GOOD TO SEE YOU. IT REALLY IS.
KORYAK, I KNOW WE'VE REALLY NEVER BEEN MUCH OF A FAMILY, BUT--
IT'S GOOD TO SEE YOU TOO, FATHER.
UMMMMM, I'M GONNA LEAVE YOU GUYS ALONE.

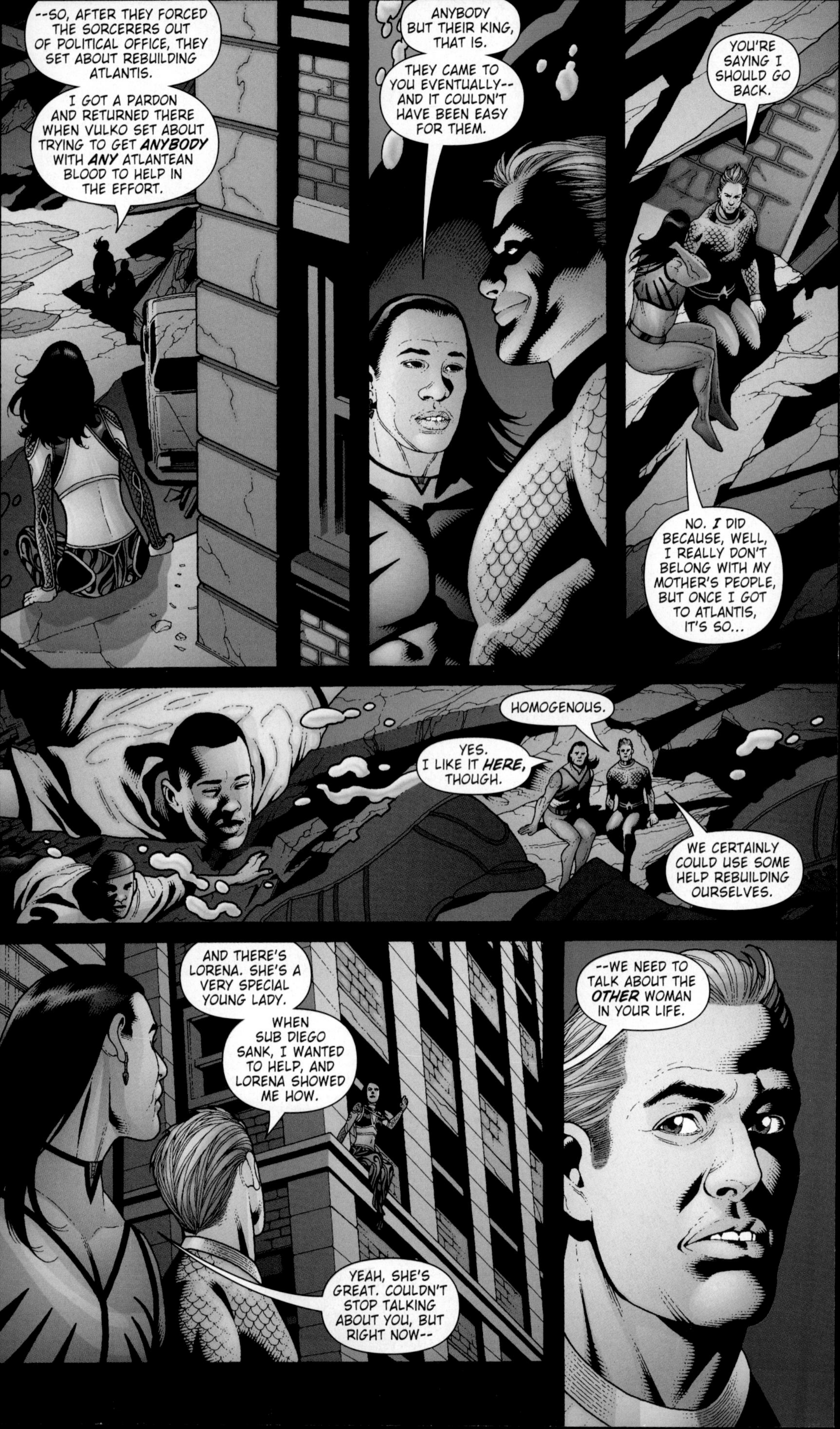
--SO, AFTER THEY FORCED THE SORCERERS OUT OF POLITICAL OFFICE, THEY SET ABOUT REBUILDING ATLANTIS.
I GOT A PARDON AND RETURNED THERE WHEN VULKO SET ABOUT TRYING TO GET ANYBODY WITH ANY ATLANTEAN BLOOD TO HELP IN THE EFFORT.
ANYBODY BUT THEIR KING, THAT IS.
THEY CAME TO YOU EVENTUALLY-- AND IT COULDN'T HAVE BEEN EASY FOR THEM.
YOU'RE SAYING I SHOULD GO BACK.
NO. I DID BECAUSE, WELL, I REALLY DON'T BELONG WITH MY MOTHER'S PEOPLE, BUT ONCE I GOT TO ATLANTIS, IT'S SO...
HOMOGENOUS.
YES. I LIKE IT HERE, THOUGH.
WE CERTAINLY COULD USE SOME HELP REBUILDING OURSELVES.
AND THERE'S LORENA. SHE'S A VERY SPECIAL YOUNG LADY.
WHEN SUB DIEGO SANK, I WANTED TO HELP, AND LORENA SHOWED ME HOW.
YEAH, SHE'S GREAT. COULDN'T STOP TALKING ABOUT YOU, BUT RIGHT NOW--
--WE NEED TO TALK ABOUT THE OTHER WOMAN IN YOUR LIFE.

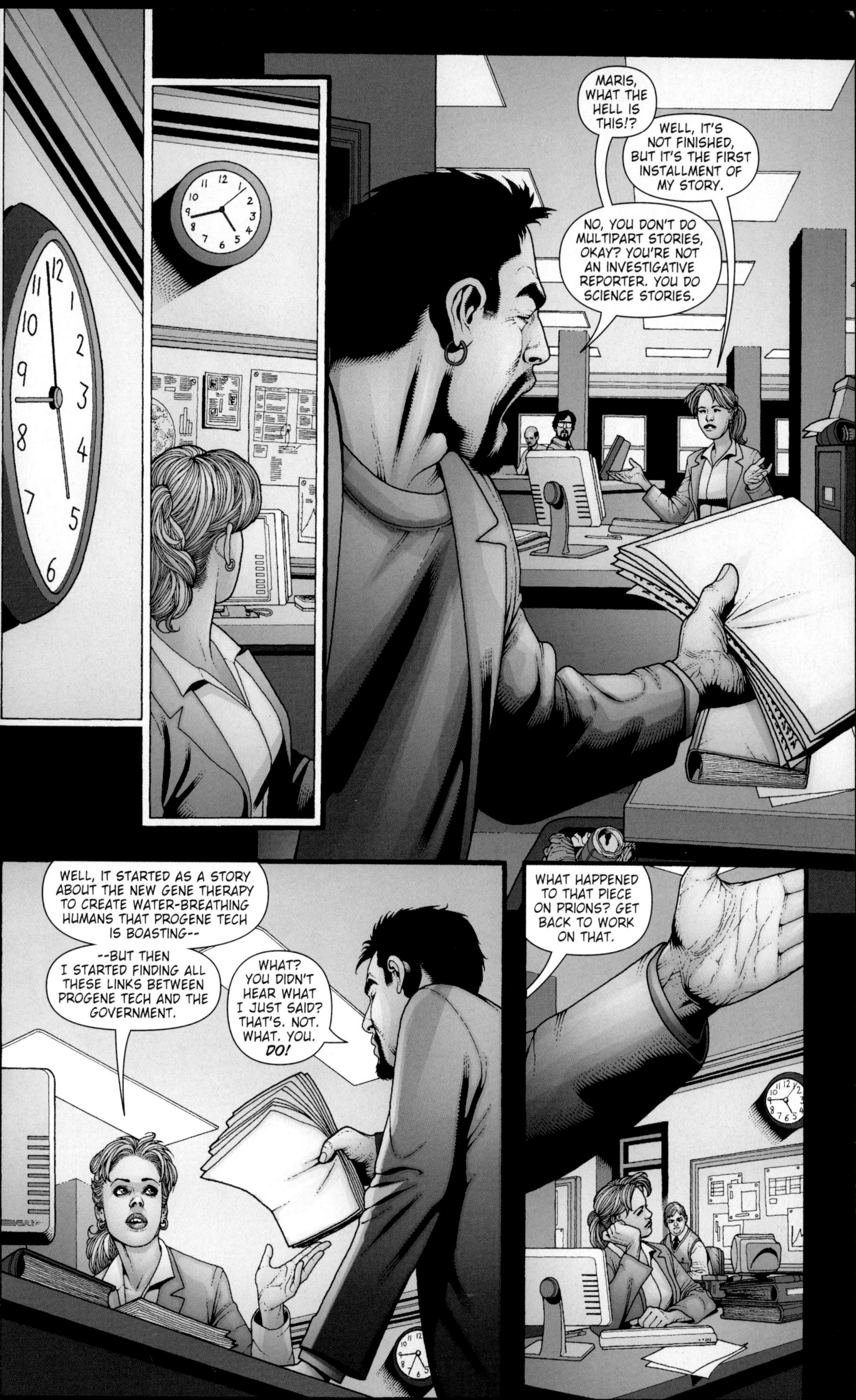
MARIS, WHAT THE HELL IS THIS!?
WELL, IT'S NOT FINISHED, BUT IT'S THE FIRST INSTALLMENT OF MY STORY.
NO, YOU DON'T DO MULTIPART STORIES, OKAY? YOU'RE NOT AN INVESTIGATIVE REPORTER. YOU DO SCIENCE STORIES.
WELL, IT STARTED AS A STORY ABOUT THE NEW GENE THERAPY TO CREATE WATER-BREATHING HUMANS THAT PROGENE TECH IS BOASTING--
--BUT THEN I STARTED FINDING ALL THESE LINKS BETWEEN PROGENE TECH AND THE GOVERNMENT.
WHAT? YOU DIDN'T HEAR WHAT I JUST SAID? THAT'S. NOT. WHAT. YOU. DO!
WHAT HAPPENED TO THAT PIECE ON PRIONS? GET BACK TO WORK ON THAT.

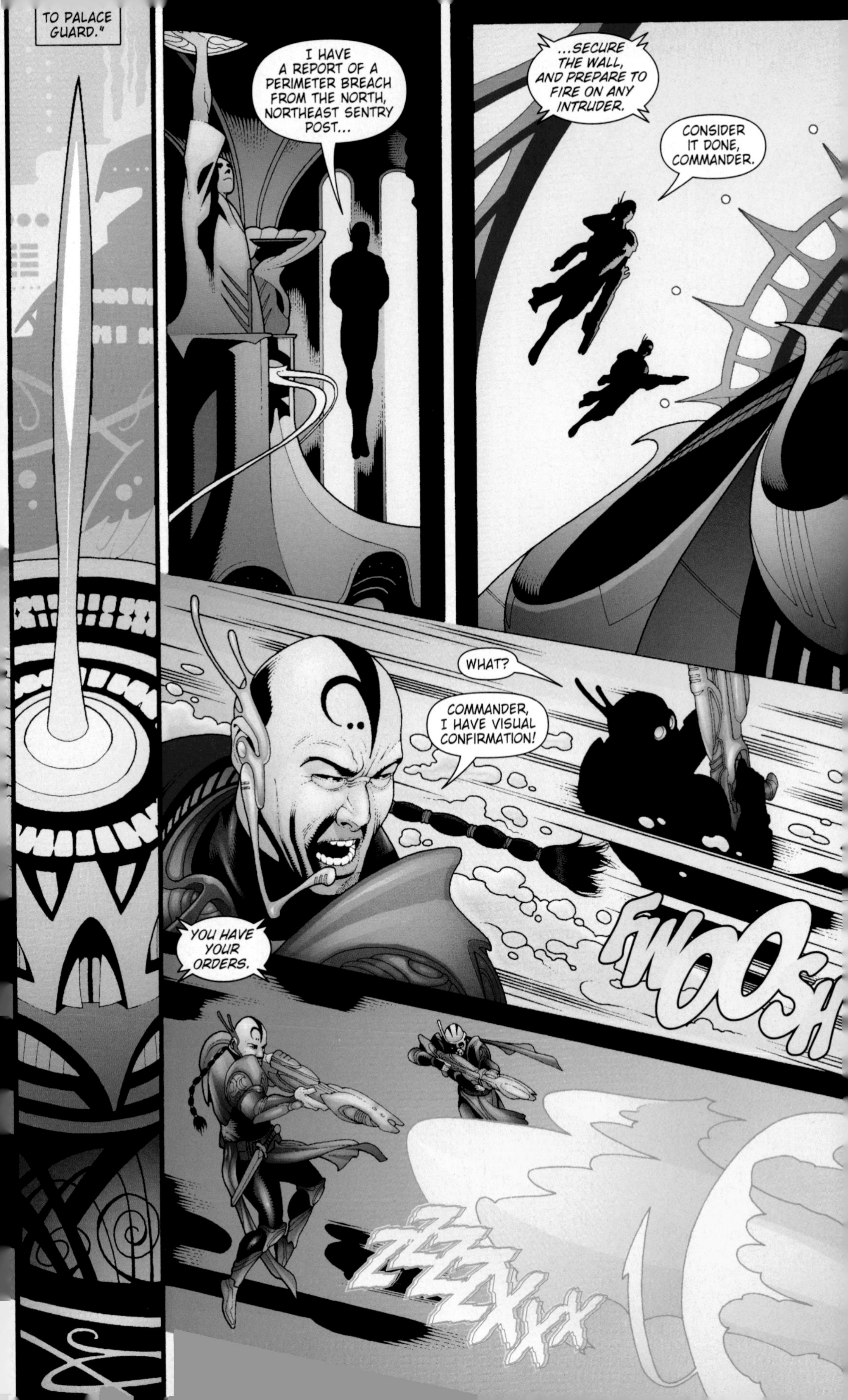
TO PALACE GUARD."
I HAVE A REPORT OF A PERIMETER BREACH FROM THE NORTH, NORTHEAST SENTRY POST...
...SECURE THE WALL, AND PREPARE TO FIRE ON ANY INTRUDER.
CONSIDER IT DONE, COMMANDER.
WHAT?
COMMANDER, I HAVE VISUAL CONFIRMATION!
YOU HAVE YOUR ORDERS.
FWOOSH
ZZZXXX

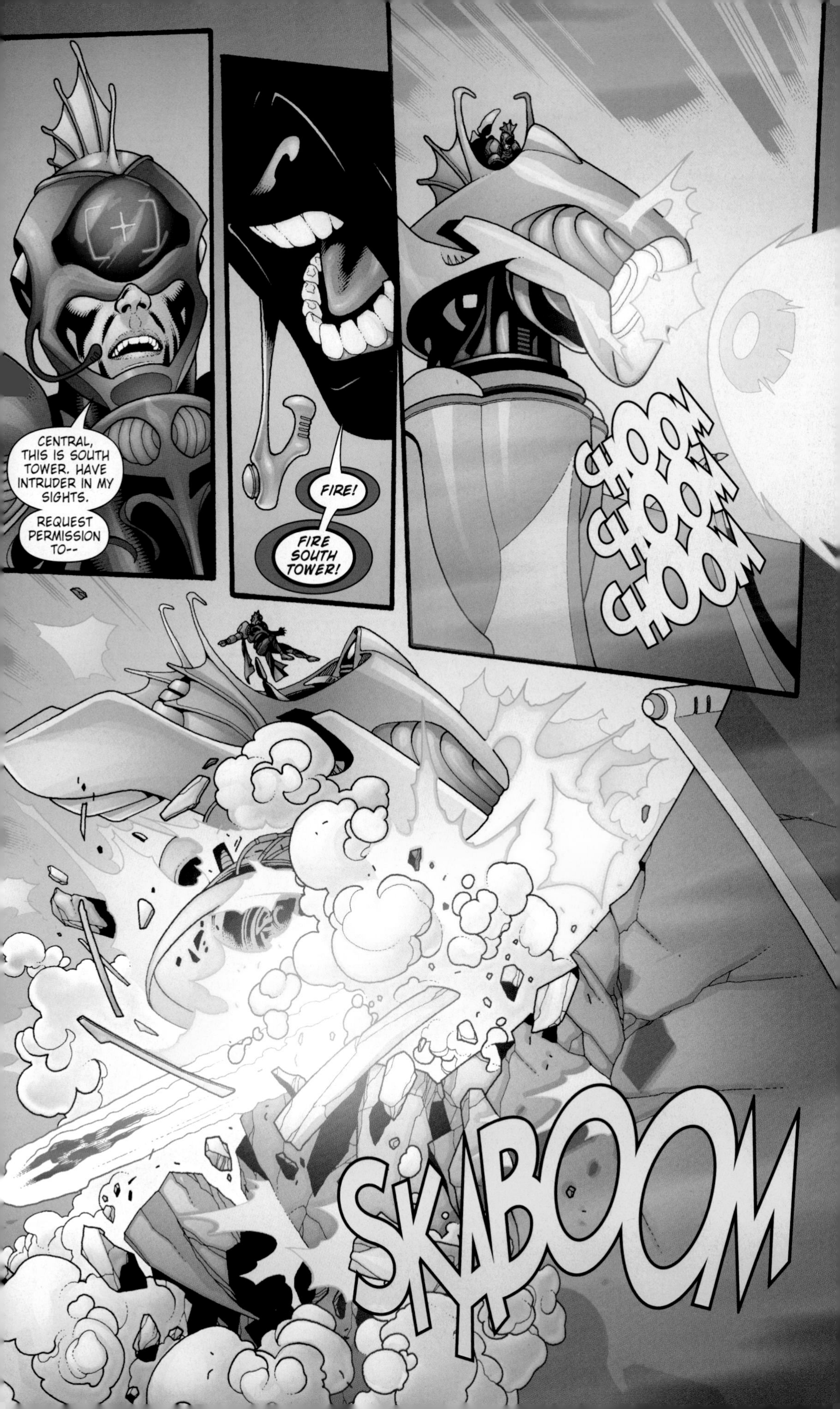
CENTRAL, THIS IS SOUTH TOWER. HAVE INTRUDER IN MY SIGHTS.
REQUEST PERMISSION TO--
FIRE!
FIRE SOUTH TOWER!
CHOOM CHOOM CHOOM
SKABOOM

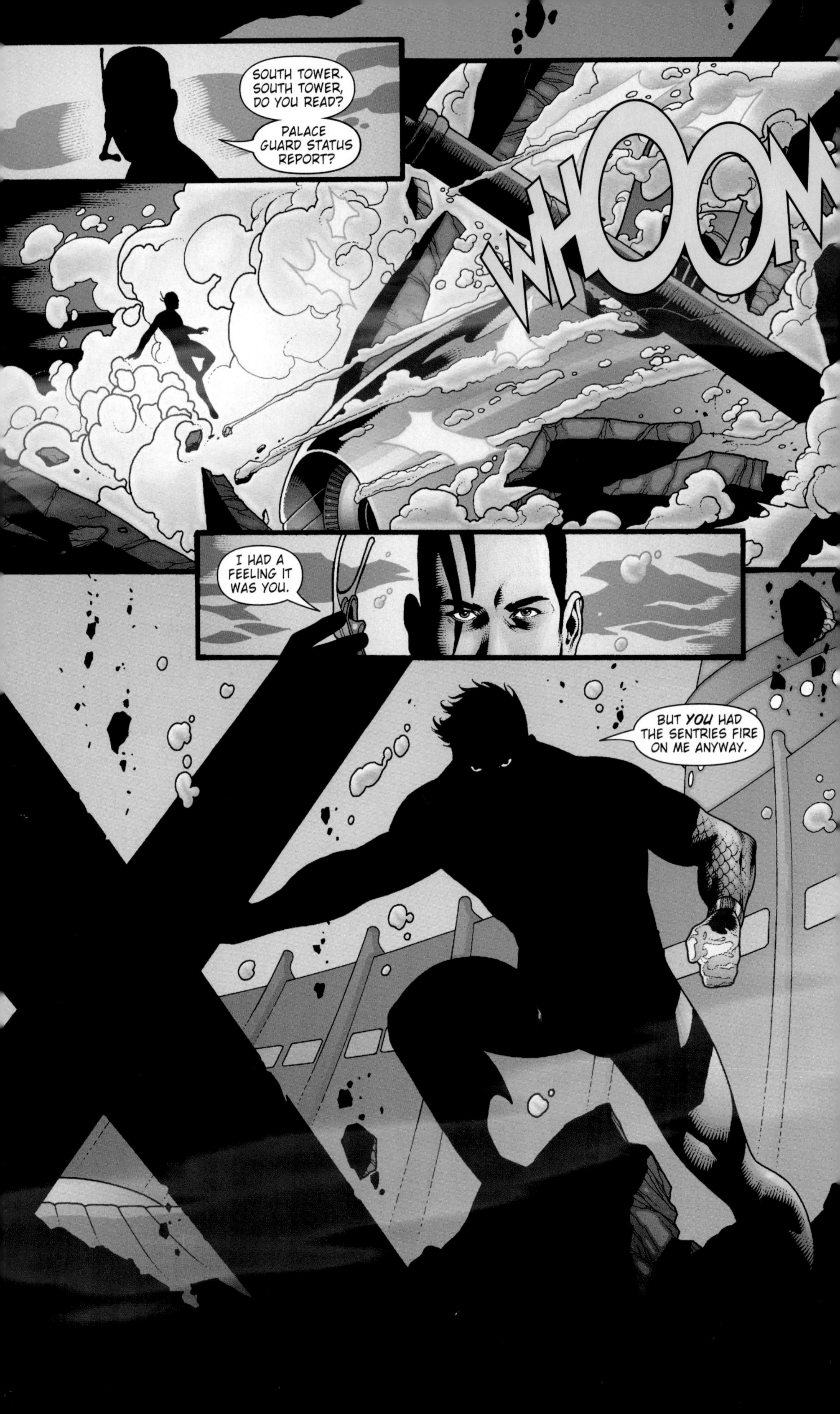
SOUTH TOWER. SOUTH TOWER, DO YOU READ?
PALACE GUARD STATUS REPORT?
WHOOM
I HAD A FEELING IT WAS YOU.
BUT *YOU* HAD THE SENTRIES FIRE ON ME ANYWAY.

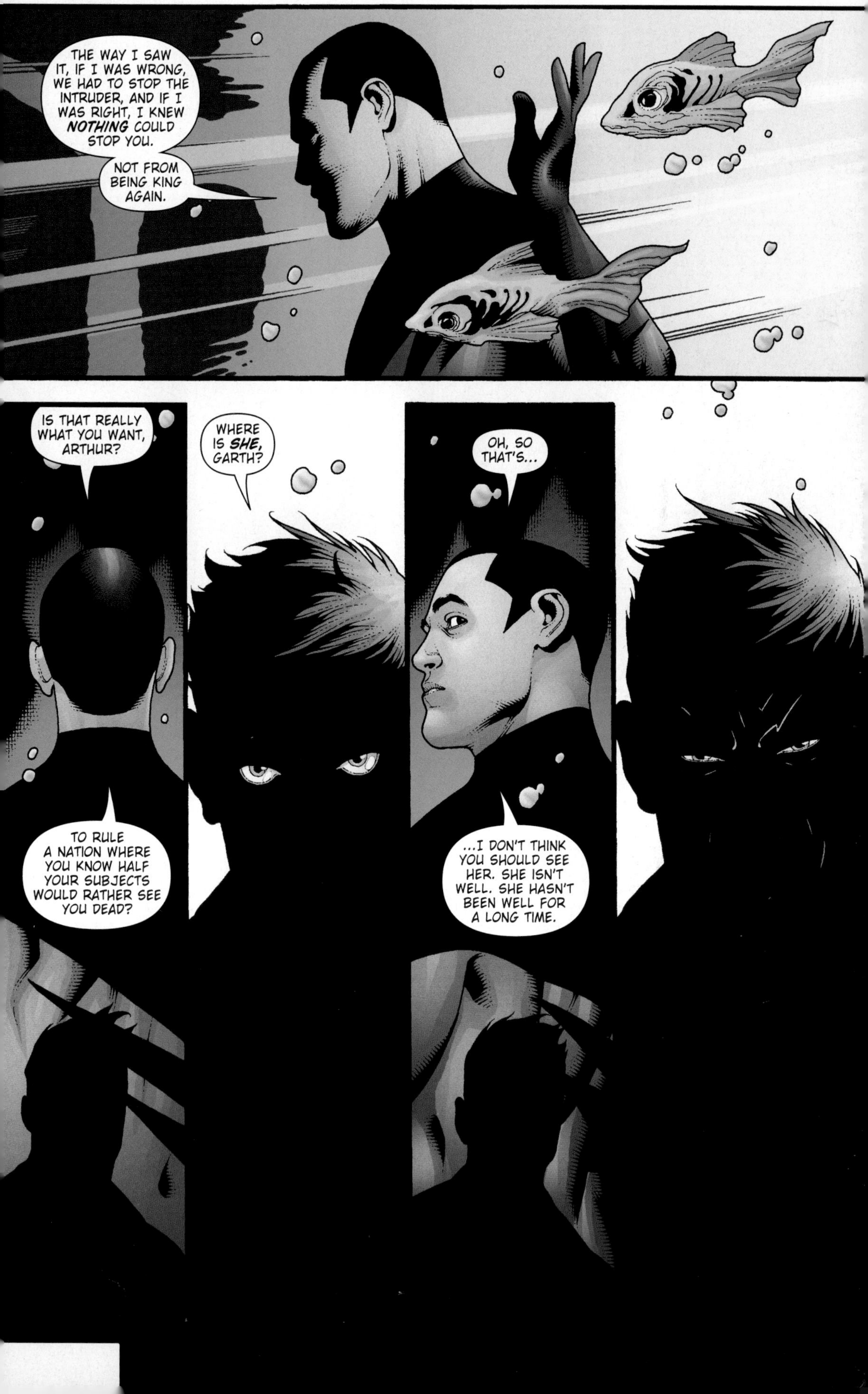
THE WAY I SAW IT, IF I WAS WRONG, WE HAD TO STOP THE INTRUDER, AND IF I WAS RIGHT, I KNEW NOTHING COULD STOP YOU.
NOT FROM BEING KING AGAIN.
IS THAT REALLY WHAT YOU WANT, ARTHUR?
TO RULE A NATION WHERE YOU KNOW HALF YOUR SUBJECTS WOULD RATHER SEE YOU DEAD?
WHERE IS SHE, GARTH?
OH, SO THAT'S...
...I DON'T THINK YOU SHOULD SEE HER. SHE ISN'T WELL. SHE HASN'T BEEN WELL FOR A LONG TIME.

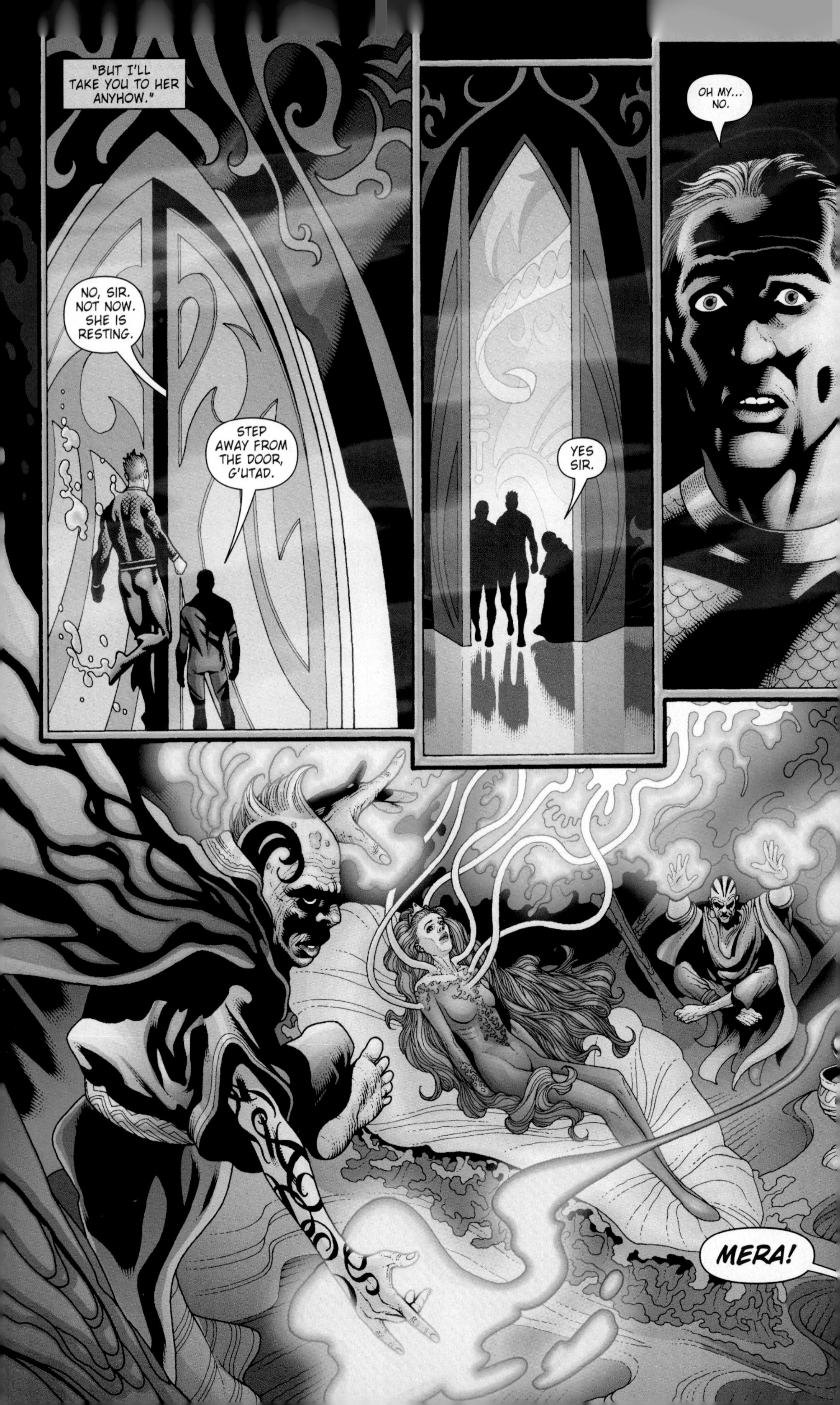
"BUT I'LL TAKE YOU TO HER ANYHOW."
NO, SIR. NOT NOW. SHE IS RESTING.
STEP AWAY FROM THE DOOR, G'UTAD.
YES SIR.
OH MY... NO.
MERA!

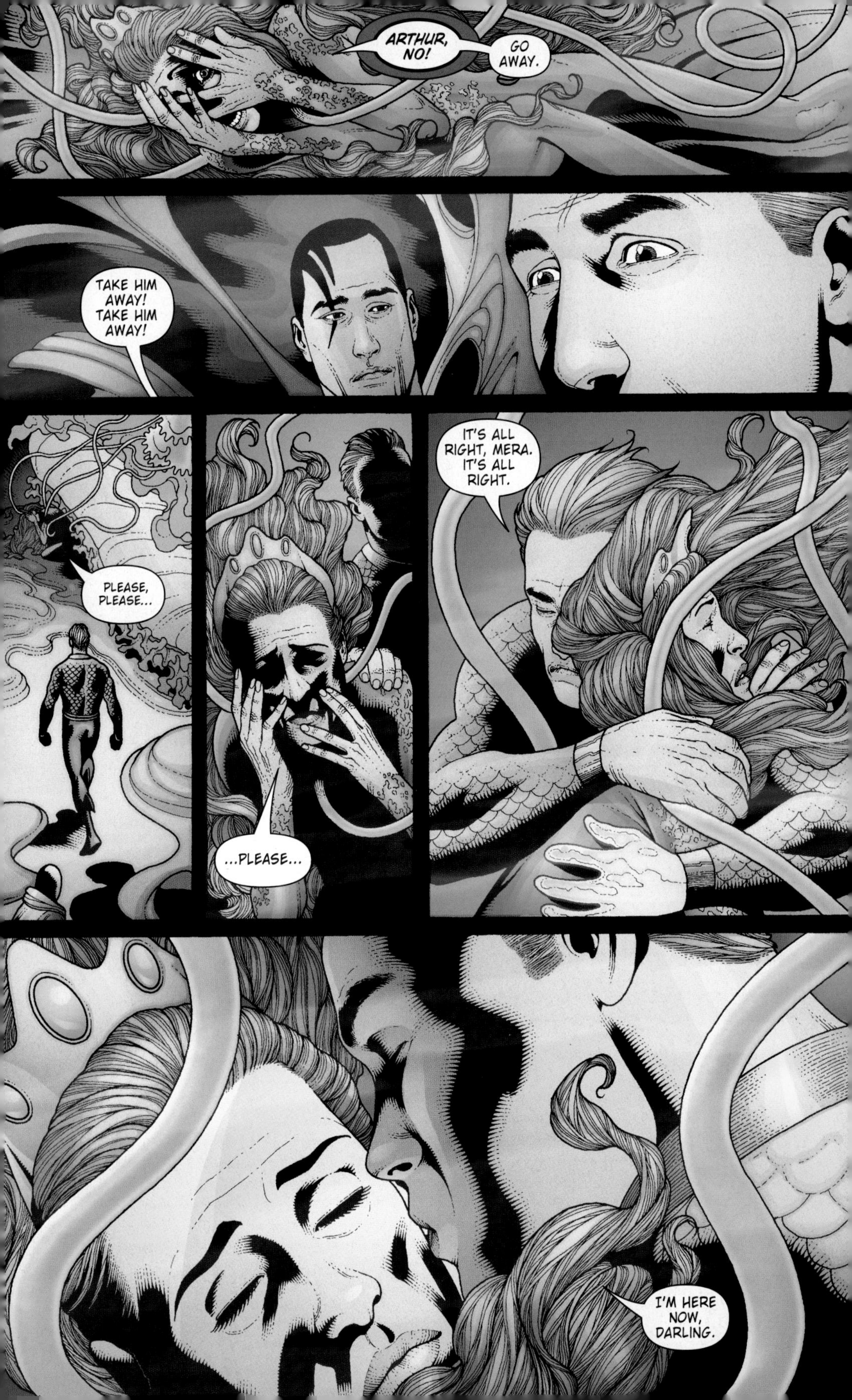
ARTHUR, NO!
GO AWAY.
TAKE HIM AWAY! TAKE HIM AWAY!
PLEASE, PLEASE...
...PLEASE...
IT'S ALL RIGHT, MERA. IT'S ALL RIGHT.
I'M HERE NOW, DARLING.

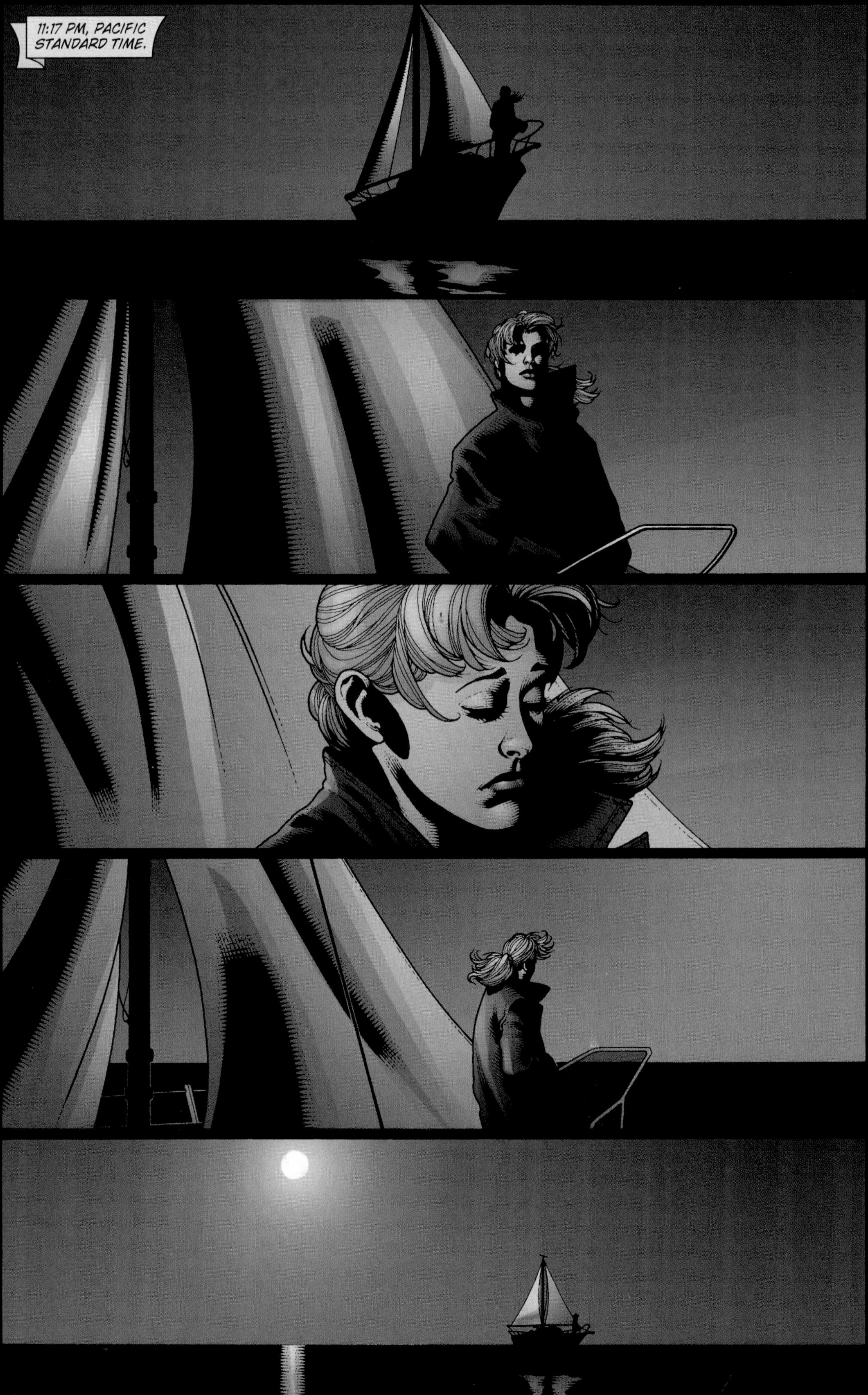
11:17 PM, PACIFIC STANDARD TIME.

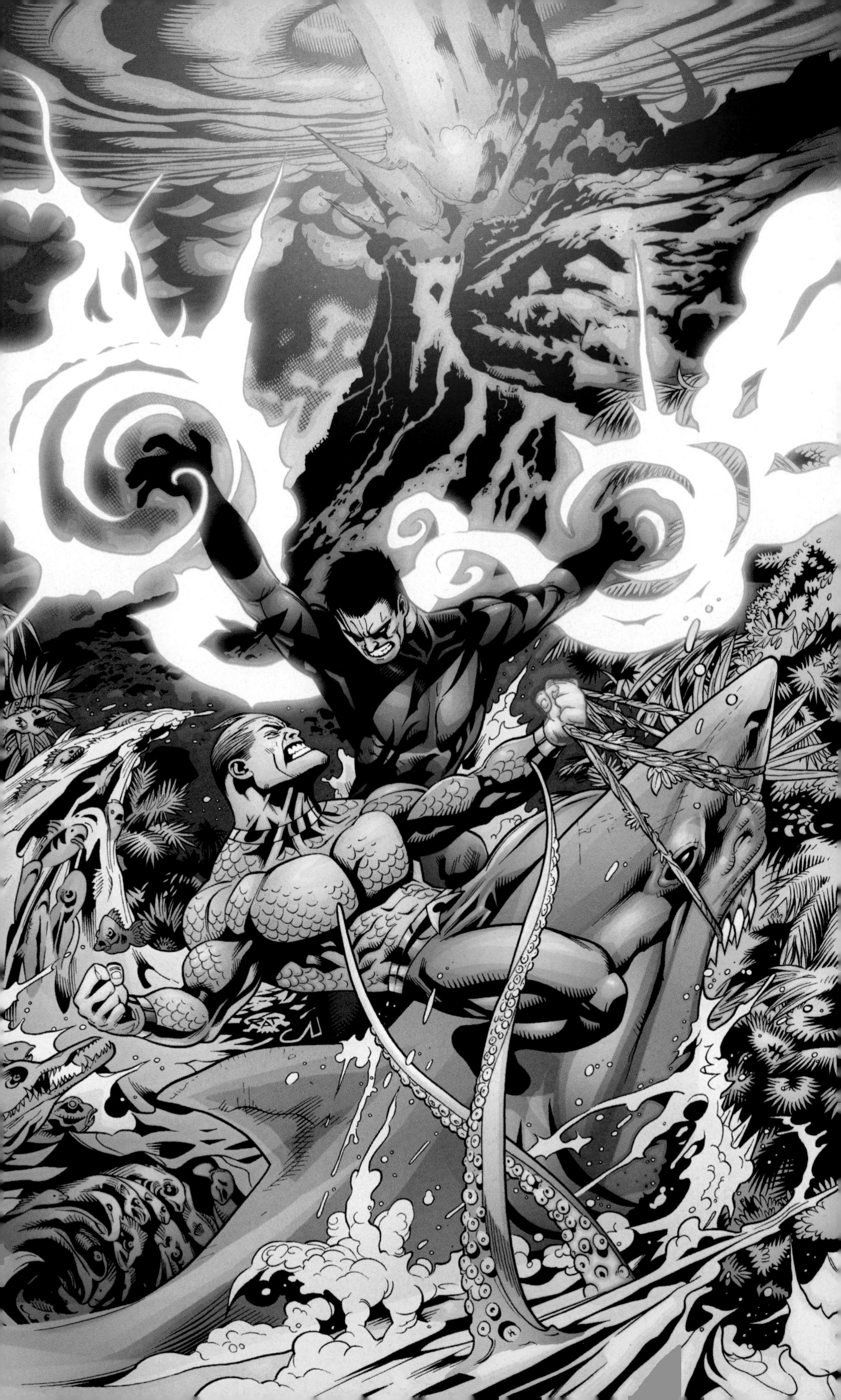

THE QUALITY OF MERCY

JOHN ARCUDI
Writer

LEONARD KIRK
Layouts

ANDY CLARKE
Finishes

NATHAN EYRING
Colorist

TRAVIS LANHAM
Letterer

PATRICK GLEASON & CHRISTIAN ALAMY
Cover

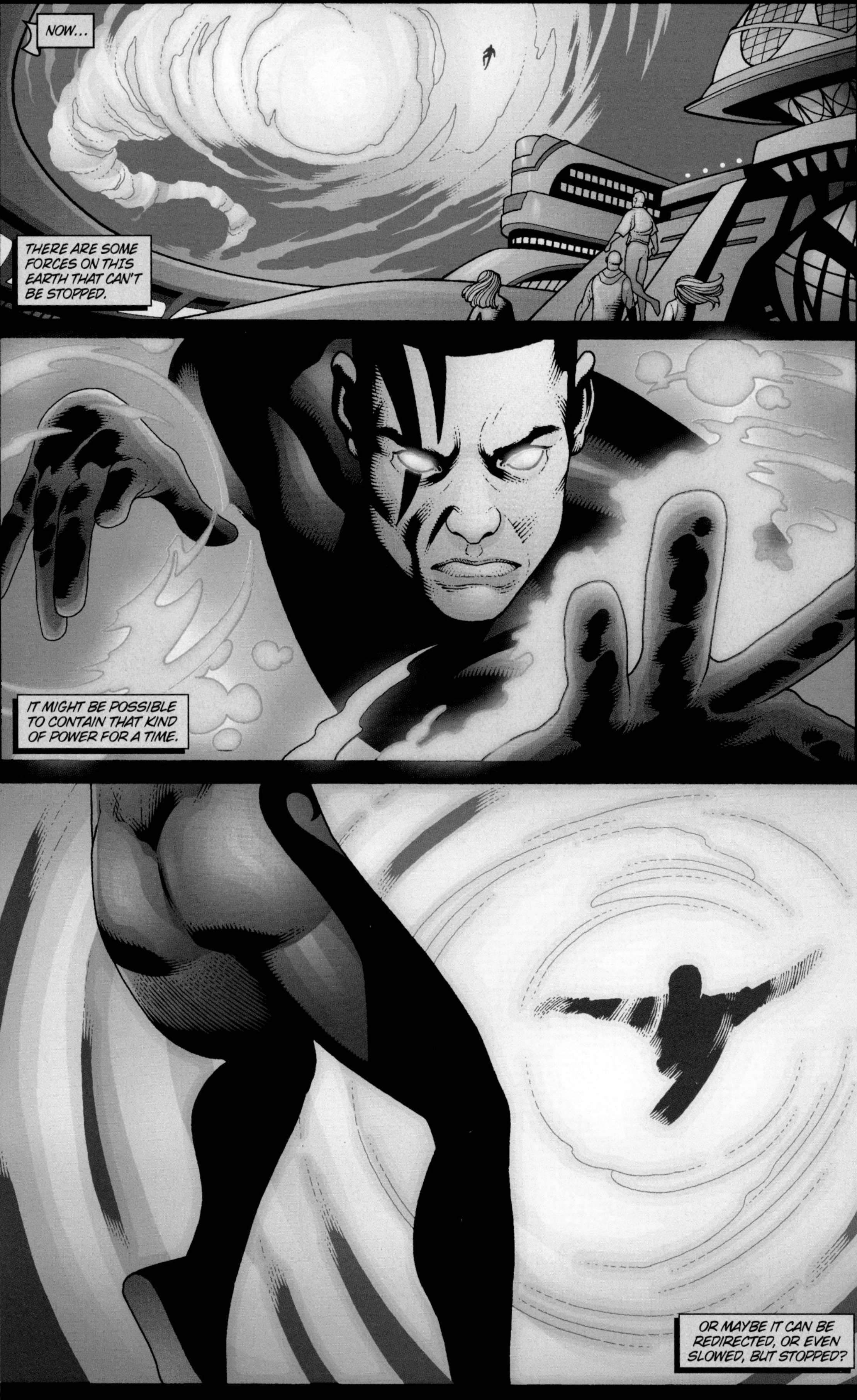
NOW...
THERE ARE SOME FORCES ON THIS EARTH THAT CAN'T BE STOPPED.
IT MIGHT BE POSSIBLE TO CONTAIN THAT KIND OF POWER FOR A TIME.
OR MAYBE IT CAN BE REDIRECTED, OR EVEN SLOWED, BUT STOPPED?

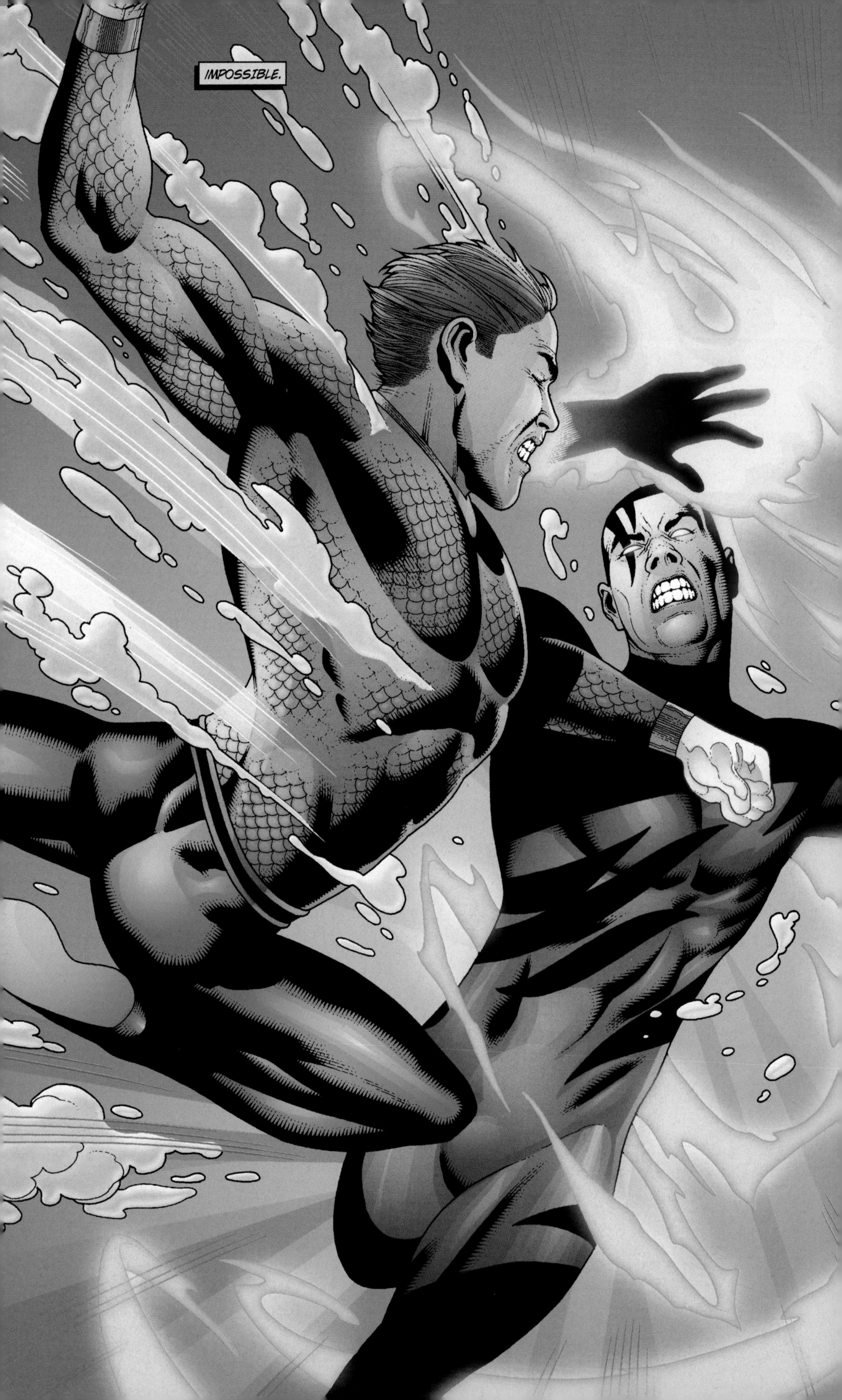
IMPOSSIBLE.

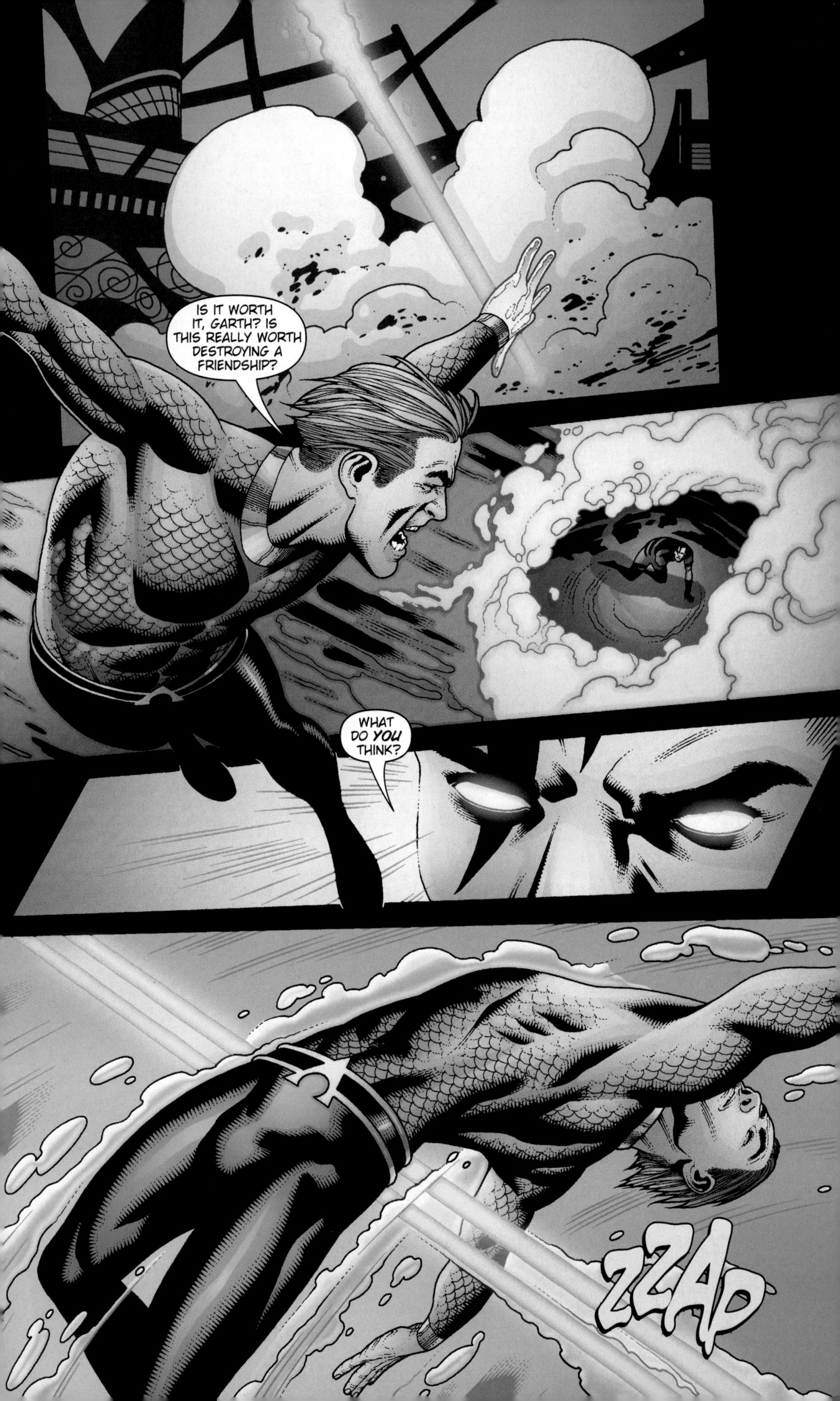
IS IT WORTH IT, GARTH? IS THIS REALLY WORTH DESTROYING A FRIENDSHIP?
WHAT DO YOU THINK?
ZZAP

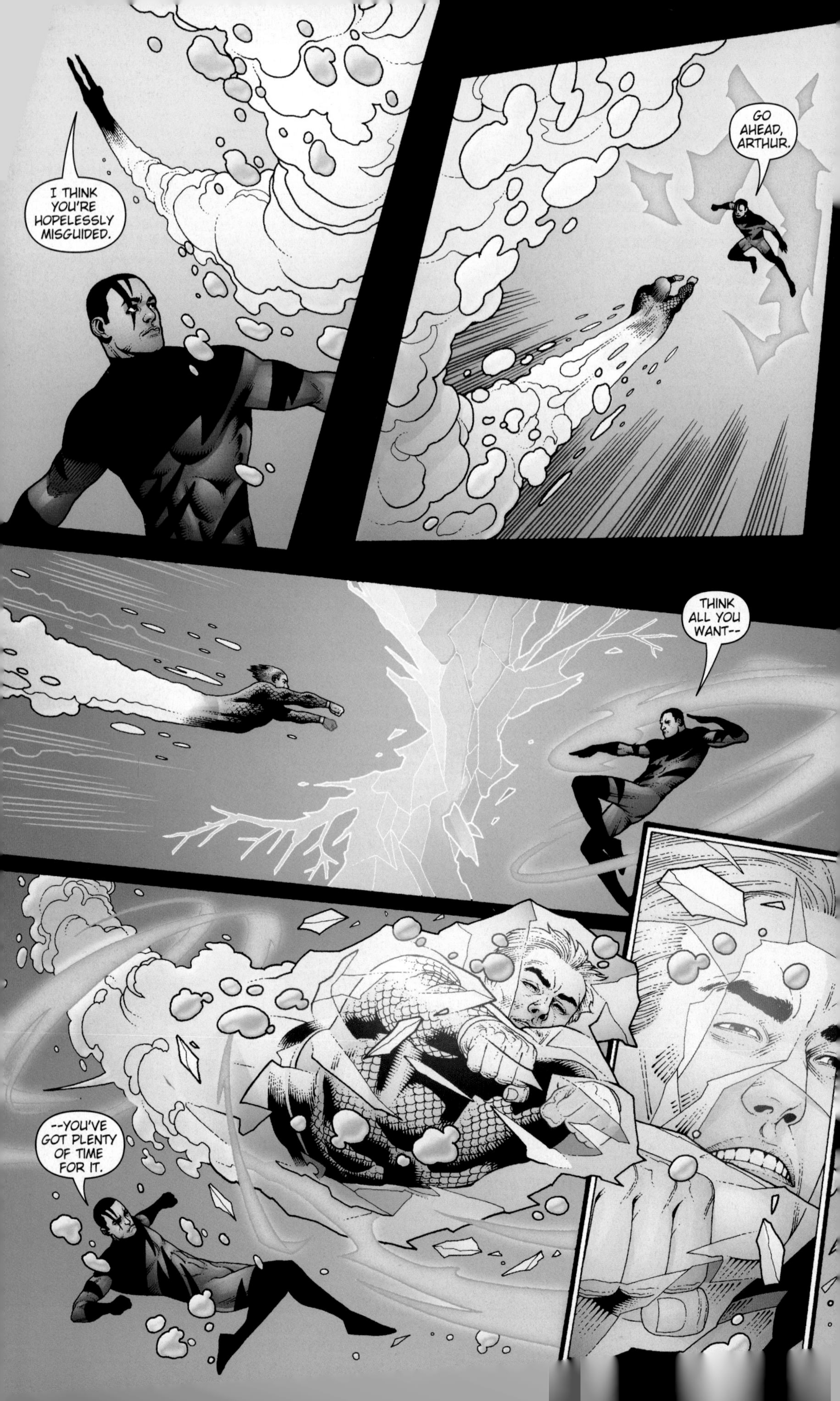
I THINK YOU'RE HOPELESSLY MISGUIDED.
GO AHEAD, ARTHUR.
THINK ALL YOU WANT--
--YOU'VE GOT PLENTY OF TIME FOR IT.

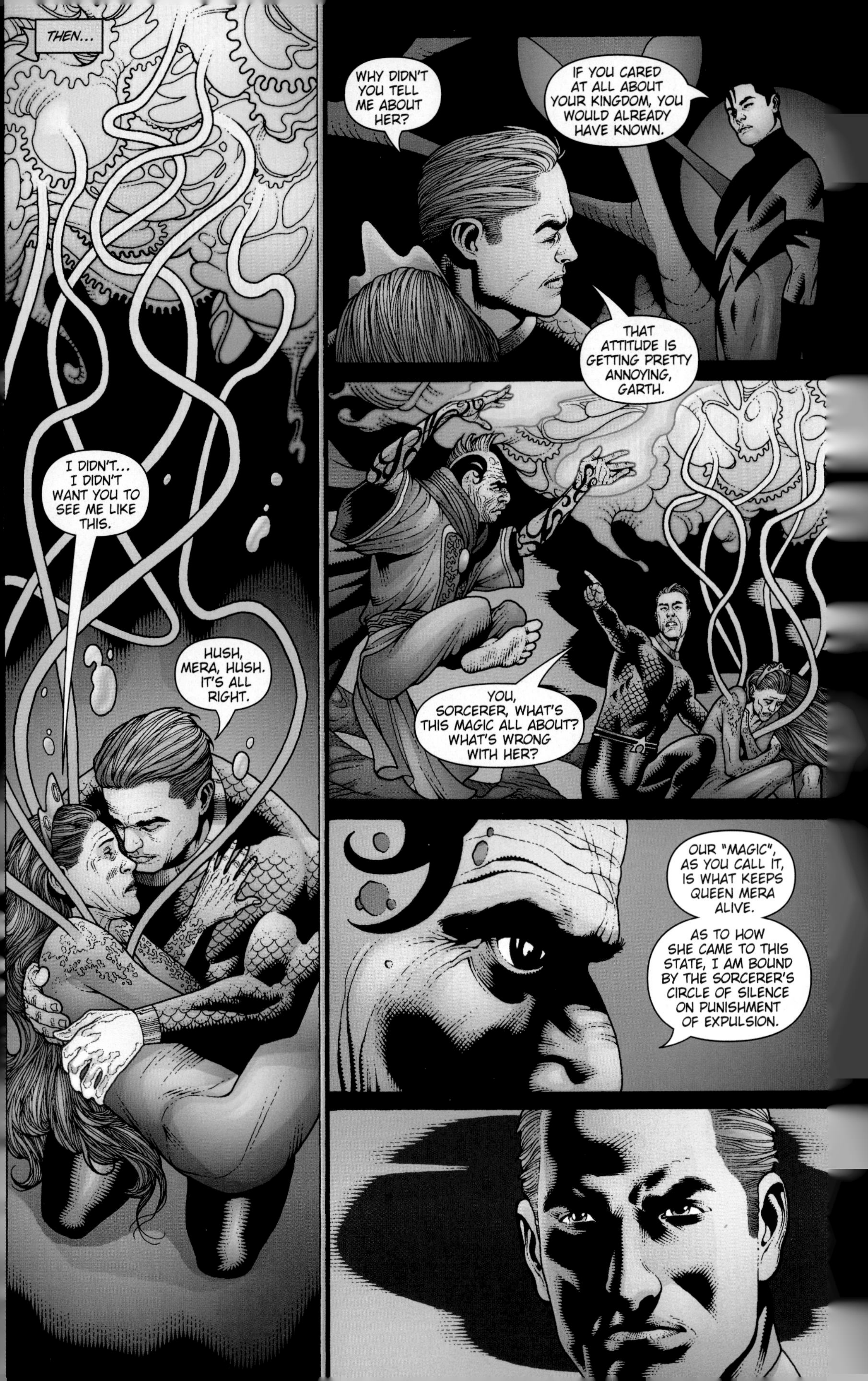
THEN...
I DIDN'T... I DIDN'T WANT YOU TO SEE ME LIKE THIS.
HUSH, MERA, HUSH. IT'S ALL RIGHT.
WHY DIDN'T YOU TELL ME ABOUT HER?
IF YOU CARED AT ALL ABOUT YOUR KINGDOM, YOU WOULD ALREADY HAVE KNOWN.
THAT ATTITUDE IS GETTING PRETTY ANNOYING, GARTH.
YOU, SORCERER, WHAT'S THIS MAGIC ALL ABOUT? WHAT'S WRONG WITH HER?
OUR "MAGIC", AS YOU CALL IT, IS WHAT KEEPS QUEEN MERA ALIVE.
AS TO HOW SHE CAME TO THIS STATE, I AM BOUND BY THE SORCERER'S CIRCLE OF SILENCE ON PUNISHMENT OF EXPULSION.

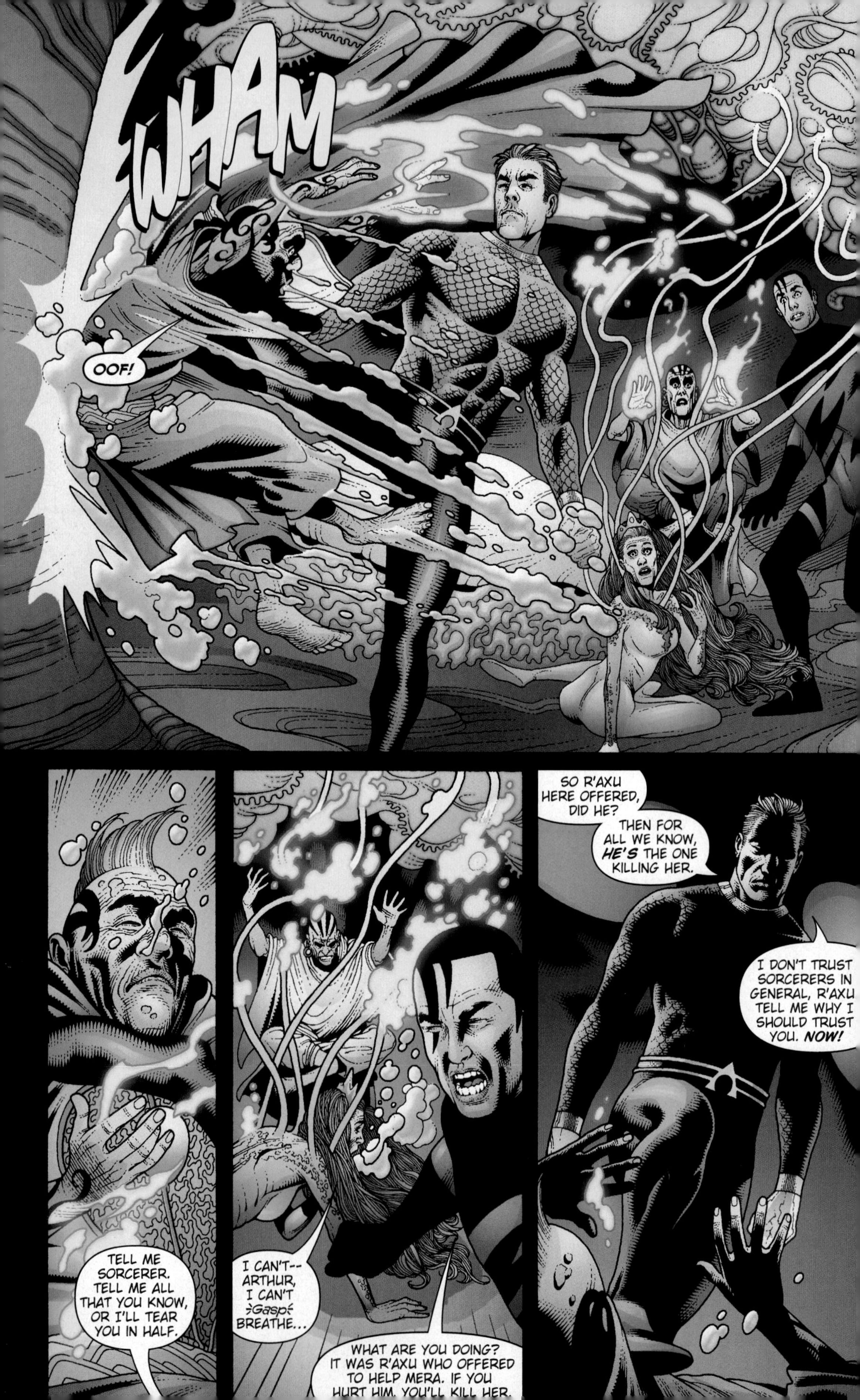
WHAM
OOF!
TELL ME SORCERER. TELL ME ALL THAT YOU KNOW, OR I'LL TEAR YOU IN HALF.
I CAN'T-- ARTHUR, I CAN'T *Gasp* BREATHE...
WHAT ARE YOU DOING? IT WAS R'AXU WHO OFFERED TO HELP MERA. IF YOU HURT HIM, YOU'LL KILL HER.
SO R'AXU HERE OFFERED, DID HE?
THEN FOR ALL WE KNOW, HE'S THE ONE KILLING HER.
I DON'T TRUST SORCERERS IN GENERAL, R'AXU TELL ME WHY I SHOULD TRUST YOU. NOW!

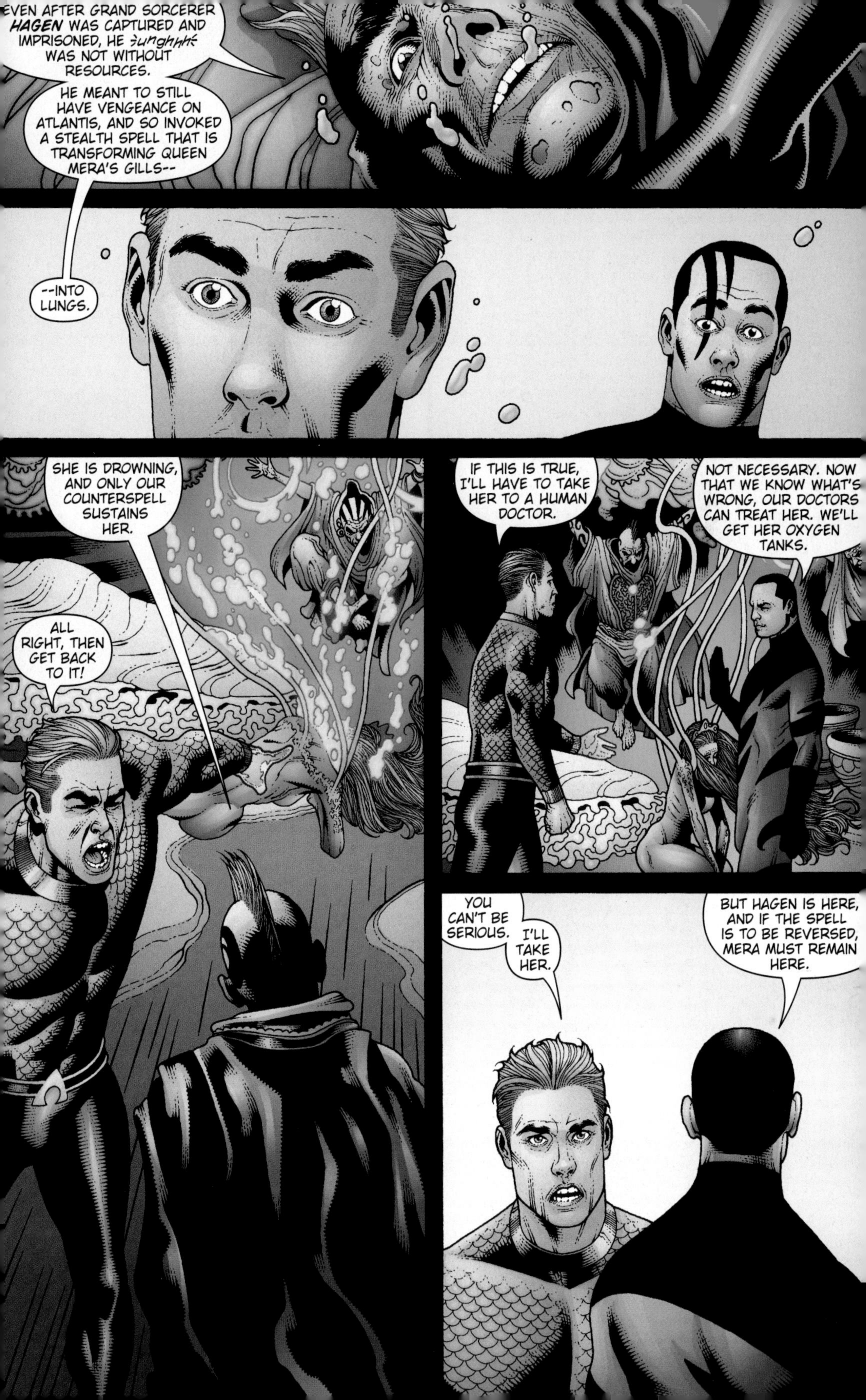
EVEN AFTER GRAND SORCERER HAGEN WAS CAPTURED AND IMPRISONED, HE ʒunghhh WAS NOT WITHOUT RESOURCES.
HE MEANT TO STILL HAVE VENGEANCE ON ATLANTIS, AND SO INVOKED A STEALTH SPELL THAT IS TRANSFORMING QUEEN MERA'S GILLS--
--INTO LUNGS.
SHE IS DROWNING, AND ONLY OUR COUNTERSPELL SUSTAINS HER.
ALL RIGHT, THEN GET BACK TO IT!
IF THIS IS TRUE, I'LL HAVE TO TAKE HER TO A HUMAN DOCTOR.
NOT NECESSARY. NOW THAT WE KNOW WHAT'S WRONG, OUR DOCTORS CAN TREAT HER. WE'LL GET HER OXYGEN TANKS.
YOU CAN'T BE SERIOUS.
I'LL TAKE HER.
BUT HAGEN IS HERE, AND IF THE SPELL IS TO BE REVERSED, MERA MUST REMAIN HERE.

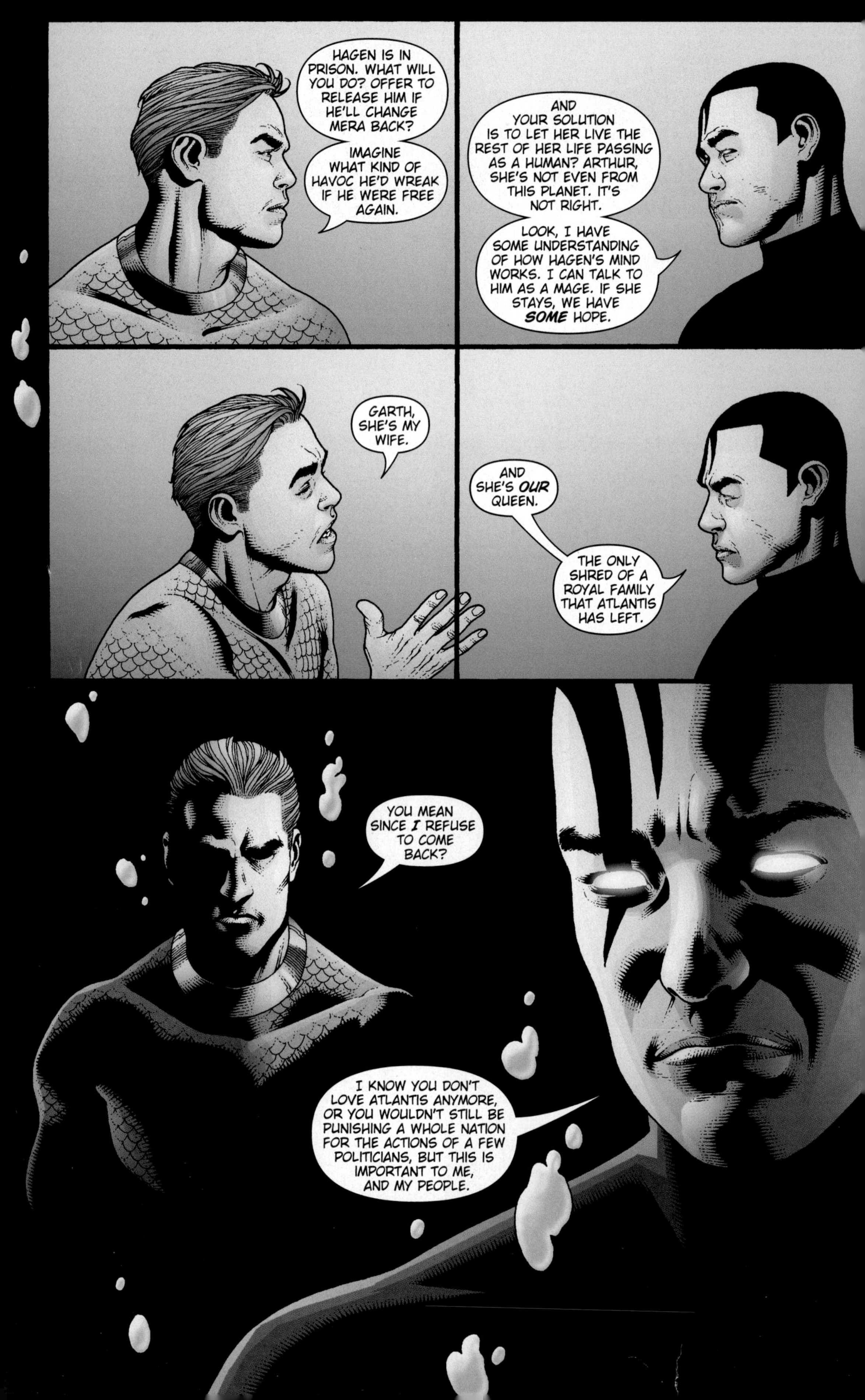
HAGEN IS IN PRISON. WHAT WILL YOU DO? OFFER TO RELEASE HIM IF HE'LL CHANGE MERA BACK?
IMAGINE WHAT KIND OF HAVOC HE'D WREAK IF HE WERE FREE AGAIN.
AND YOUR SOLUTION IS TO LET HER LIVE THE REST OF HER LIFE PASSING AS A HUMAN? ARTHUR, SHE'S NOT EVEN FROM THIS PLANET. IT'S NOT RIGHT.
LOOK, I HAVE SOME UNDERSTANDING OF HOW HAGEN'S MIND WORKS. I CAN TALK TO HIM AS A MAGE. IF SHE STAYS, WE HAVE *SOME* HOPE.
GARTH, SHE'S MY WIFE.
AND SHE'S *OUR* QUEEN.
THE ONLY SHRED OF A ROYAL FAMILY THAT ATLANTIS HAS LEFT.
YOU MEAN SINCE *I* REFUSE TO COME BACK?
I KNOW YOU DON'T LOVE ATLANTIS ANYMORE, OR YOU WOULDN'T STILL BE PUNISHING A WHOLE NATION FOR THE ACTIONS OF A FEW POLITICIANS, BUT THIS IS IMPORTANT TO ME, AND MY PEOPLE.

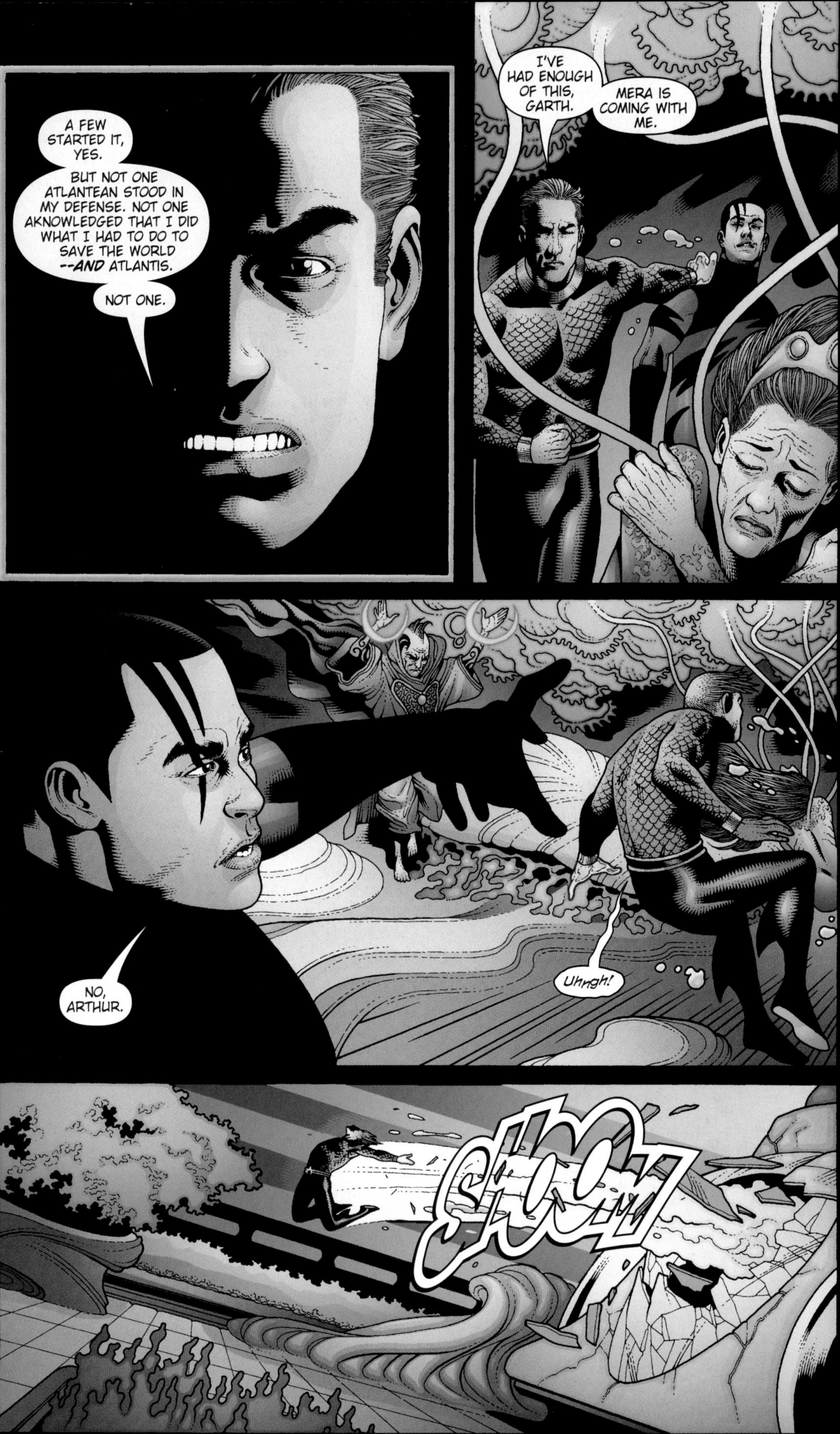
A FEW STARTED IT, YES.
BUT NOT ONE ATLANTEAN STOOD IN MY DEFENSE. NOT ONE AKNOWLEDGED THAT I DID WHAT I HAD TO DO TO SAVE THE WORLD --AND ATLANTIS.
NOT ONE.
I'VE HAD ENOUGH OF THIS, GARTH.
MERA IS COMING WITH ME.
NO, ARTHUR.
Uhngh!
SHOOM

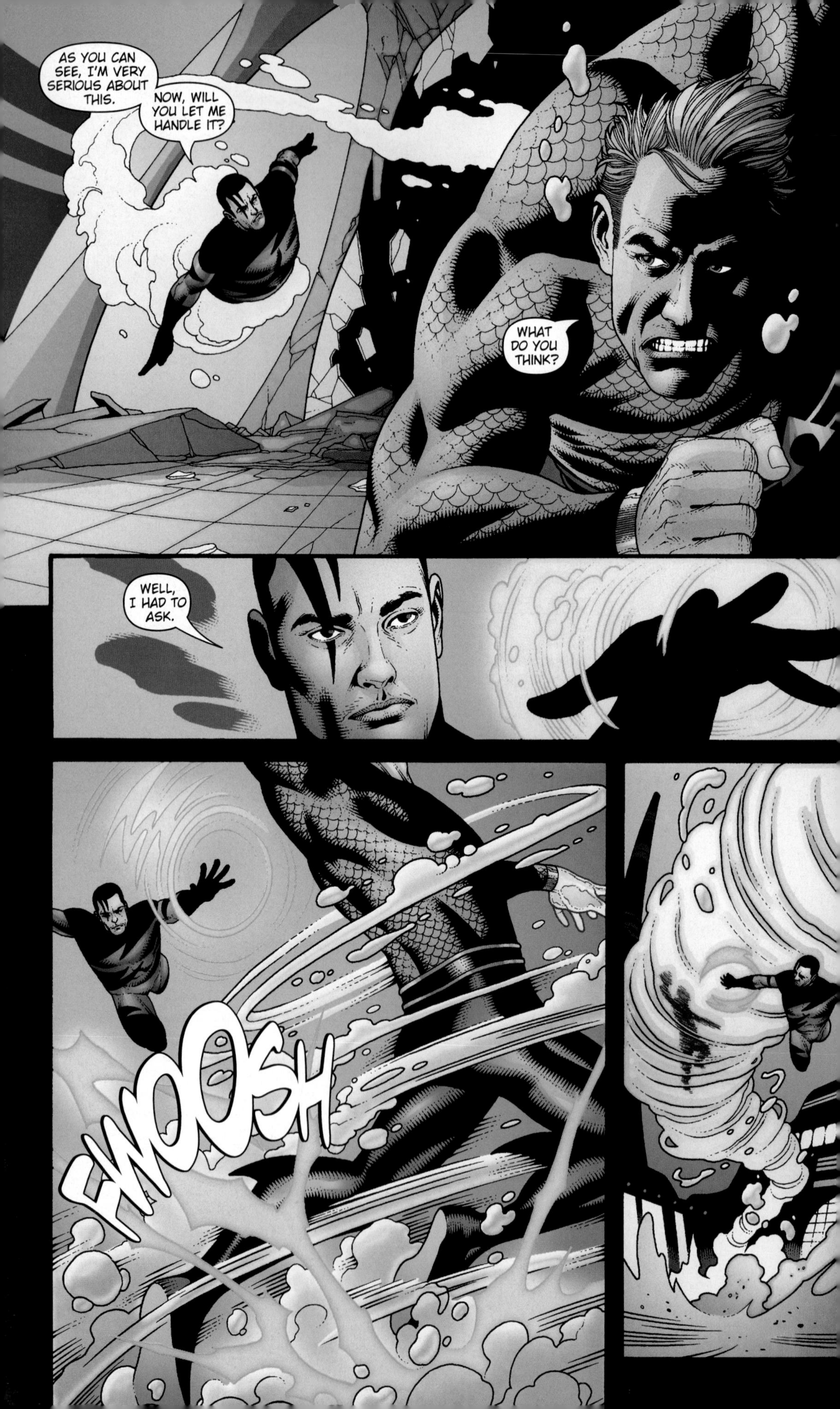

AS YOU CAN SEE, I'M VERY SERIOUS ABOUT THIS.
NOW, WILL YOU LET ME HANDLE IT?
WHAT DO YOU THINK?
WELL, I HAD TO ASK.
FWOOSH

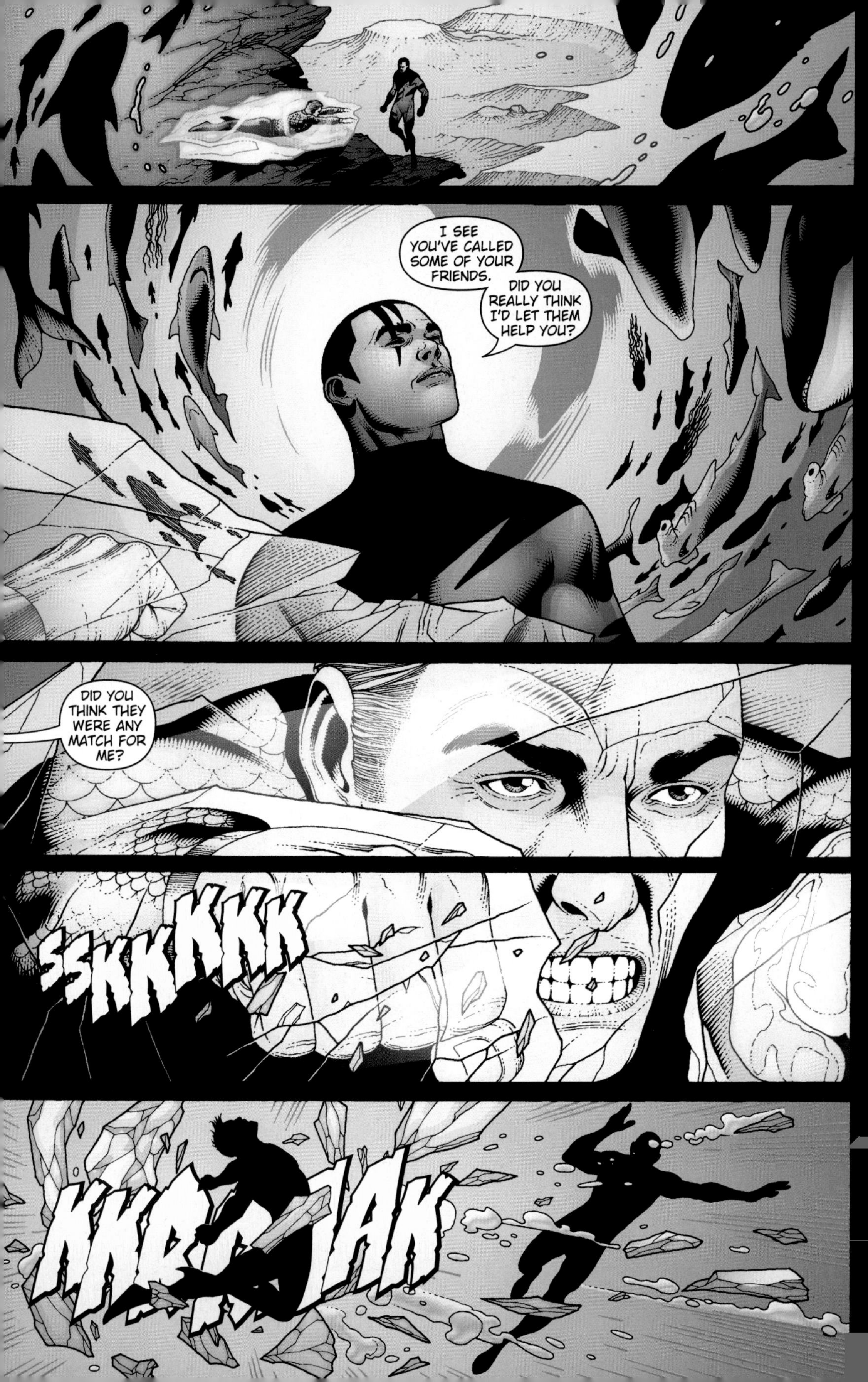
I SEE YOU'VE CALLED SOME OF YOUR FRIENDS.
DID YOU REALLY THINK I'D LET THEM HELP YOU?
DID YOU THINK THEY WERE ANY MATCH FOR ME?
SSKKKKK

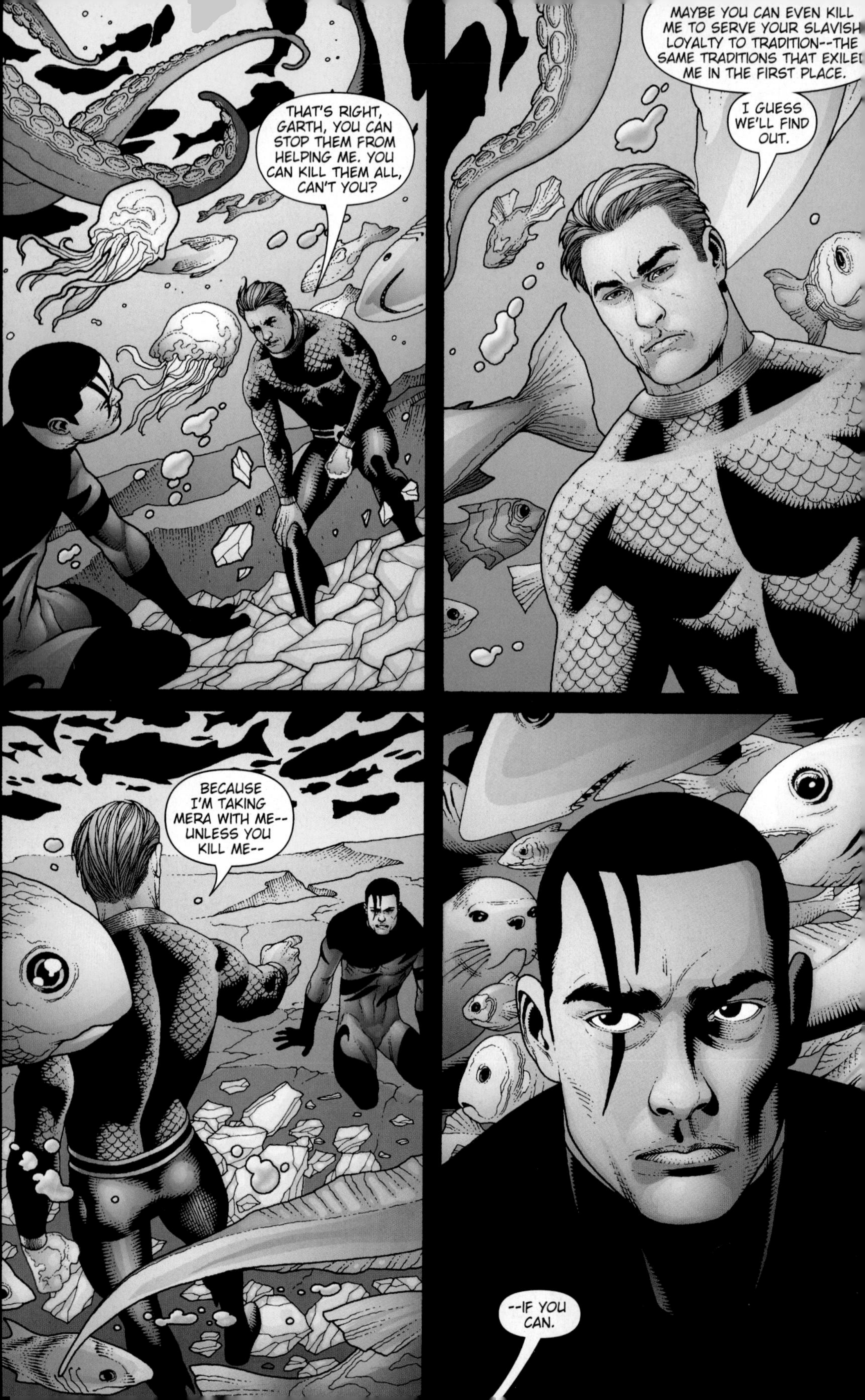
THAT'S RIGHT, GARTH, YOU CAN STOP THEM FROM HELPING ME. YOU CAN KILL THEM ALL, CAN'T YOU?
MAYBE YOU CAN EVEN KILL ME TO SERVE YOUR SLAVISH LOYALTY TO TRADITION--THE SAME TRADITIONS THAT EXILED ME IN THE FIRST PLACE.
I GUESS WE'LL FIND OUT.
BECAUSE I'M TAKING MERA WITH ME--UNLESS YOU KILL ME--
--IF YOU CAN.

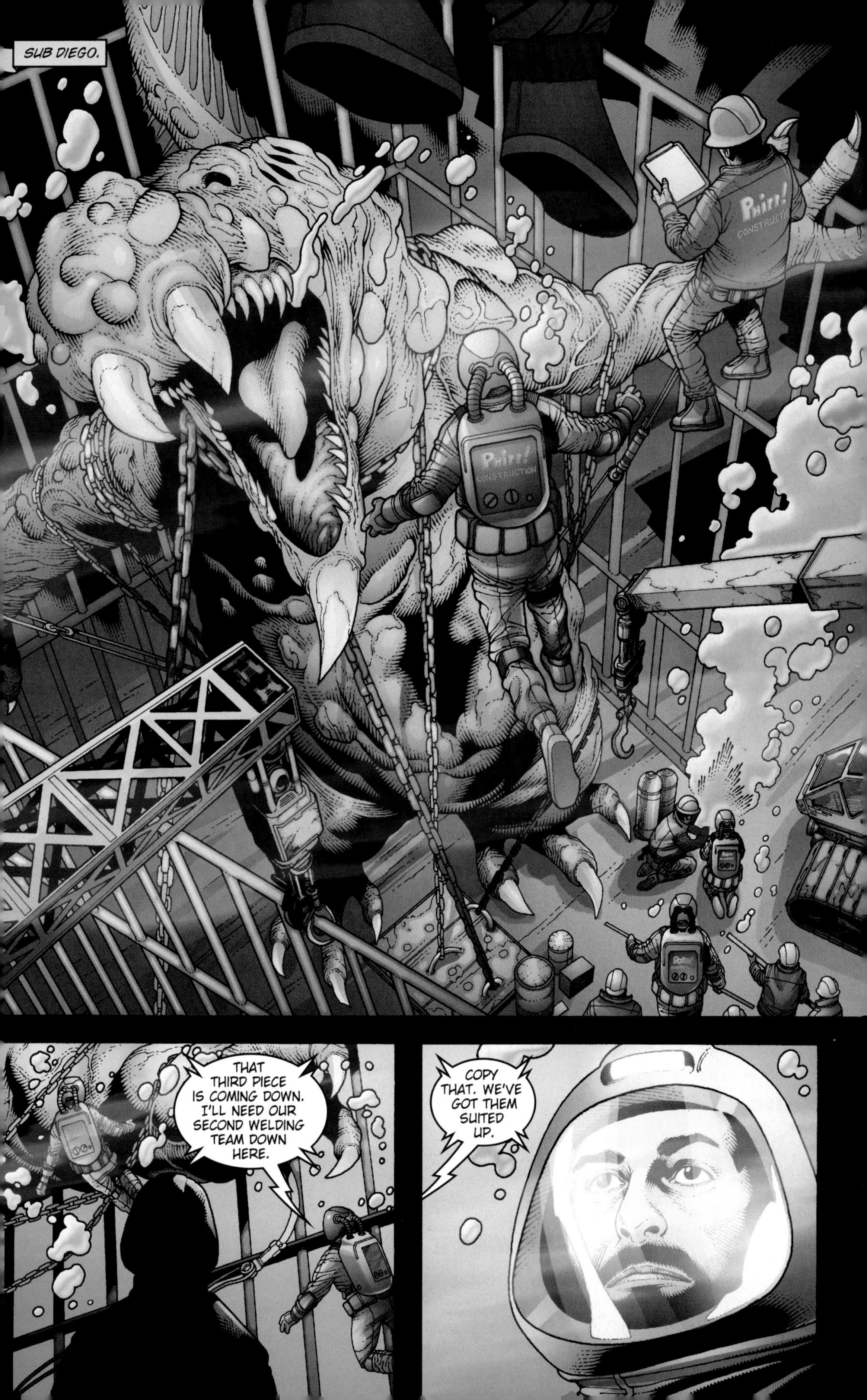
SUB DIEGO.
THAT THIRD PIECE IS COMING DOWN. I'LL NEED OUR SECOND WELDING TEAM DOWN HERE.
COPY THAT. WE'VE GOT THEM SUITED UP.

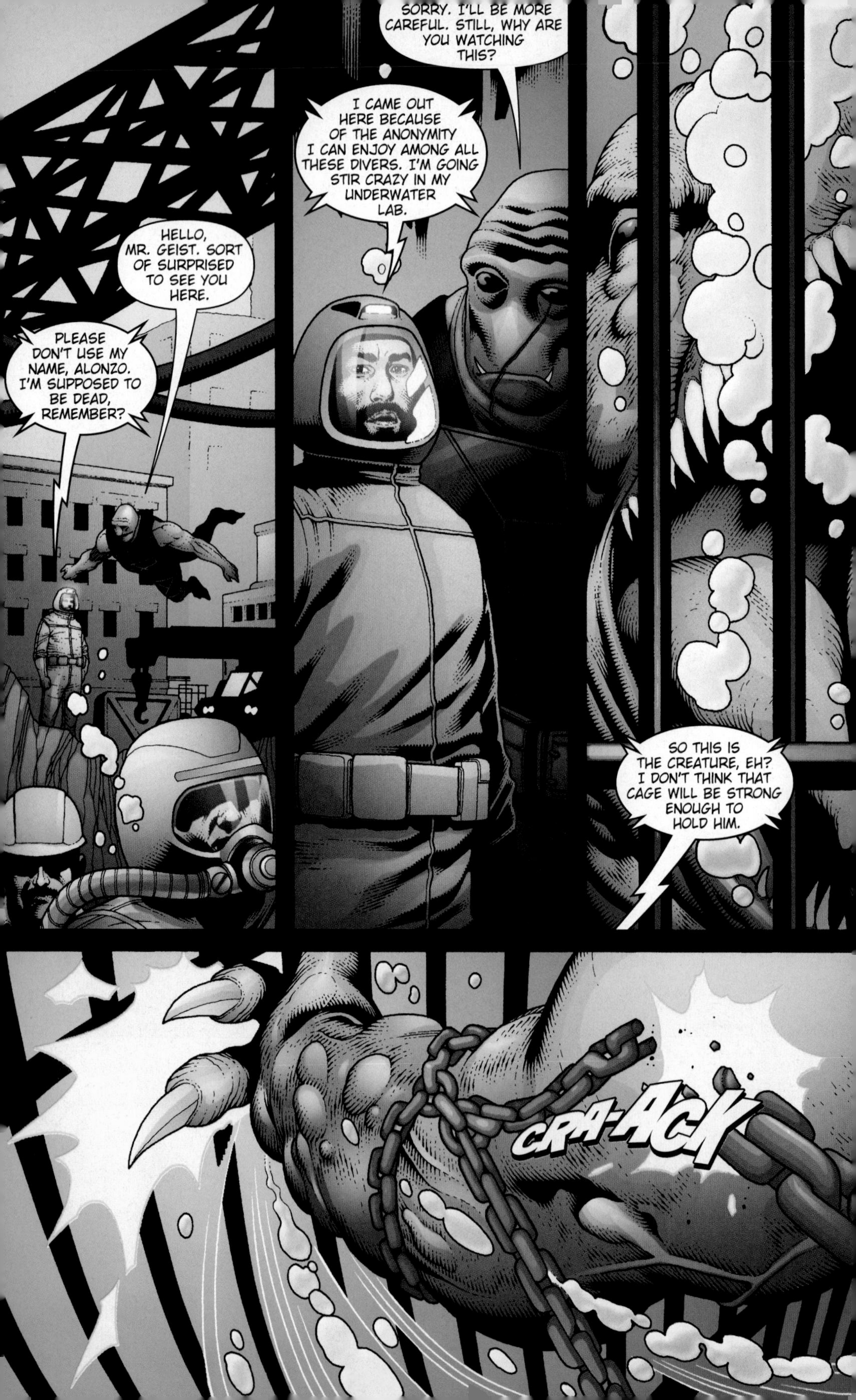
PLEASE DON'T USE MY NAME, ALONZO. I'M SUPPOSED TO BE DEAD, REMEMBER?
HELLO, MR. GEIST. SORT OF SURPRISED TO SEE YOU HERE.
SORRY. I'LL BE MORE CAREFUL. STILL, WHY ARE YOU WATCHING THIS?
I CAME OUT HERE BECAUSE OF THE ANONYMITY I CAN ENJOY AMONG ALL THESE DIVERS. I'M GOING STIR CRAZY IN MY UNDERWATER LAB.
SO THIS IS THE CREATURE, EH? I DON'T THINK THAT CAGE WILL BE STRONG ENOUGH TO HOLD HIM.
CRA-ACK

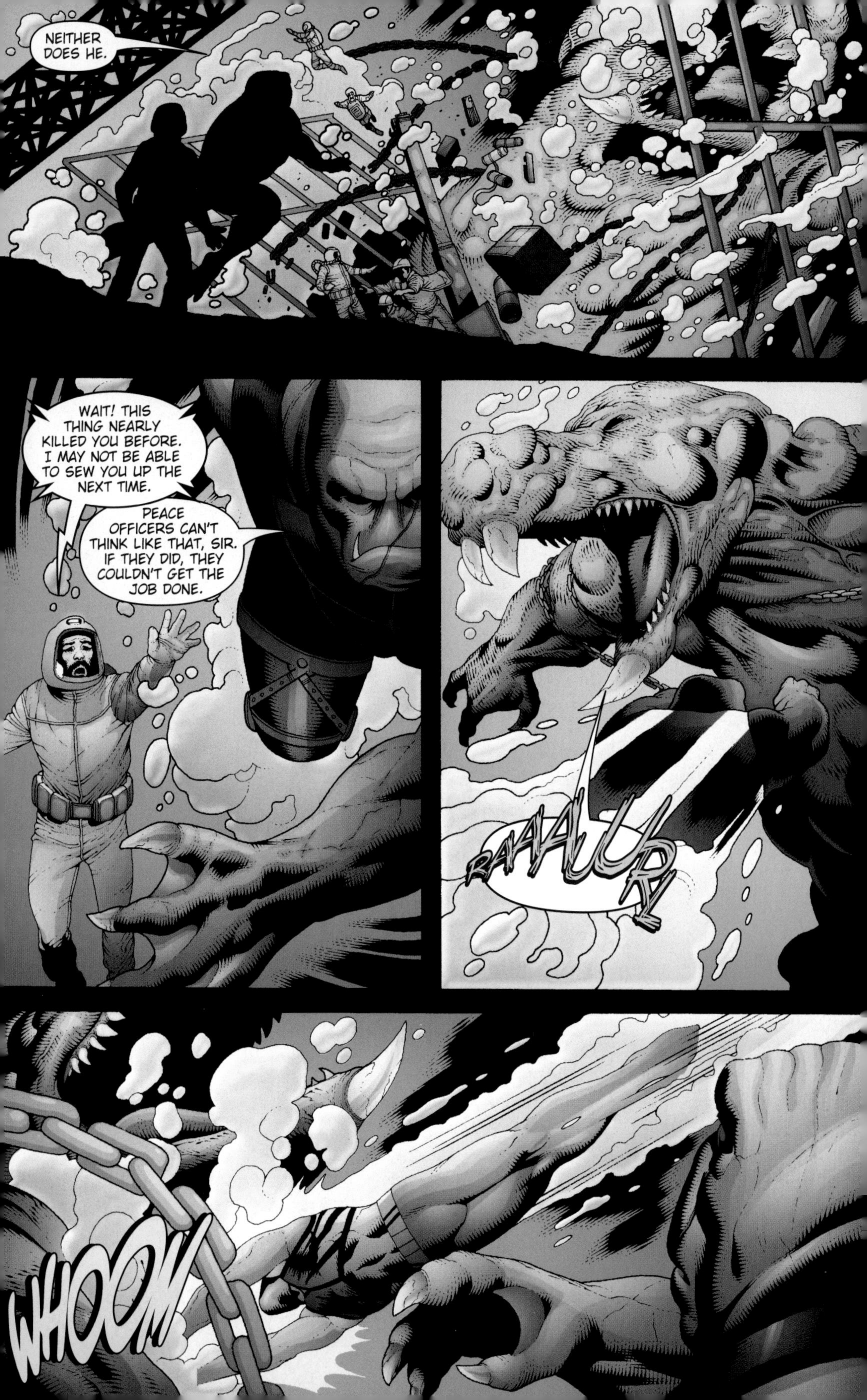
NEITHER DOES HE.
WAIT! THIS THING NEARLY KILLED YOU BEFORE. I MAY NOT BE ABLE TO SEW YOU UP THE NEXT TIME.
PEACE OFFICERS CAN'T THINK LIKE THAT, SIR. IF THEY DID, THEY COULDN'T GET THE JOB DONE.
RAAUR!
WHOOM

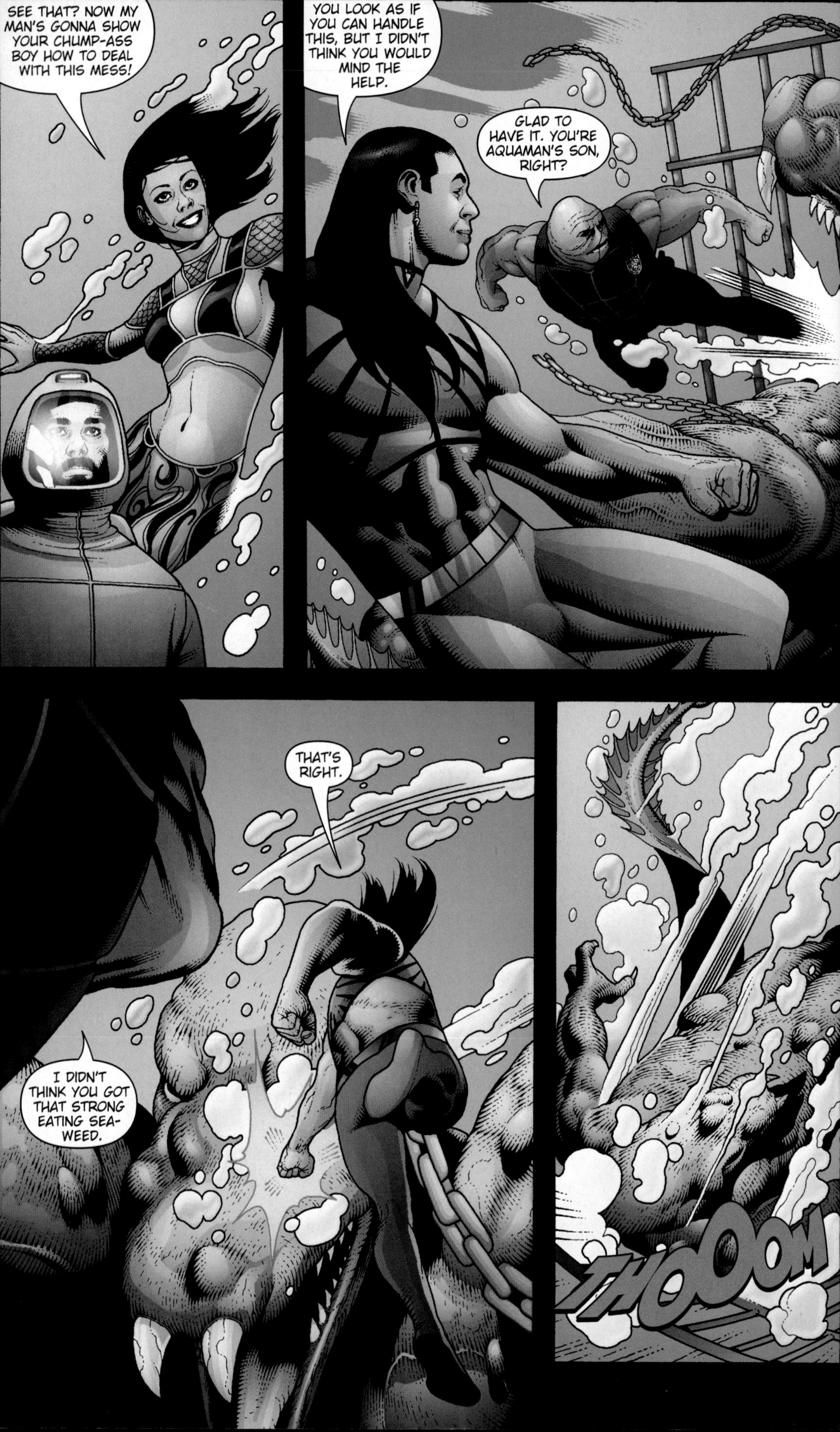
SEE THAT? NOW MY MAN'S GONNA SHOW YOUR CHUMP-ASS BOY HOW TO DEAL WITH THIS MESS!
YOU LOOK AS IF YOU CAN HANDLE THIS, BUT I DIDN'T THINK YOU WOULD MIND THE HELP.
GLAD TO HAVE IT. YOU'RE AQUAMAN'S SON, RIGHT?
THAT'S RIGHT.
I DIDN'T THINK YOU GOT THAT STRONG EATING SEA-WEED.
THOOOM

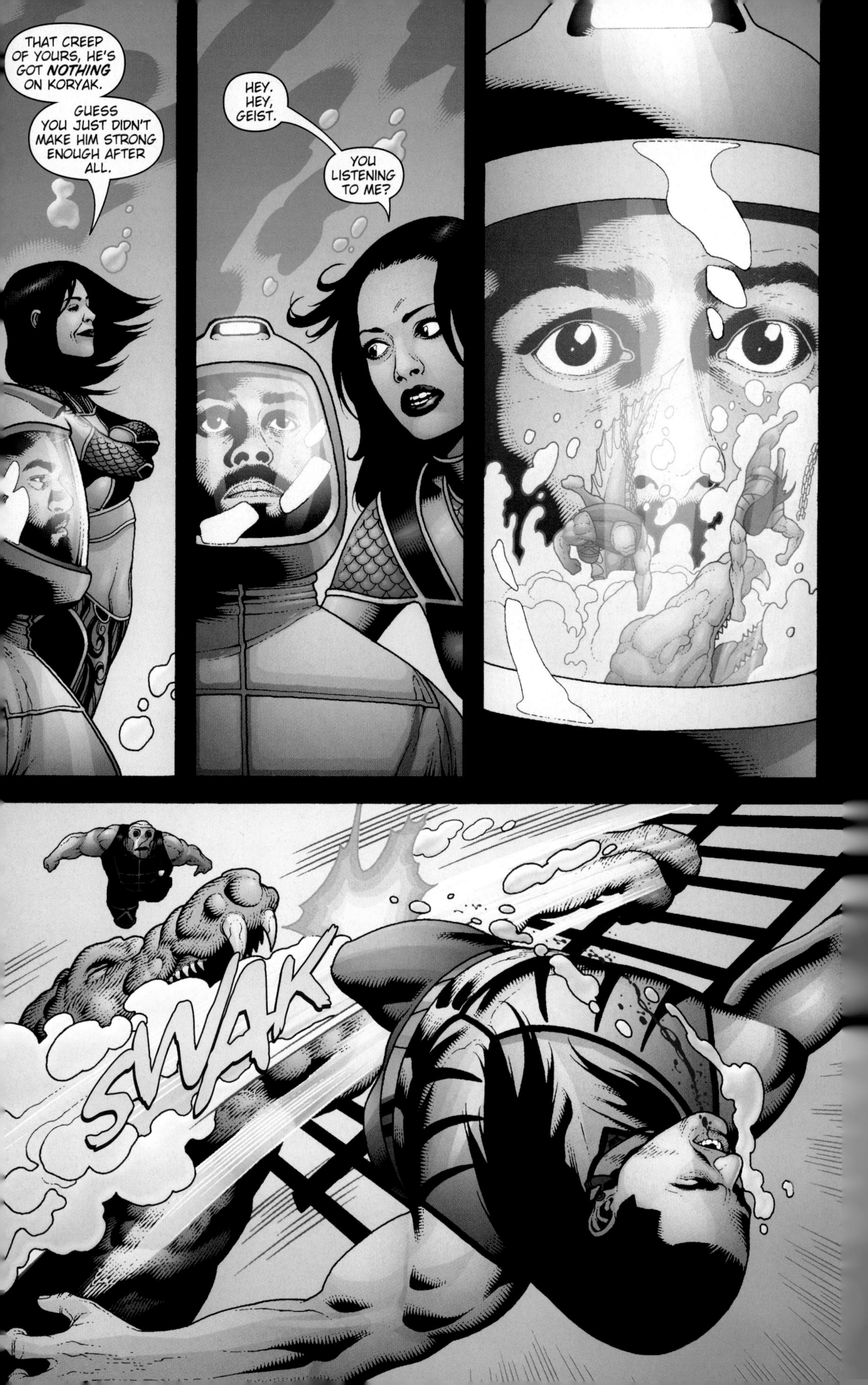
THAT CREEP OF YOURS, HE'S GOT **NOTHING** ON KORYAK.
GUESS YOU JUST DIDN'T MAKE HIM STRONG ENOUGH AFTER ALL.
HEY. HEY, GEIST.
YOU LISTENING TO ME?
SWAK

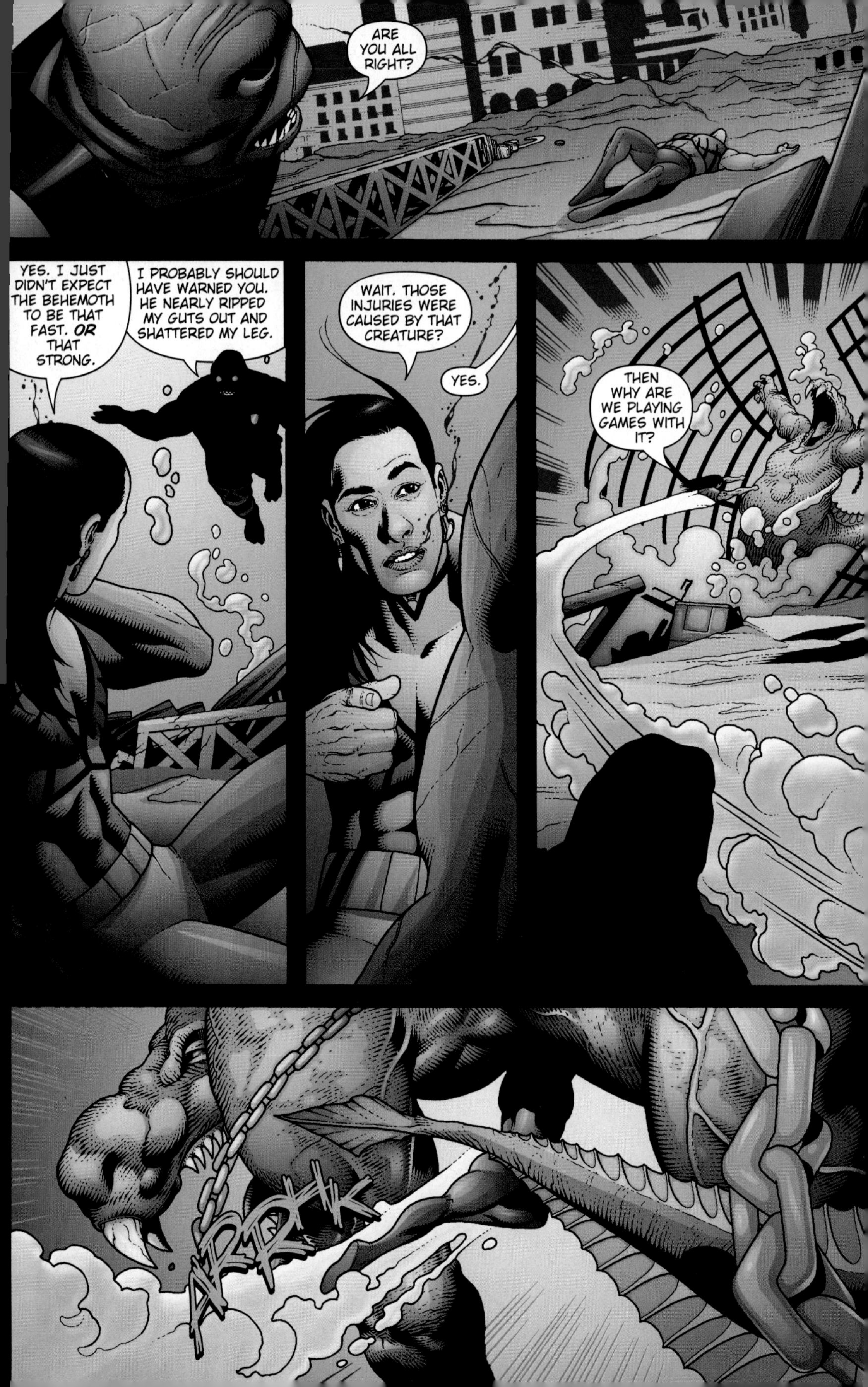
ARE YOU ALL RIGHT?
YES. I JUST DIDN'T EXPECT THE BEHEMOTH TO BE THAT FAST. OR THAT STRONG.
I PROBABLY SHOULD HAVE WARNED YOU. HE NEARLY RIPPED MY GUTS OUT AND SHATTERED MY LEG.
WAIT. THOSE INJURIES WERE CAUSED BY THAT CREATURE?
YES.
THEN WHY ARE WE PLAYING GAMES WITH IT?
ARRKK

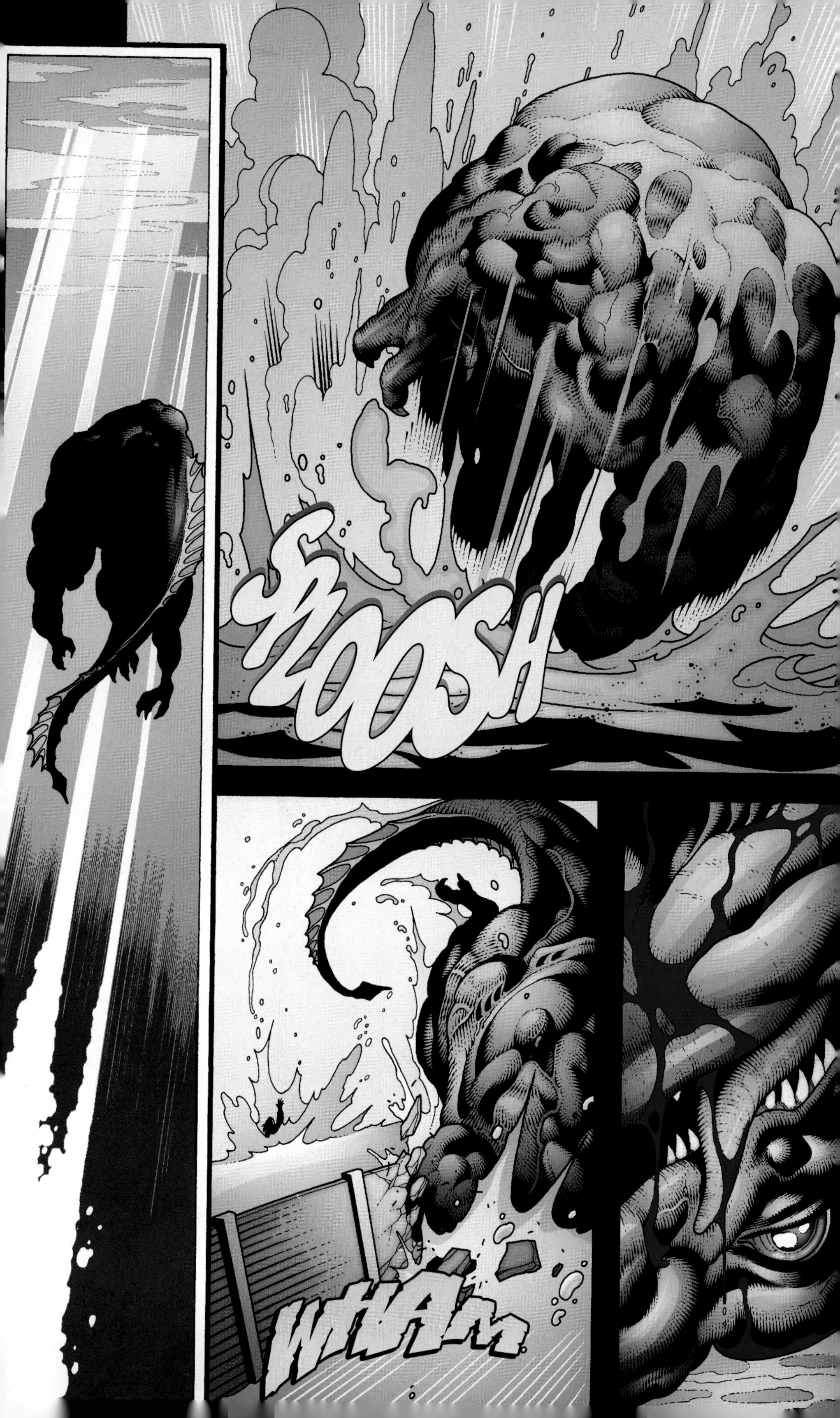
SWOOSH
WHAM

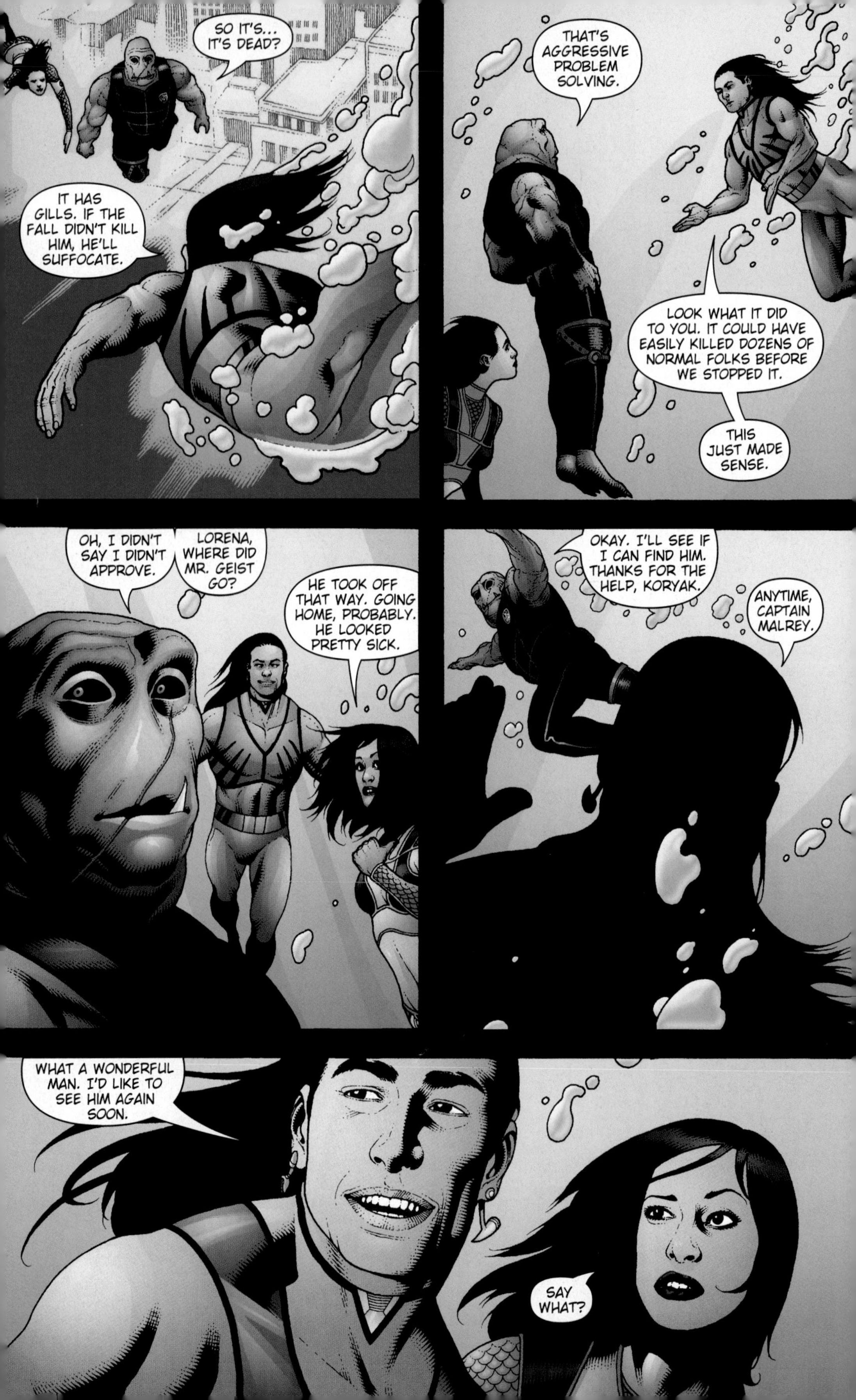
SO IT'S... IT'S DEAD?
IT HAS GILLS. IF THE FALL DIDN'T KILL HIM, HE'LL SUFFOCATE.
THAT'S AGGRESSIVE PROBLEM SOLVING.
LOOK WHAT IT DID TO YOU. IT COULD HAVE EASILY KILLED DOZENS OF NORMAL FOLKS BEFORE WE STOPPED IT.
THIS JUST MADE SENSE.
OH, I DIDN'T SAY I DIDN'T APPROVE.
LORENA, WHERE DID MR. GEIST GO?
HE TOOK OFF THAT WAY. GOING HOME, PROBABLY. HE LOOKED PRETTY SICK.
OKAY. I'LL SEE IF I CAN FIND HIM. THANKS FOR THE HELP, KORYAK.
ANYTIME, CAPTAIN MALREY.
WHAT A WONDERFUL MAN. I'D LIKE TO SEE HIM AGAIN SOON.
SAY WHAT?

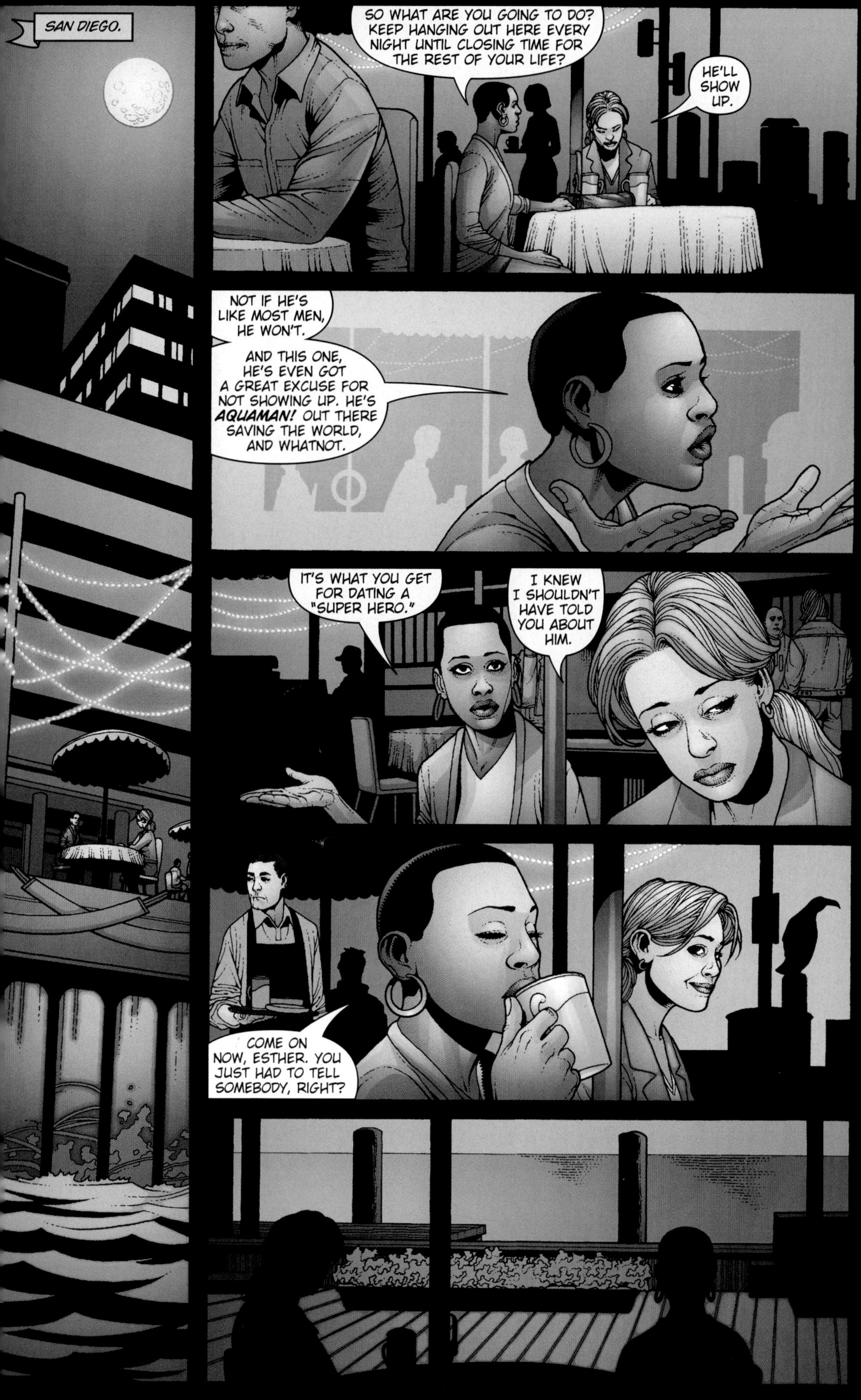
SAN DIEGO.
SO WHAT ARE YOU GOING TO DO? KEEP HANGING OUT HERE EVERY NIGHT UNTIL CLOSING TIME FOR THE REST OF YOUR LIFE?
HE'LL SHOW UP.
NOT IF HE'S LIKE MOST MEN, HE WON'T.
AND THIS ONE, HE'S EVEN GOT A GREAT EXCUSE FOR NOT SHOWING UP. HE'S AQUAMAN! OUT THERE SAVING THE WORLD, AND WHATNOT.
IT'S WHAT YOU GET FOR DATING A "SUPER HERO."
I KNEW I SHOULDN'T HAVE TOLD YOU ABOUT HIM.
COME ON NOW, ESTHER. YOU JUST HAD TO TELL SOMEBODY, RIGHT?

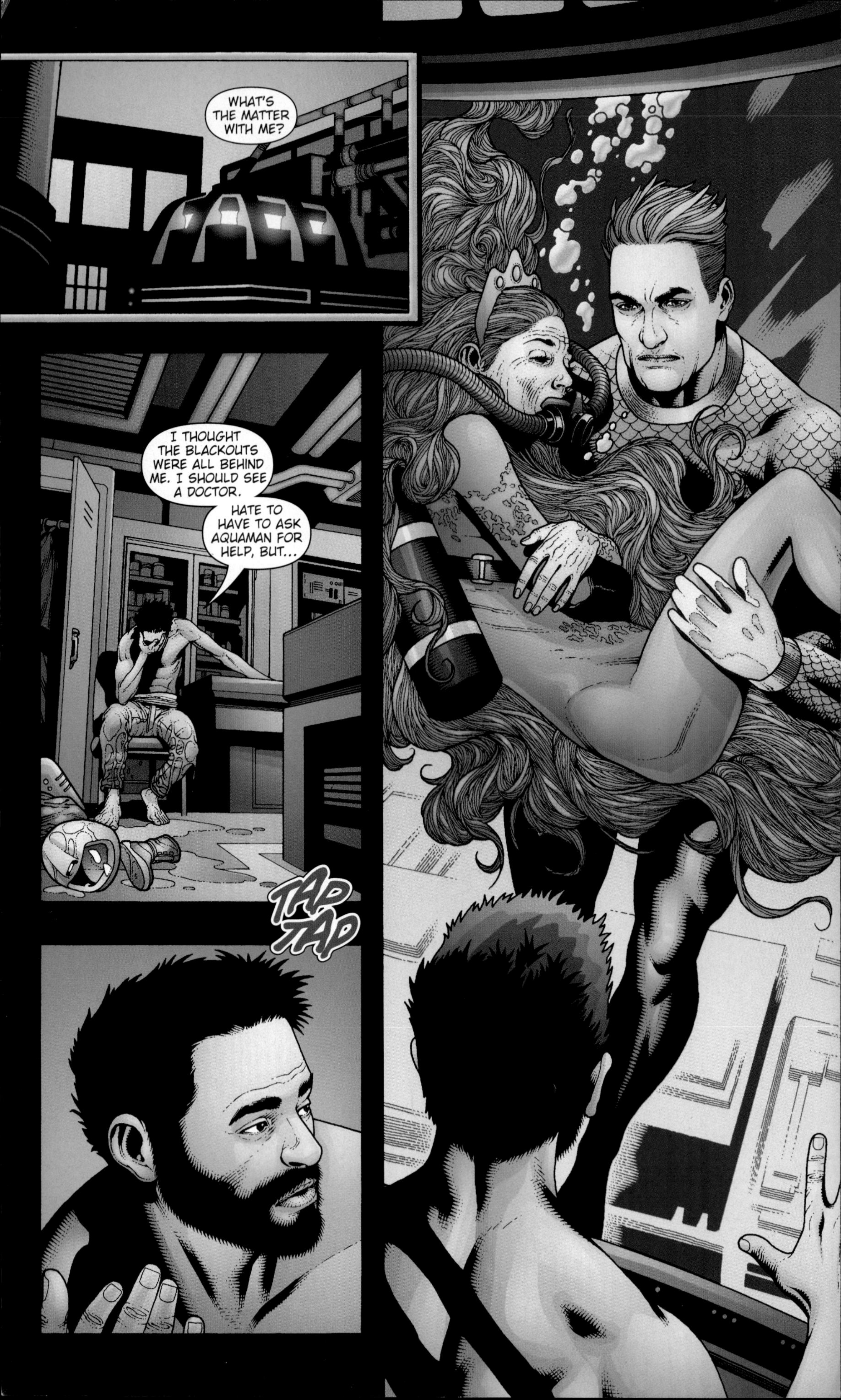
WHAT'S THE MATTER WITH ME?
I THOUGHT THE BLACKOUTS WERE ALL BEHIND ME. I SHOULD SEE A DOCTOR.
HATE TO HAVE TO ASK AQUAMAN FOR HELP, BUT...
TAP TAP

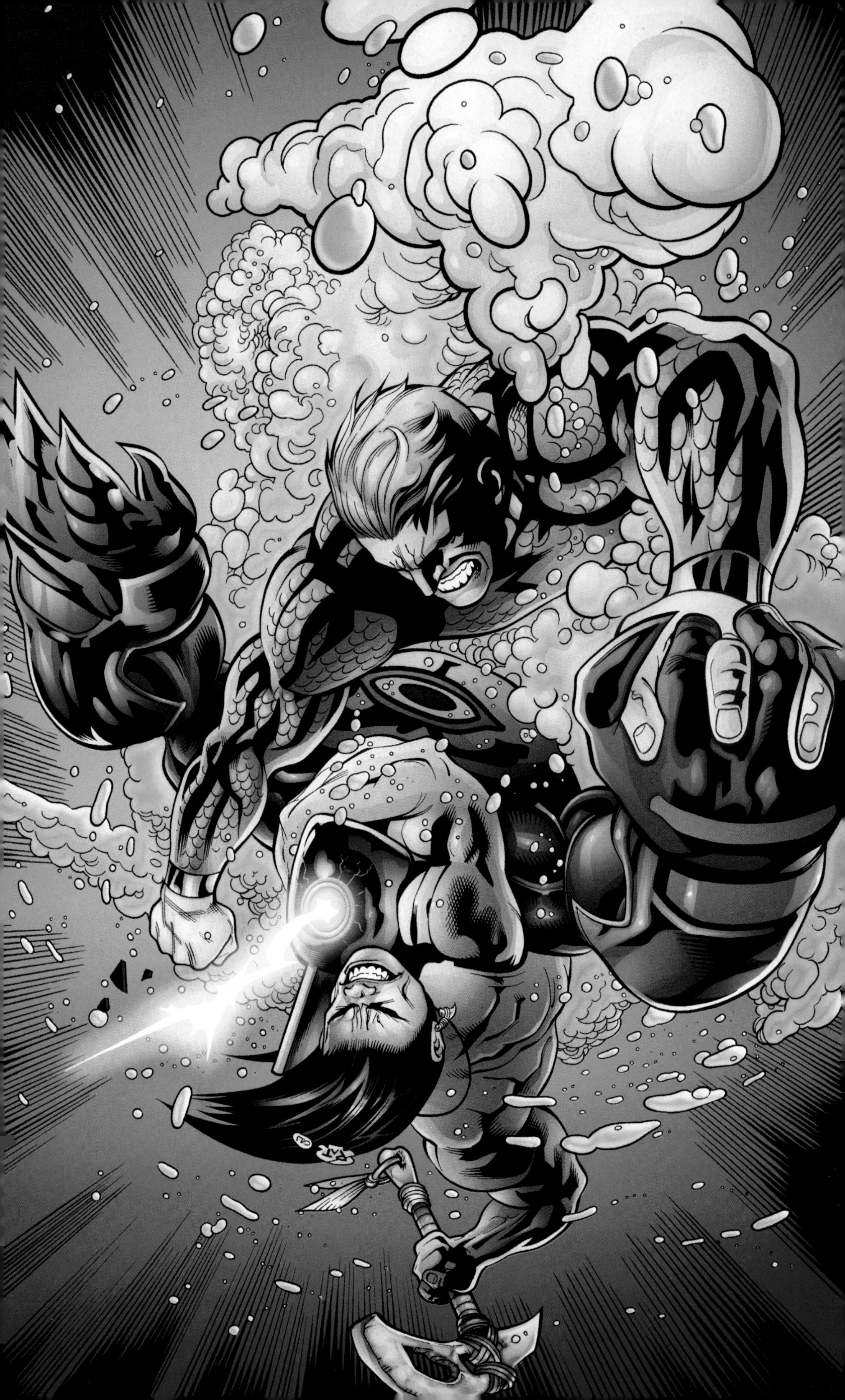

A WALK-ON PART IN THE WAR

JOHN ARCUDI
Writer

LEONARD KIRK
Layouts

ANDY CLARKE
Finishes

NATHAN EYRING
Colorist

TRAVIS LANHAM
Letterer

**PATRICK GLEASON &
CHRISTIAN ALAMY**
Cover

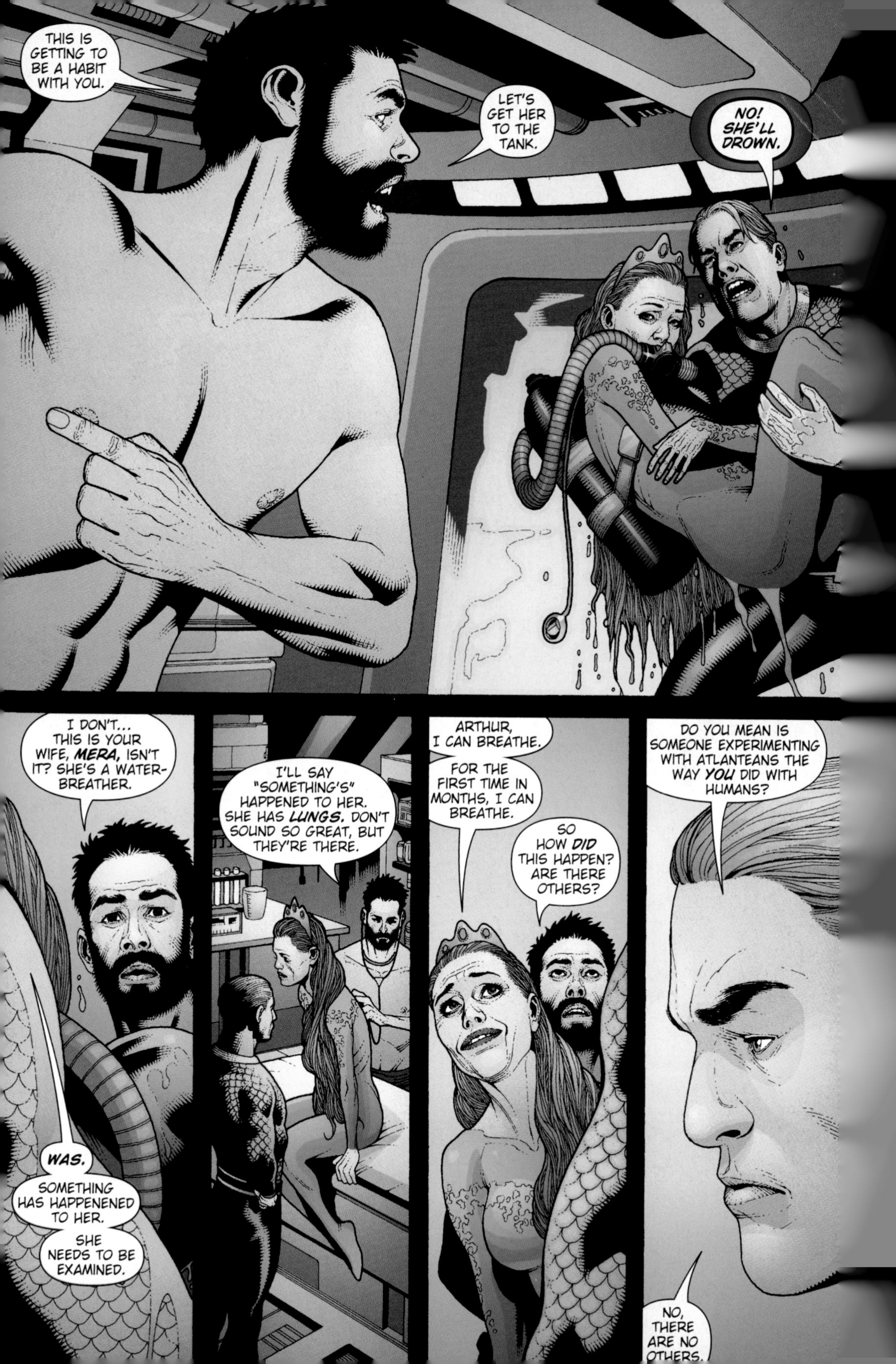
THIS IS GETTING TO BE A HABIT WITH YOU.
LET'S GET HER TO THE TANK.
NO! SHE'LL DROWN.
I DON'T... THIS IS YOUR WIFE, MERA, ISN'T IT? SHE'S A WATER-BREATHER.
WAS.
SOMETHING HAS HAPPENENED TO HER.
SHE NEEDS TO BE EXAMINED.
I'LL SAY "SOMETHING'S" HAPPENED TO HER. SHE HAS LUNGS. DON'T SOUND SO GREAT, BUT THEY'RE THERE.
ARTHUR, I CAN BREATHE.
FOR THE FIRST TIME IN MONTHS, I CAN BREATHE.
SO HOW DID THIS HAPPEN? ARE THERE OTHERS?
DO YOU MEAN IS SOMEONE EXPERIMENTING WITH ATLANTEANS THE WAY YOU DID WITH HUMANS?
NO, THERE ARE NO OTHERS.

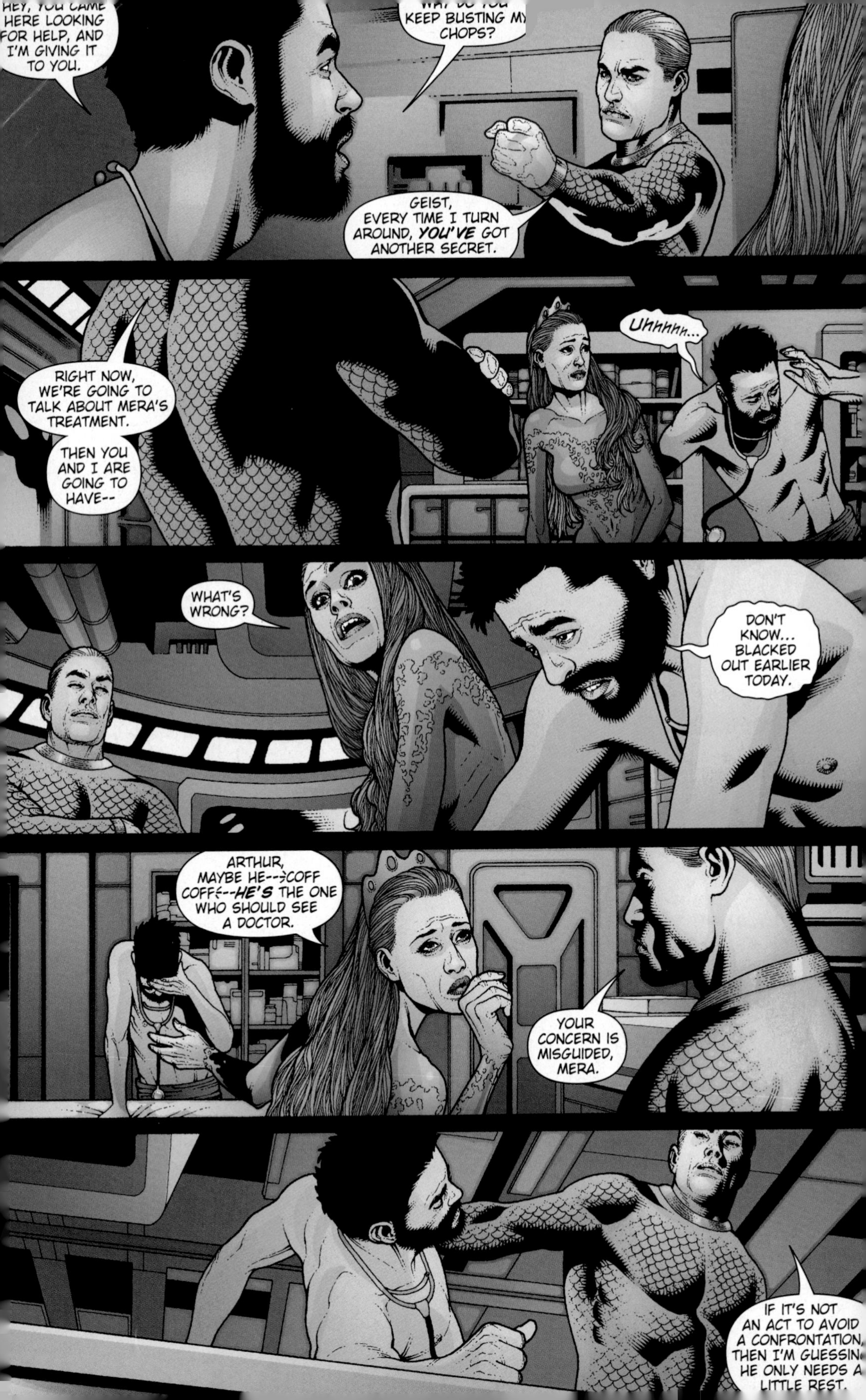
HEY, YOU CAME HERE LOOKING FOR HELP, AND I'M GIVING IT TO YOU.
KEEP BUSTING MY CHOPS?
GEIST, EVERY TIME I TURN AROUND, ***YOU'VE*** GOT ANOTHER SECRET.
RIGHT NOW, WE'RE GOING TO TALK ABOUT MERA'S TREATMENT.
THEN YOU AND I ARE GOING TO HAVE--
Uhhhhh...
WHAT'S WRONG?
DON'T KNOW... BLACKED OUT EARLIER TODAY.
ARTHUR, MAYBE HE--*COFF COFF*--***HE'S*** THE ONE WHO SHOULD SEE A DOCTOR.
YOUR CONCERN IS MISGUIDED, MERA.
IF IT'S NOT AN ACT TO AVOID A CONFRONTATION, THEN I'M GUESSIN HE ONLY NEEDS A LITTLE REST.

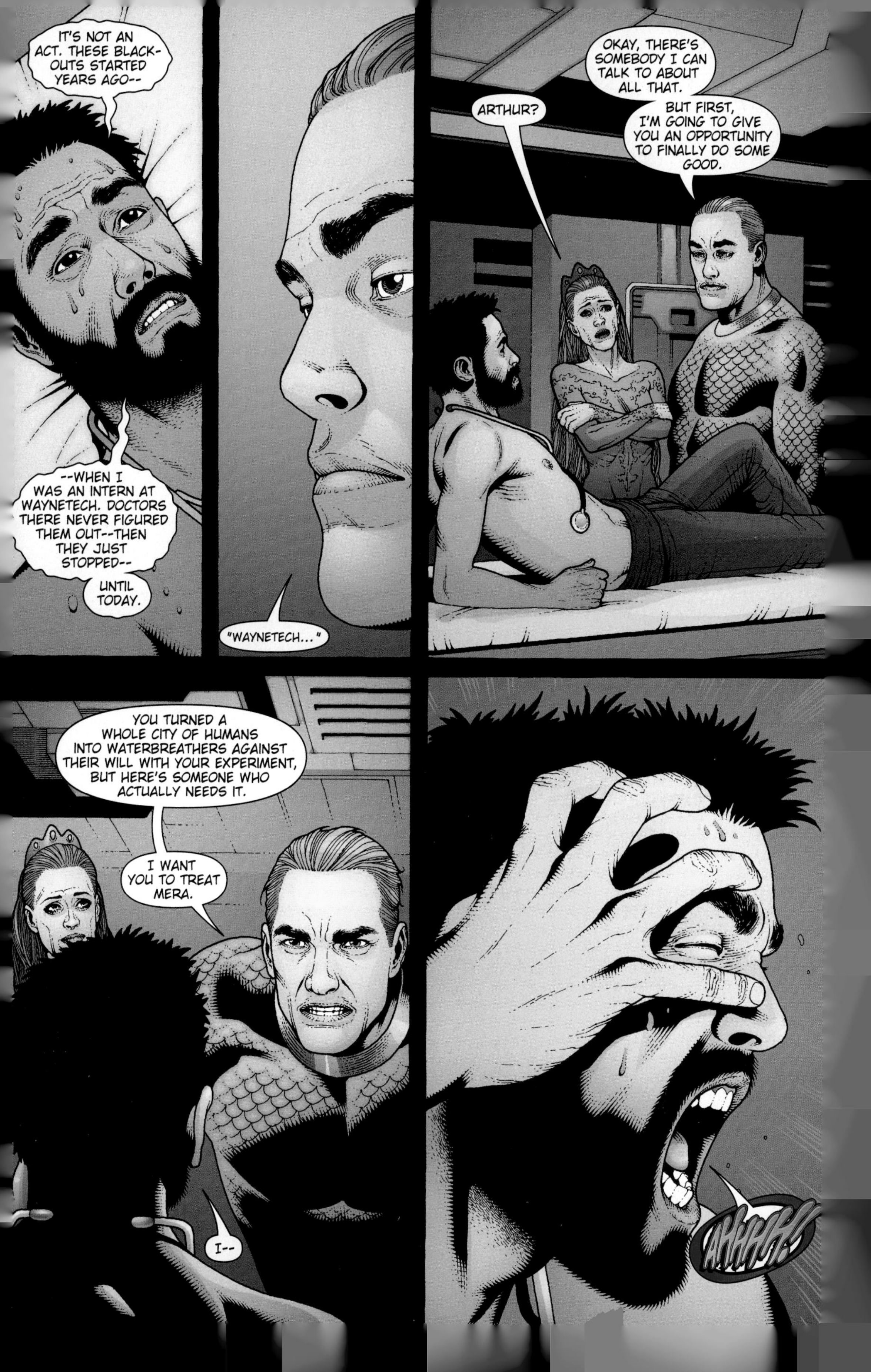
IT'S NOT AN ACT. THESE BLACK-OUTS STARTED YEARS AGO--
--WHEN I WAS AN INTERN AT WAYNETECH. DOCTORS THERE NEVER FIGURED THEM OUT--THEN THEY JUST STOPPED--
UNTIL TODAY.
"WAYNETECH..."
OKAY, THERE'S SOMEBODY I CAN TALK TO ABOUT ALL THAT.
ARTHUR?
BUT FIRST, I'M GOING TO GIVE YOU AN OPPORTUNITY TO FINALLY DO SOME GOOD.
YOU TURNED A WHOLE CITY OF HUMANS INTO WATERBREATHERS AGAINST THEIR WILL WITH YOUR EXPERIMENT, BUT HERE'S SOMEONE WHO ACTUALLY NEEDS IT.
I WANT YOU TO TREAT MERA.
I--
AHHHH!

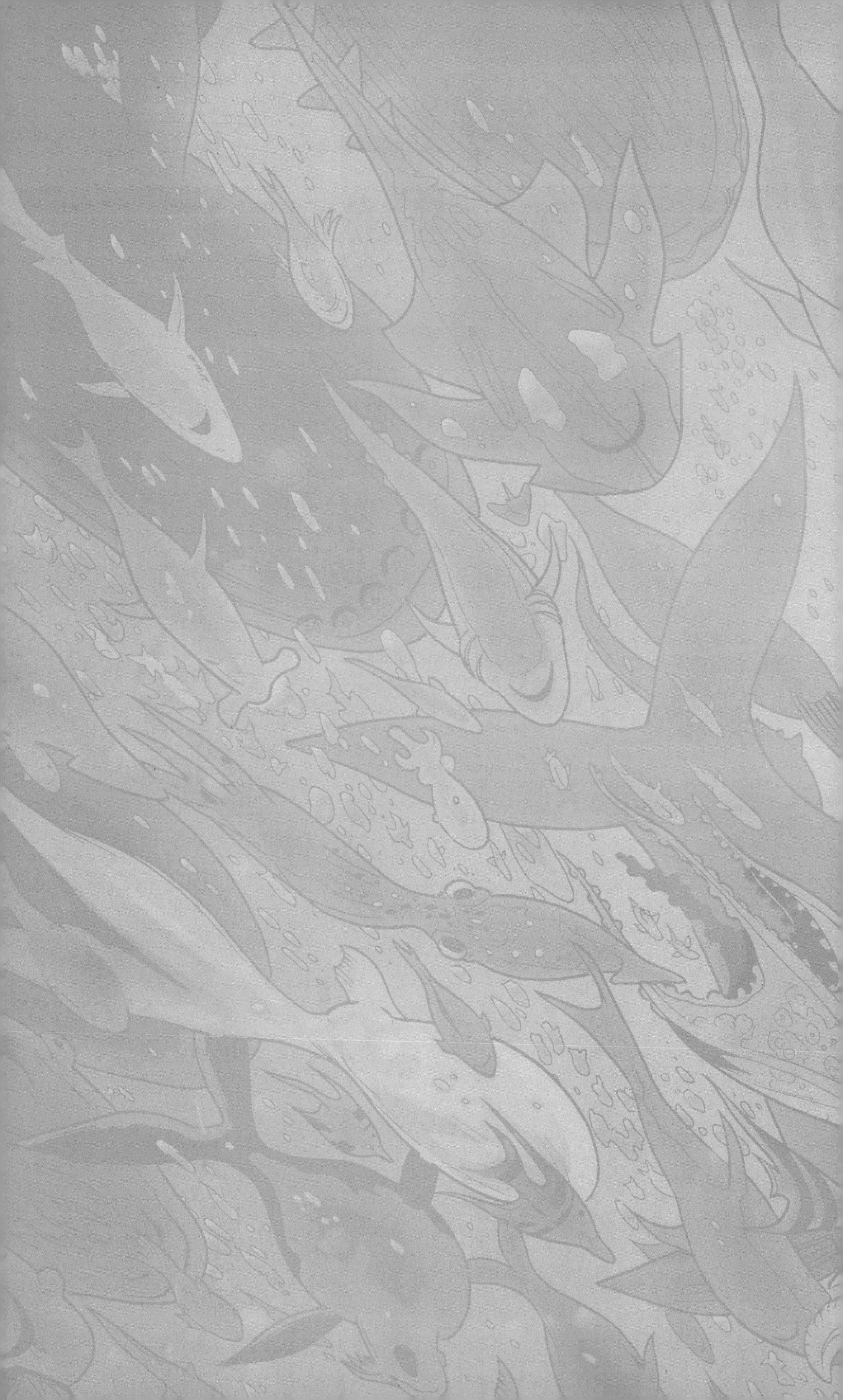

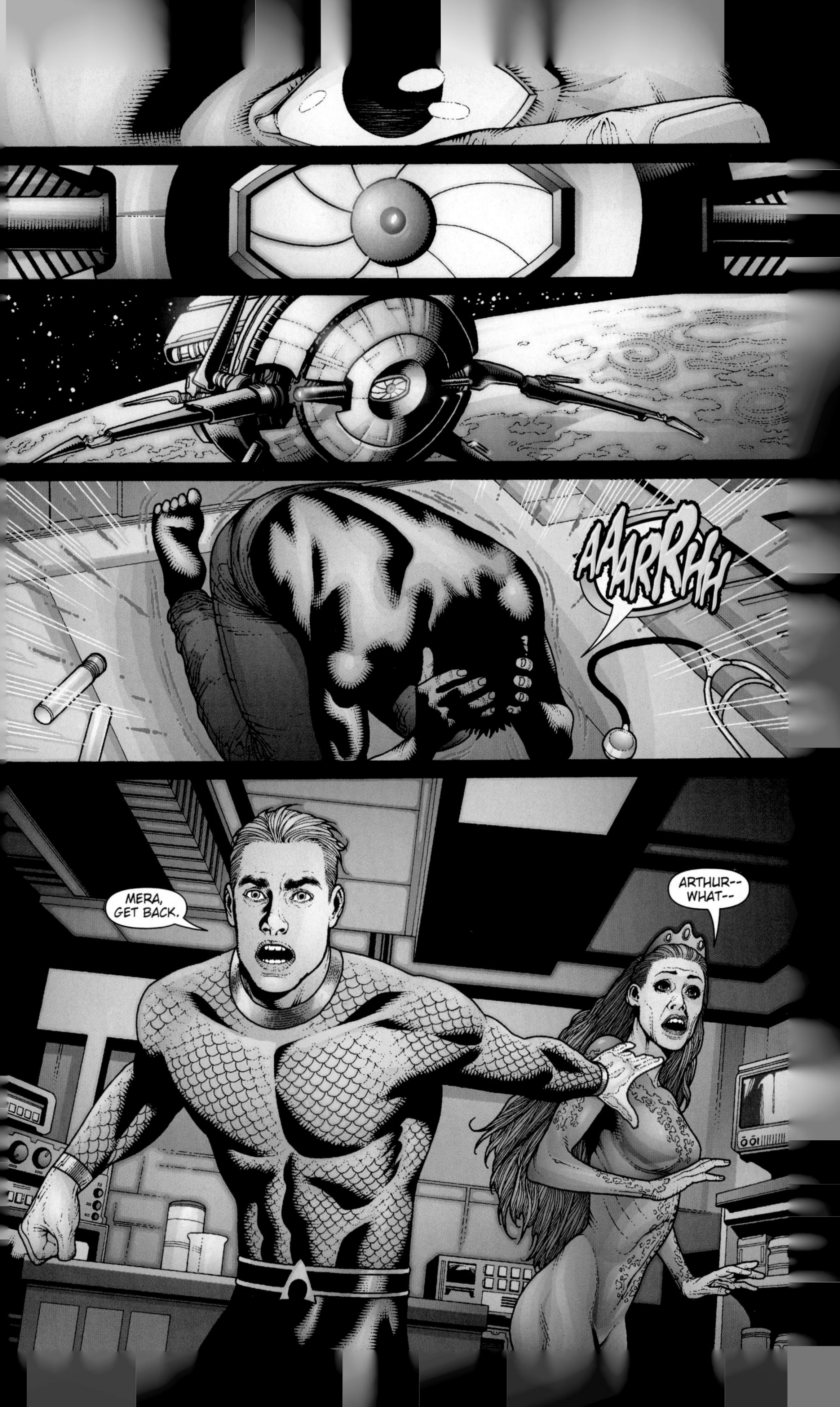
AAARRHH
MERA, GET BACK.
ARTHUR-- WHAT--

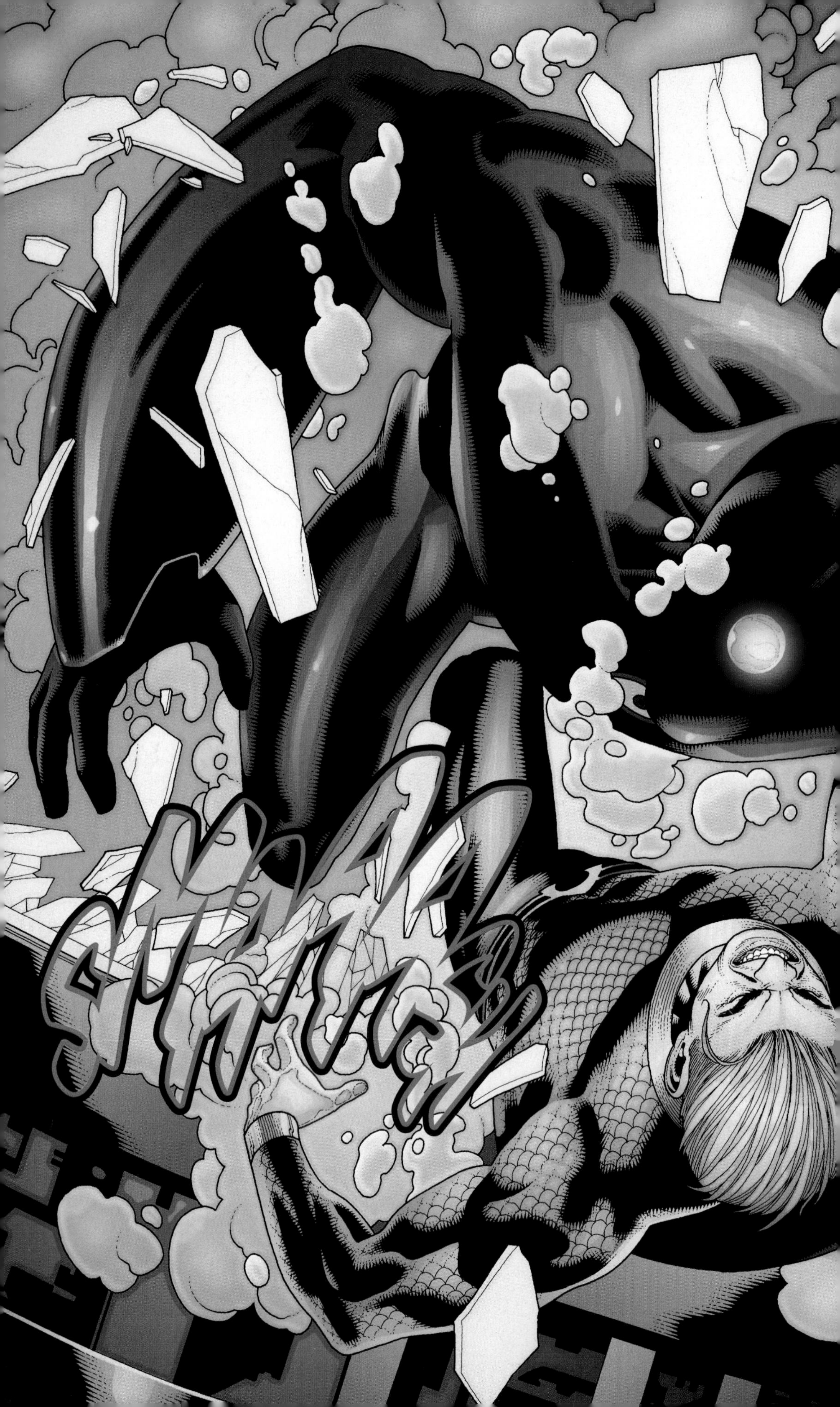

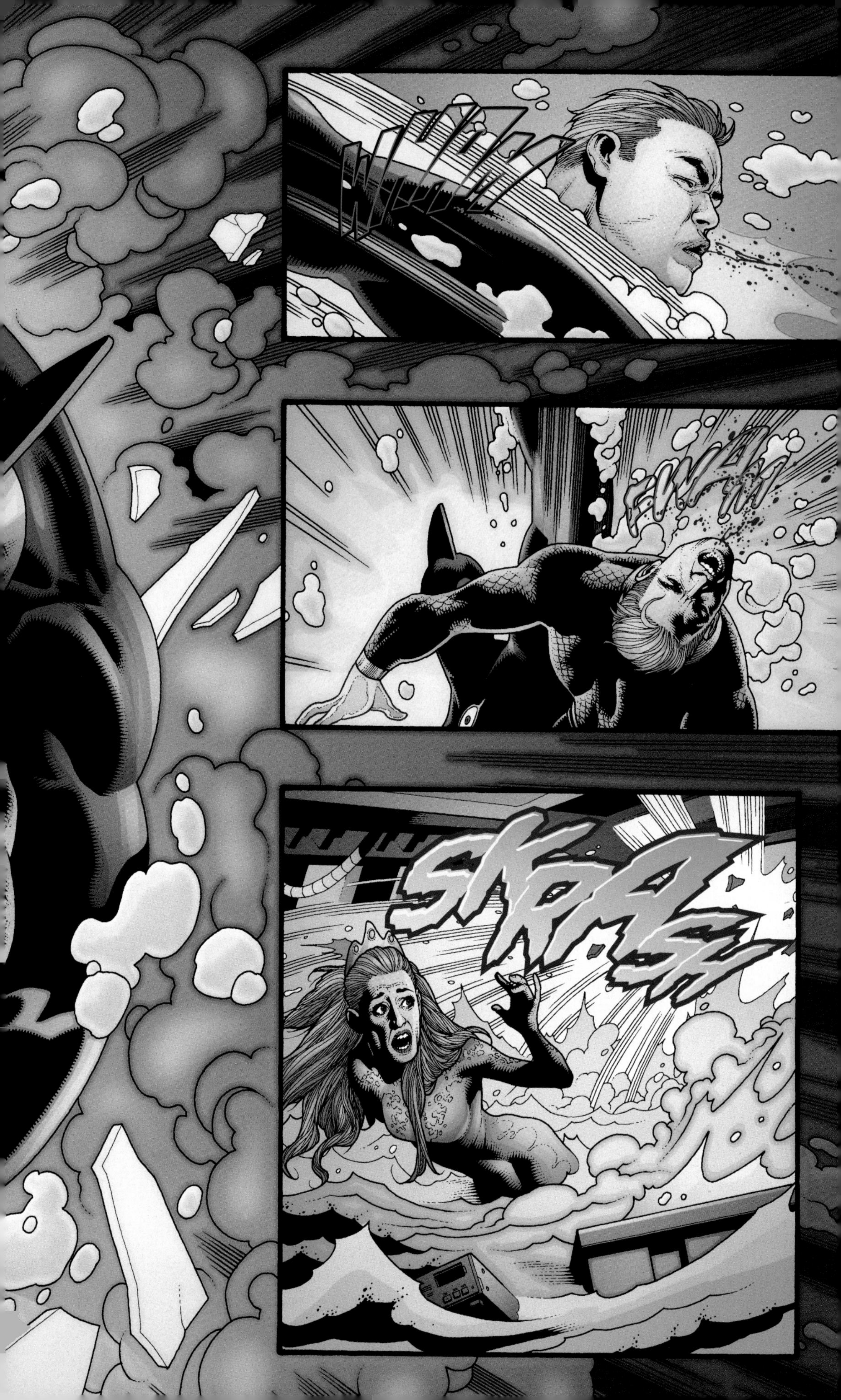
SKRASH

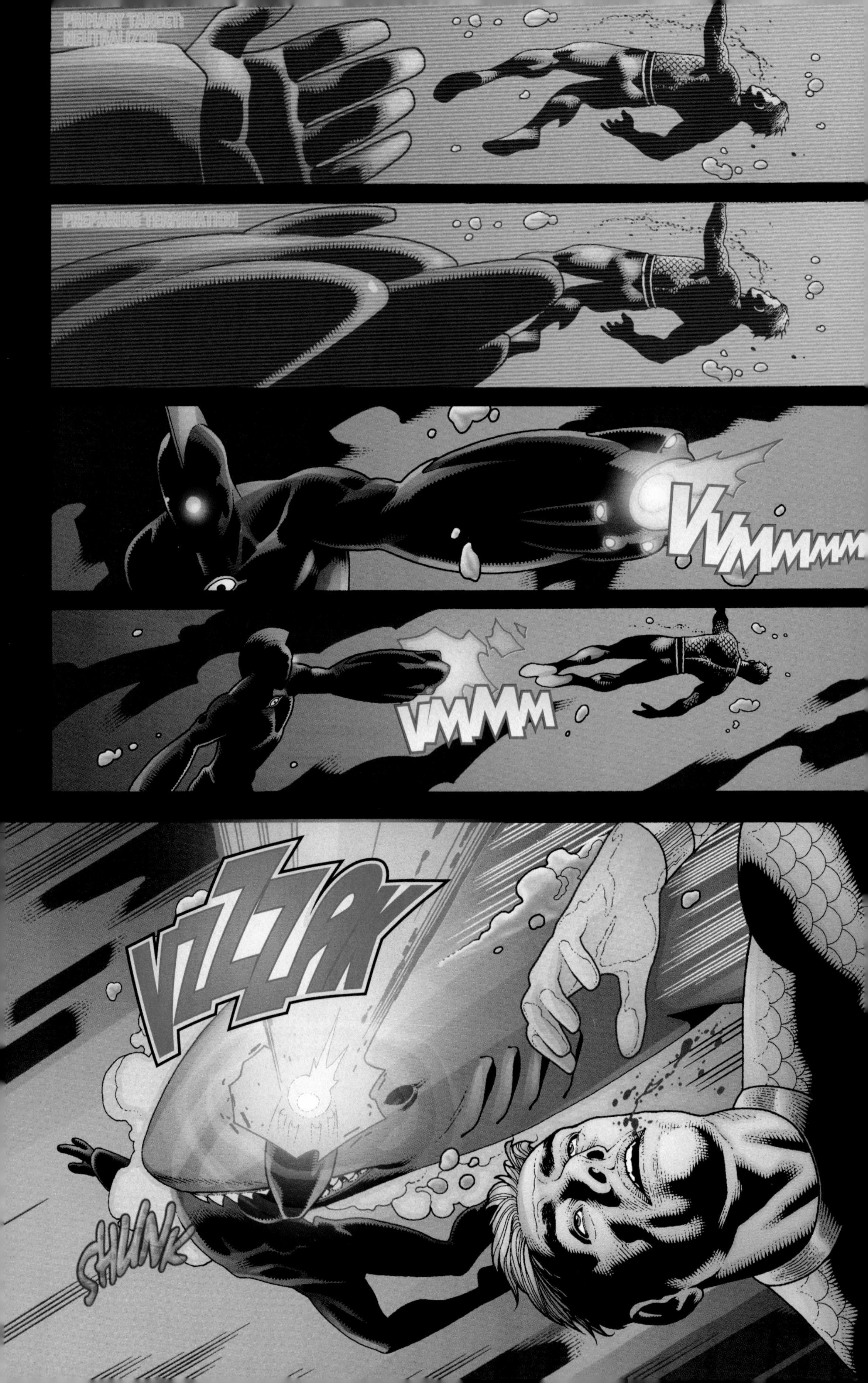
PRIMARY TARGET: NEUTRALIZED
PREPARING TERMINATION
VVMMMMM
VMMM
VZZZAK
SHUNK

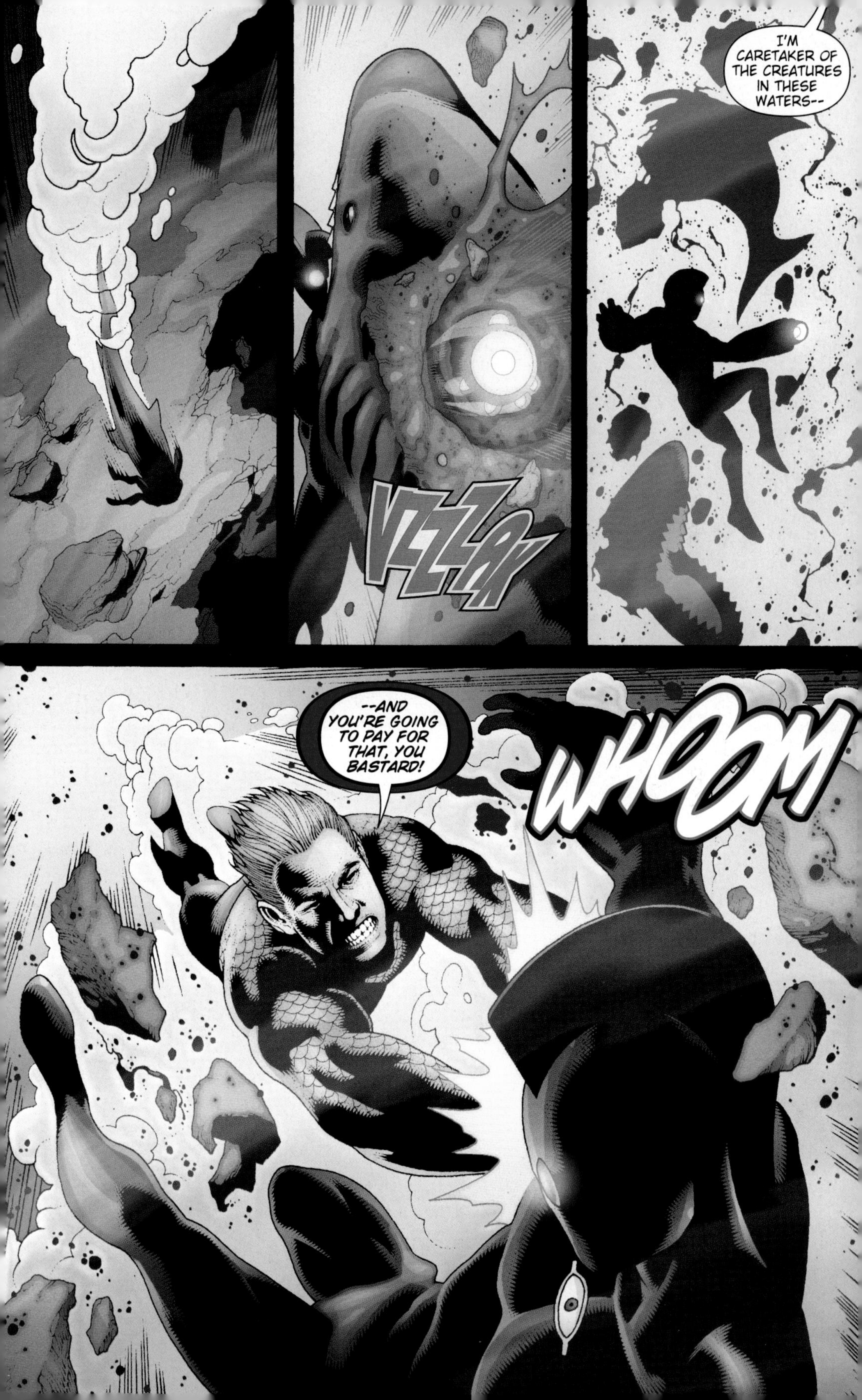
I'M CARETAKER OF THE CREATURES IN THESE WATERS--
VZZZAK
--AND YOU'RE GOING TO PAY FOR THAT, YOU BASTARD!
WHOOM

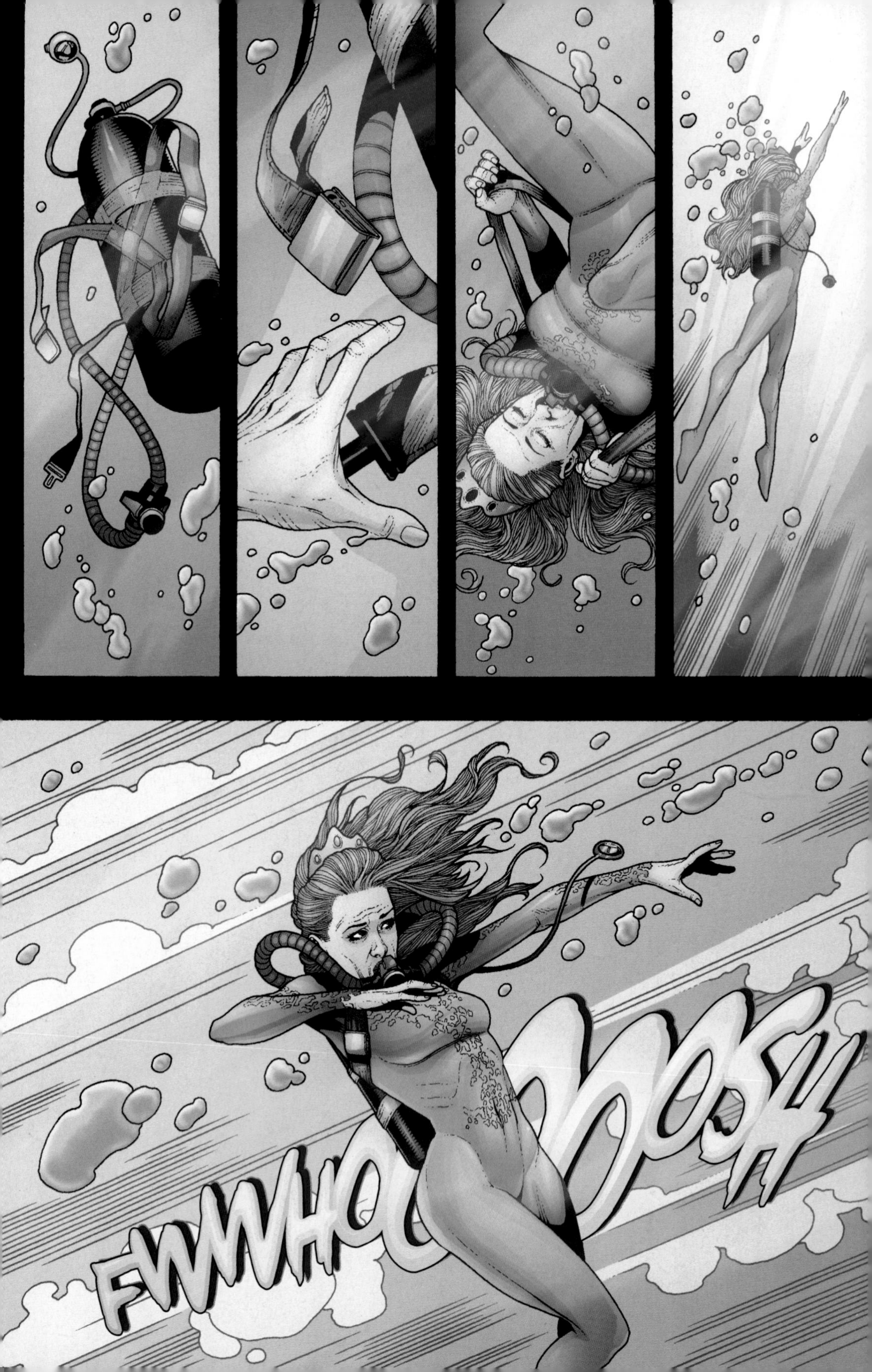
FWHOOOOOSH

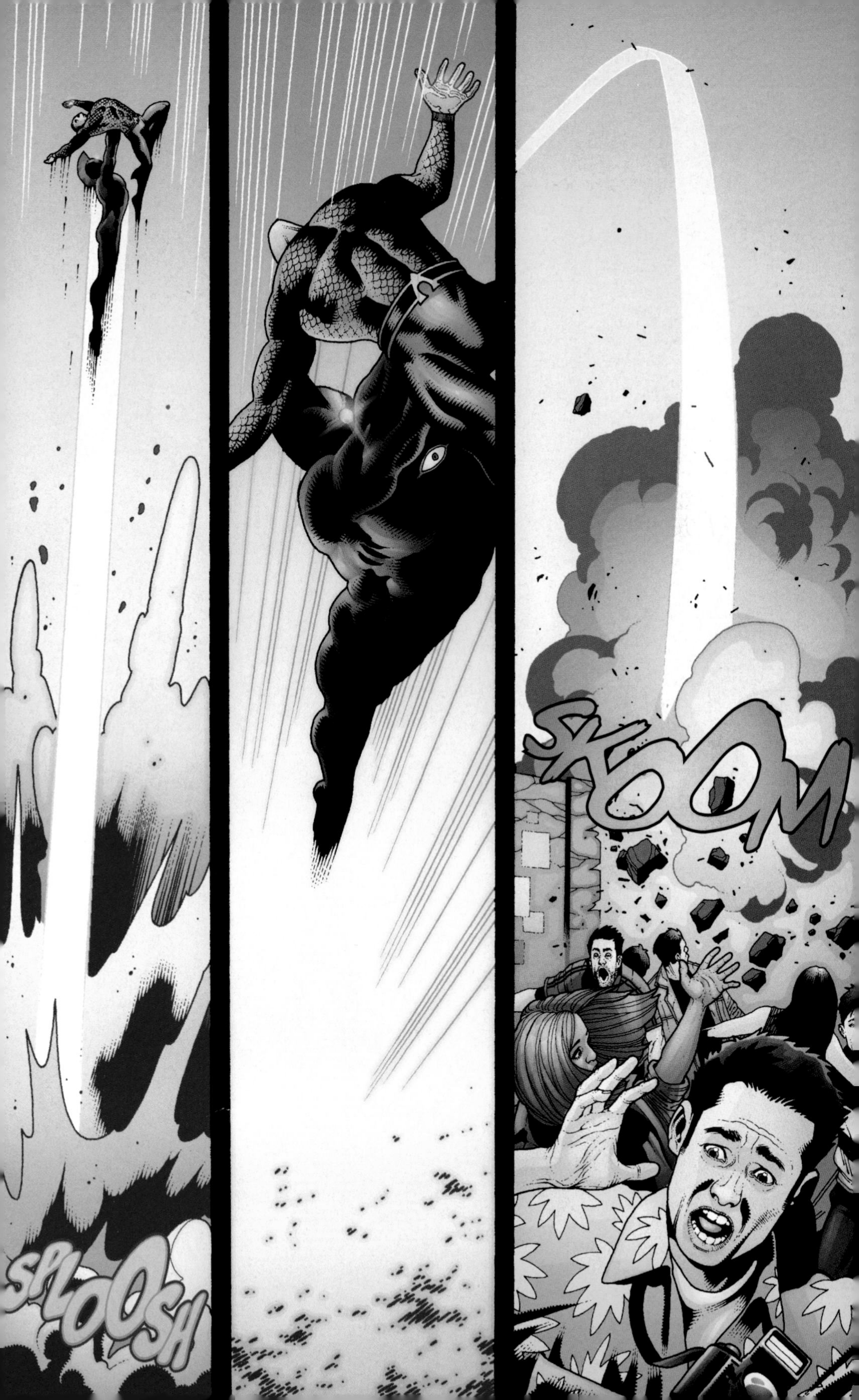
SPLOOSH
SKOOM

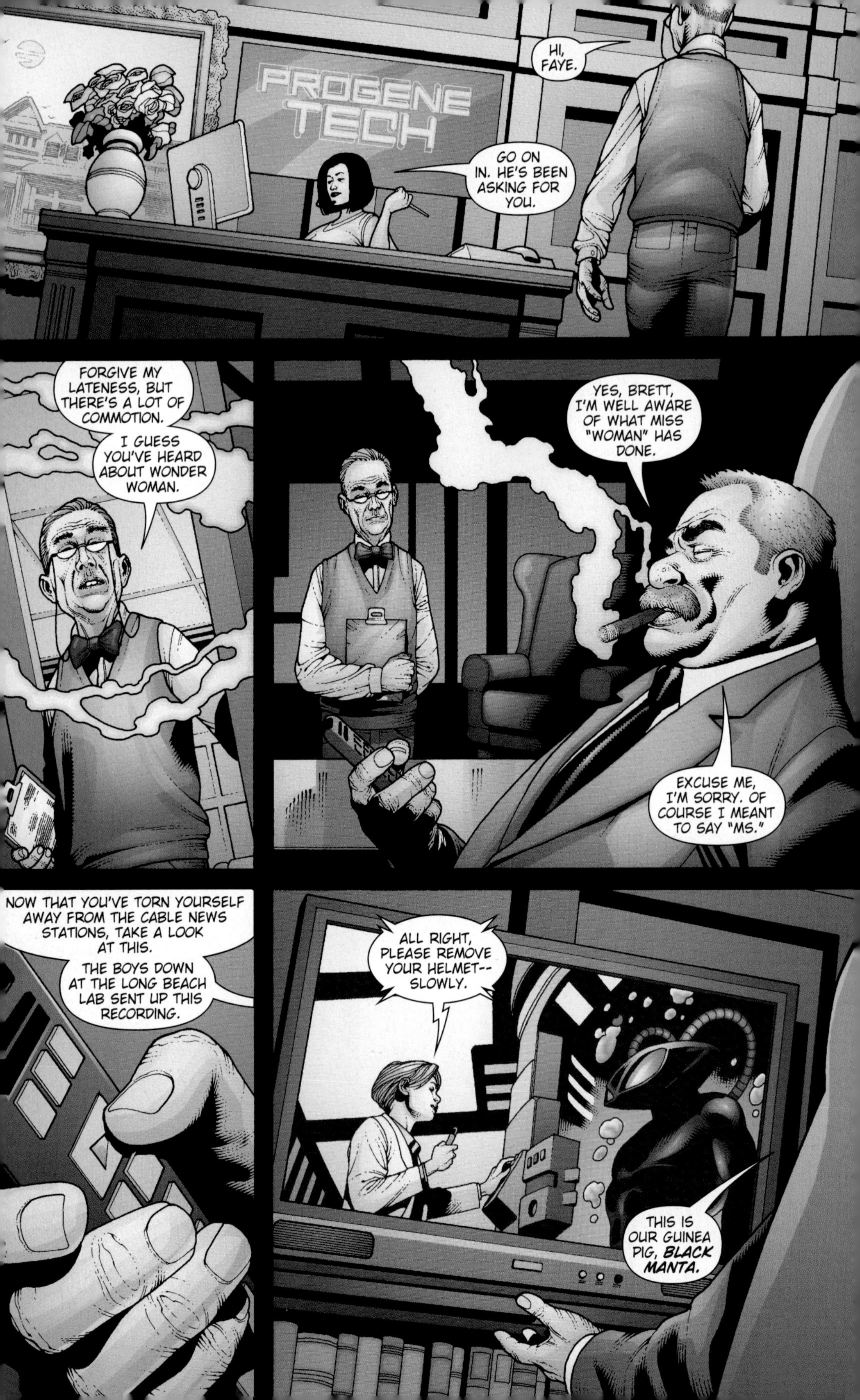
PROGENE TECH
HI, FAYE.
GO ON IN. HE'S BEEN ASKING FOR YOU.
FORGIVE MY LATENESS, BUT THERE'S A LOT OF COMMOTION.
I GUESS YOU'VE HEARD ABOUT WONDER WOMAN.
YES, BRETT, I'M WELL AWARE OF WHAT MISS "WOMAN" HAS DONE.
EXCUSE ME, I'M SORRY. OF COURSE I MEANT TO SAY "MS."
NOW THAT YOU'VE TORN YOURSELF AWAY FROM THE CABLE NEWS STATIONS, TAKE A LOOK AT THIS.
THE BOYS DOWN AT THE LONG BEACH LAB SENT UP THIS RECORDING.
ALL RIGHT, PLEASE REMOVE YOUR HELMET-- SLOWLY.
THIS IS OUR GUINEA PIG, ***BLACK MANTA.***

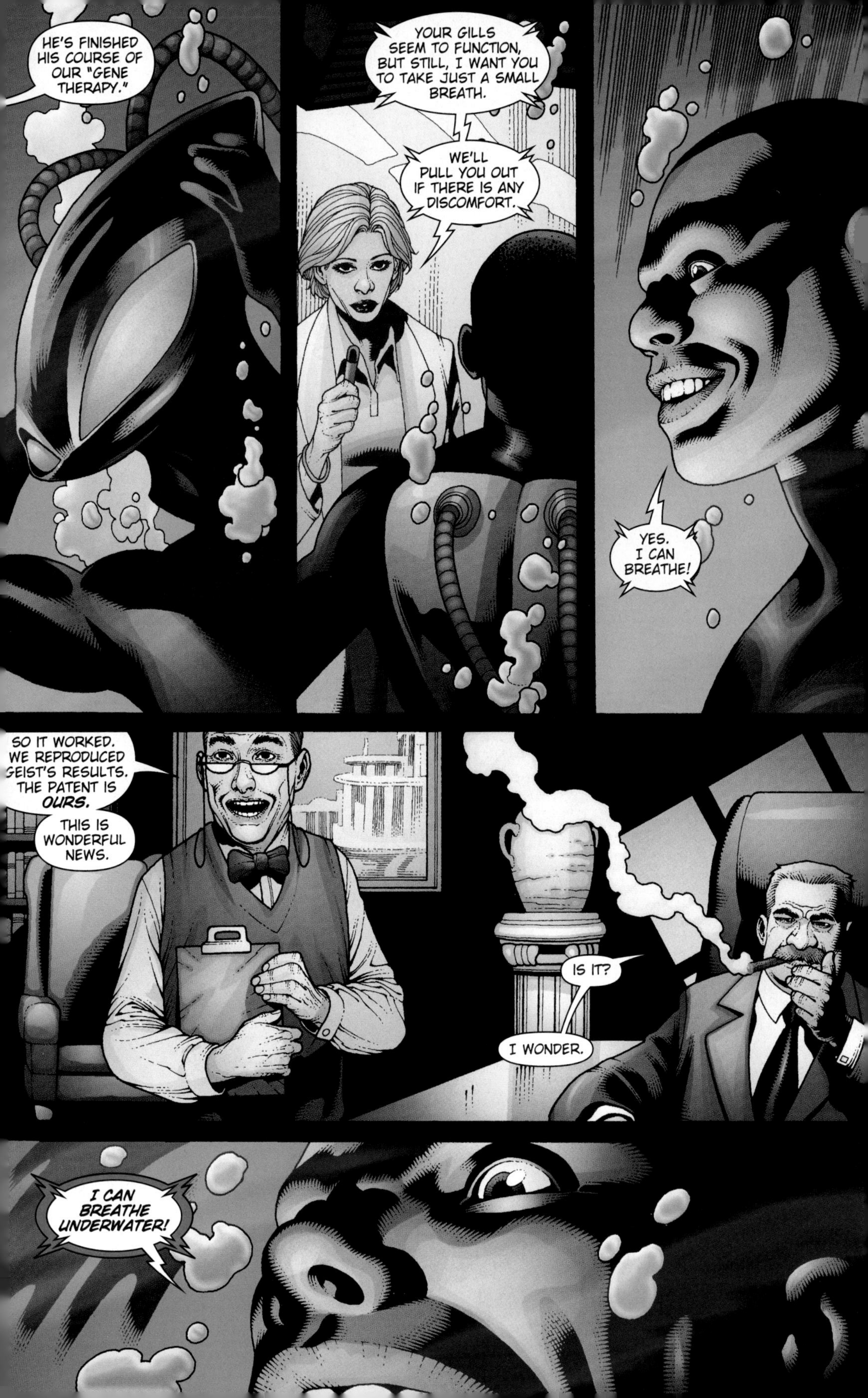
HE'S FINISHED HIS COURSE OF OUR "GENE THERAPY."
YOUR GILLS SEEM TO FUNCTION, BUT STILL, I WANT YOU TO TAKE JUST A SMALL BREATH.
WE'LL PULL YOU OUT IF THERE IS ANY DISCOMFORT.
YES. I CAN BREATHE!
SO IT WORKED. WE REPRODUCED GEIST'S RESULTS. THE PATENT IS OURS.
THIS IS WONDERFUL NEWS.
IS IT?
I WONDER.
I CAN BREATHE UNDERWATER!

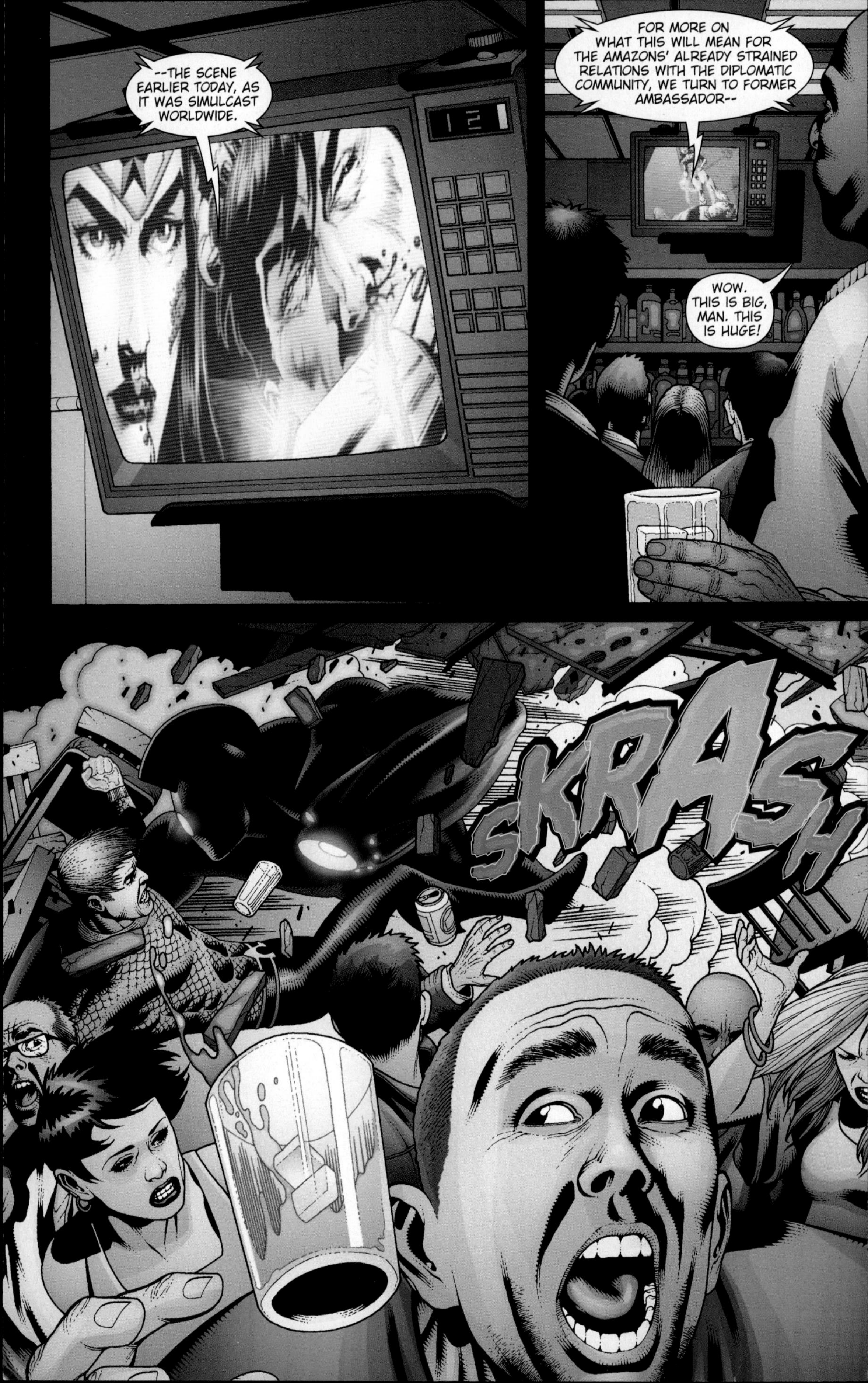
--THE SCENE EARLIER TODAY, AS IT WAS SIMULCAST WORLDWIDE.
FOR MORE ON WHAT THIS WILL MEAN FOR THE AMAZONS' ALREADY STRAINED RELATIONS WITH THE DIPLOMATIC COMMUNITY, WE TURN TO FORMER AMBASSADOR--
WOW. THIS IS BIG, MAN. THIS IS HUGE!
SKRASH

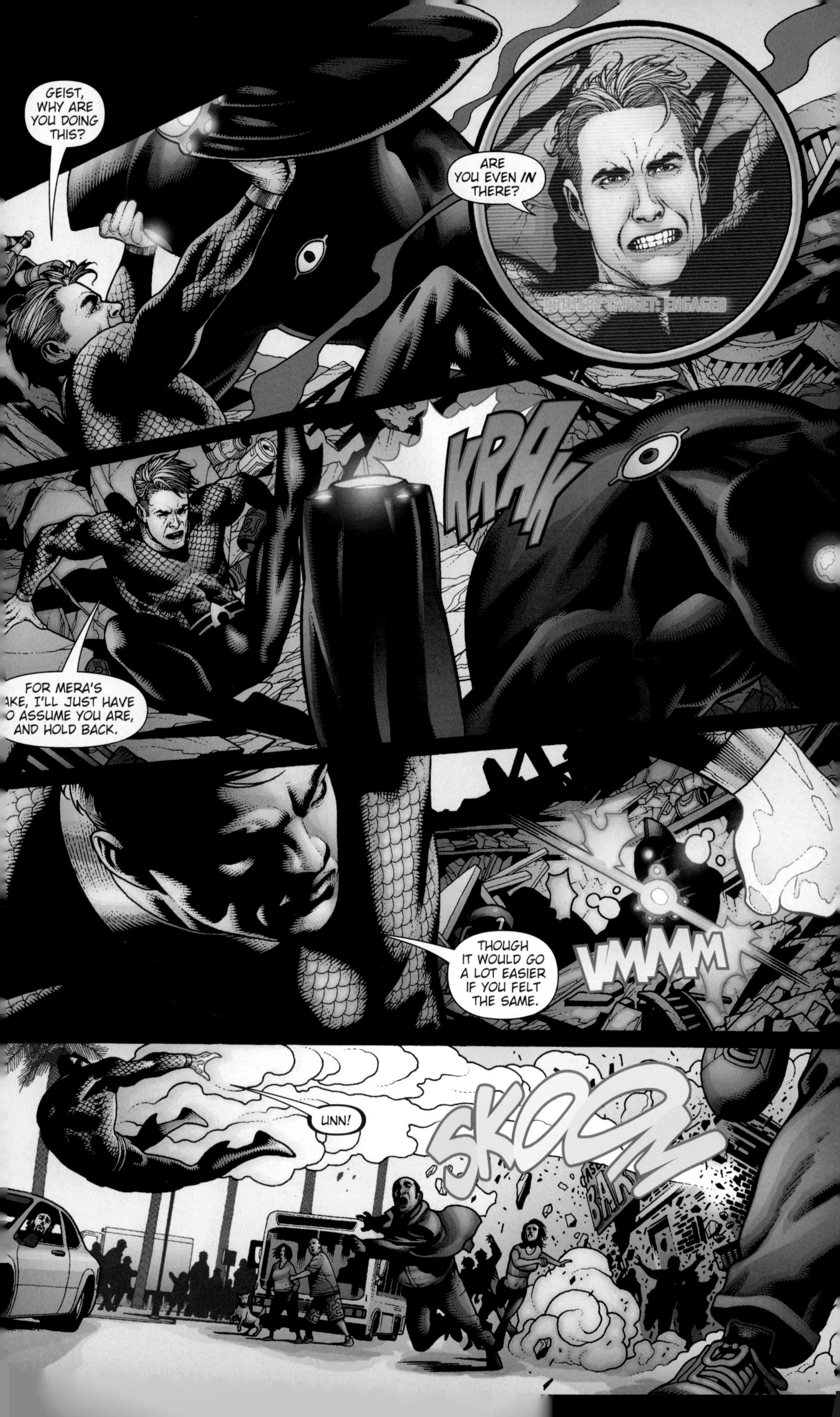
GEIST, WHY ARE YOU DOING THIS?
ARE YOU EVEN *IN* THERE?
TARGET: ENGAGED
KRAK
FOR MERA'S AKE, I'LL JUST HAVE O ASSUME YOU ARE, AND HOLD BACK.
THOUGH IT WOULD GO A LOT EASIER IF YOU FELT THE SAME.
VMMM
UNN!
SKOOM

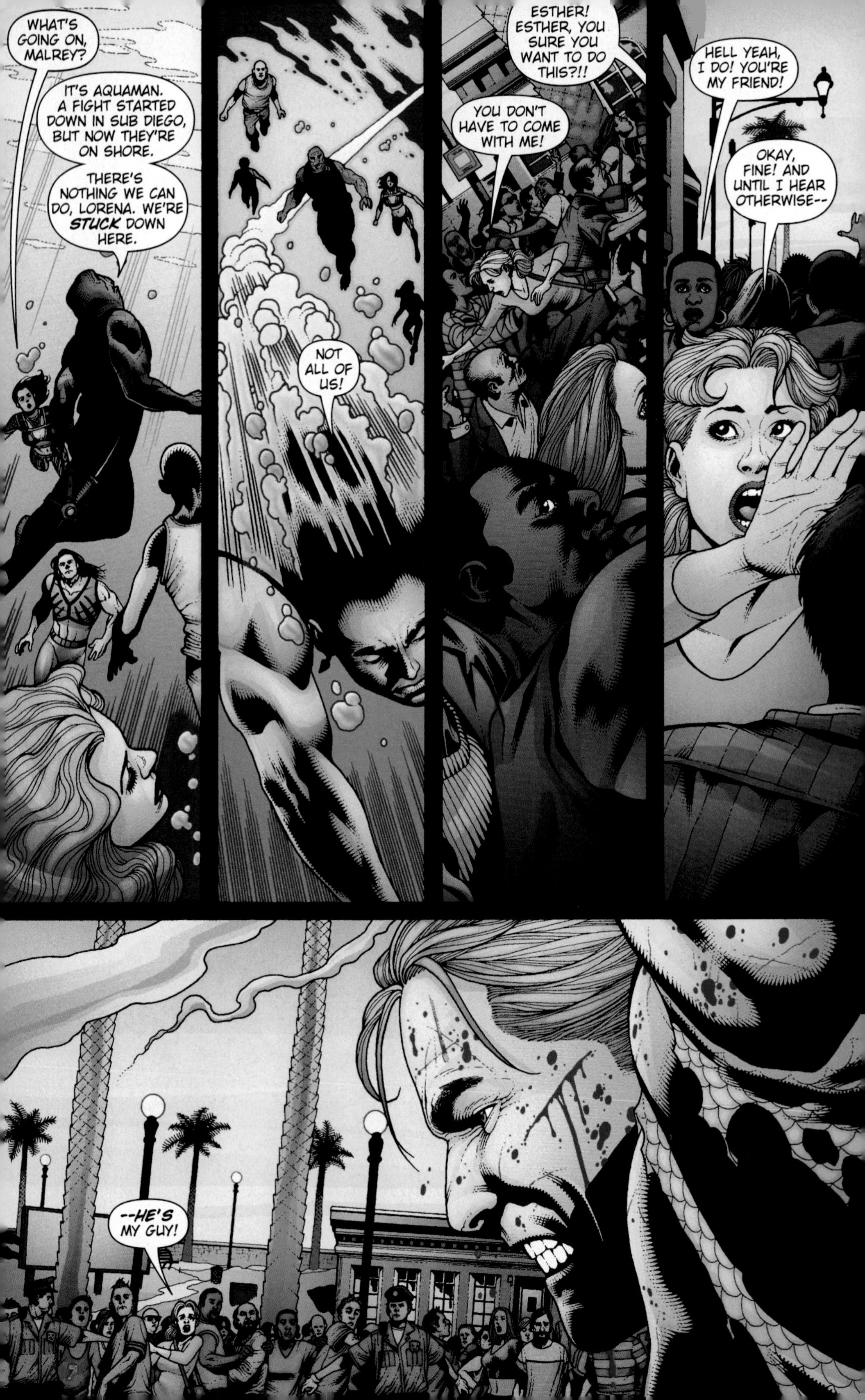
WHAT'S GOING ON, MALREY?
IT'S AQUAMAN. A FIGHT STARTED DOWN IN SUB DIEGO, BUT NOW THEY'RE ON SHORE.
THERE'S NOTHING WE CAN DO, LORENA. WE'RE STUCK DOWN HERE.
NOT ALL OF US!
ESTHER! ESTHER, YOU SURE YOU WANT TO DO THIS?!!
YOU DON'T HAVE TO COME WITH ME!
HELL YEAH, I DO! YOU'RE MY FRIEND!
OKAY, FINE! AND UNTIL I HEAR OTHERWISE--
--HE'S MY GUY!

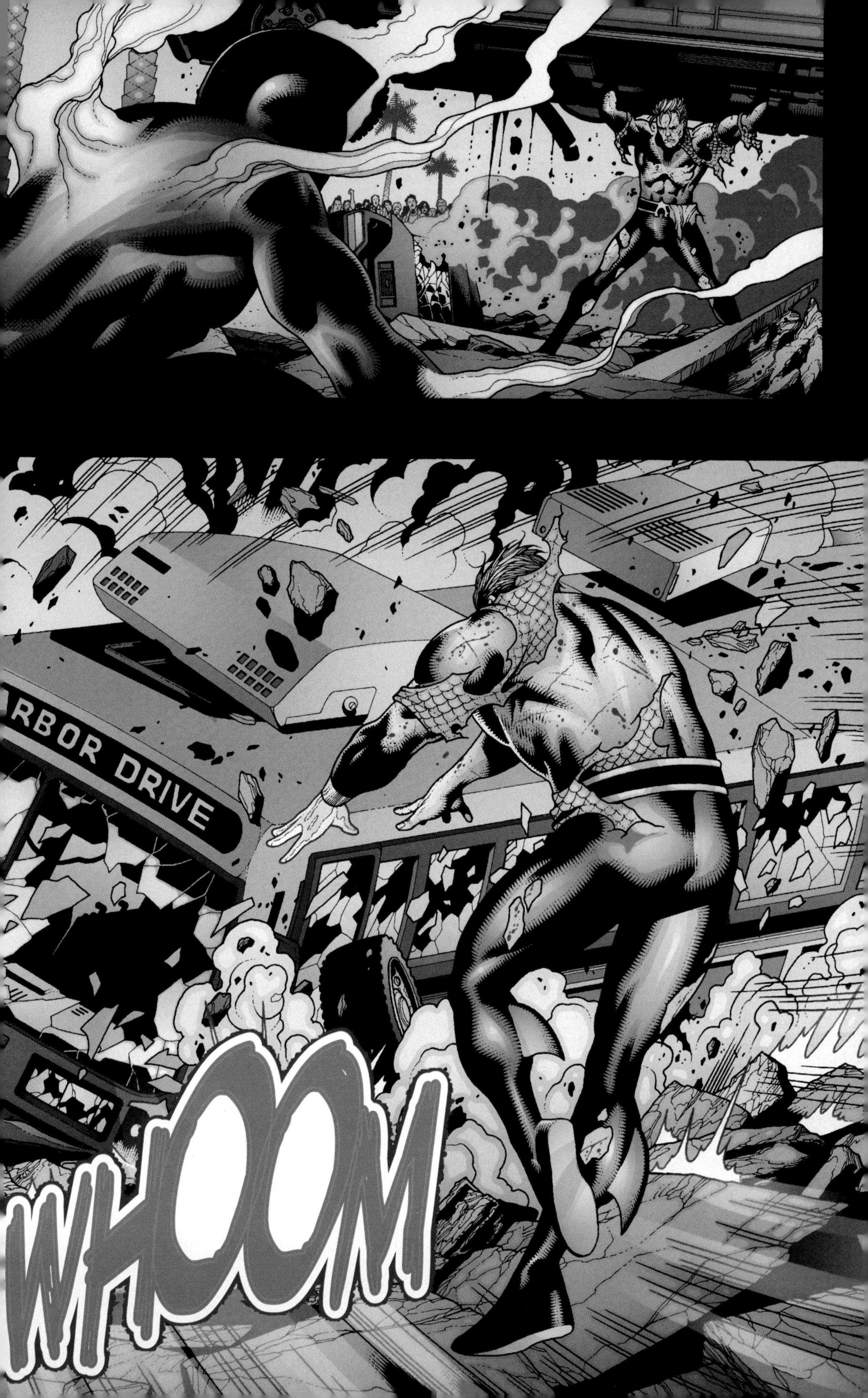
RBOR DRIVE
WHOOM

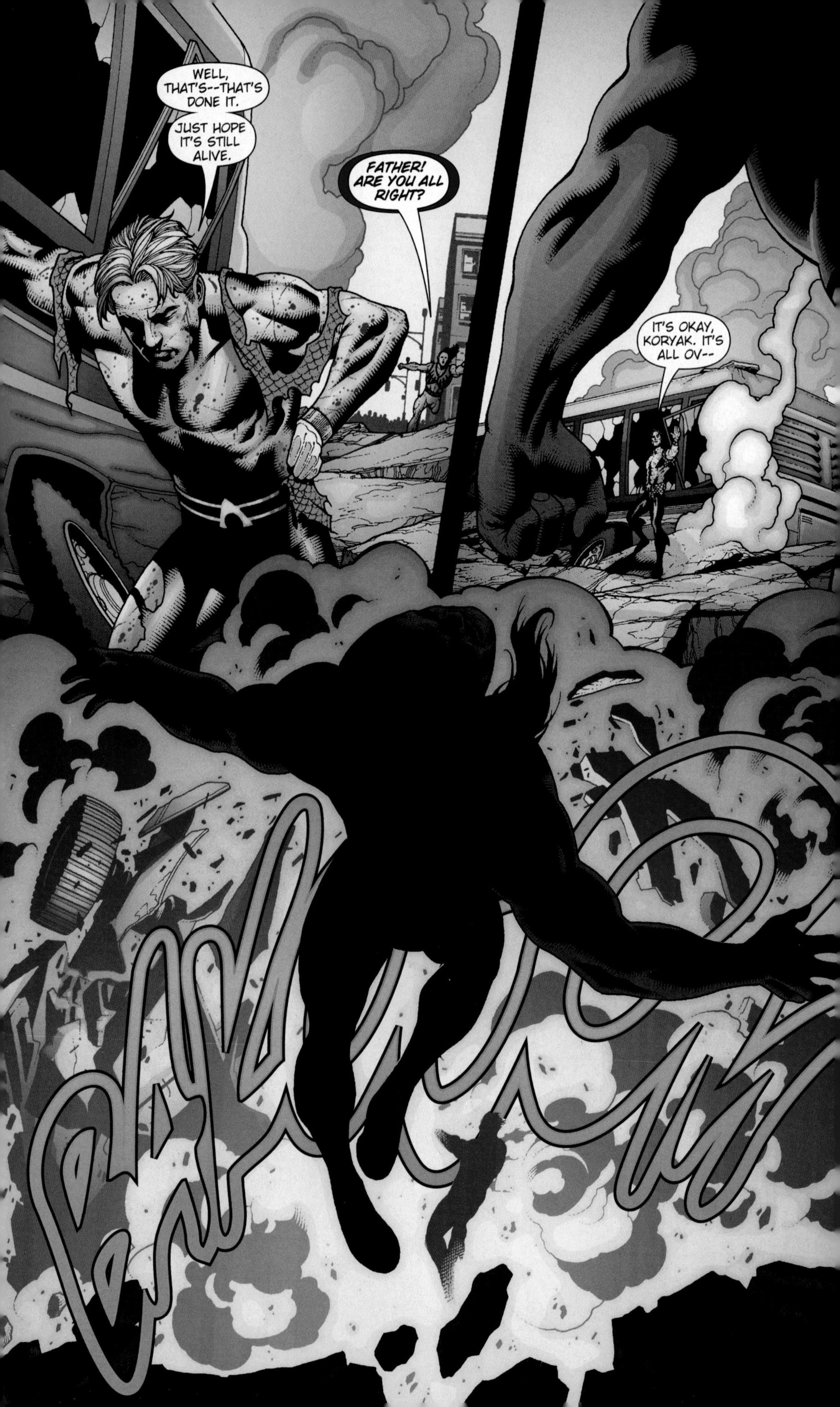
WELL, THAT'S--THAT'S DONE IT.
JUST HOPE IT'S STILL ALIVE.
FATHER! ARE YOU ALL RIGHT?
IT'S OKAY, KORYAK. IT'S ALL OV--

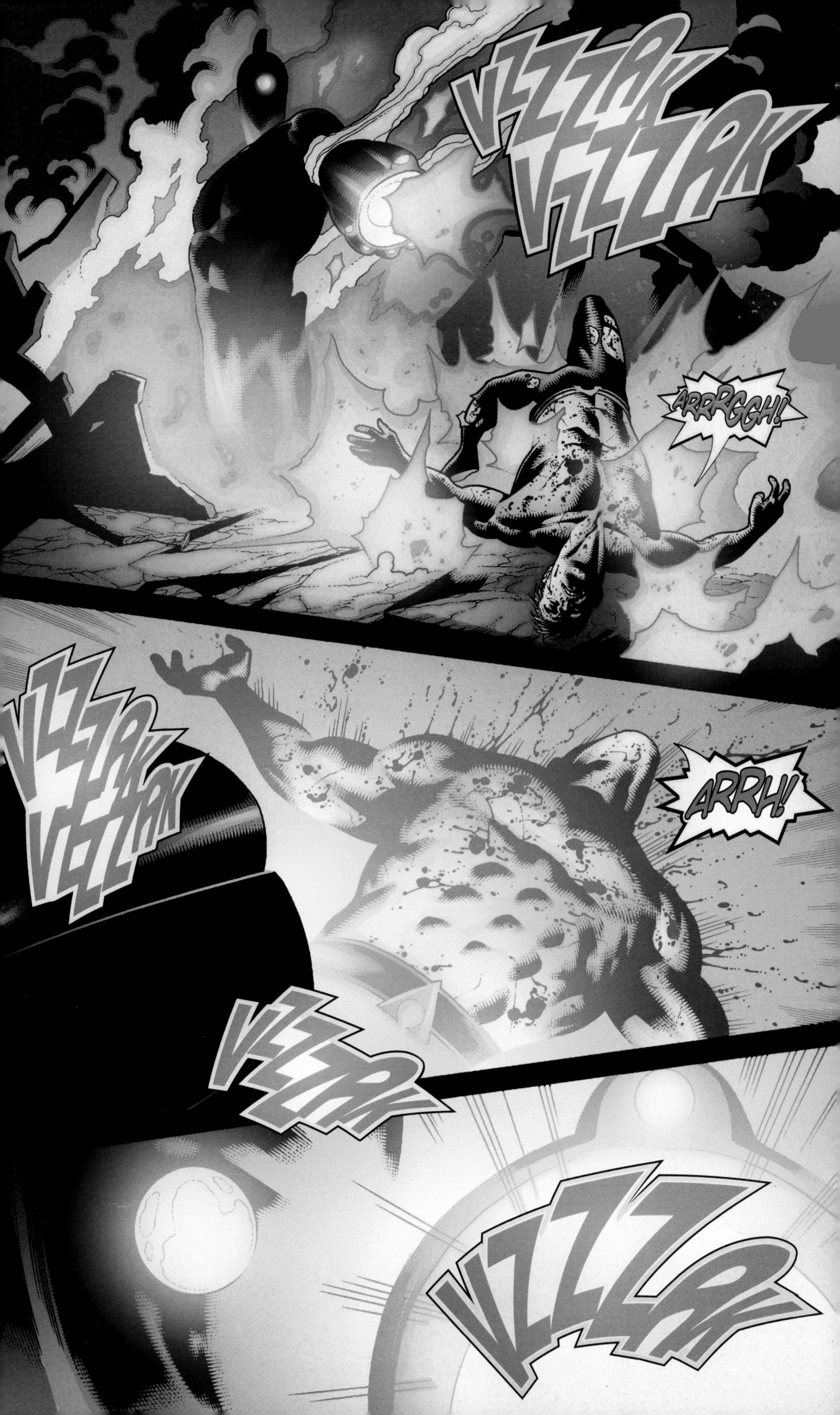
VZZZAK VZZZAK
ARRRGGH!
VZZZAK VZZZAK
ARRH!
VZZZAK
VZZZAK

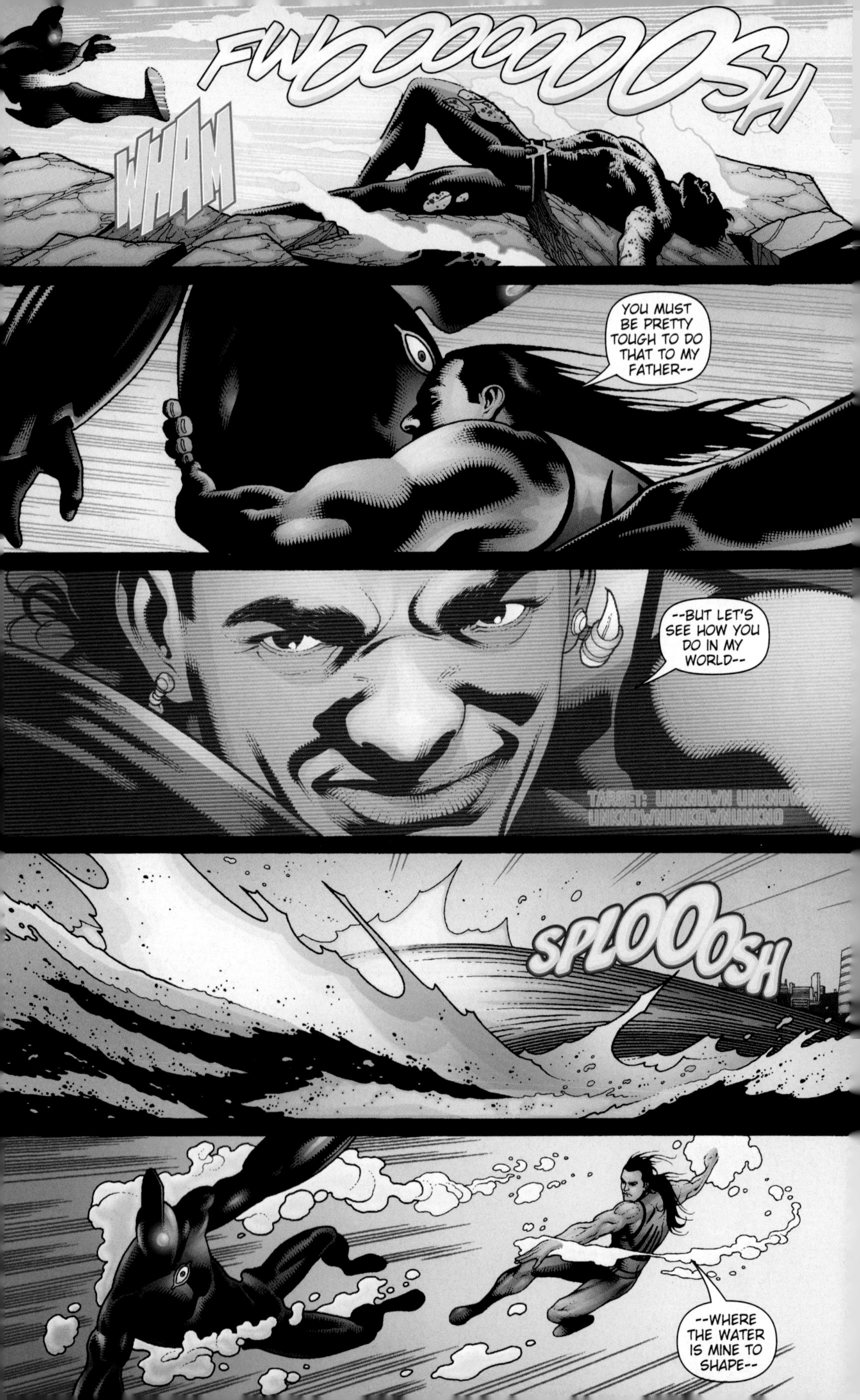
FWOOOOOOOSH
WHAM
YOU MUST BE PRETTY TOUGH TO DO THAT TO MY FATHER--
--BUT LET'S SEE HOW YOU DO IN MY WORLD--
TARGET: UNKNOWN UNKNOW
UNKNOWNUNKOWNUNKNO
SPLOOOSH
--WHERE THE WATER IS MINE TO SHAPE--

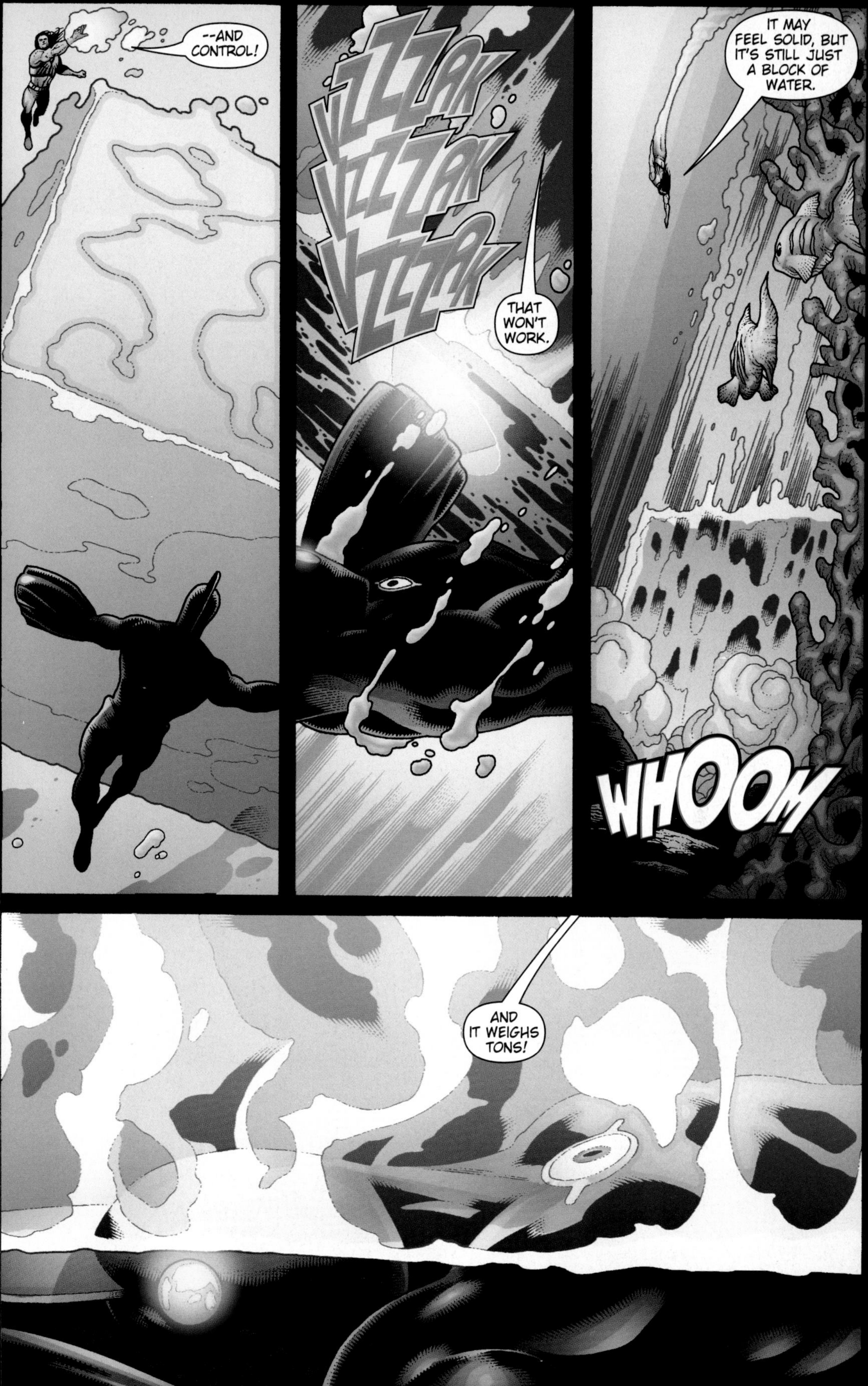
--AND CONTROL!
VIZZZAK VIZZZAK VIZZZAK
THAT WON'T WORK.
IT MAY FEEL SOLID, BUT IT'S STILL JUST A BLOCK OF WATER.
WHOOM
AND IT WEIGHS TONS!

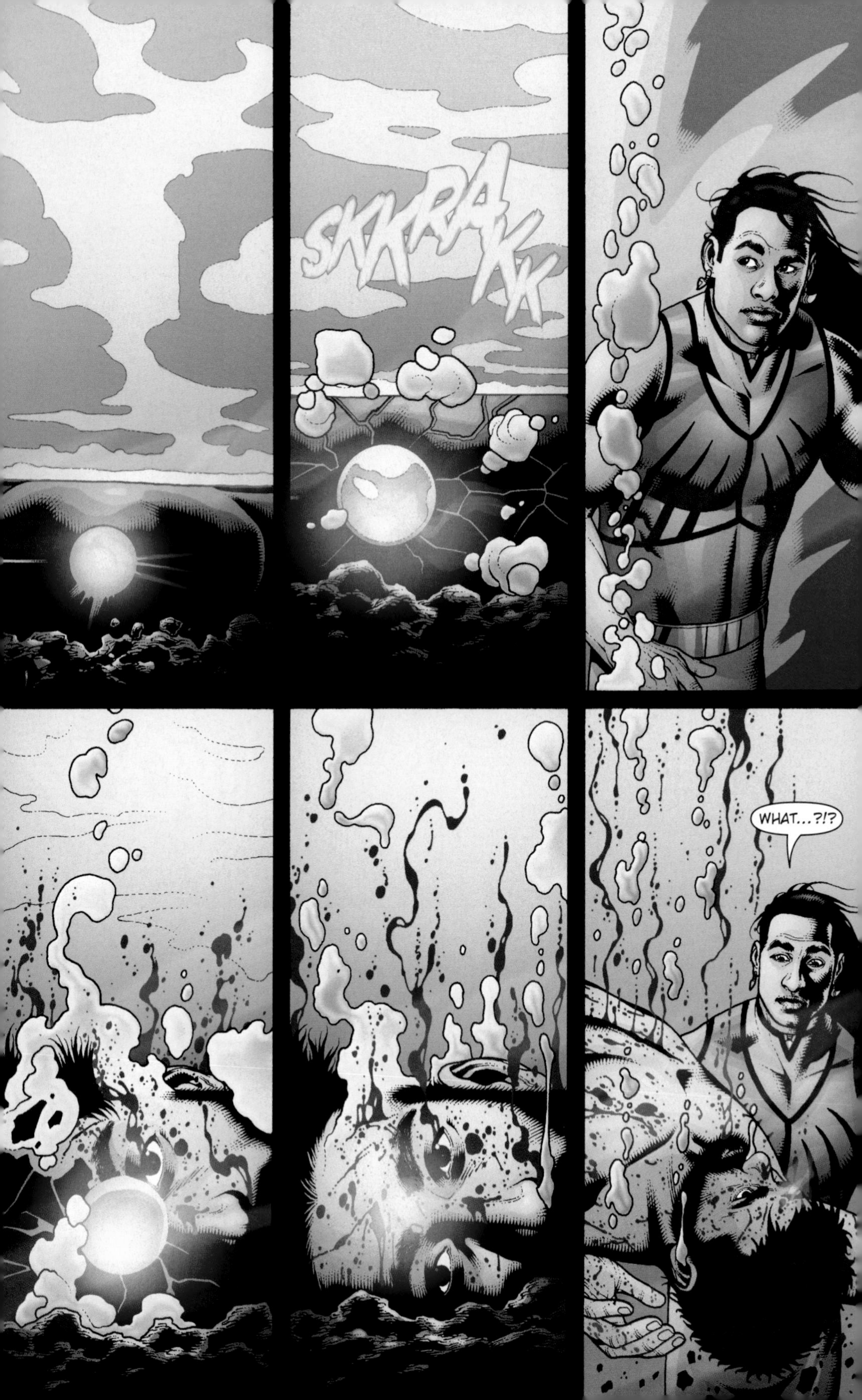
SKKRAKK
WHAT...?!?

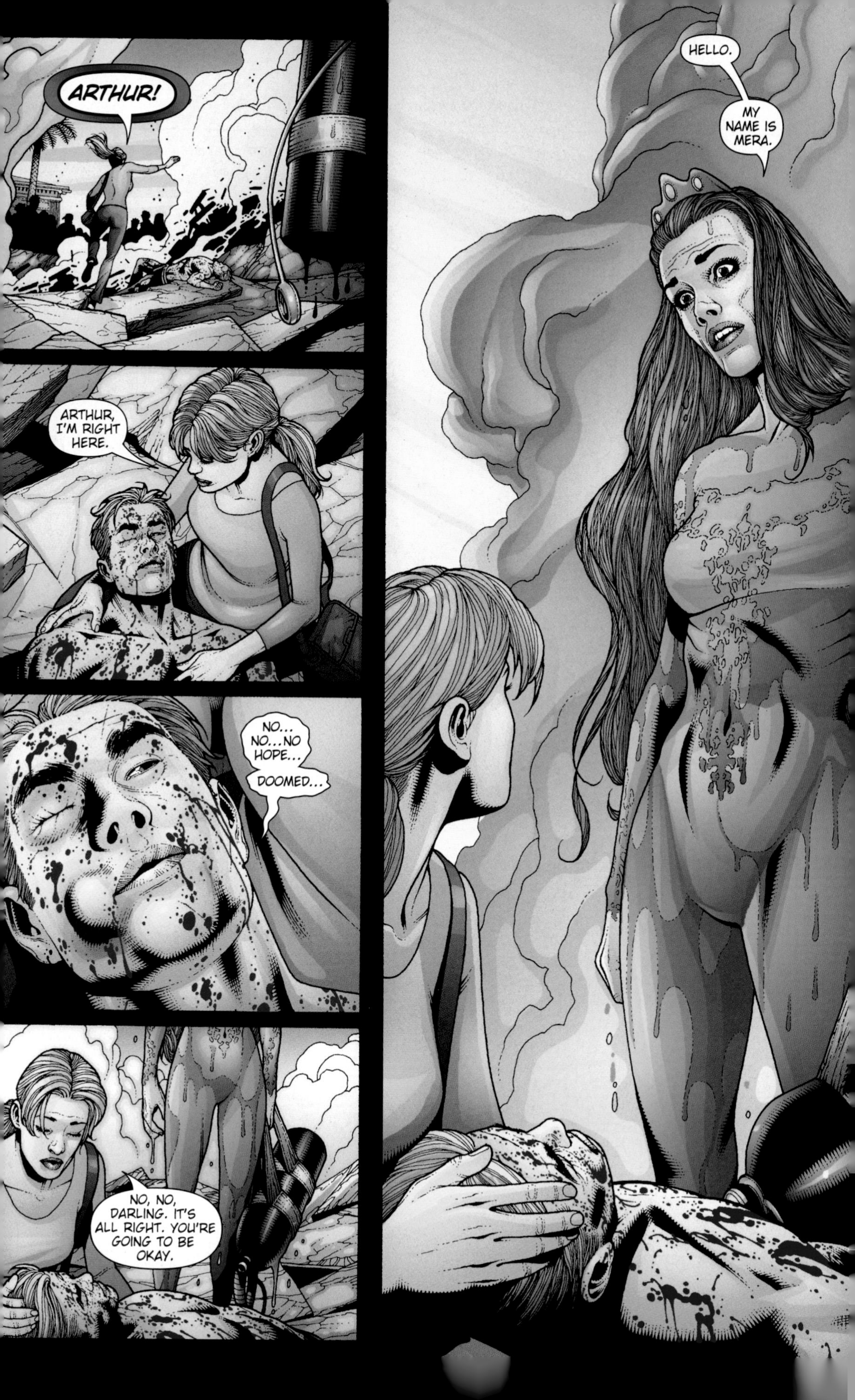
ARTHUR!
ARTHUR, I'M RIGHT HERE.
NO... NO...NO HOPE...
DOOMED...
NO, NO, DARLING. IT'S ALL RIGHT. YOU'RE GOING TO BE OKAY.
HELLO.
MY NAME IS MERA.

AQUAMAN *sketch by* **PATRICK GLEASON**

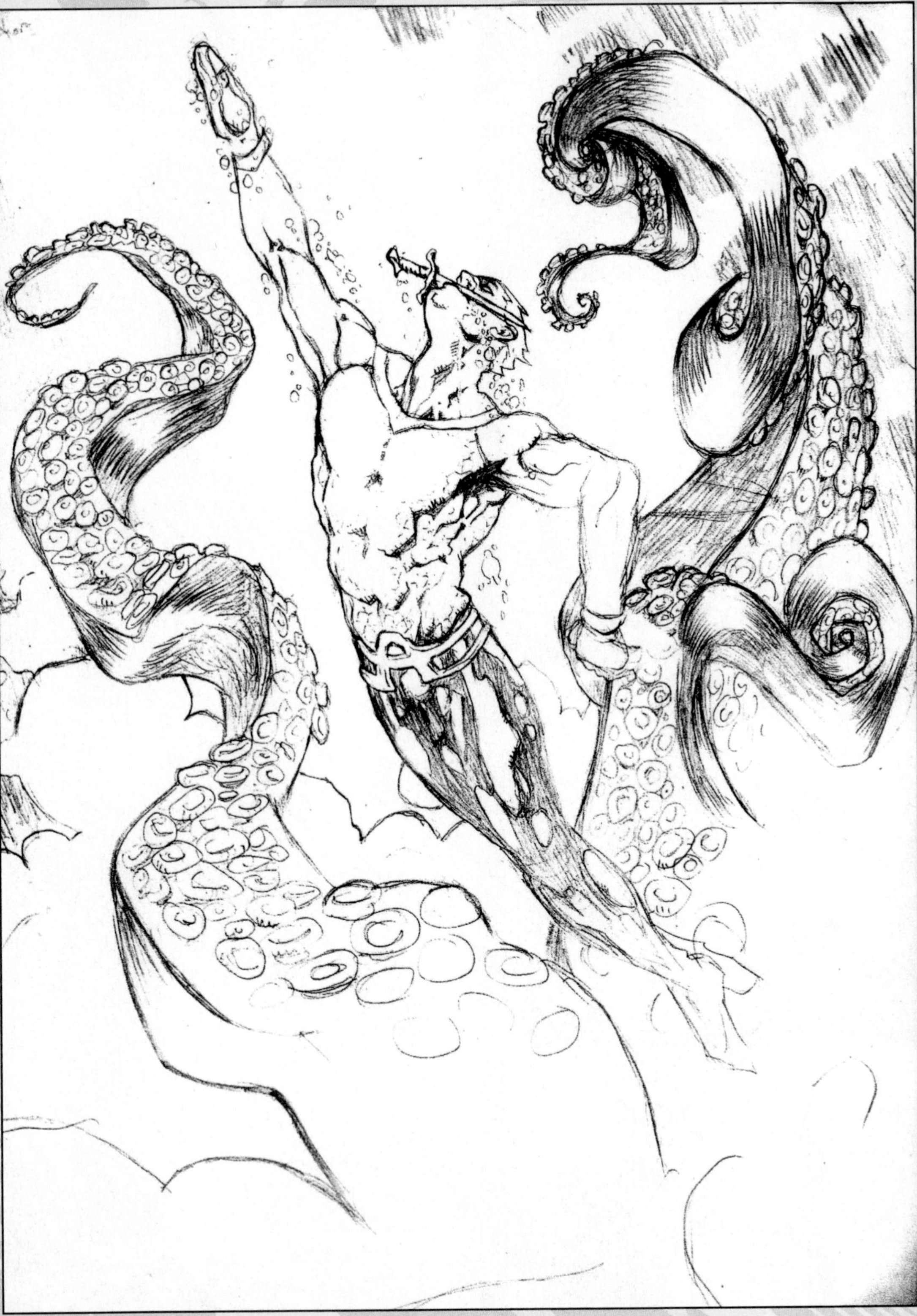

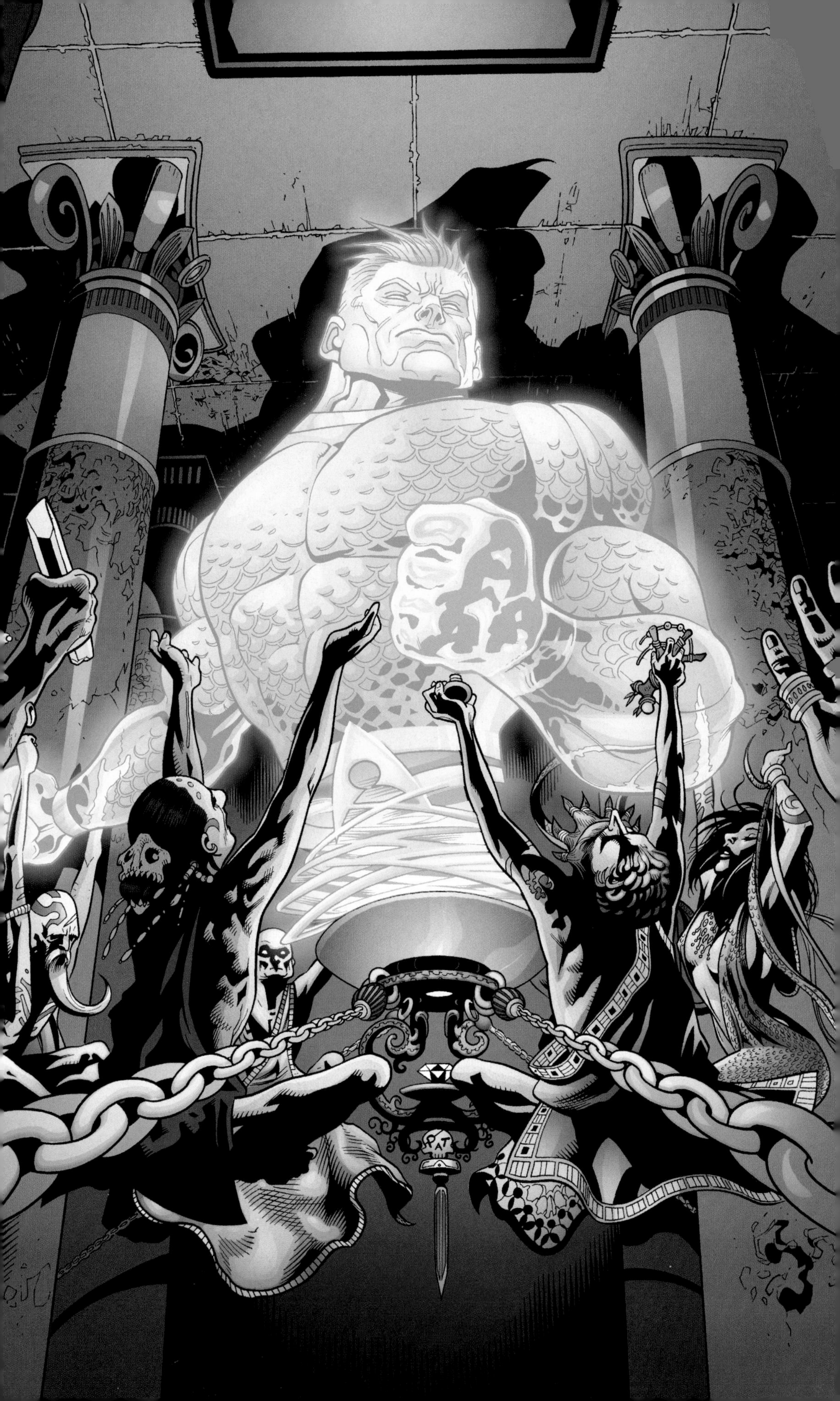

THE FAILURE OF SUCCESS

JOHN ARCUDI
Writer

LEONARD KIRK
Layouts

ANDY CLARKE
Finishes

NATHAN EYRING
Colorist

TRAVIS LANHAM
Letterer

**PATRICK GLEASON &
CHRISTIAN ALAMY**
Cover

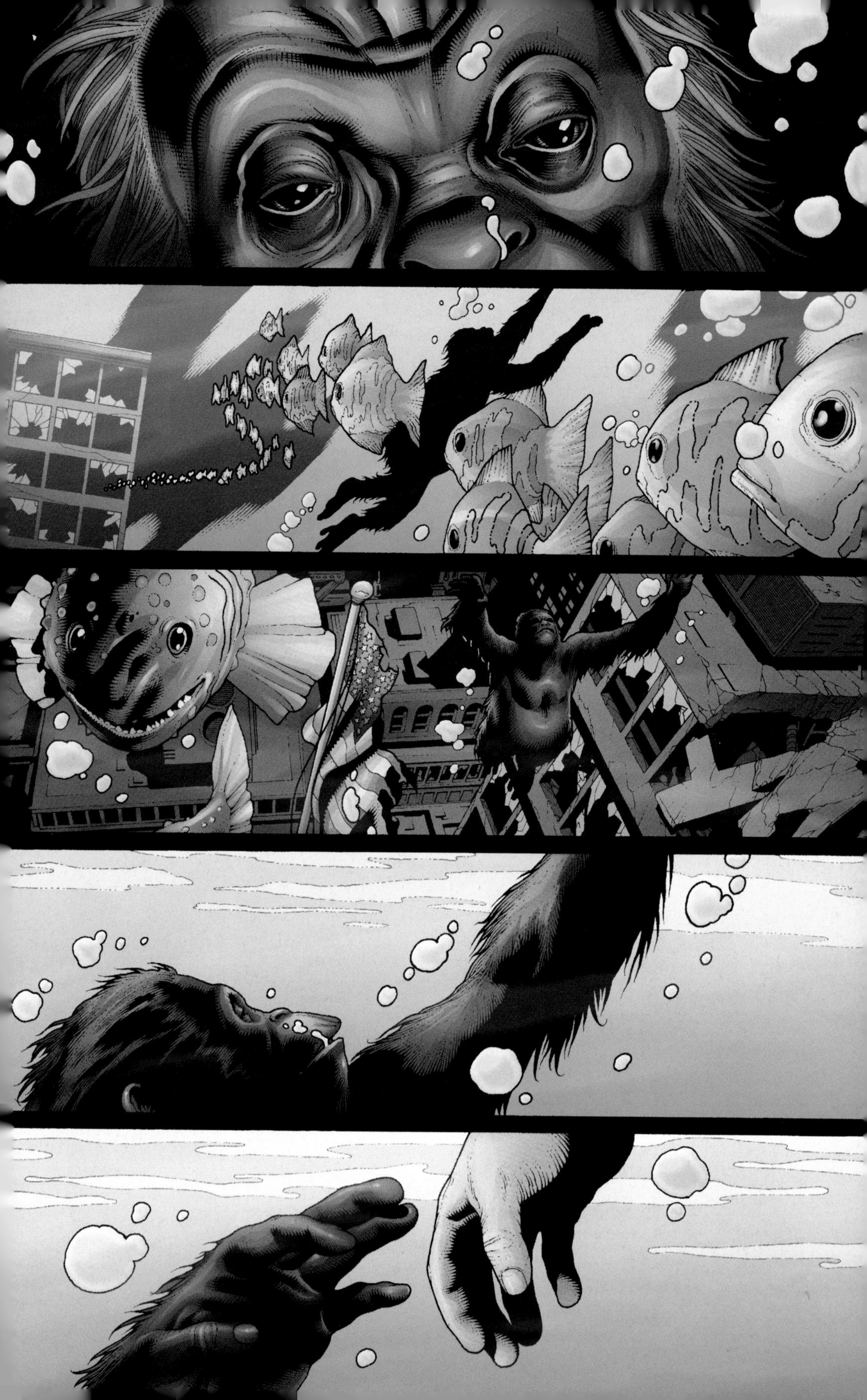

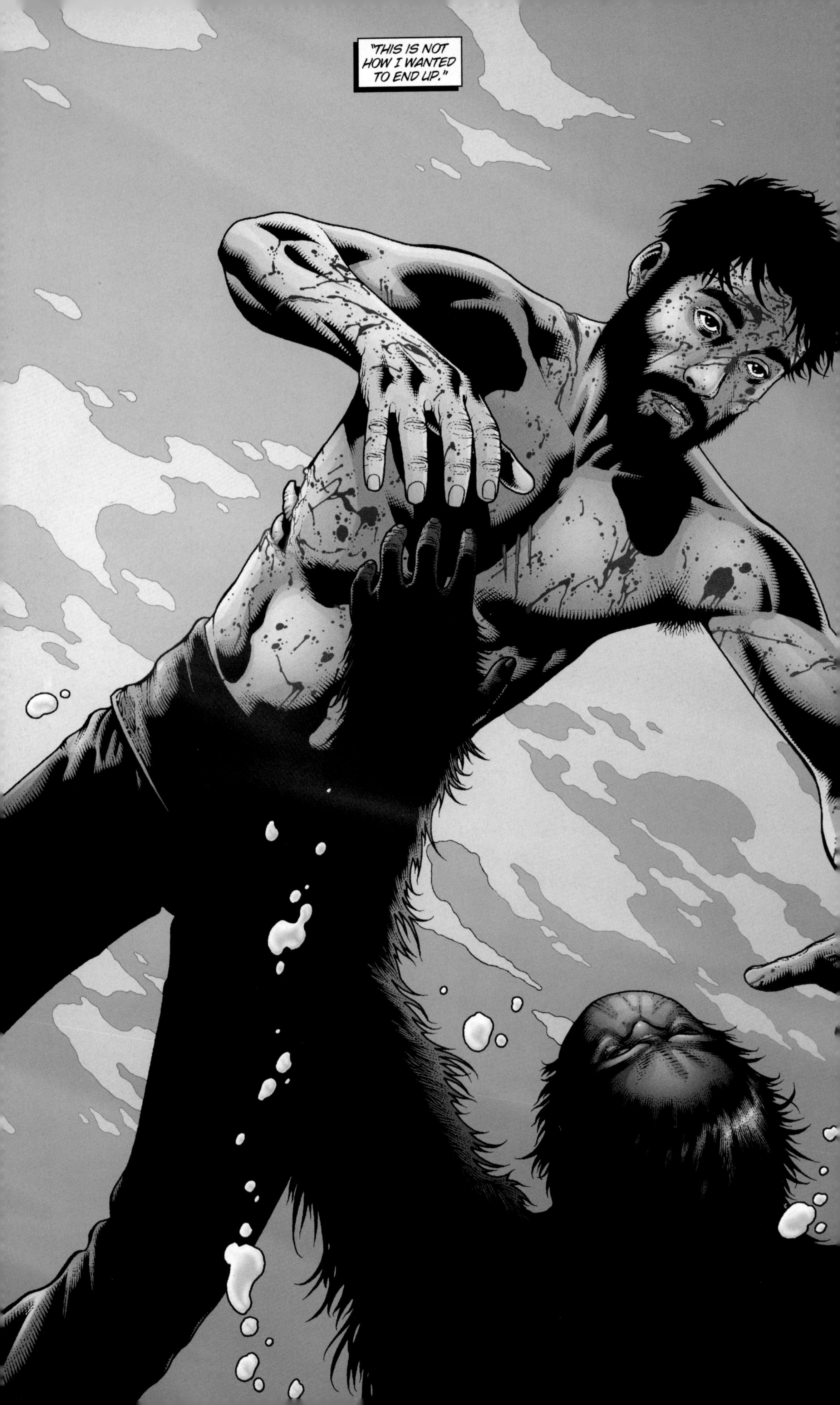
"THIS IS NOT HOW I WANTED TO END UP."

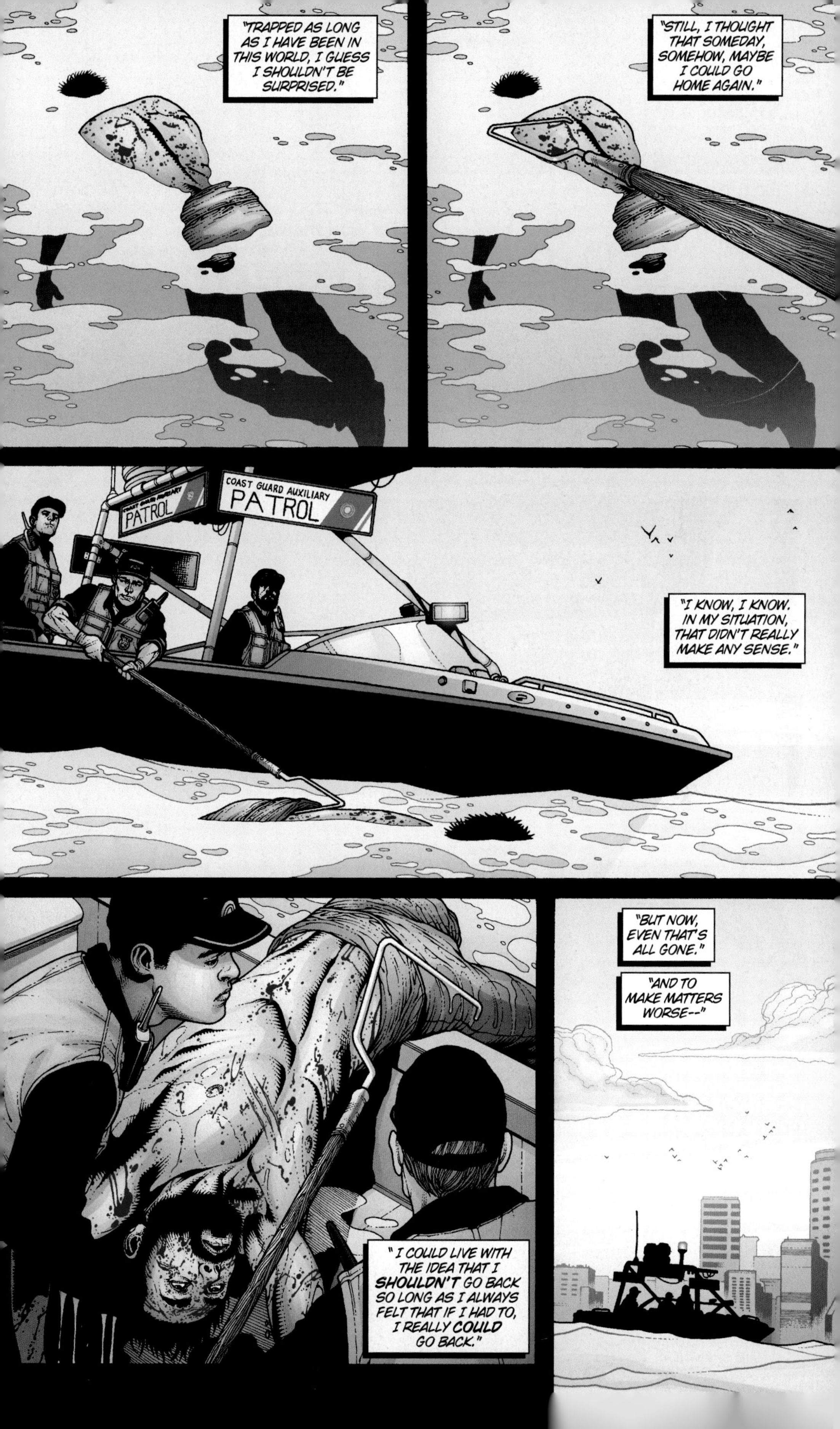
"TRAPPED AS LONG AS I HAVE BEEN IN THIS WORLD, I GUESS I SHOULDN'T BE SURPRISED."
"STILL, I THOUGHT THAT SOMEDAY, SOMEHOW, MAYBE I COULD GO HOME AGAIN."
COAST GUARD AUXILIARY PATROL
PATROL
"I KNOW, I KNOW. IN MY SITUATION, THAT DIDN'T REALLY MAKE ANY SENSE."
"I COULD LIVE WITH THE IDEA THAT I SHOULDN'T GO BACK SO LONG AS I ALWAYS FELT THAT IF I HAD TO, I REALLY COULD GO BACK."
"BUT NOW, EVEN THAT'S ALL GONE."
"AND TO MAKE MATTERS WORSE--"

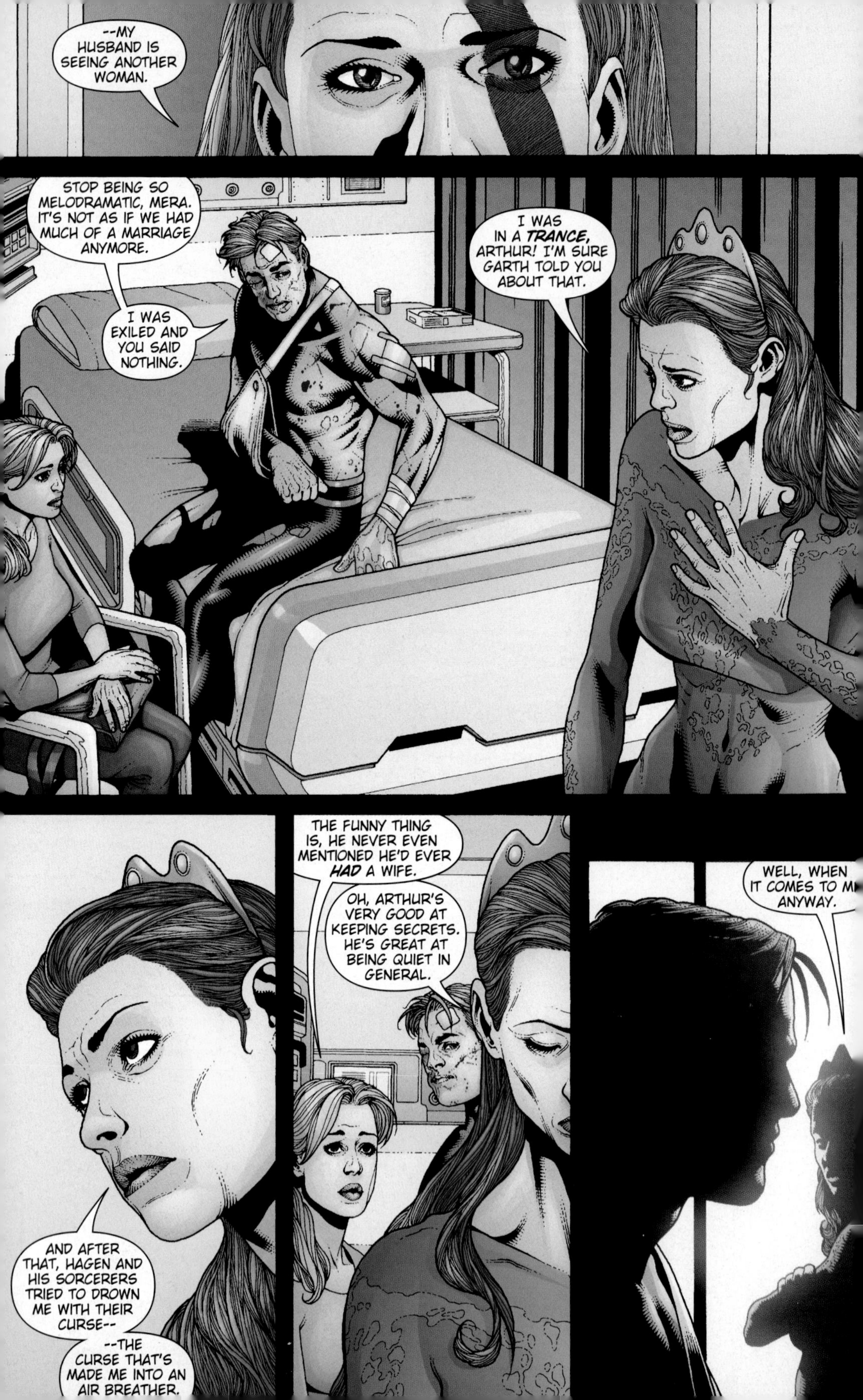
--MY HUSBAND IS SEEING ANOTHER WOMAN.
STOP BEING SO MELODRAMATIC, MERA. IT'S NOT AS IF WE HAD MUCH OF A MARRIAGE ANYMORE.
I WAS EXILED AND YOU SAID NOTHING.
I WAS IN A TRANCE, ARTHUR! I'M SURE GARTH TOLD YOU ABOUT THAT.
AND AFTER THAT, HAGEN AND HIS SORCERERS TRIED TO DROWN ME WITH THEIR CURSE--
--THE CURSE THAT'S MADE ME INTO AN AIR BREATHER.
THE FUNNY THING IS, HE NEVER EVEN MENTIONED HE'D EVER HAD A WIFE.
OH, ARTHUR'S VERY GOOD AT KEEPING SECRETS. HE'S GREAT AT BEING QUIET IN GENERAL.
WELL, WHEN IT COMES TO ME ANYWAY.

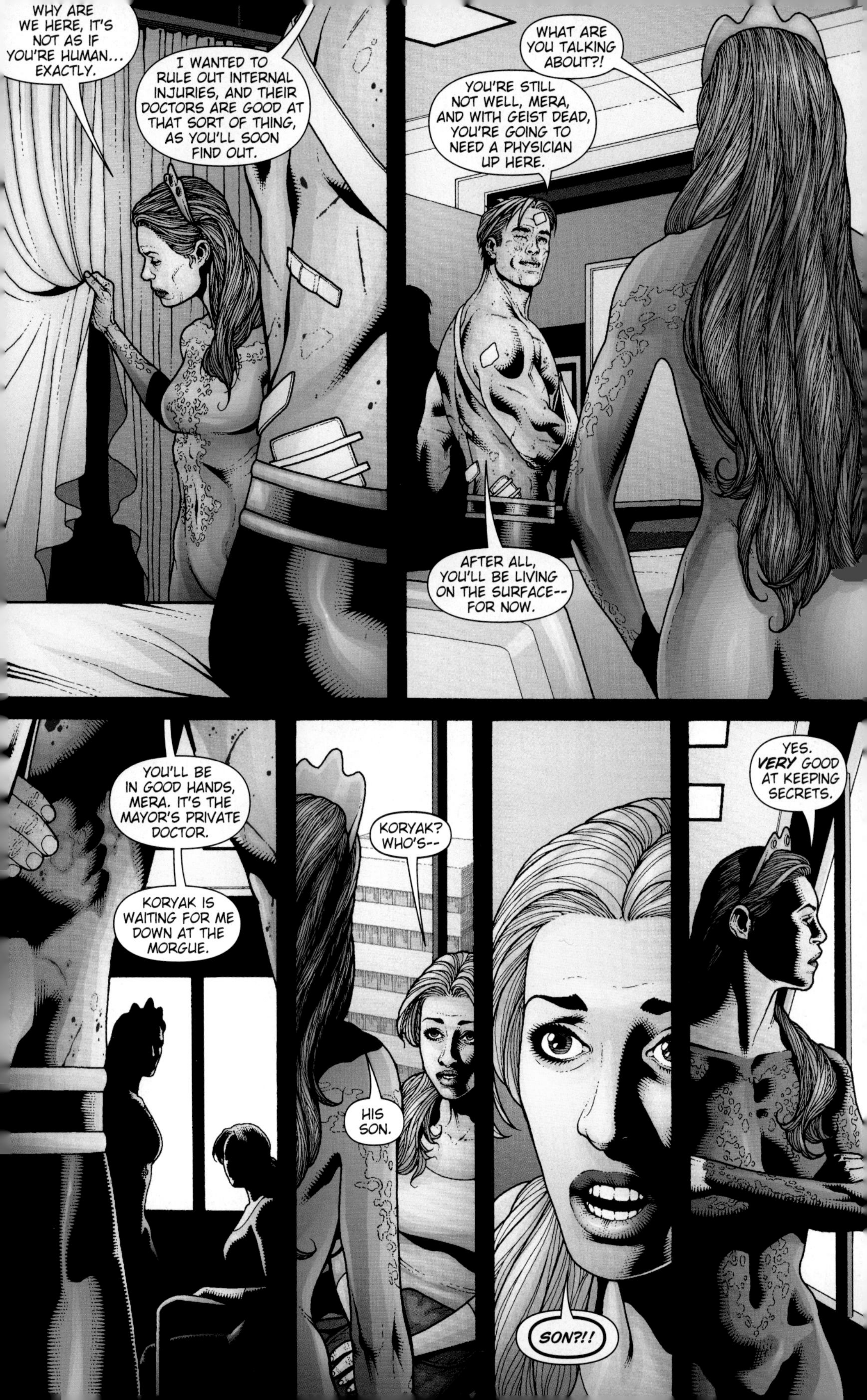
WHY ARE WE HERE, IT'S NOT AS IF YOU'RE HUMAN... EXACTLY.
I WANTED TO RULE OUT INTERNAL INJURIES, AND THEIR DOCTORS ARE GOOD AT THAT SORT OF THING, AS YOU'LL SOON FIND OUT.
WHAT ARE YOU TALKING ABOUT?!
YOU'RE STILL NOT WELL, MERA, AND WITH GEIST DEAD, YOU'RE GOING TO NEED A PHYSICIAN UP HERE.
AFTER ALL, YOU'LL BE LIVING ON THE SURFACE-- FOR NOW.
YOU'LL BE IN GOOD HANDS, MERA. IT'S THE MAYOR'S PRIVATE DOCTOR.
KORYAK IS WAITING FOR ME DOWN AT THE MORGUE.
KORYAK? WHO'S--
HIS SON.
SON?!!
YES. VERY GOOD AT KEEPING SECRETS.

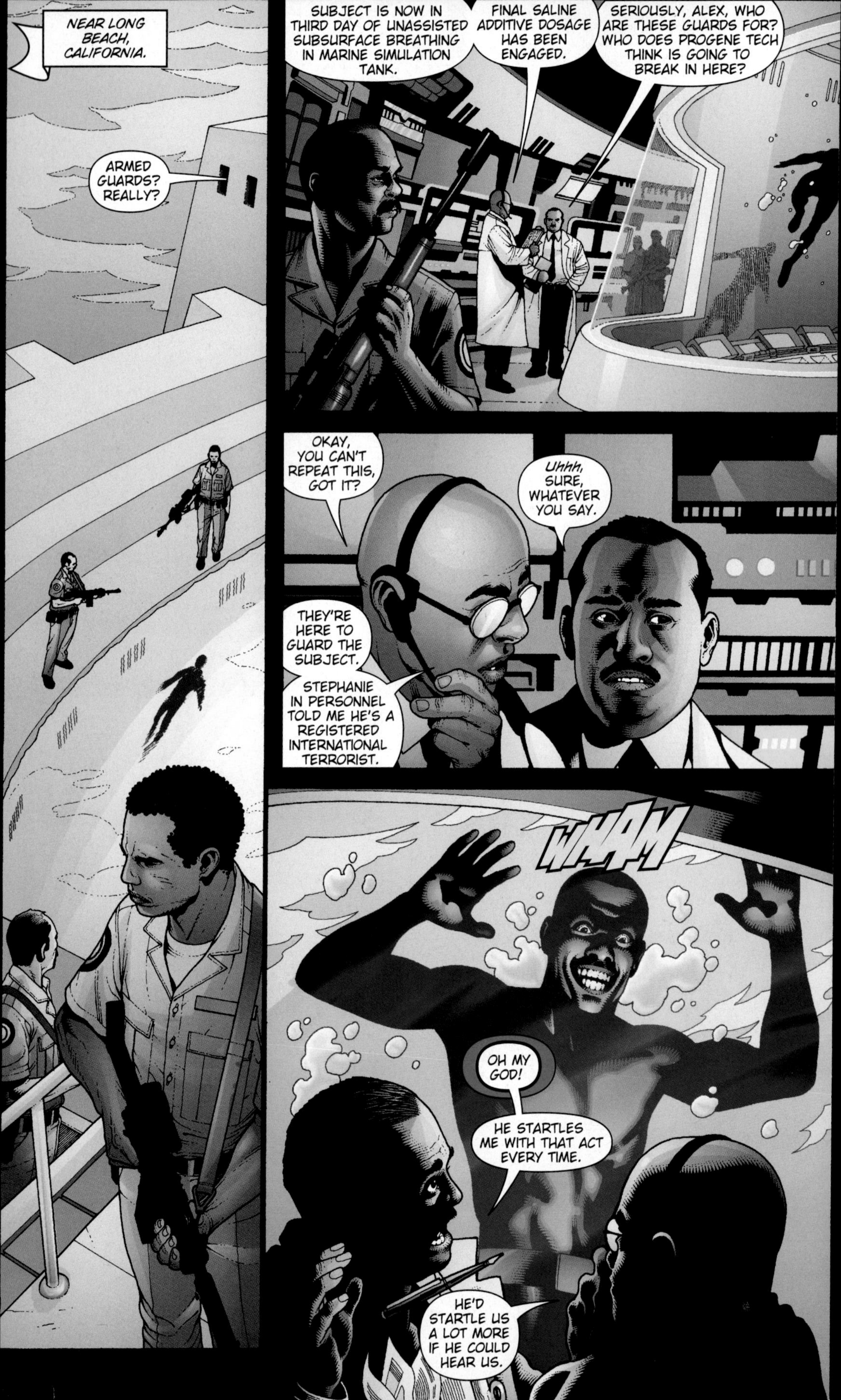
NEAR LONG BEACH, CALIFORNIA.
ARMED GUARDS? REALLY?
SUBJECT IS NOW IN THIRD DAY OF UNASSISTED SUBSURFACE BREATHING IN MARINE SIMULATION TANK.
FINAL SALINE ADDITIVE DOSAGE HAS BEEN ENGAGED.
SERIOUSLY, ALEX, WHO ARE THESE GUARDS FOR? WHO DOES PROGENE TECH THINK IS GOING TO BREAK IN HERE?
OKAY, YOU CAN'T REPEAT THIS, GOT IT?
Uhhh, SURE, WHATEVER YOU SAY.
THEY'RE HERE TO GUARD THE SUBJECT.
STEPHANIE IN PERSONNEL TOLD ME HE'S A REGISTERED INTERNATIONAL TERRORIST.
WHAM
OH MY GOD!
HE STARTLES ME WITH THAT ACT EVERY TIME.
HE'D STARTLE US A LOT MORE IF HE COULD HEAR US.

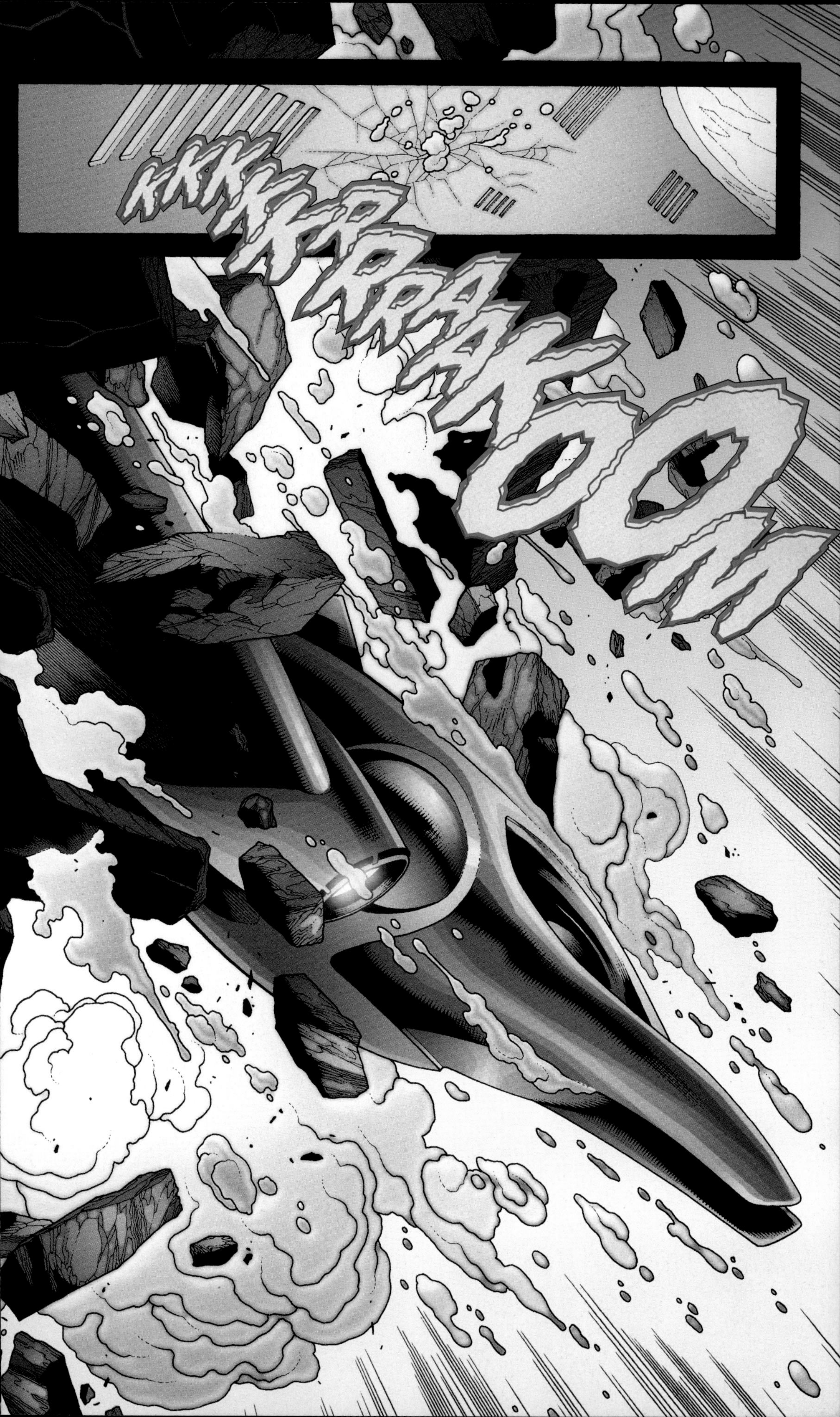
K-K-K-KRRAKOOM

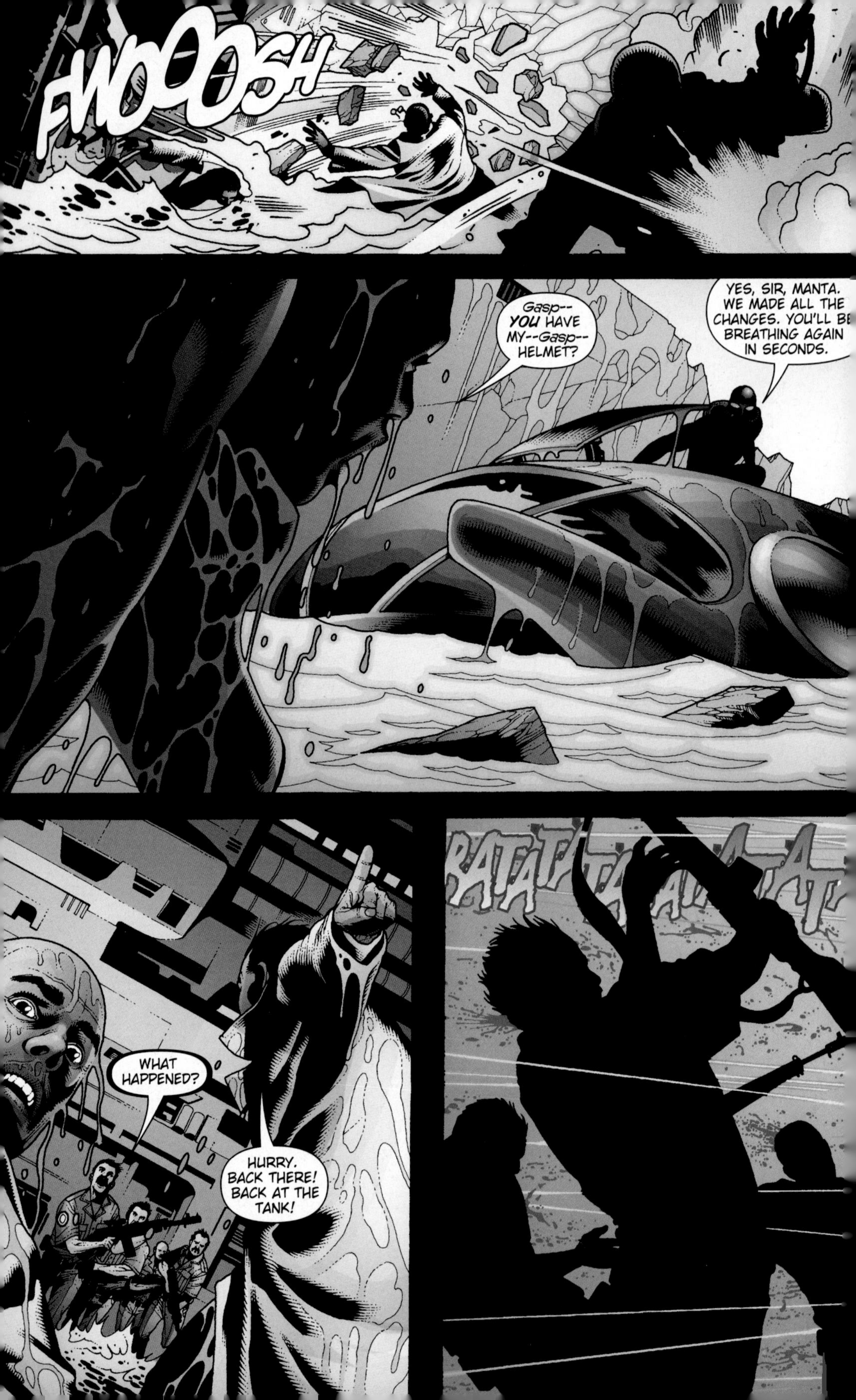
FWOOOSH
Gasp-- YOU HAVE MY--Gasp-- HELMET?
YES, SIR, MANTA. WE MADE ALL THE CHANGES. YOU'LL BE BREATHING AGAIN IN SECONDS.
WHAT HAPPENED?
HURRY. BACK THERE! BACK AT THE TANK!

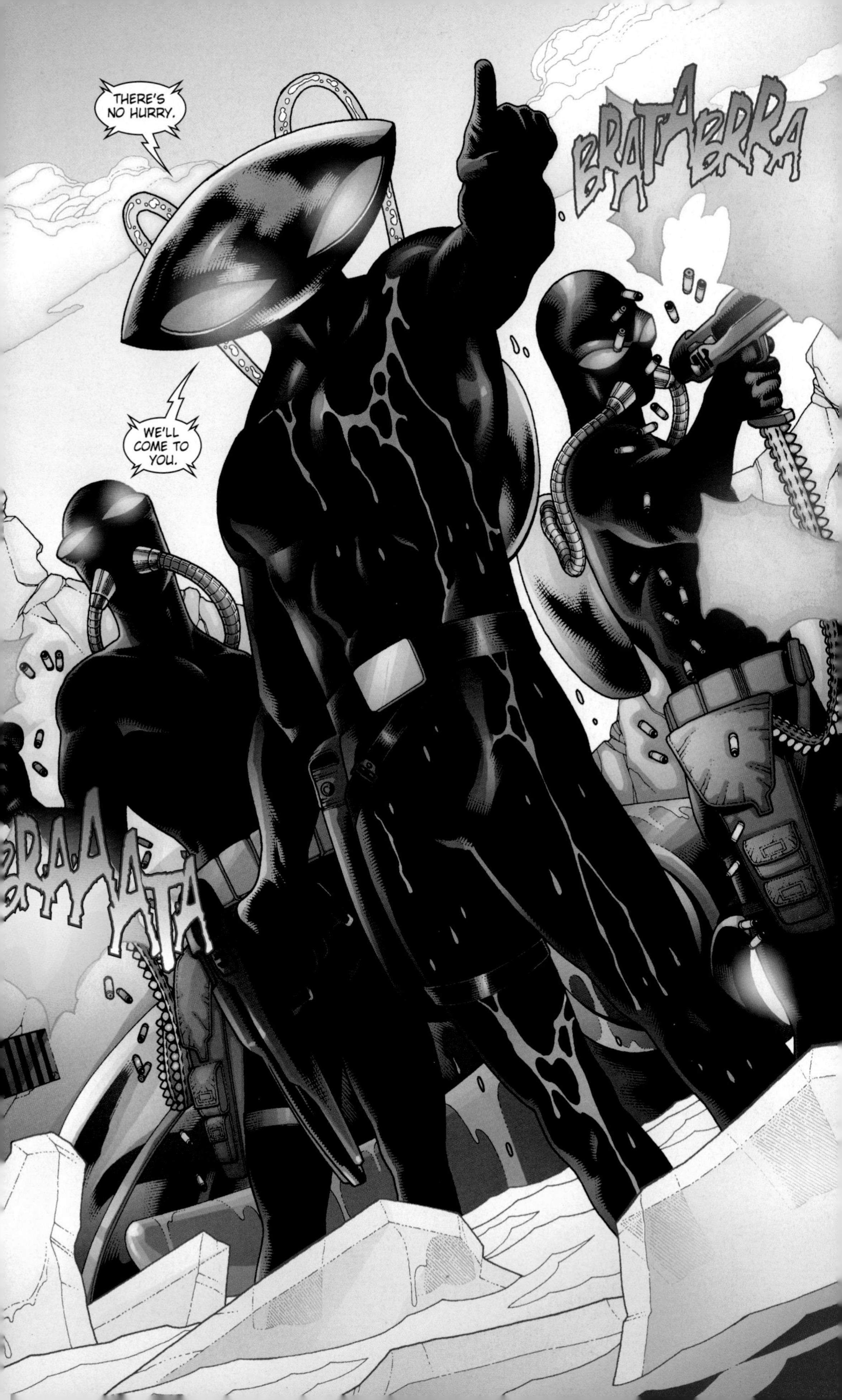
THERE'S NO HURRY.
WE'LL COME TO YOU.
BRATARRA
BRAAATA

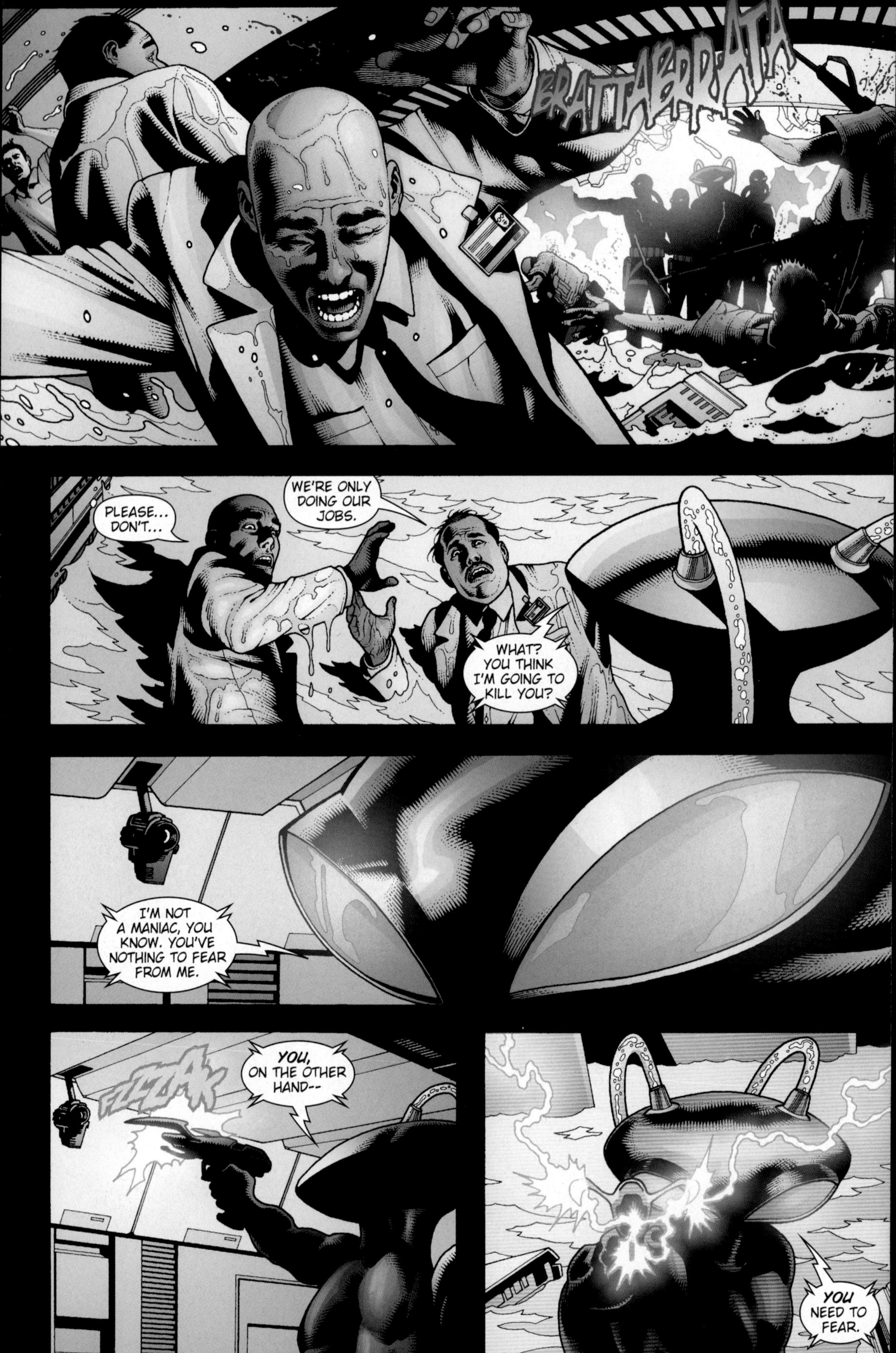
BRATTABDDATA
PLEASE... DON'T...
WE'RE ONLY DOING OUR JOBS.
WHAT? YOU THINK I'M GOING TO KILL YOU?
I'M NOT A MANIAC, YOU KNOW. YOU'VE NOTHING TO FEAR FROM ME.
YOU, ON THE OTHER HAND--
YOU NEED TO FEAR.

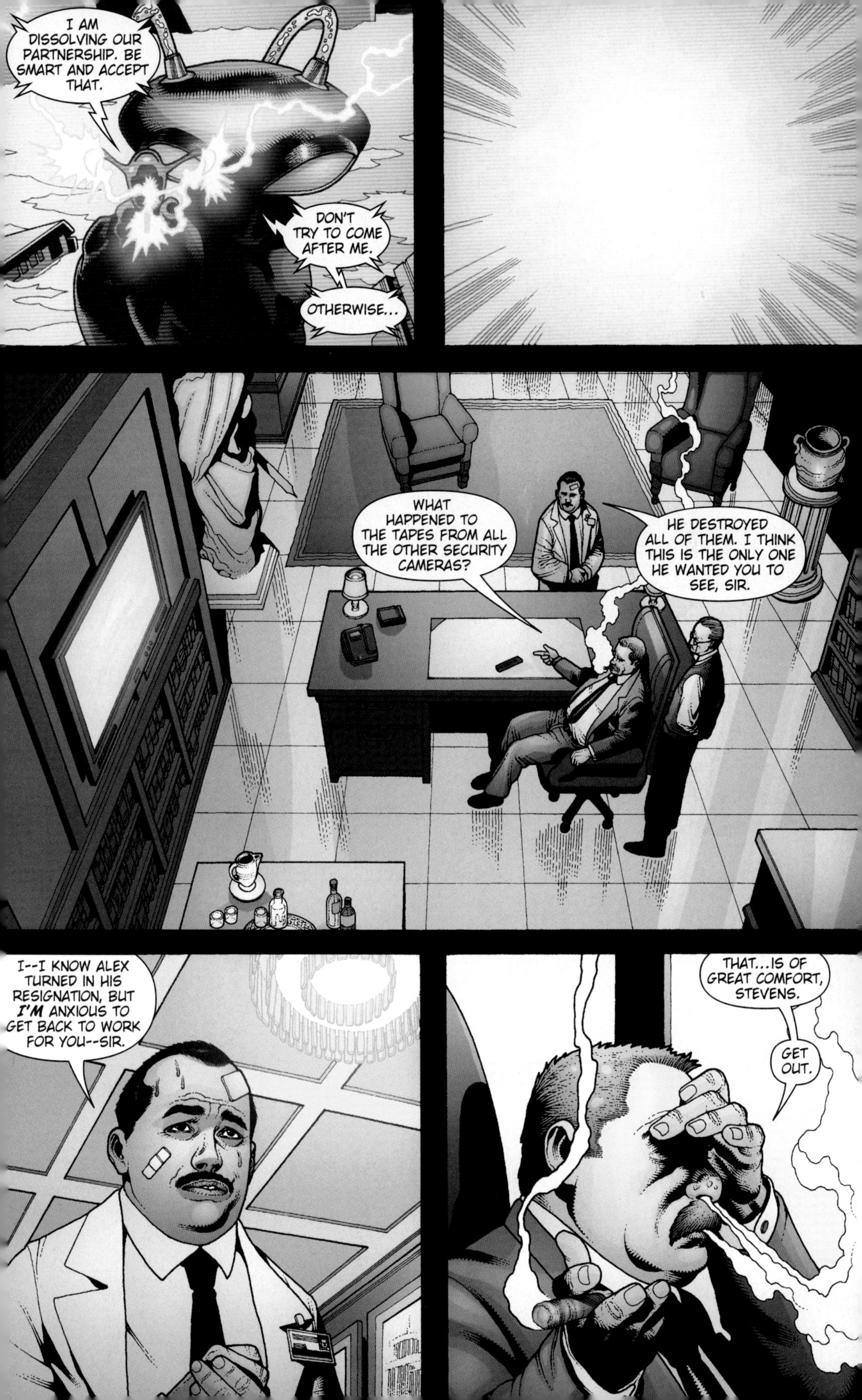
I AM DISSOLVING OUR PARTNERSHIP. BE SMART AND ACCEPT THAT.
DON'T TRY TO COME AFTER ME.
OTHERWISE...
WHAT HAPPENED TO THE TAPES FROM ALL THE OTHER SECURITY CAMERAS?
HE DESTROYED ALL OF THEM. I THINK THIS IS THE ONLY ONE HE WANTED YOU TO SEE, SIR.
I--I KNOW ALEX TURNED IN HIS RESIGNATION, BUT I'M ANXIOUS TO GET BACK TO WORK FOR YOU--SIR.
THAT...IS OF GREAT COMFORT, STEVENS.
GET OUT.

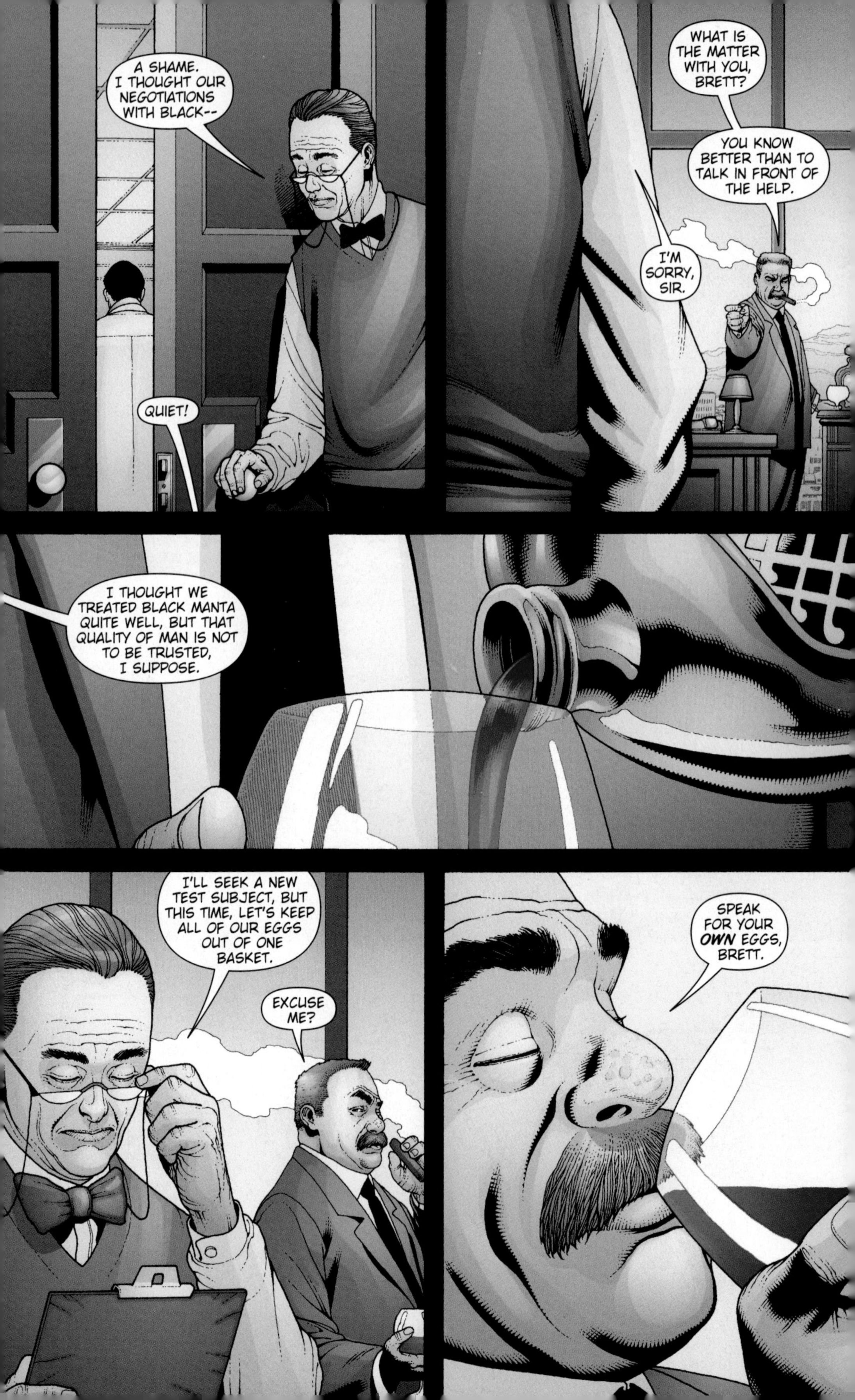
A SHAME. I THOUGHT OUR NEGOTIATIONS WITH BLACK--
QUIET!
WHAT IS THE MATTER WITH YOU, BRETT?
YOU KNOW BETTER THAN TO TALK IN FRONT OF THE HELP.
I'M SORRY, SIR.
I THOUGHT WE TREATED BLACK MANTA QUITE WELL, BUT THAT QUALITY OF MAN IS NOT TO BE TRUSTED, I SUPPOSE.
I'LL SEEK A NEW TEST SUBJECT, BUT THIS TIME, LET'S KEEP ALL OF OUR EGGS OUT OF ONE BASKET.
EXCUSE ME?
SPEAK FOR YOUR *OWN* EGGS, BRETT.

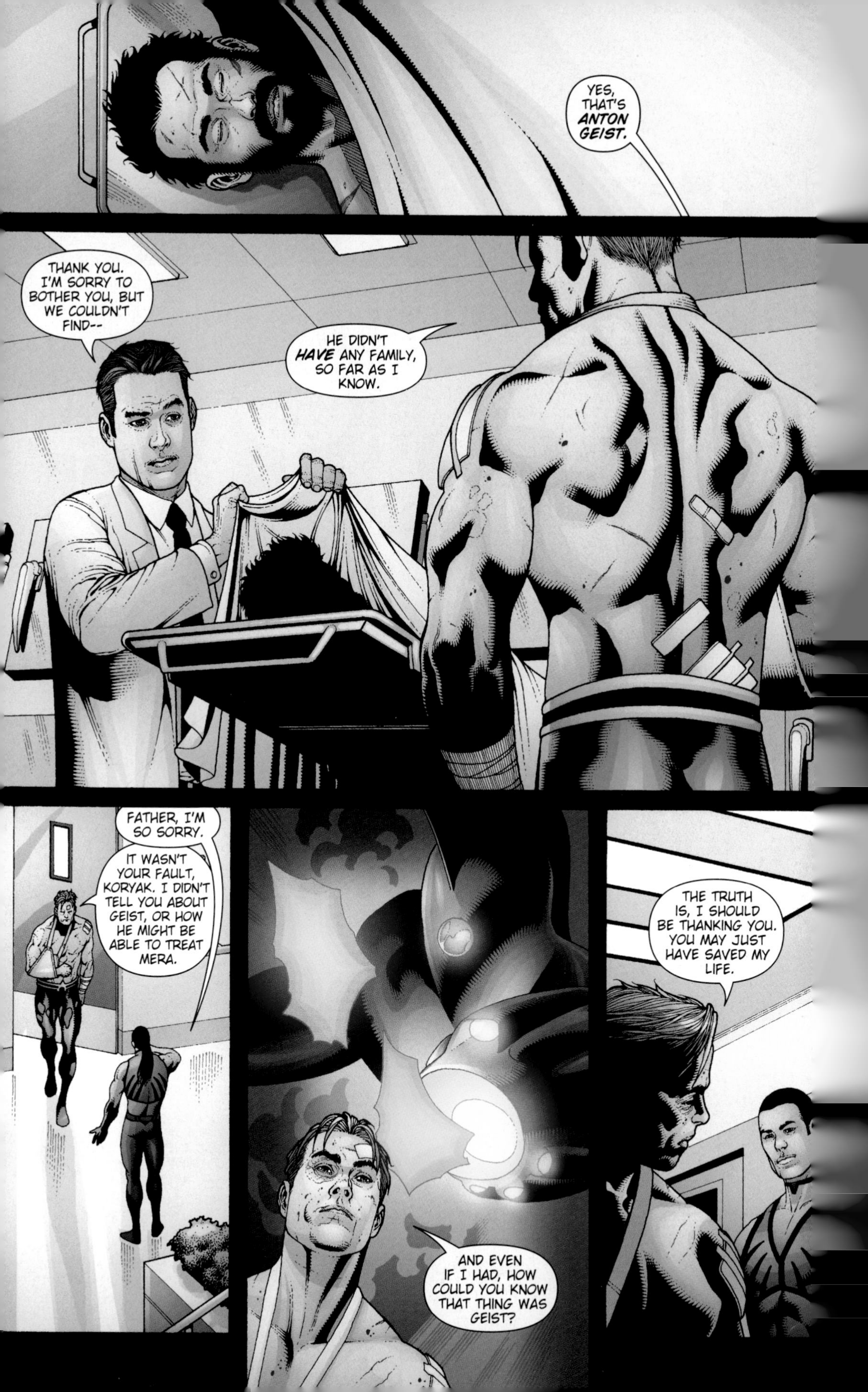
YES, THAT'S ANTON GEIST.
THANK YOU. I'M SORRY TO BOTHER YOU, BUT WE COULDN'T FIND--
HE DIDN'T HAVE ANY FAMILY, SO FAR AS I KNOW.
FATHER, I'M SO SORRY.
IT WASN'T YOUR FAULT, KORYAK. I DIDN'T TELL YOU ABOUT GEIST, OR HOW HE MIGHT BE ABLE TO TREAT MERA.
AND EVEN IF I HAD, HOW COULD YOU KNOW THAT THING WAS GEIST?
THE TRUTH IS, I SHOULD BE THANKING YOU. YOU MAY JUST HAVE SAVED MY LIFE.

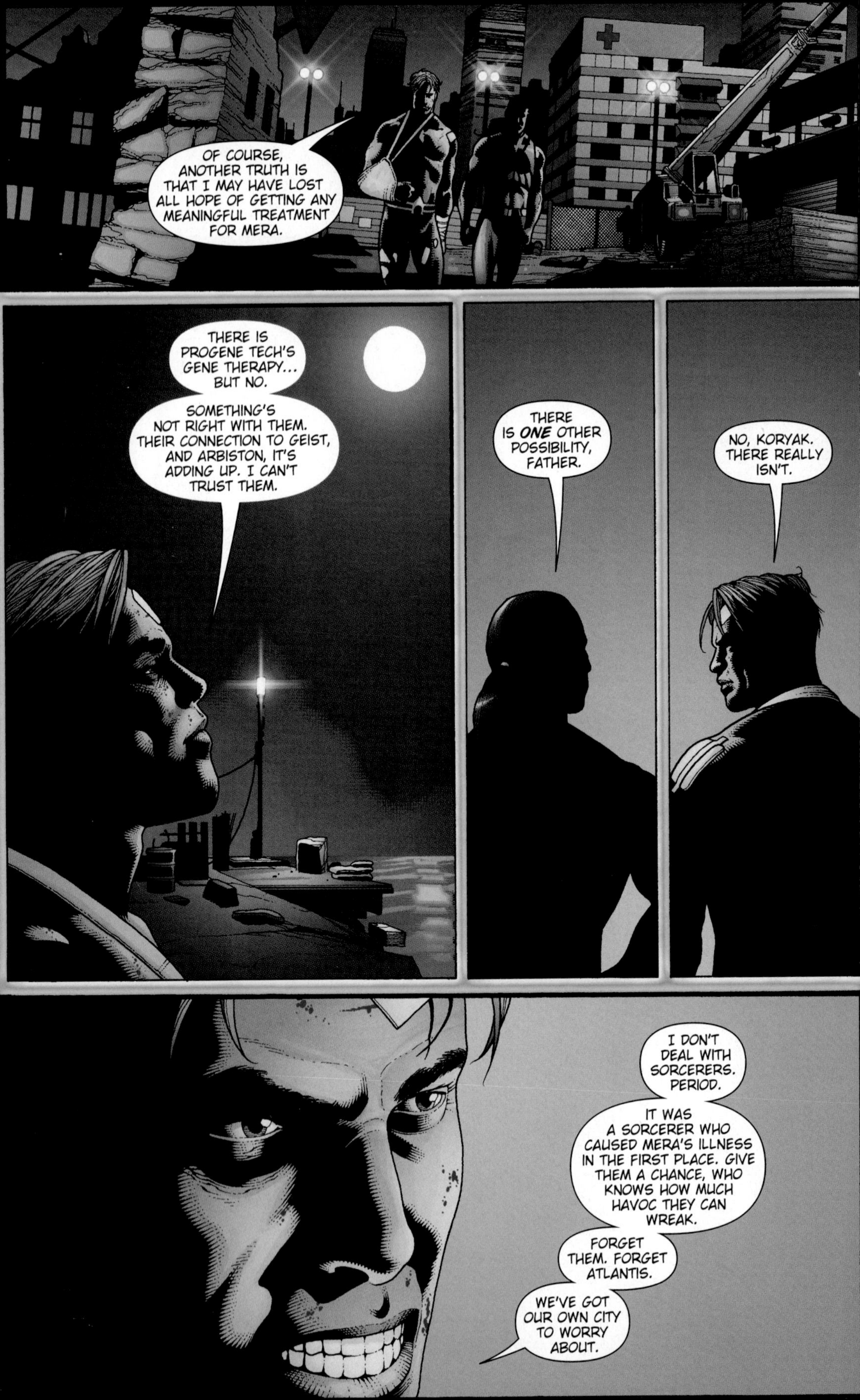

OF COURSE, ANOTHER TRUTH IS THAT I MAY HAVE LOST ALL HOPE OF GETTING ANY MEANINGFUL TREATMENT FOR MERA.
THERE IS PROGENE TECH'S GENE THERAPY... BUT NO.
SOMETHING'S NOT RIGHT WITH THEM. THEIR CONNECTION TO GEIST, AND ARBISTON, IT'S ADDING UP. I CAN'T TRUST THEM.
THERE IS *ONE* OTHER POSSIBILITY, FATHER.
NO, KORYAK. THERE REALLY ISN'T.
I DON'T DEAL WITH SORCERERS. PERIOD.
IT WAS A SORCERER WHO CAUSED MERA'S ILLNESS IN THE FIRST PLACE. GIVE THEM A CHANCE, WHO KNOWS HOW MUCH HAVOC THEY CAN WREAK.
FORGET THEM. FORGET ATLANTIS.
WE'VE GOT OUR OWN CITY TO WORRY ABOUT.

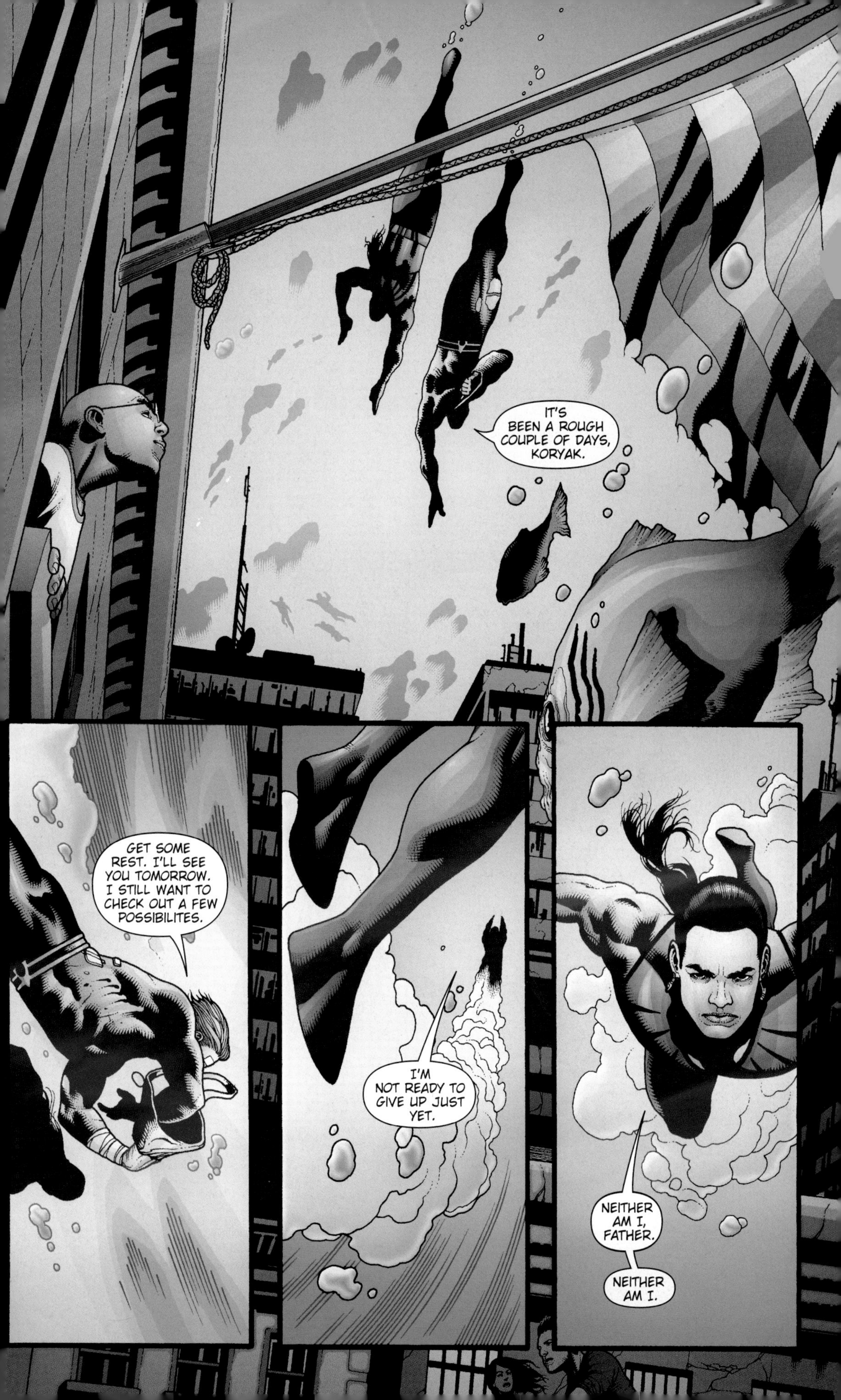
IT'S BEEN A ROUGH COUPLE OF DAYS, KORYAK.
GET SOME REST. I'LL SEE YOU TOMORROW. I STILL WANT TO CHECK OUT A FEW POSSIBILITES.
I'M NOT READY TO GIVE UP JUST YET.
NEITHER AM I, FATHER.
NEITHER AM I.

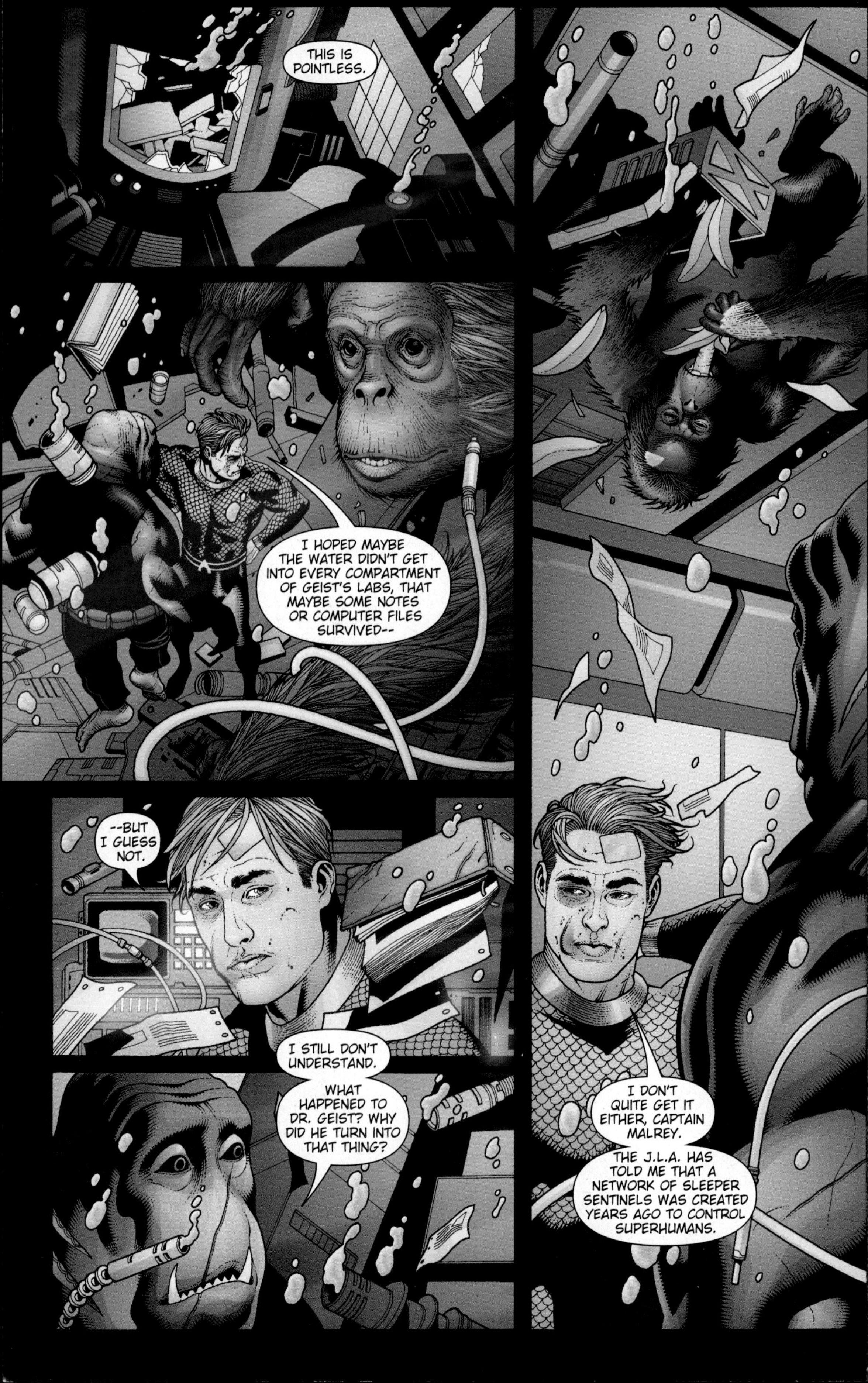

THIS IS POINTLESS.
I HOPED MAYBE THE WATER DIDN'T GET INTO EVERY COMPARTMENT OF GEIST'S LABS, THAT MAYBE SOME NOTES OR COMPUTER FILES SURVIVED--
--BUT I GUESS NOT.
I STILL DON'T UNDERSTAND.
WHAT HAPPENED TO DR. GEIST? WHY DID HE TURN INTO THAT THING?
I DON'T QUITE GET IT EITHER, CAPTAIN MALREY.
THE J.L.A. HAS TOLD ME THAT A NETWORK OF SLEEPER SENTINELS WAS CREATED YEARS AGO TO CONTROL SUPERHUMANS.

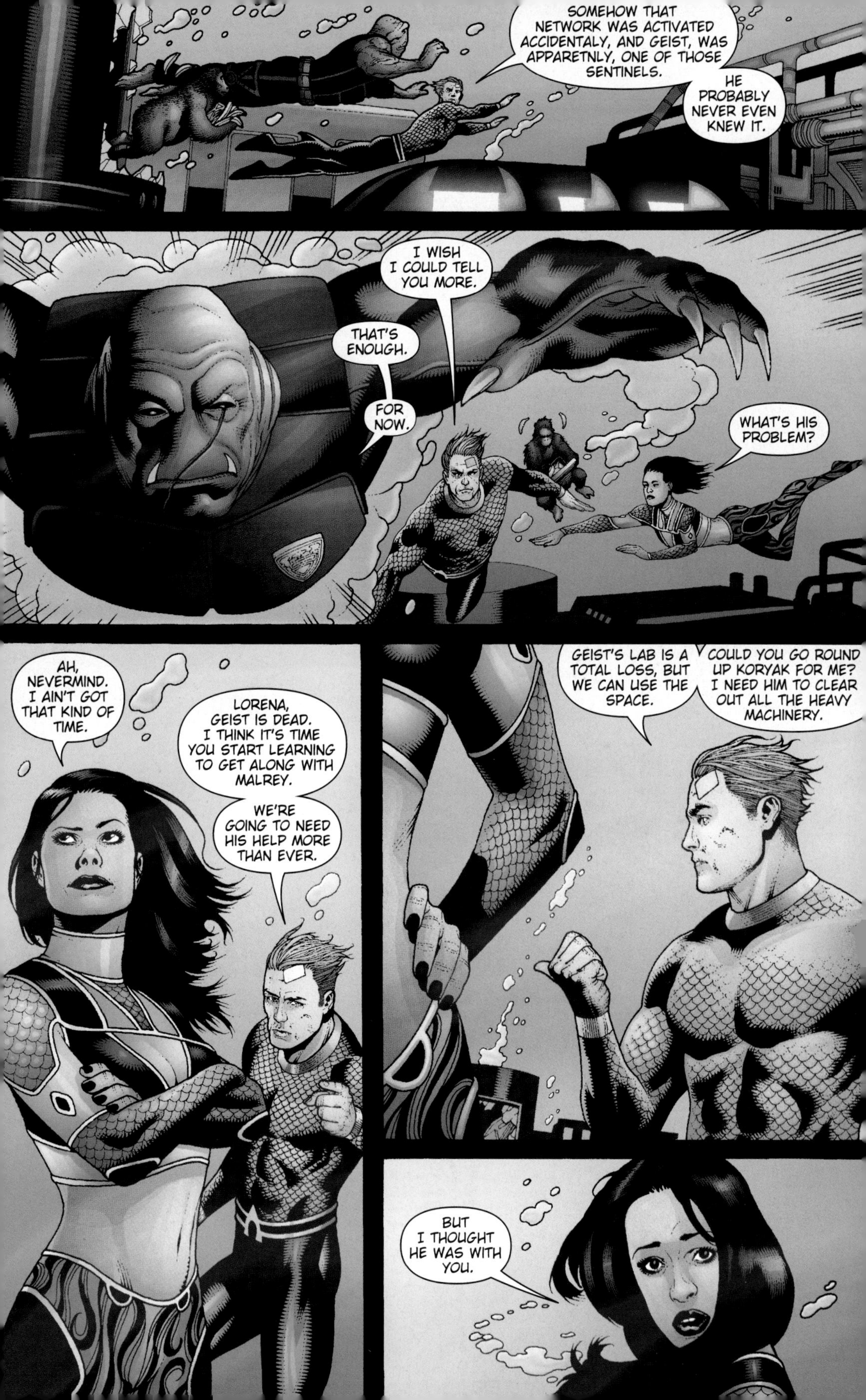
SOMEHOW THAT NETWORK WAS ACTIVATED ACCIDENTALY, AND GEIST, WAS APPARETNLY, ONE OF THOSE SENTINELS.
HE PROBABLY NEVER EVEN KNEW IT.
I WISH I COULD TELL YOU MORE.
THAT'S ENOUGH.
FOR NOW.
WHAT'S HIS PROBLEM?
AH, NEVERMIND. I AIN'T GOT THAT KIND OF TIME.
LORENA, GEIST IS DEAD. I THINK IT'S TIME YOU START LEARNING TO GET ALONG WITH MALREY.
WE'RE GOING TO NEED HIS HELP MORE THAN EVER.
GEIST'S LAB IS A TOTAL LOSS, BUT WE CAN USE THE SPACE.
COULD YOU GO ROUND UP KORYAK FOR ME? I NEED HIM TO CLEAR OUT ALL THE HEAVY MACHINERY.
BUT I THOUGHT HE WAS WITH YOU.

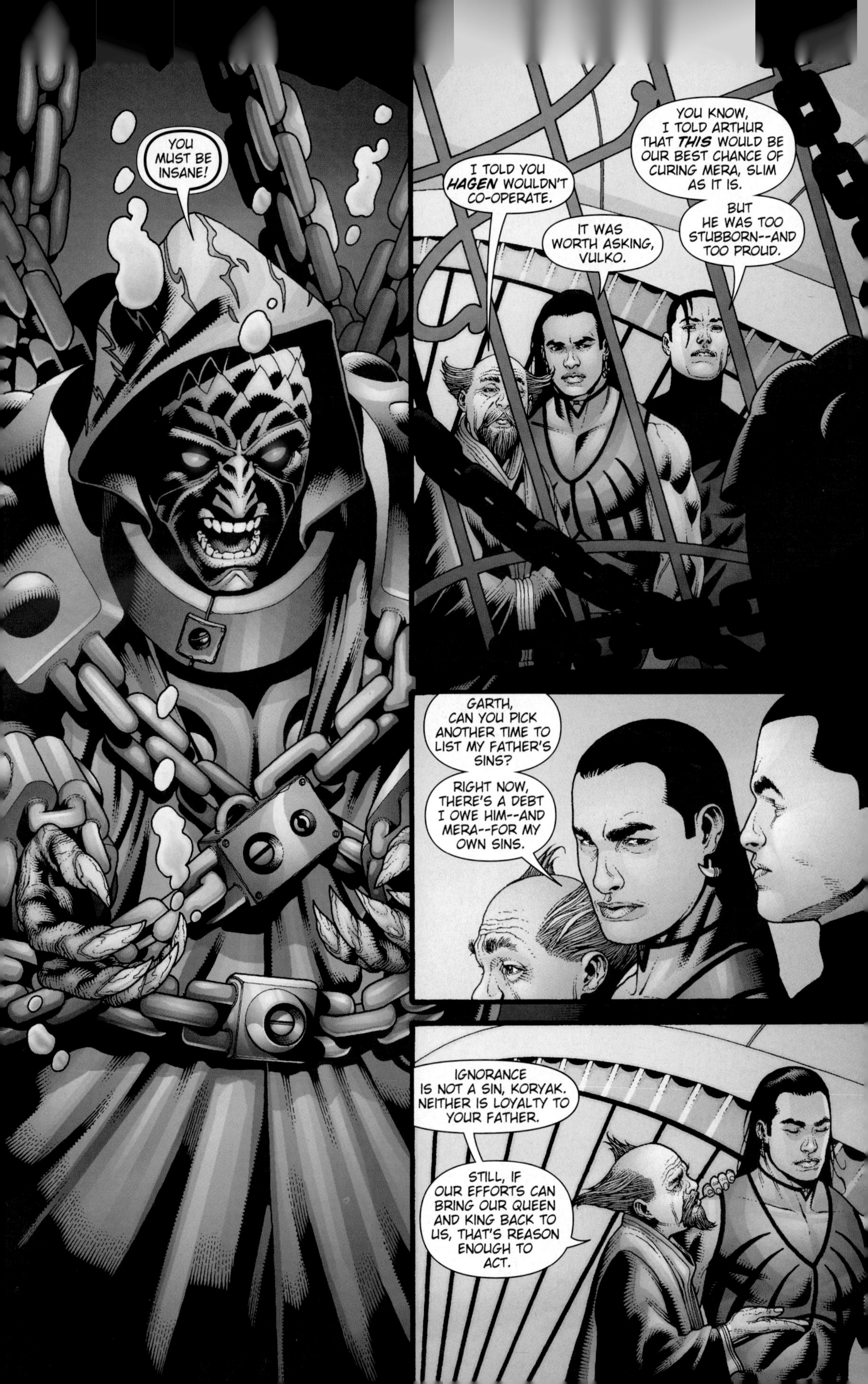
YOU MUST BE INSANE!
I TOLD YOU HAGEN WOULDN'T CO-OPERATE.
IT WAS WORTH ASKING, VULKO.
YOU KNOW, I TOLD ARTHUR THAT THIS WOULD BE OUR BEST CHANCE OF CURING MERA, SLIM AS IT IS.
BUT HE WAS TOO STUBBORN--AND TOO PROUD.
GARTH, CAN YOU PICK ANOTHER TIME TO LIST MY FATHER'S SINS?
RIGHT NOW, THERE'S A DEBT I OWE HIM--AND MERA--FOR MY OWN SINS.
IGNORANCE IS NOT A SIN, KORYAK. NEITHER IS LOYALTY TO YOUR FATHER.
STILL, IF OUR EFFORTS CAN BRING OUR QUEEN AND KING BACK TO US, THAT'S REASON ENOUGH TO ACT.

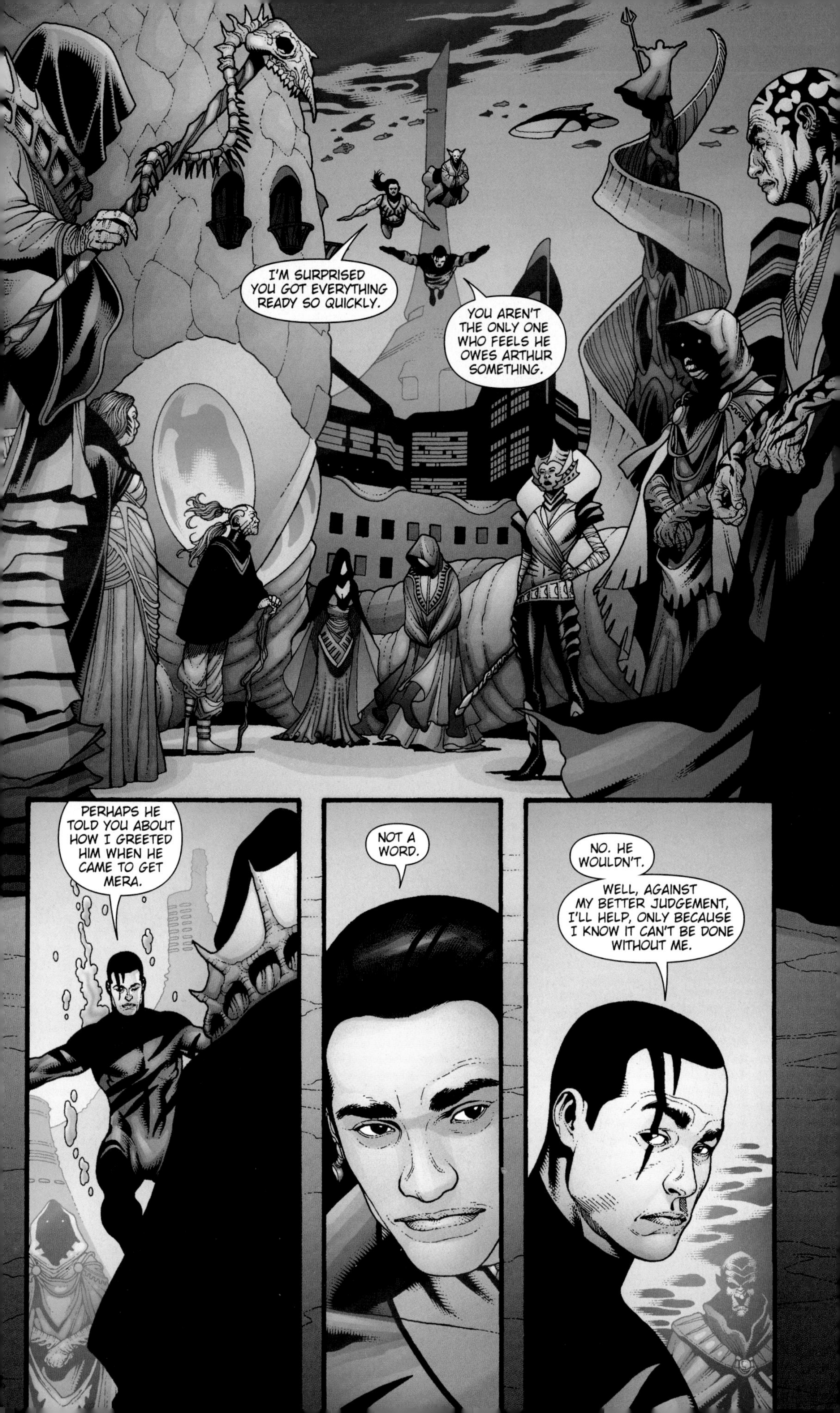
I'M SURPRISED YOU GOT EVERYTHING READY SO QUICKLY.
YOU AREN'T THE ONLY ONE WHO FEELS HE OWES ARTHUR SOMETHING.
PERHAPS HE TOLD YOU ABOUT HOW I GREETED HIM WHEN HE CAME TO GET MERA.
NOT A WORD.
NO. HE WOULDN'T.
WELL, AGAINST MY BETTER JUDGEMENT, I'LL HELP, ONLY BECAUSE I KNOW IT CAN'T BE DONE WITHOUT ME.

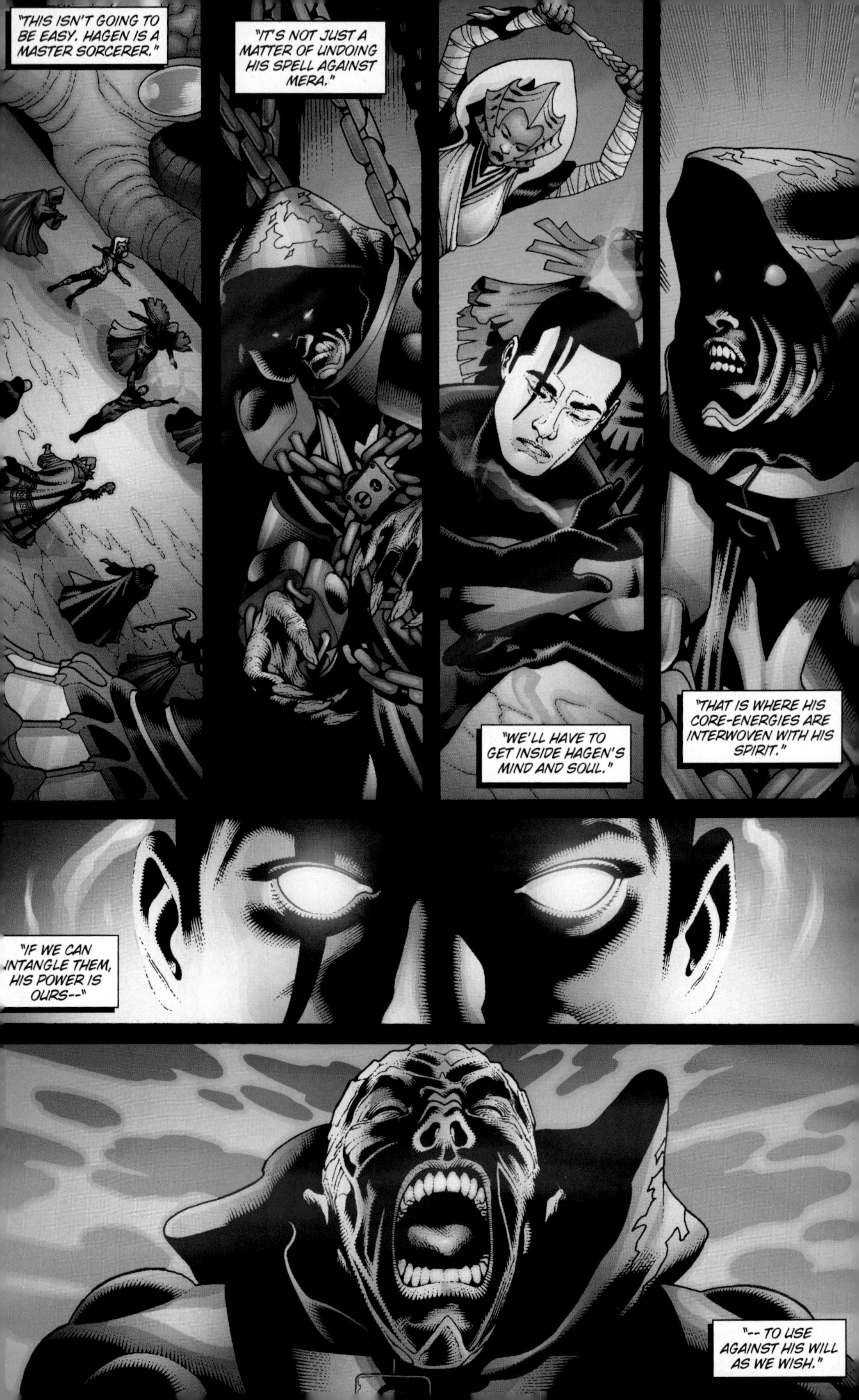
"THIS ISN'T GOING TO BE EASY. HAGEN IS A MASTER SORCERER."
"IT'S NOT JUST A MATTER OF UNDOING HIS SPELL AGAINST MERA."
"WE'LL HAVE TO GET INSIDE HAGEN'S MIND AND SOUL."
"THAT IS WHERE HIS CORE-ENERGIES ARE INTERWOVEN WITH HIS SPIRIT."
"IF WE CAN INTANGLE THEM, HIS POWER IS OURS--"
"-- TO USE AGAINST HIS WILL AS WE WISH."

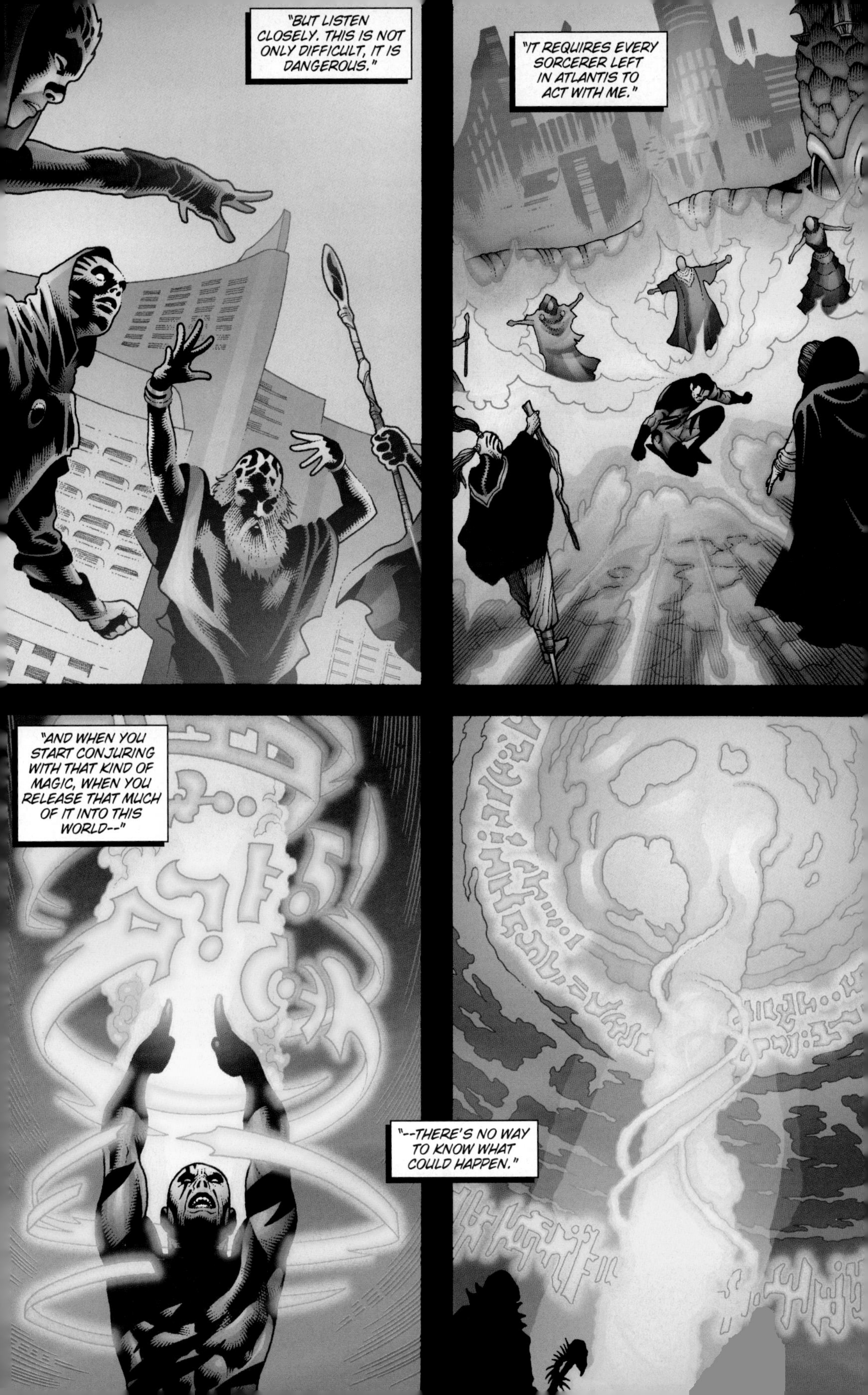
"BUT LISTEN CLOSELY. THIS IS NOT ONLY DIFFICULT, IT IS DANGEROUS."
"IT REQUIRES EVERY SORCERER LEFT IN ATLANTIS TO ACT WITH ME."
"AND WHEN YOU START CONJURING WITH THAT KIND OF MAGIC, WHEN YOU RELEASE THAT MUCH OF IT INTO THIS WORLD--"
"--THERE'S NO WAY TO KNOW WHAT COULD HAPPEN."

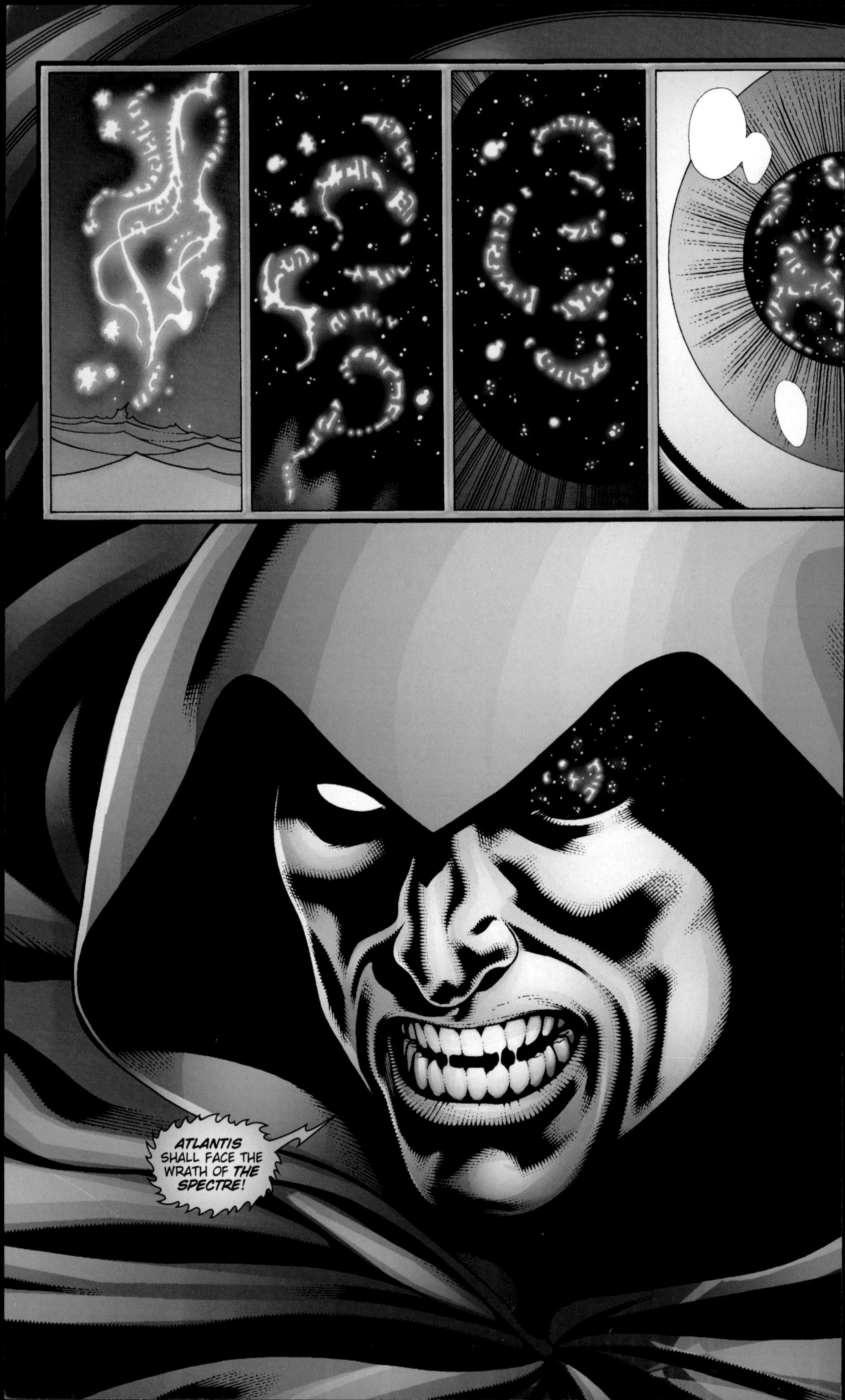
ATLANTIS SHALL FACE THE WRATH OF THE SPECTRE!

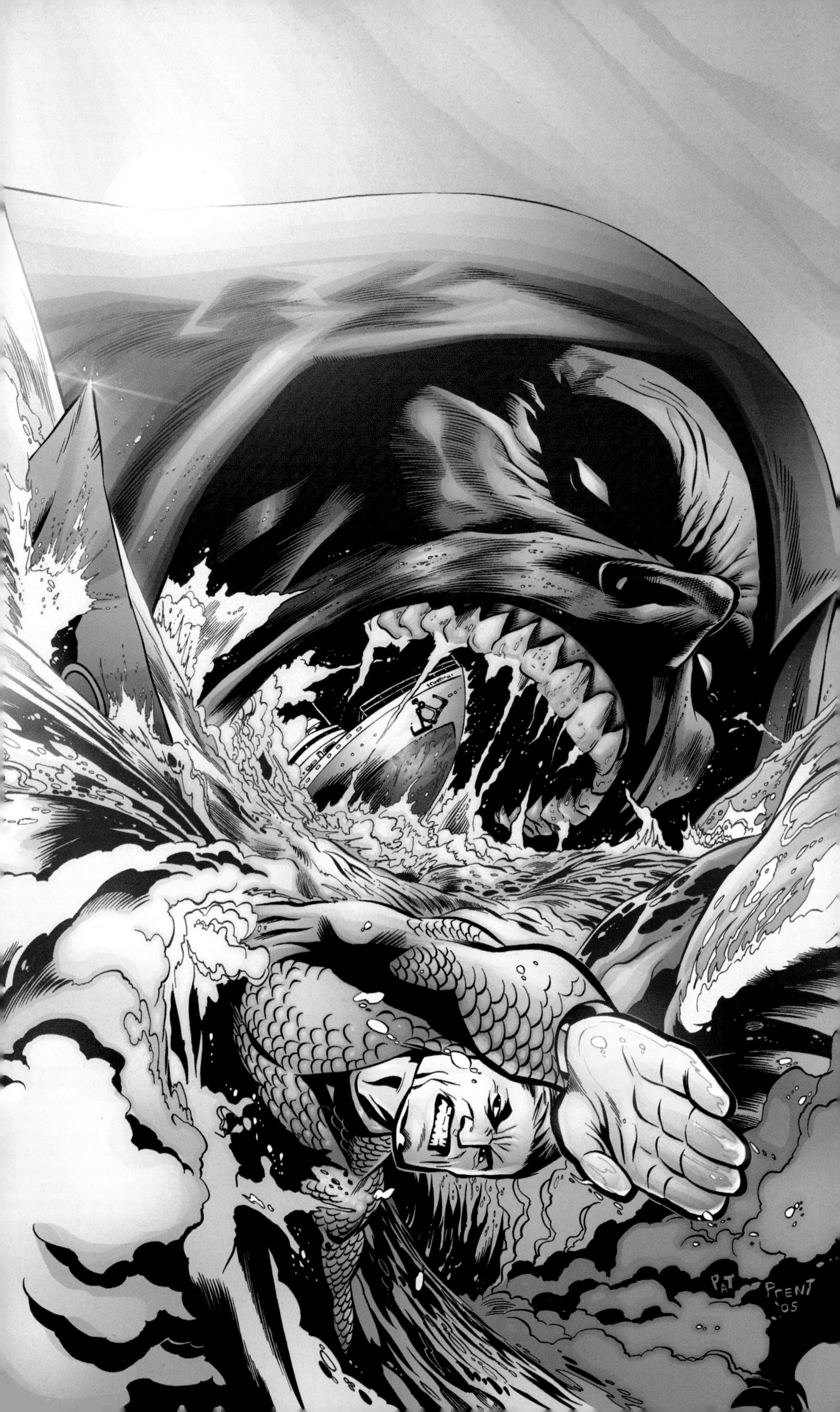

ALL FALL DOWN

JOHN ARCUDI
Writer

LEONARD KIRK
Layouts

ANDY CLARKE
Finishes

NATHAN EYRING
Colorist

TRAVIS LANHAM
Letterer

**PATRICK GLEASON &
PRENTIS ROLLINS**
Cover

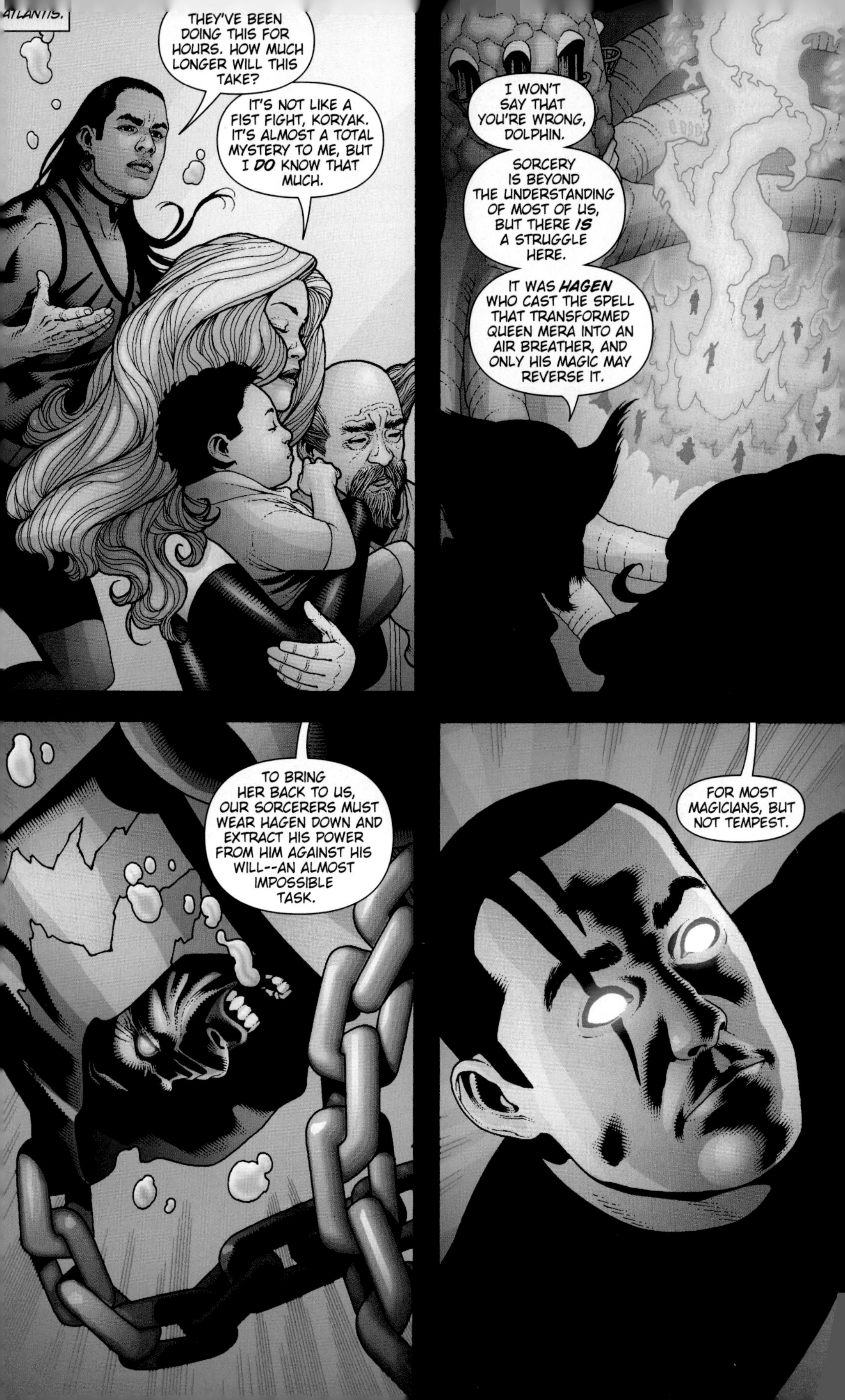
ATLANTIS.
THEY'VE BEEN DOING THIS FOR HOURS. HOW MUCH LONGER WILL THIS TAKE?
IT'S NOT LIKE A FIST FIGHT, KORYAK. IT'S ALMOST A TOTAL MYSTERY TO ME, BUT I DO KNOW THAT MUCH.
I WON'T SAY THAT YOU'RE WRONG, DOLPHIN.
SORCERY IS BEYOND THE UNDERSTANDING OF MOST OF US, BUT THERE IS A STRUGGLE HERE.
IT WAS HAGEN WHO CAST THE SPELL THAT TRANSFORMED QUEEN MERA INTO AN AIR BREATHER, AND ONLY HIS MAGIC MAY REVERSE IT.
TO BRING HER BACK TO US, OUR SORCERERS MUST WEAR HAGEN DOWN AND EXTRACT HIS POWER FROM HIM AGAINST HIS WILL--AN ALMOST IMPOSSIBLE TASK.
FOR MOST MAGICIANS, BUT NOT TEMPEST.

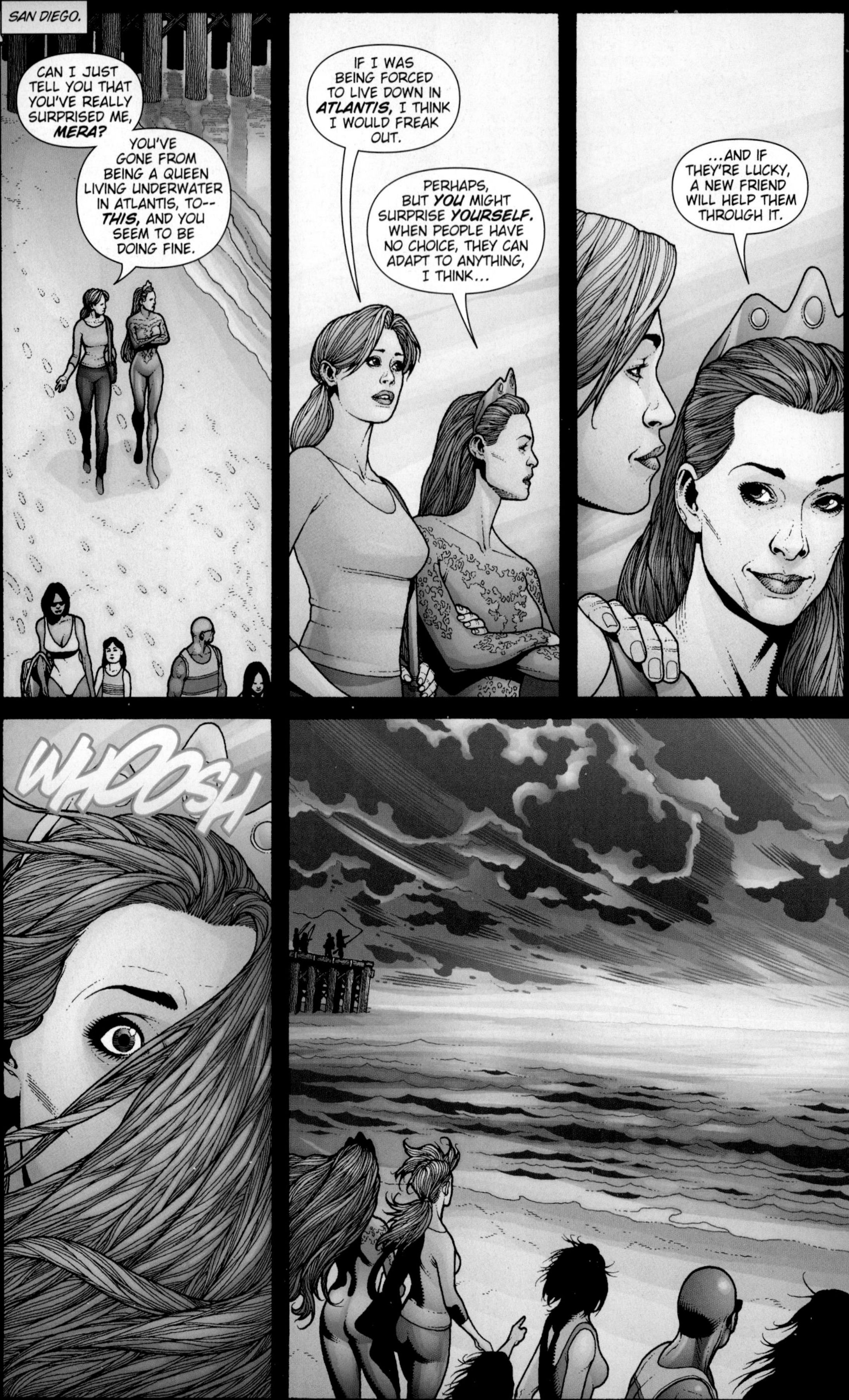
SAN DIEGO.
CAN I JUST TELL YOU THAT YOU'VE REALLY SURPRISED ME, MERA?
YOU'VE GONE FROM BEING A QUEEN LIVING UNDERWATER IN ATLANTIS, TO-- THIS, AND YOU SEEM TO BE DOING FINE.
IF I WAS BEING FORCED TO LIVE DOWN IN ATLANTIS, I THINK I WOULD FREAK OUT.
PERHAPS, BUT YOU MIGHT SURPRISE YOURSELF. WHEN PEOPLE HAVE NO CHOICE, THEY CAN ADAPT TO ANYTHING, I THINK...
...AND IF THEY'RE LUCKY, A NEW FRIEND WILL HELP THEM THROUGH IT.
WHOOSH

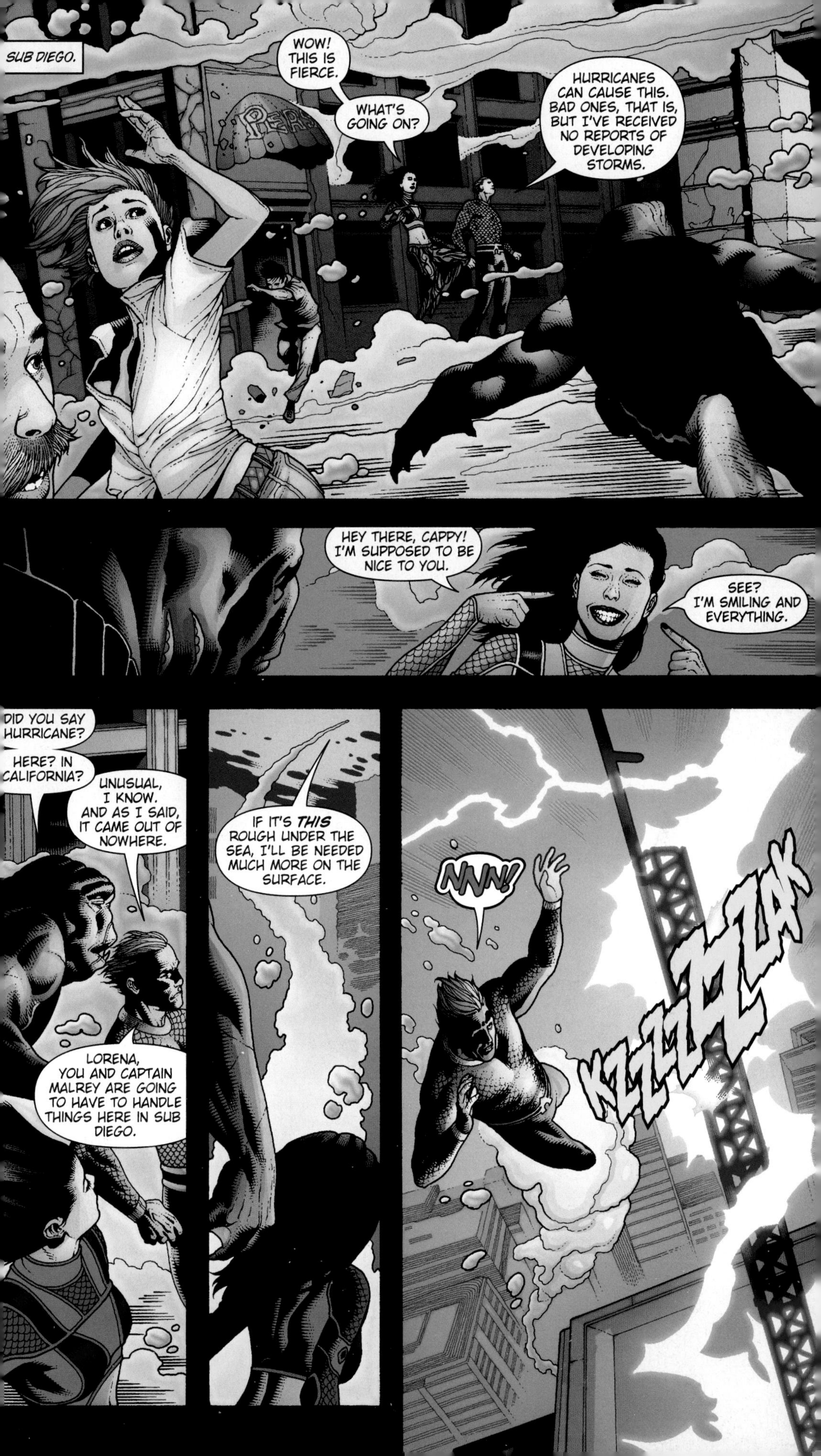
SUB DIEGO.
WOW! THIS IS FIERCE.
WHAT'S GOING ON?
HURRICANES CAN CAUSE THIS. BAD ONES, THAT IS, BUT I'VE RECEIVED NO REPORTS OF DEVELOPING STORMS.
HEY THERE, CAPPY! I'M SUPPOSED TO BE NICE TO YOU.
SEE? I'M SMILING AND EVERYTHING.
DID YOU SAY HURRICANE?
HERE? IN CALIFORNIA?
UNUSUAL, I KNOW. AND AS I SAID, IT CAME OUT OF NOWHERE.
LORENA, YOU AND CAPTAIN MALREY ARE GOING TO HAVE TO HANDLE THINGS HERE IN SUB DIEGO.
IF IT'S THIS ROUGH UNDER THE SEA, I'LL BE NEEDED MUCH MORE ON THE SURFACE.
NNN!
KZZZZZZAK

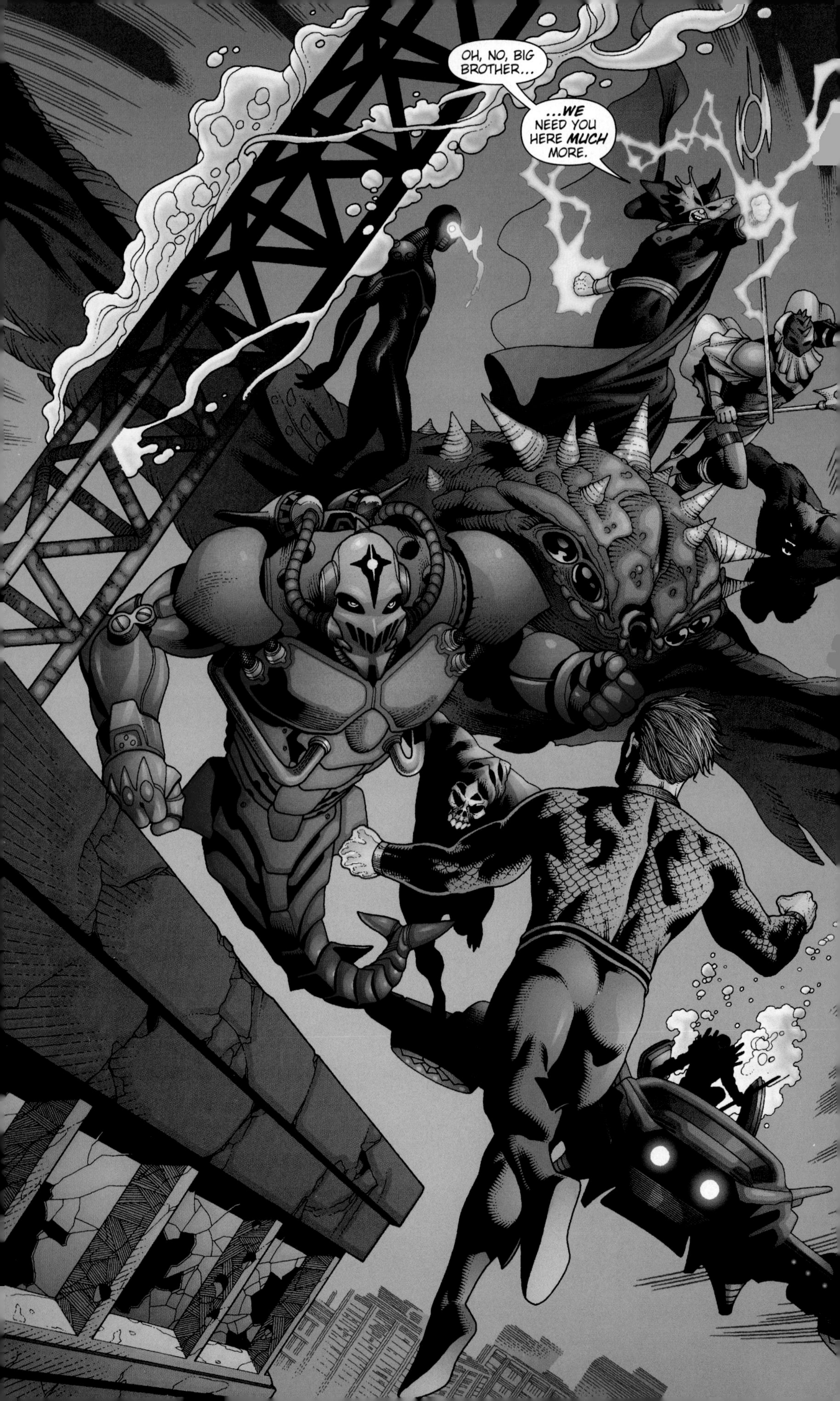
OH, NO, BIG BROTHER...
...WE NEED YOU HERE MUCH MORE.

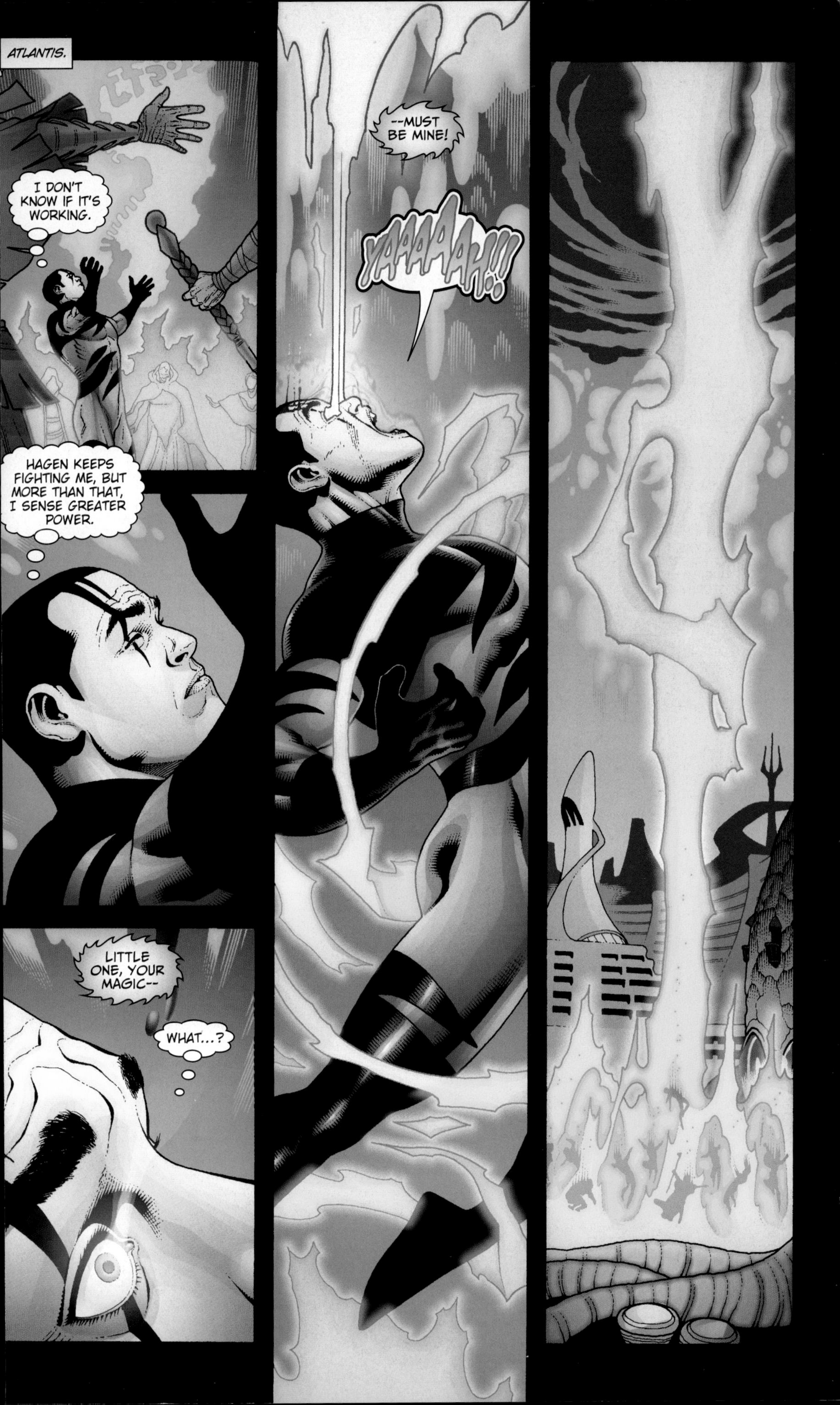
ATLANTIS.
I DON'T KNOW IF IT'S WORKING.
HAGEN KEEPS FIGHTING ME, BUT MORE THAN THAT, I SENSE GREATER POWER.
LITTLE ONE, YOUR MAGIC--
WHAT...?
--MUST BE MINE!
YAAAAAH!!

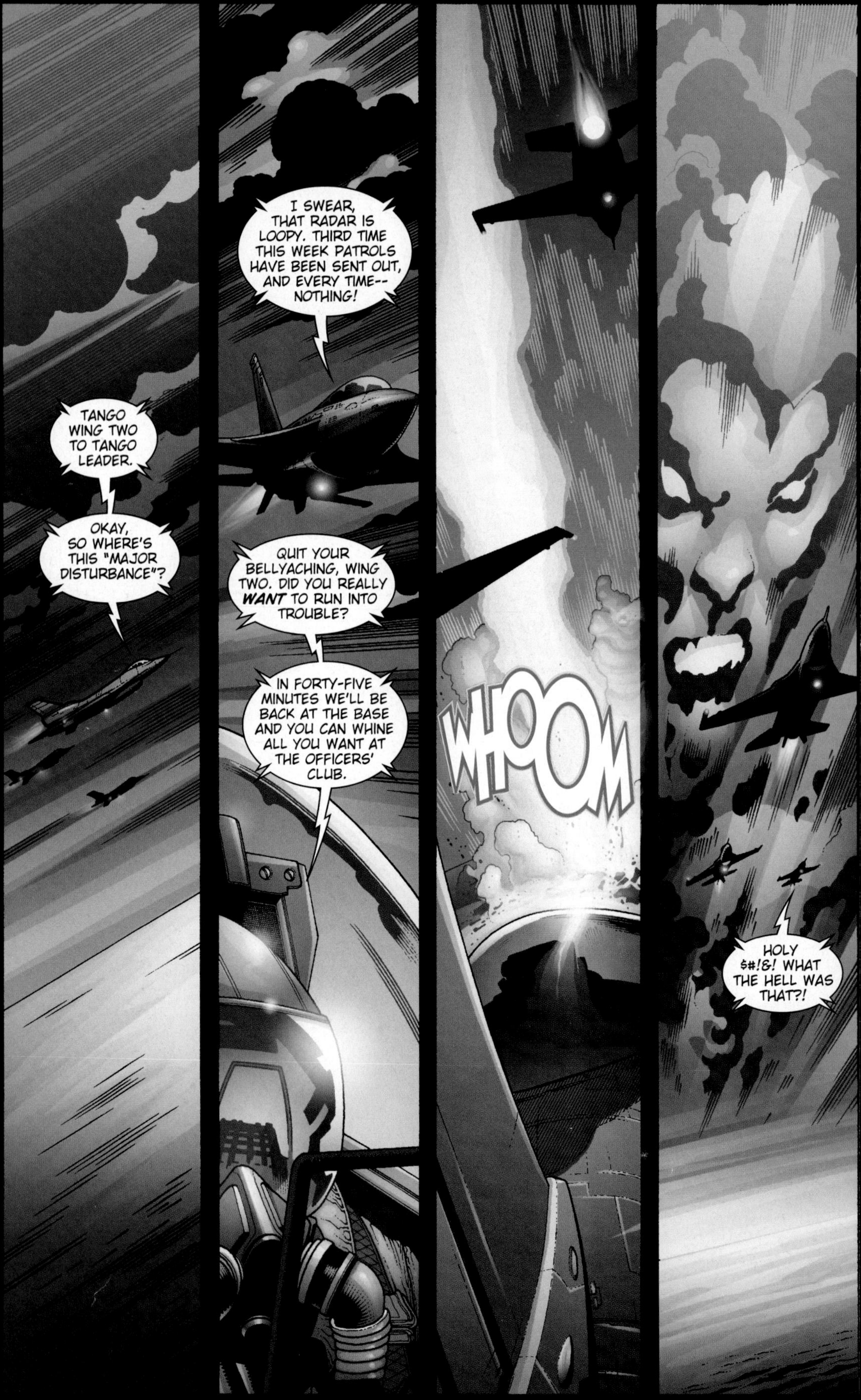
TANGO WING TWO TO TANGO LEADER.
OKAY, SO WHERE'S THIS "MAJOR DISTURBANCE"?
I SWEAR, THAT RADAR IS LOOPY. THIRD TIME THIS WEEK PATROLS HAVE BEEN SENT OUT, AND EVERY TIME-- NOTHING!
QUIT YOUR BELLYACHING, WING TWO. DID YOU REALLY WANT TO RUN INTO TROUBLE?
IN FORTY-FIVE MINUTES WE'LL BE BACK AT THE BASE AND YOU CAN WHINE ALL YOU WANT AT THE OFFICERS' CLUB.
WHOOM
HOLY $#!&! WHAT THE HELL WAS THAT?!

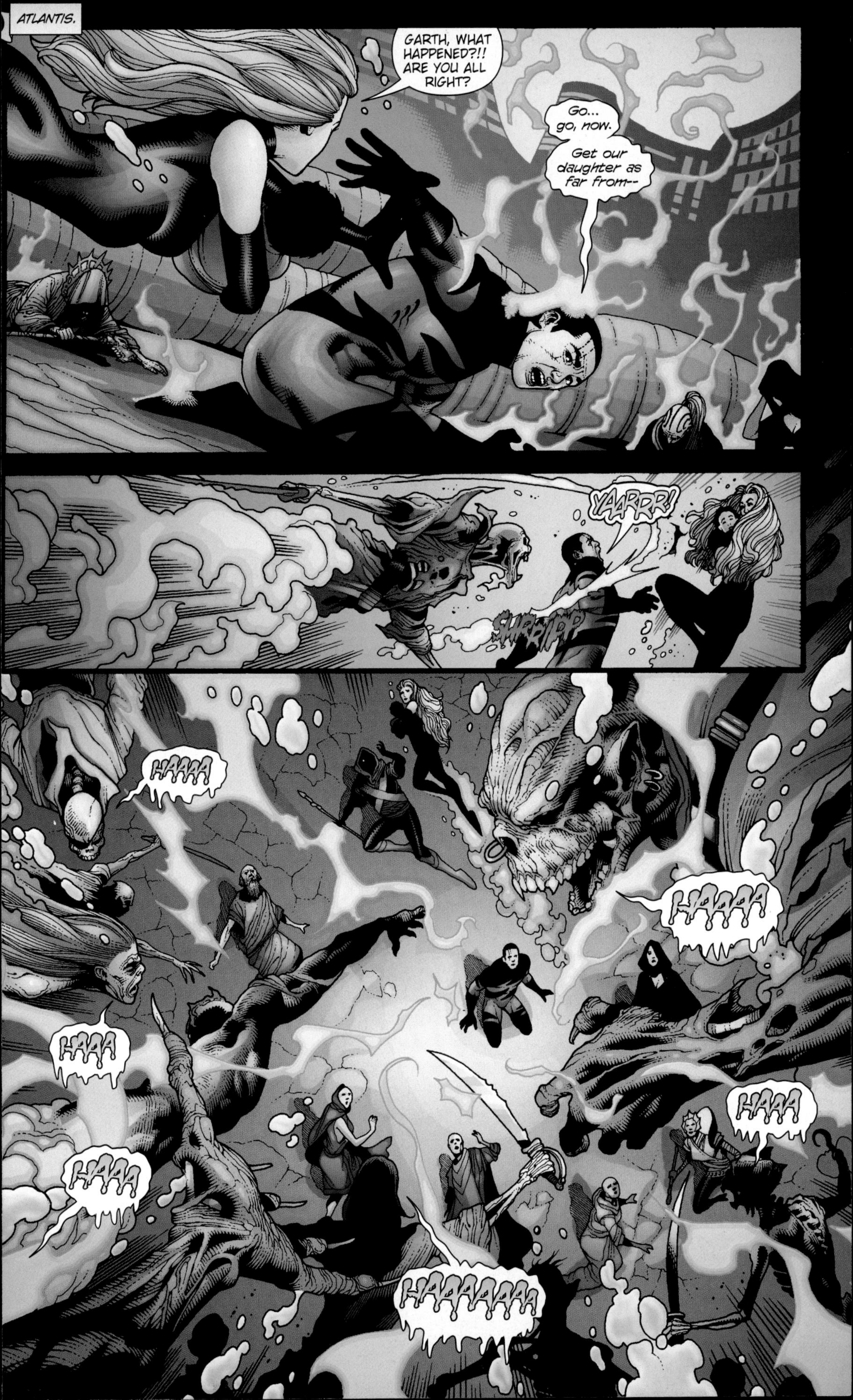
ATLANTIS.
GARTH, WHAT HAPPENED?!! ARE YOU ALL RIGHT?
Go... go, now.
Get our daughter as far from--
YAARRR!
SHRIPP
HAAAA
HAAAA
HAAA
HAAA
HAAA
HAAAAAAAA

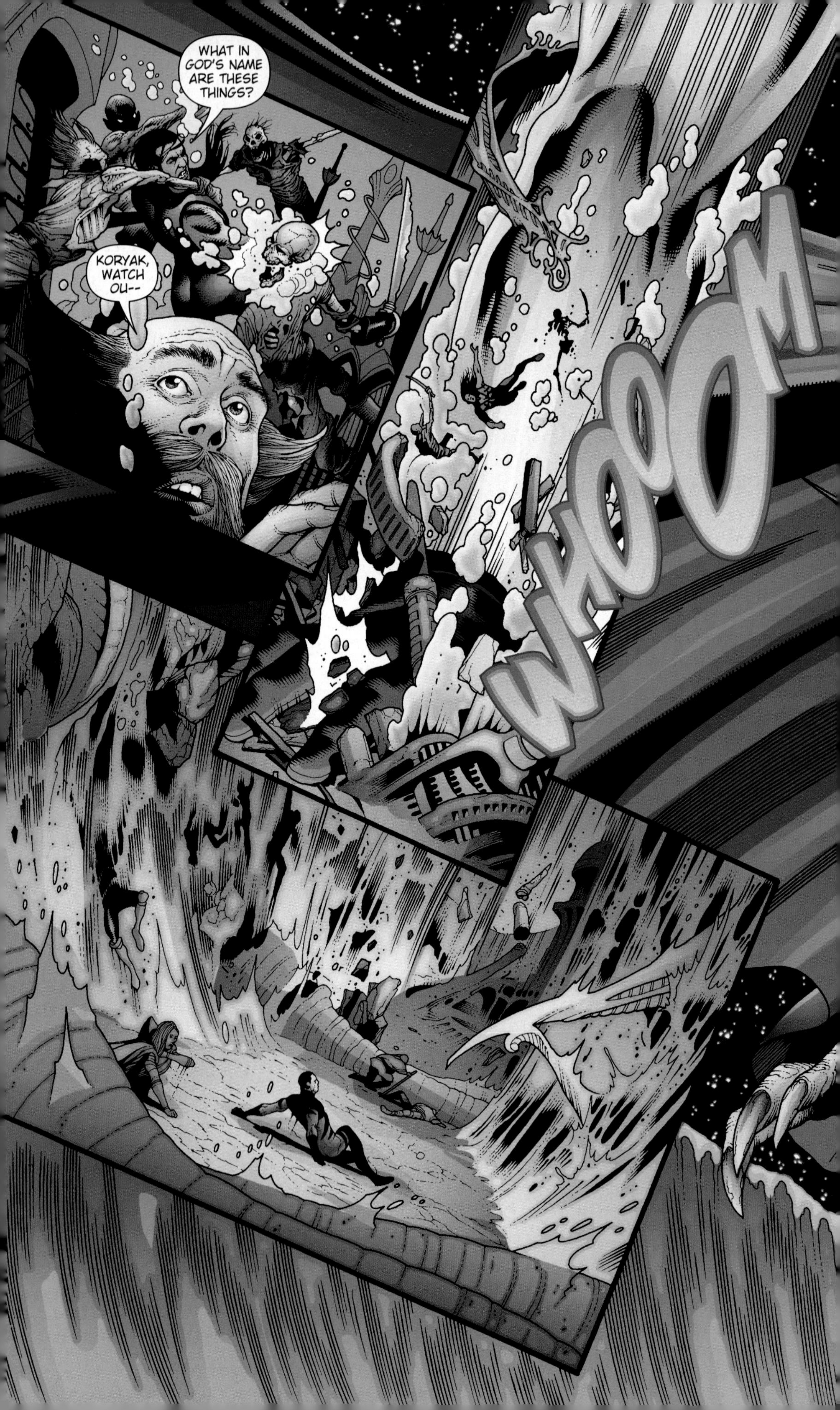
WHAT IN GOD'S NAME ARE THESE THINGS?
KORYAK, WATCH OU--
WHOOOOM

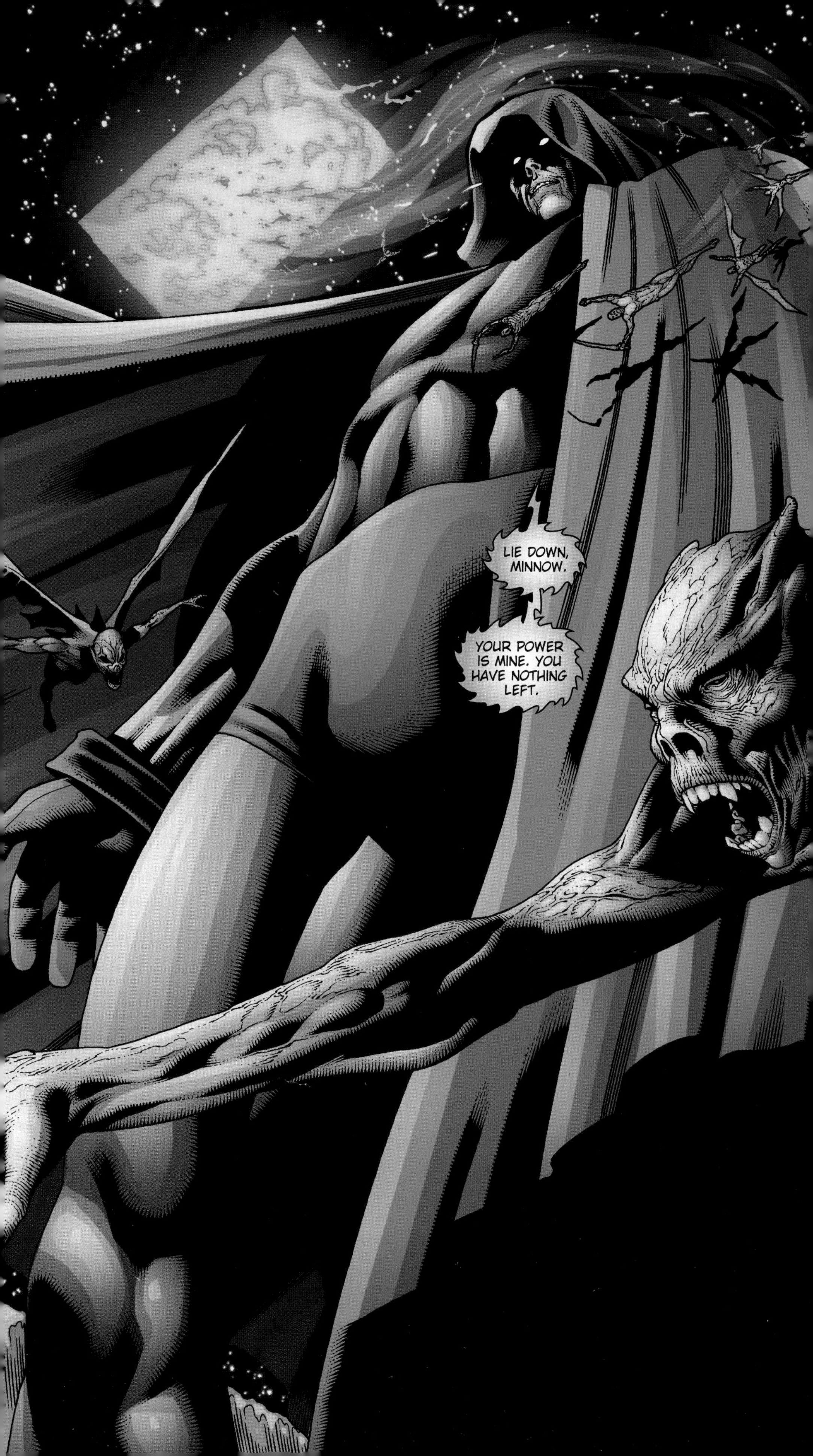
LIE DOWN, MINNOW.
YOUR POWER IS MINE. YOU HAVE NOTHING LEFT.

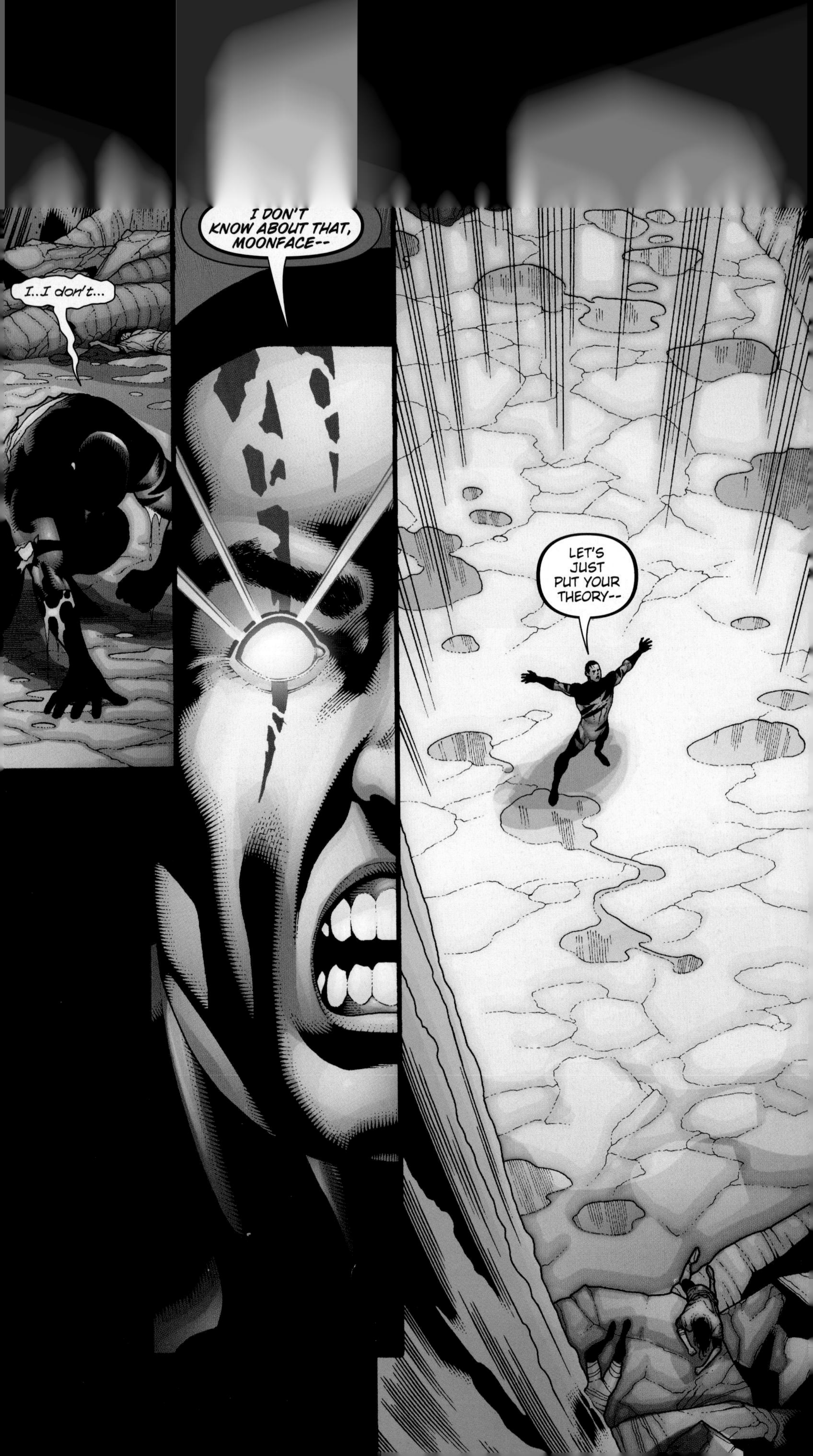
I..I don't...
I DON'T KNOW ABOUT THAT, MOONFACE--
LET'S JUST PUT YOUR THEORY--

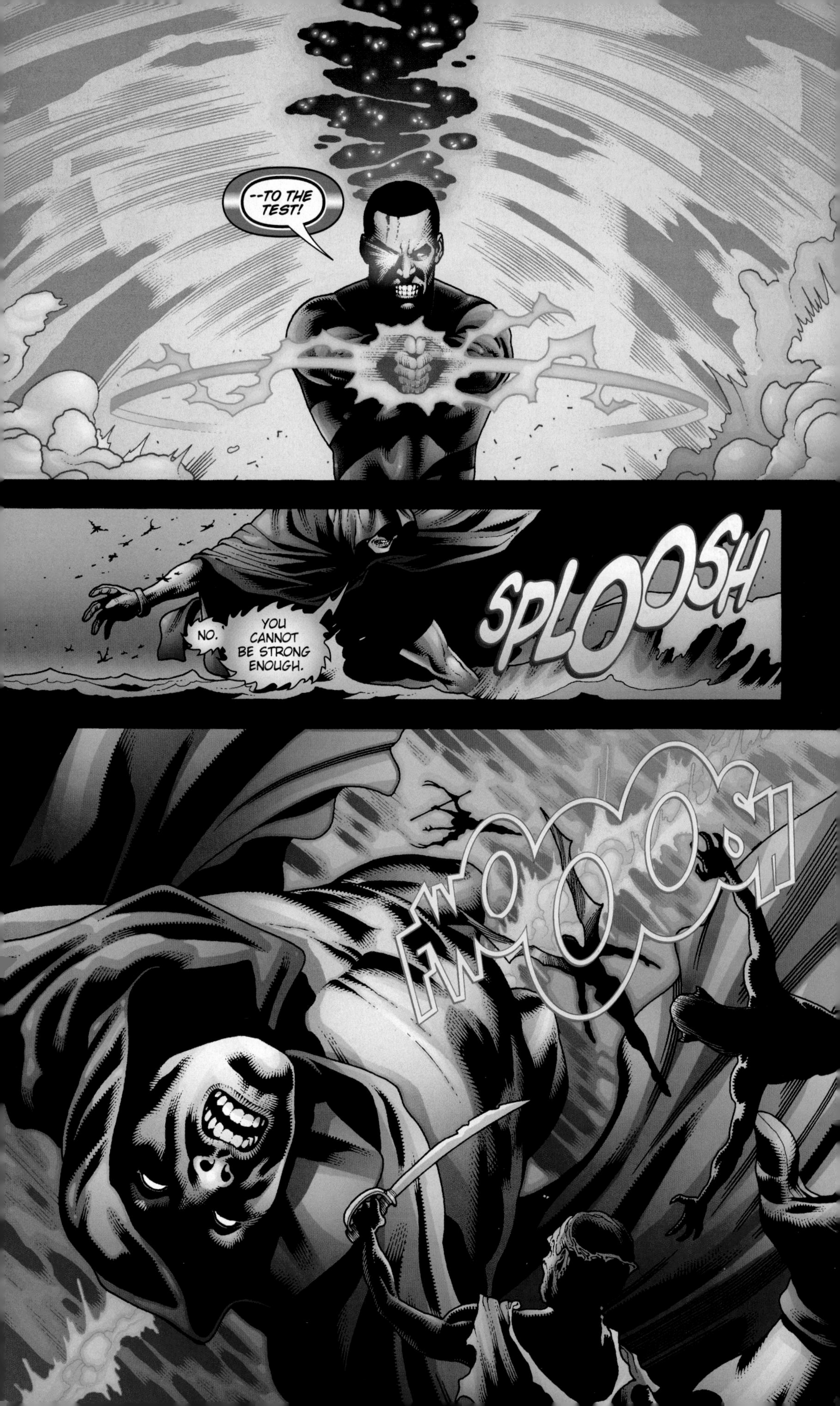
--TO THE TEST!
SPLOOSH
NO.
YOU CANNOT BE STRONG ENOUGH.
FWOOOOSH

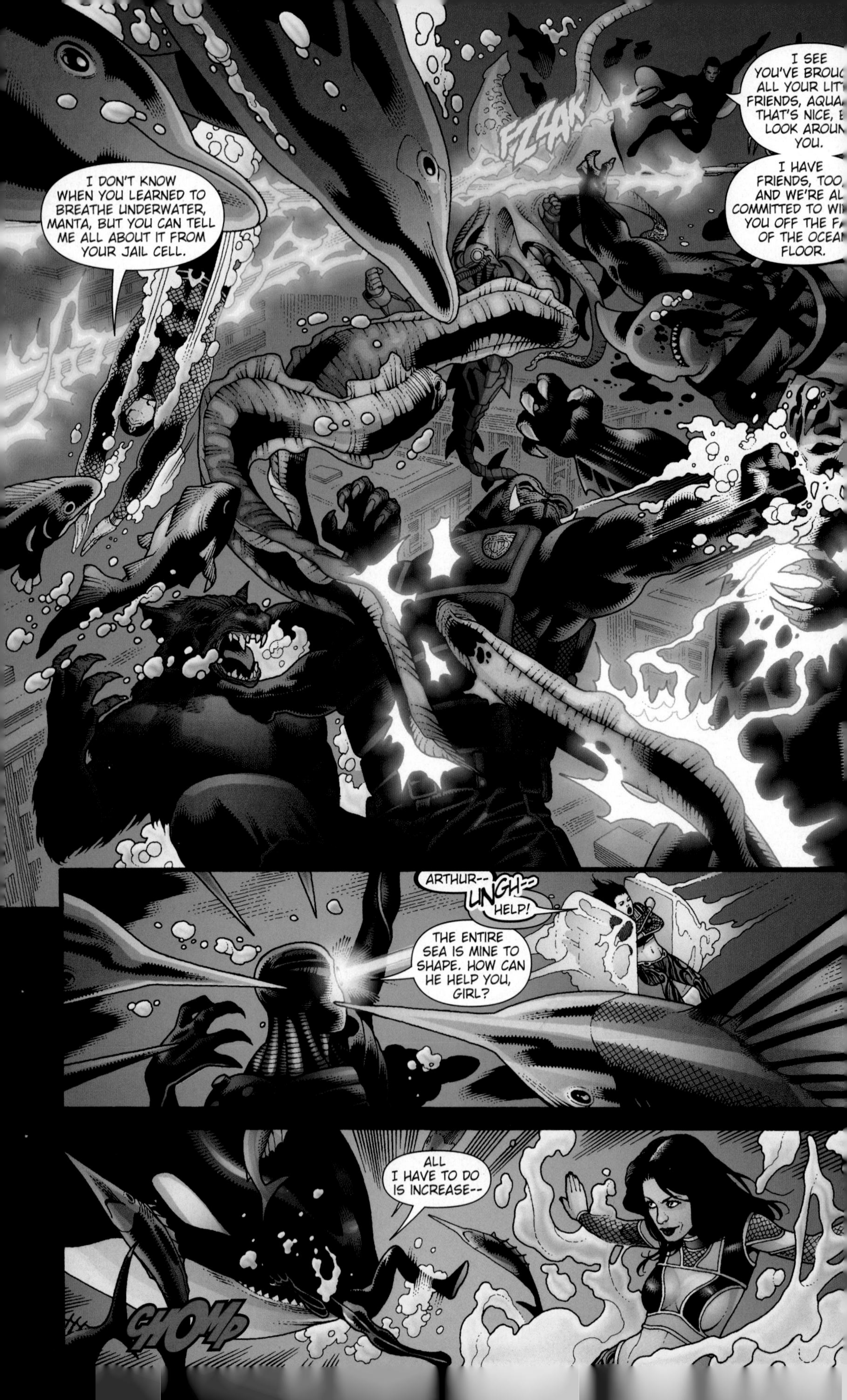
I SEE YOU'VE BROUG
ALL YOUR LIT
FRIENDS, AQUA
THAT'S NICE,
LOOK AROUN
YOU.
I HAVE FRIENDS, TOO,
AND WE'RE AL
COMMITTED TO WI
YOU OFF THE FA
OF THE OCEAN
FLOOR.
FZZAK
I DON'T KNOW WHEN YOU LEARNED TO BREATHE UNDERWATER, MANTA, BUT YOU CAN TELL ME ALL ABOUT IT FROM YOUR JAIL CELL.
ARTHUR--
UNGH--
HELP!
THE ENTIRE SEA IS MINE TO SHAPE. HOW CAN HE HELP YOU, GIRL?
ALL I HAVE TO DO IS INCREASE--
CHOMP

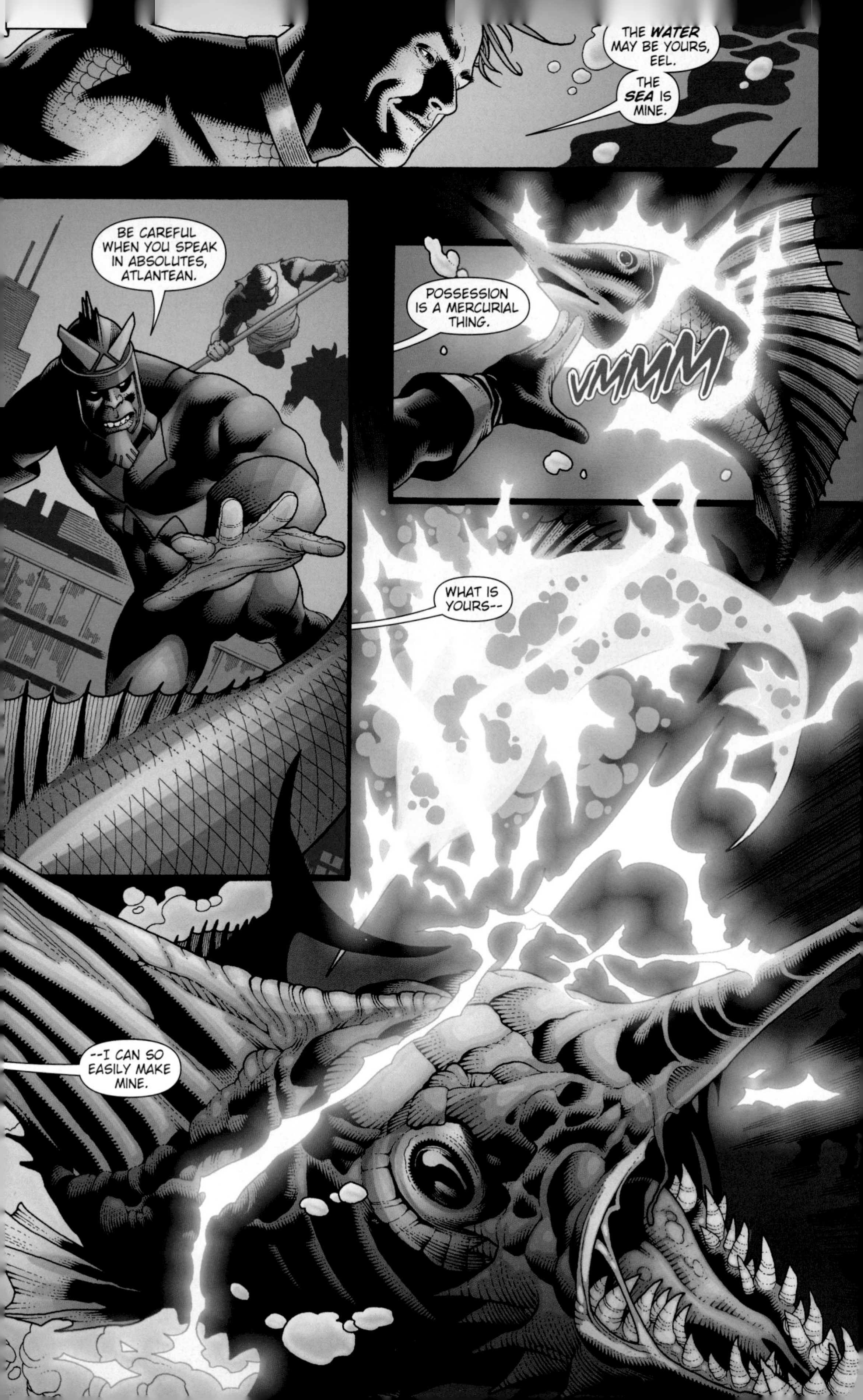
THE **WATER** MAY BE YOURS, EEL.
THE **SEA** IS MINE.
BE CAREFUL WHEN YOU SPEAK IN ABSOLUTES, ATLANTEAN.
POSSESSION IS A MERCURIAL THING.
VMMM
WHAT IS YOURS--
--I CAN SO EASILY MAKE MINE.

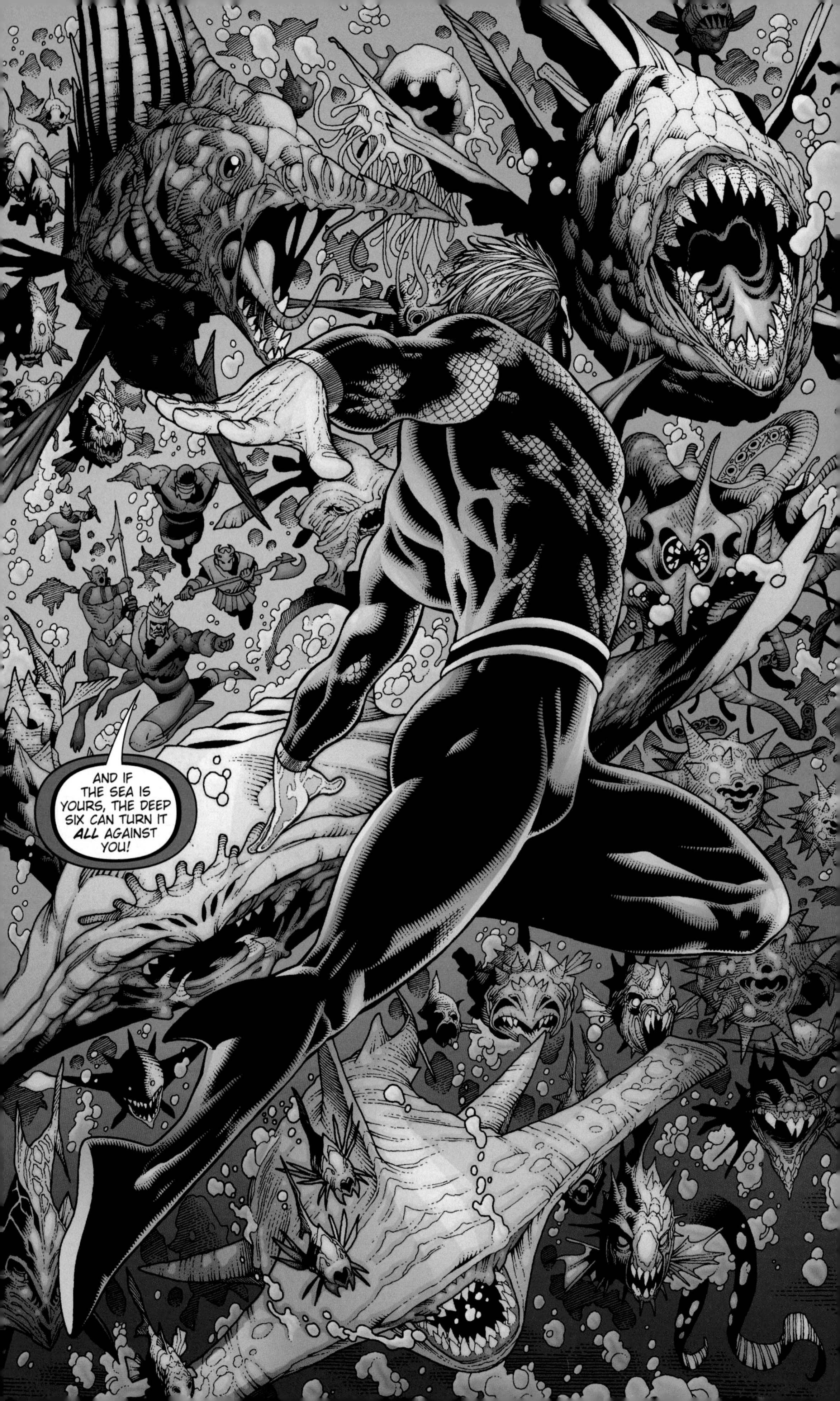
AND IF THE SEA IS YOURS, THE DEEP SIX CAN TURN IT ALL AGAINST YOU!

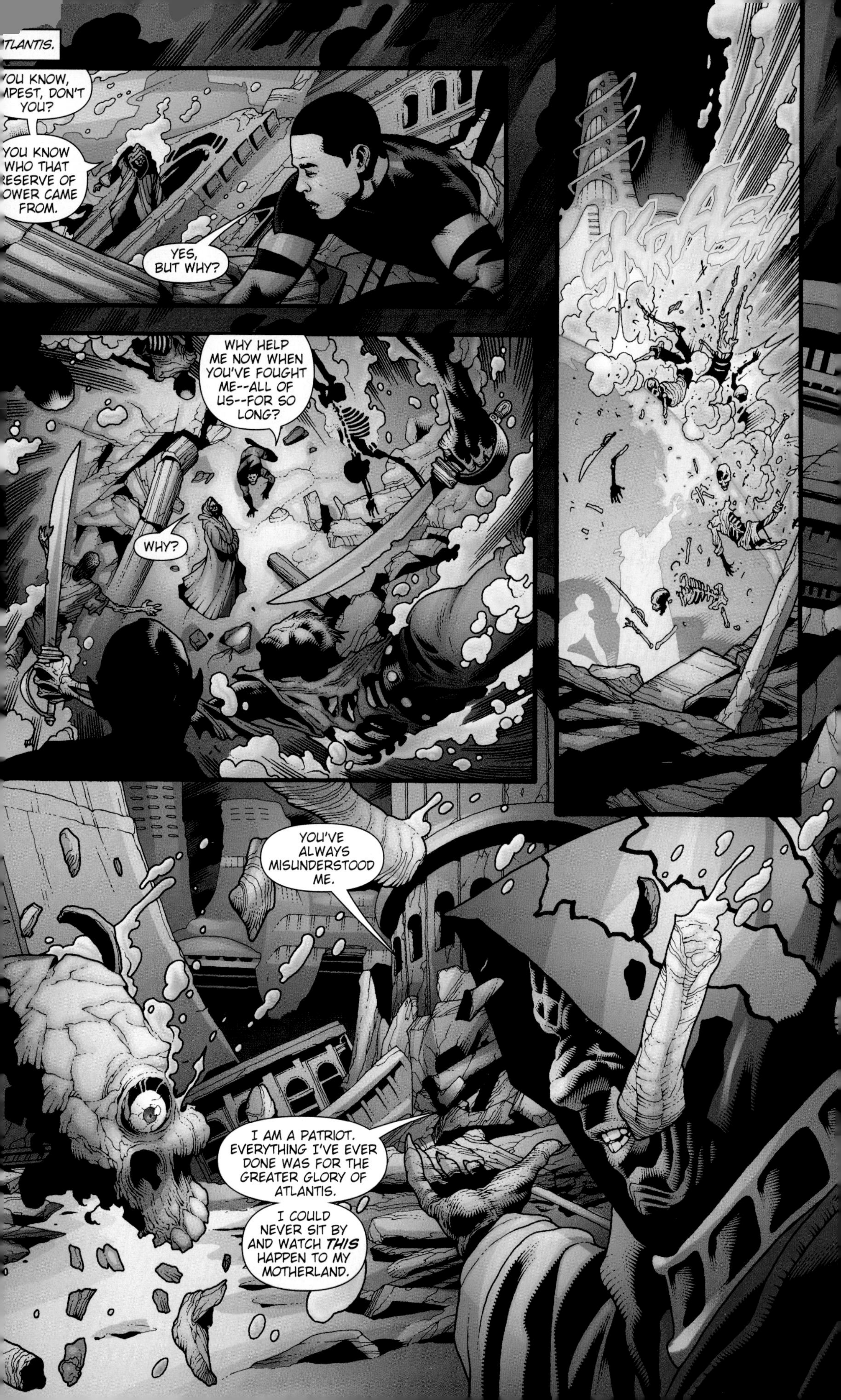
TLANTIS.
YOU KNOW, MPEST, DON'T YOU?
YOU KNOW WHO THAT RESERVE OF OWER CAME FROM.
YES, BUT WHY?
SKRASH
WHY HELP ME NOW WHEN YOU'VE FOUGHT ME--ALL OF US--FOR SO LONG?
WHY?
YOU'VE ALWAYS MISUNDERSTOOD ME.
I AM A PATRIOT. EVERYTHING I'VE EVER DONE WAS FOR THE GREATER GLORY OF ATLANTIS.
I COULD NEVER SIT BY AND WATCH *THIS* HAPPEN TO MY MOTHERLAND.

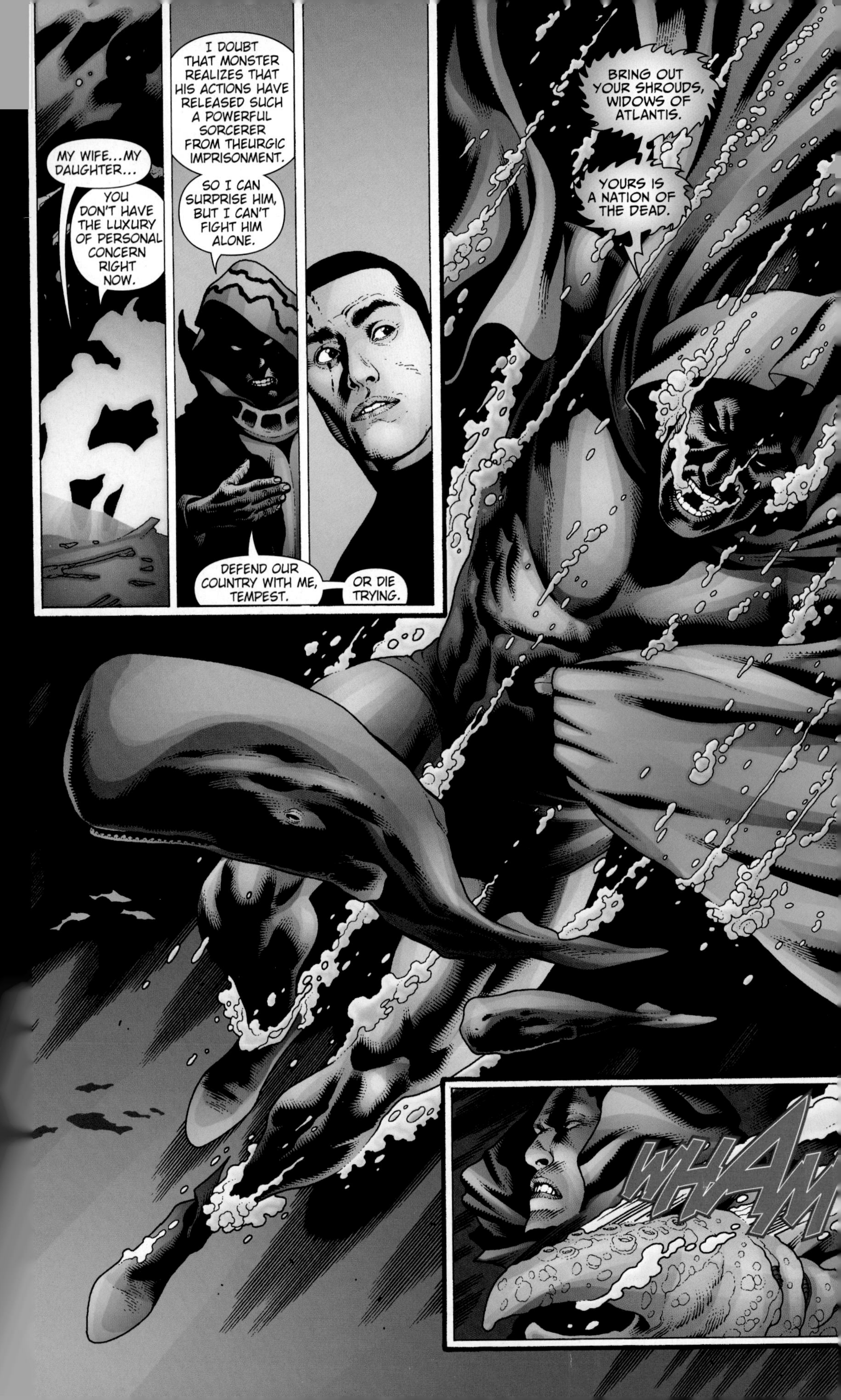
MY WIFE...MY DAUGHTER...
YOU DON'T HAVE THE LUXURY OF PERSONAL CONCERN RIGHT NOW.
I DOUBT THAT MONSTER REALIZES THAT HIS ACTIONS HAVE RELEASED SUCH A POWERFUL SORCERER FROM THEURGIC IMPRISONMENT.
SO I CAN SURPRISE HIM, BUT I CAN'T FIGHT HIM ALONE.
DEFEND OUR COUNTRY WITH ME, TEMPEST.
OR DIE TRYING.
BRING OUT YOUR SHROUDS, WIDOWS OF ATLANTIS.
YOURS IS A NATION OF THE DEAD.
WHAM

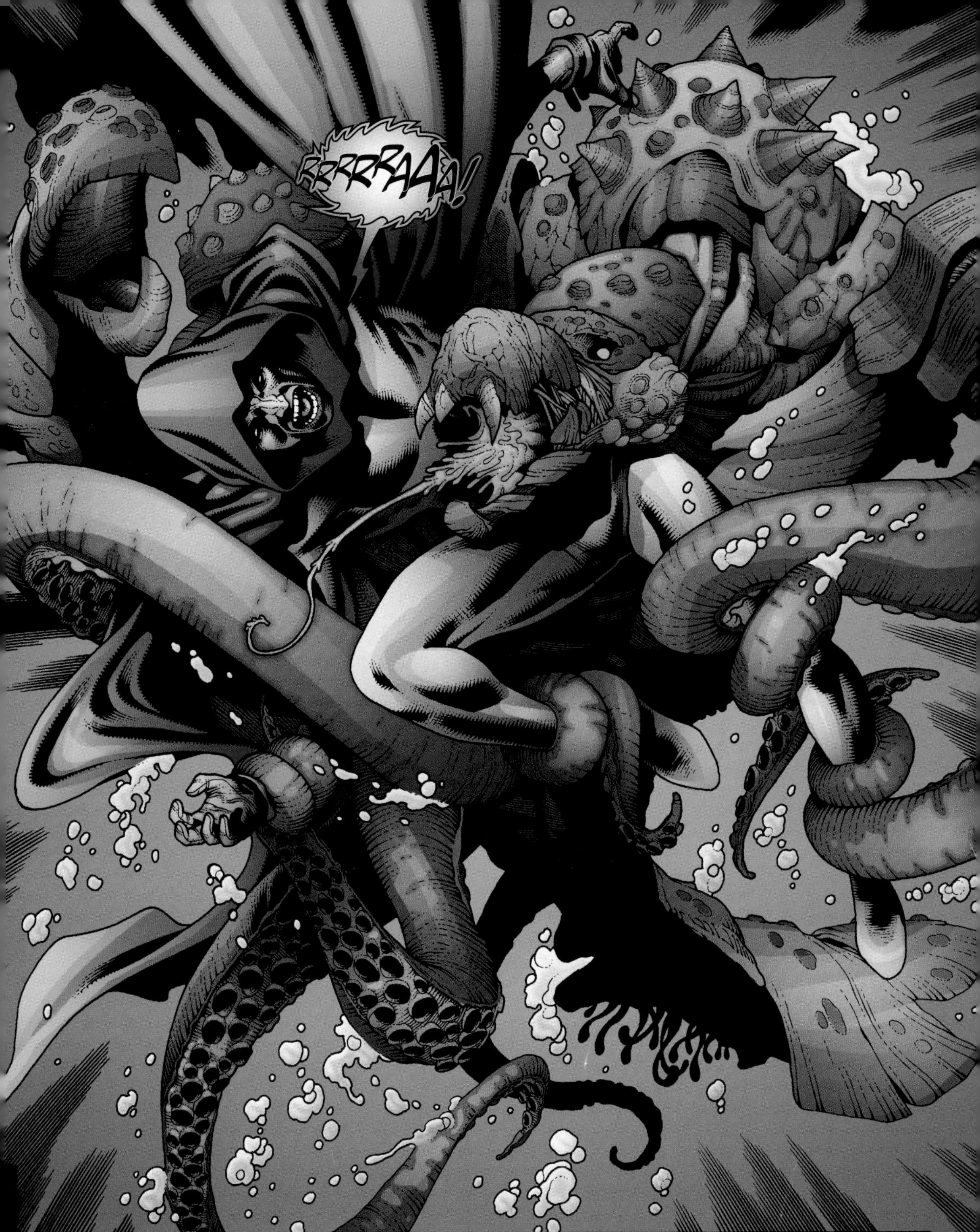
RRRRRAAA!

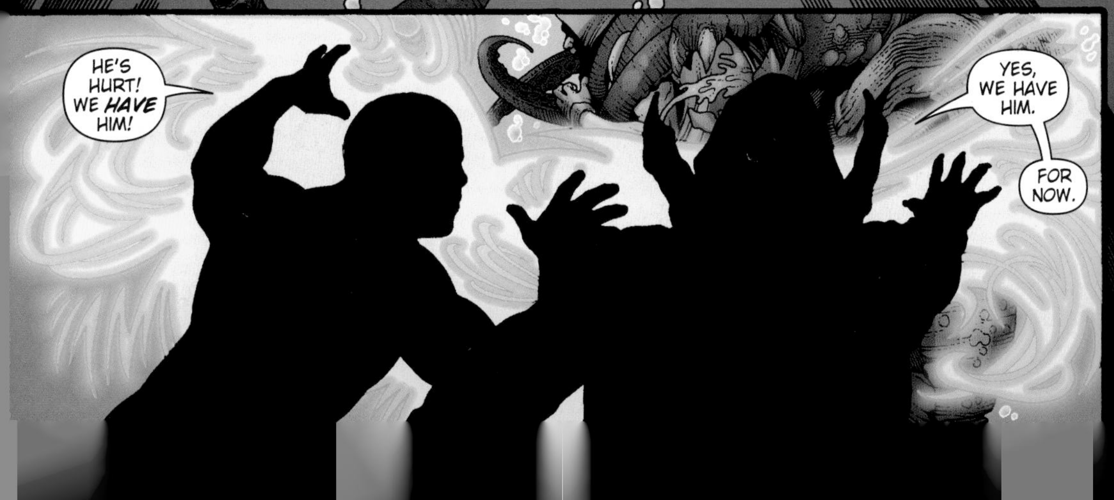
HE'S HURT! WE *HAVE* HIM!
YES, WE HAVE HIM.
FOR NOW.

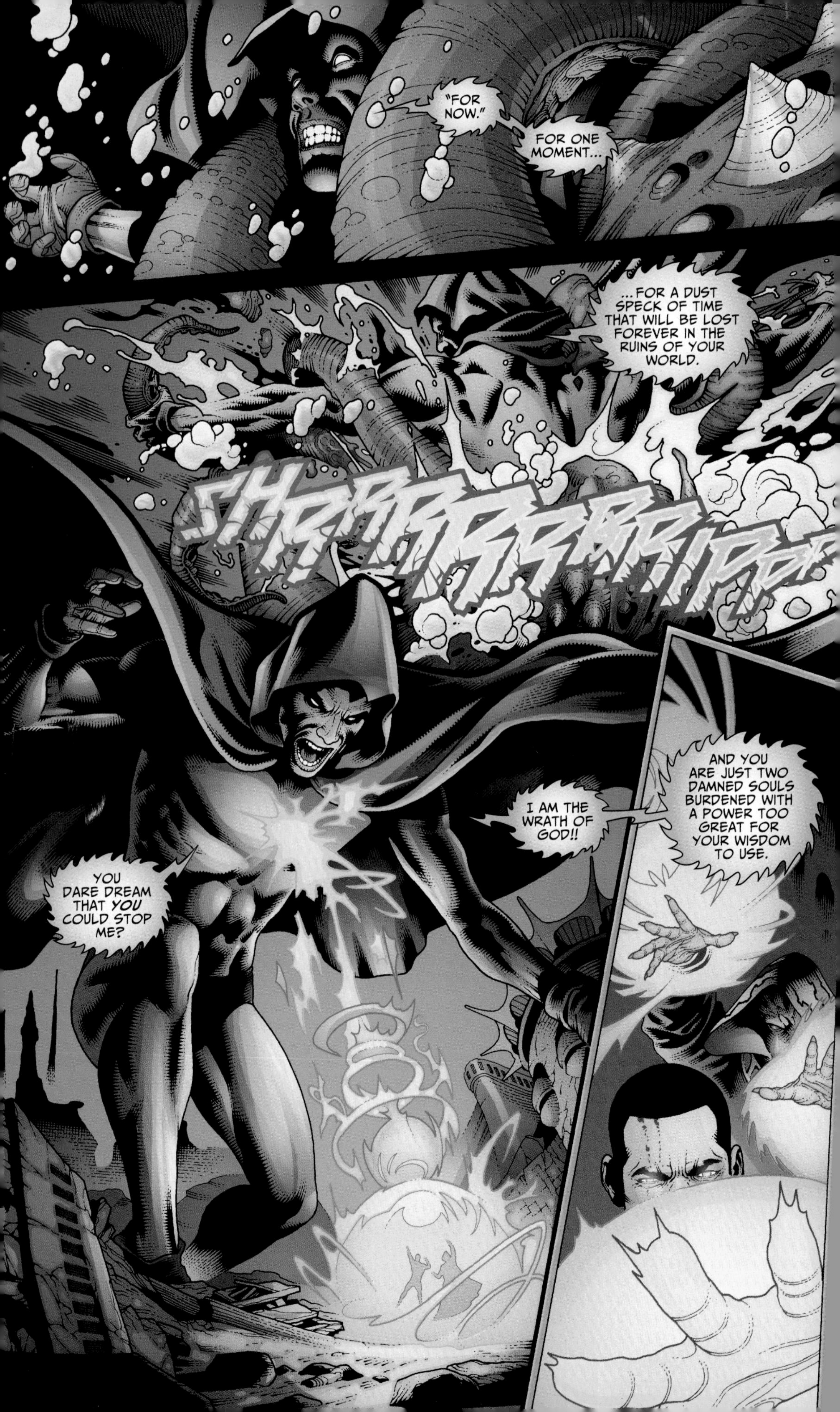
"FOR NOW."
FOR ONE MOMENT...
...FOR A DUST SPECK OF TIME THAT WILL BE LOST FOREVER IN THE RUINS OF YOUR WORLD.
SHRRRRRRRIPP
YOU DARE DREAM THAT YOU COULD STOP ME?
I AM THE WRATH OF GOD!!
AND YOU ARE JUST TWO DAMNED SOULS BURDENED WITH A POWER TOO GREAT FOR YOUR WISDOM TO USE.

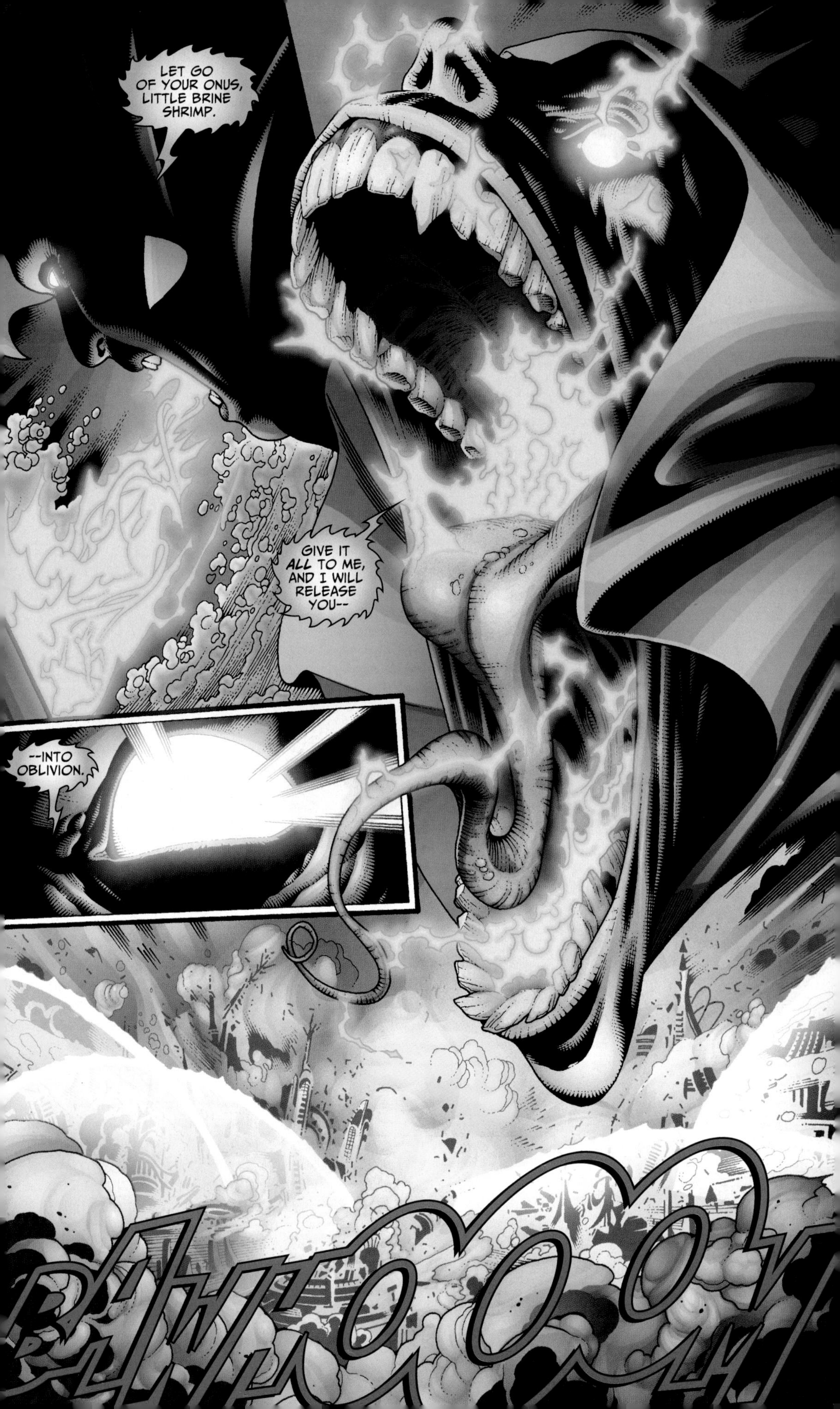
LET GO OF YOUR ONUS, LITTLE BRINE SHRIMP.
GIVE IT ALL TO ME, AND I WILL RELEASE YOU--
--INTO OBLIVION.
BHWOOOM

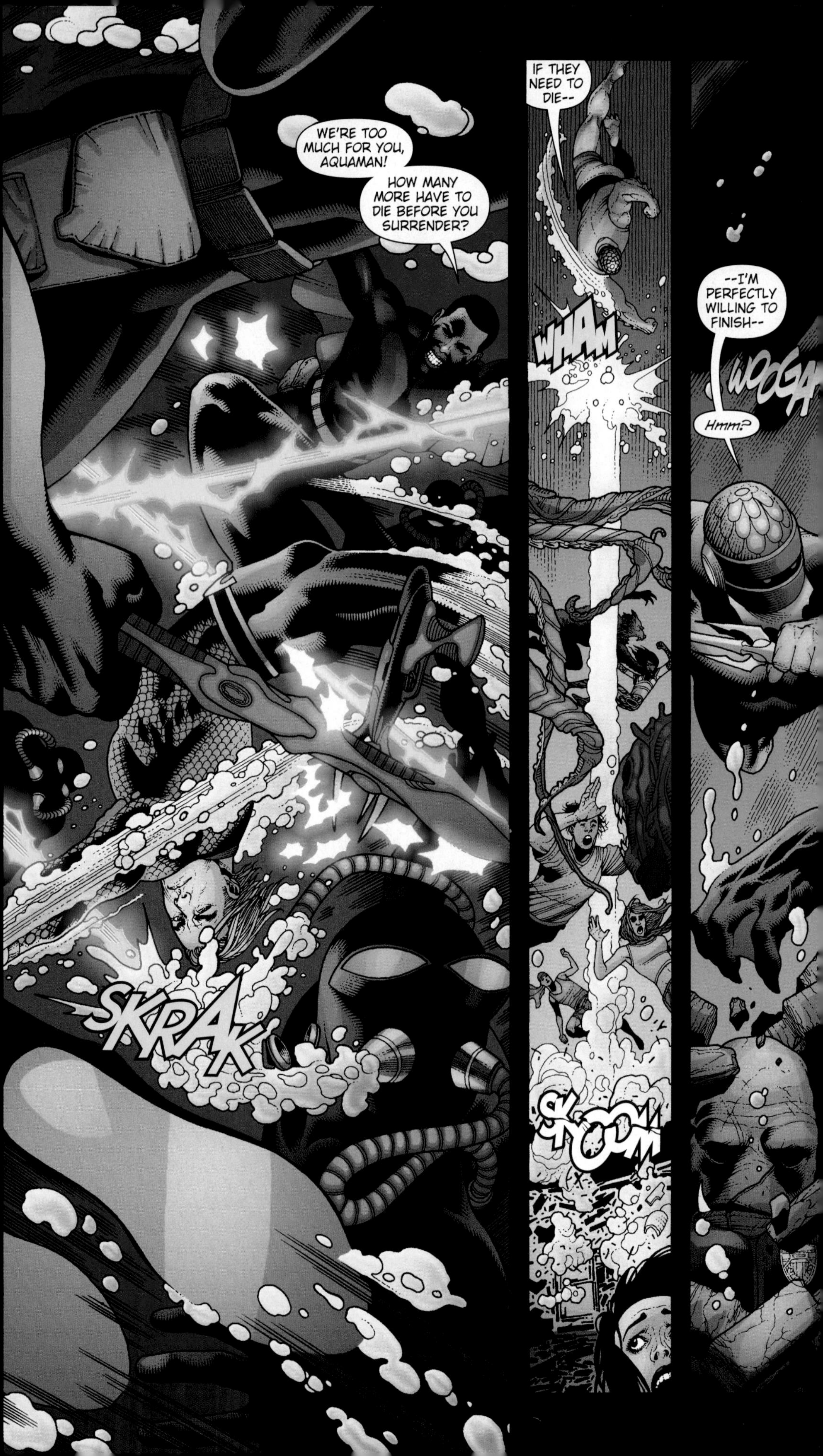
WE'RE TOO MUCH FOR YOU, AQUAMAN!
HOW MANY MORE HAVE TO DIE BEFORE YOU SURRENDER?
SKRAK
IF THEY NEED TO DIE--
WHAM
SKOOM
--I'M PERFECTLY WILLING TO FINISH--
WOOGA
Hmm?

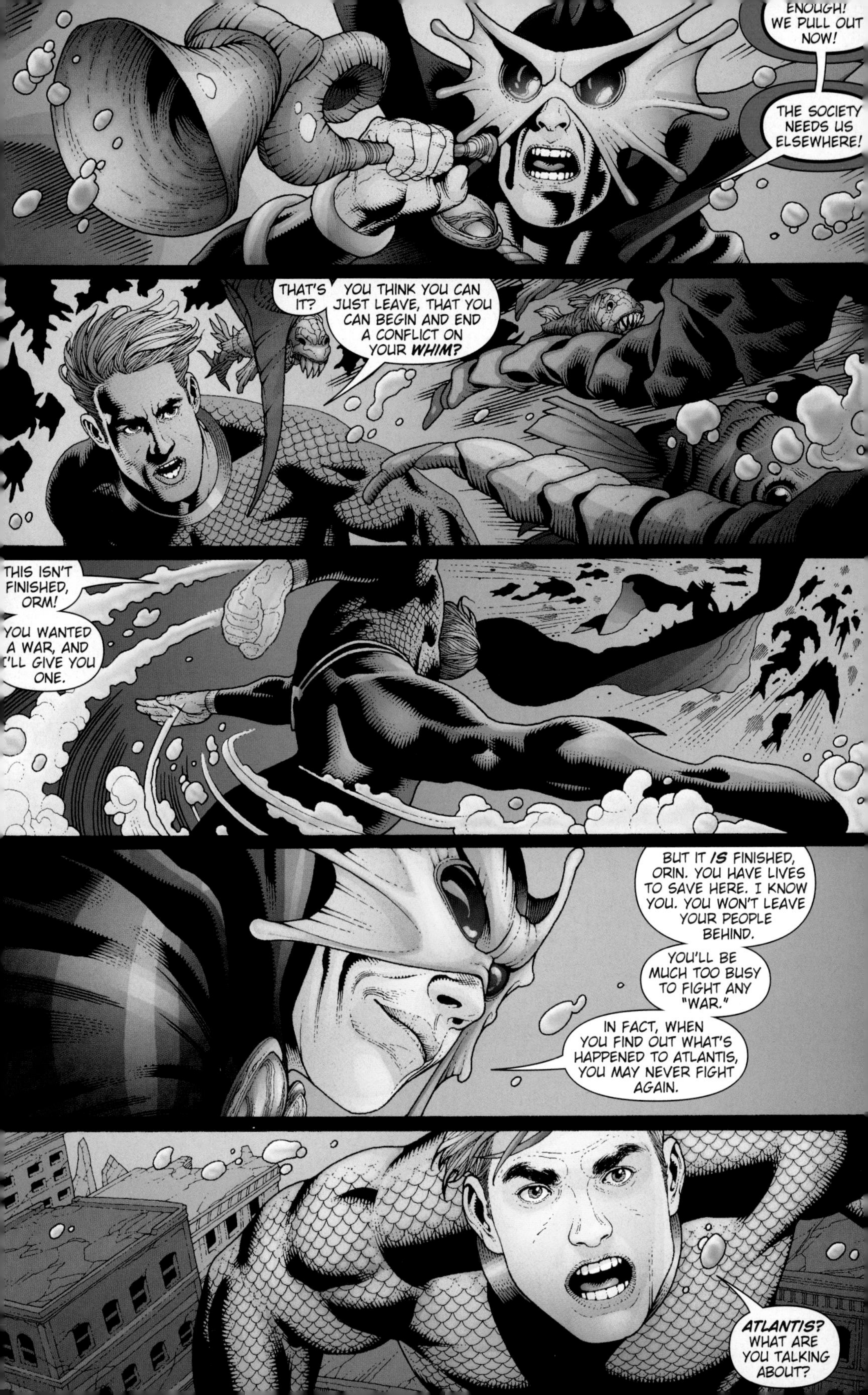
ENOUGH! WE PULL OUT NOW!
THE SOCIETY NEEDS US ELSEWHERE!
THAT'S IT?
YOU THINK YOU CAN JUST LEAVE, THAT YOU CAN BEGIN AND END A CONFLICT ON YOUR **WHIM?**
THIS ISN'T FINISHED, ORM!
YOU WANTED A WAR, AND I'LL GIVE YOU ONE.
BUT IT *IS* FINISHED, ORIN. YOU HAVE LIVES TO SAVE HERE. I KNOW YOU. YOU WON'T LEAVE YOUR PEOPLE BEHIND.
YOU'LL BE MUCH TOO BUSY TO FIGHT ANY "WAR."
IN FACT, WHEN YOU FIND OUT WHAT'S HAPPENED TO ATLANTIS, YOU MAY NEVER FIGHT AGAIN.
ATLANTIS? WHAT ARE YOU TALKING ABOUT?

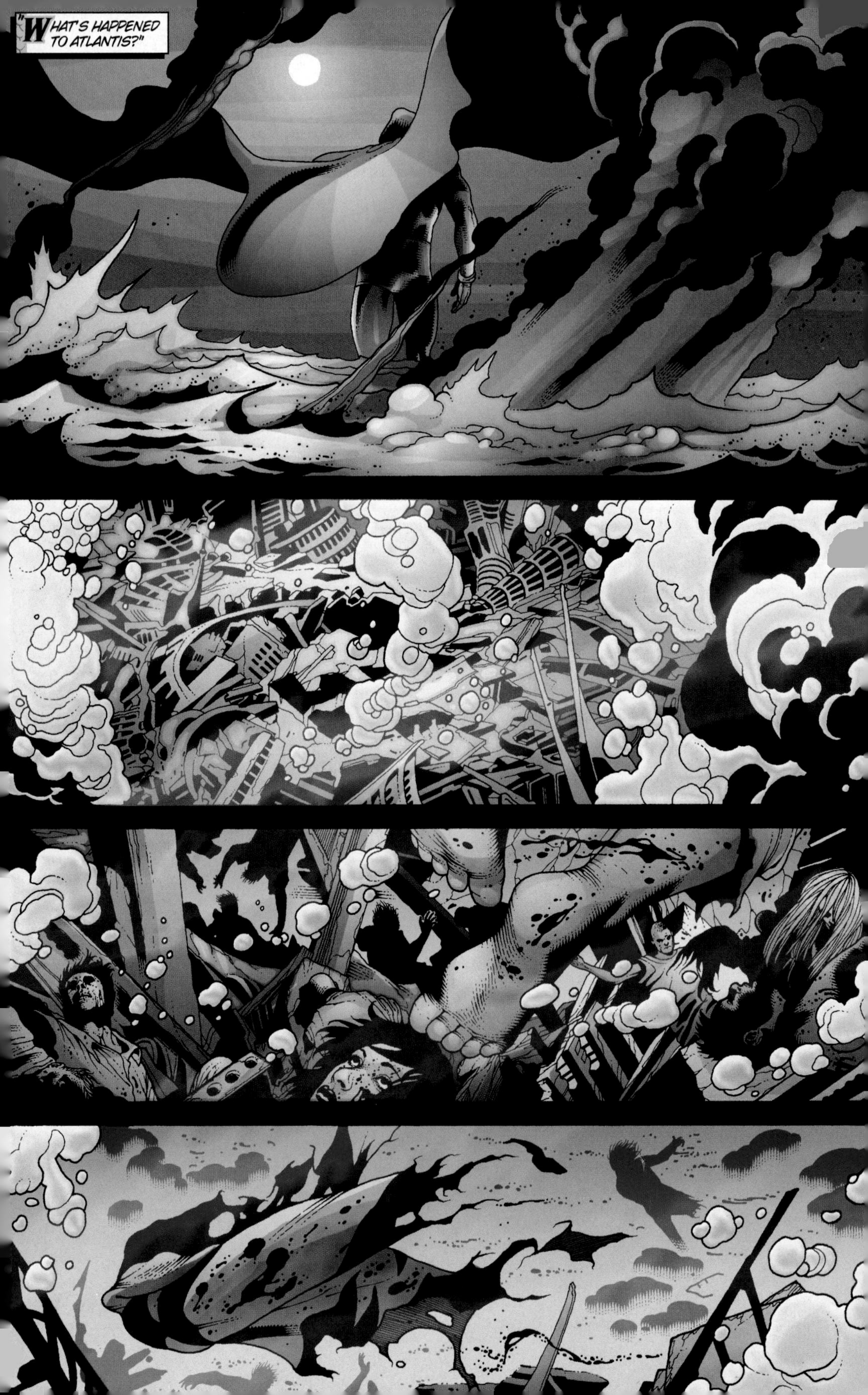
"WHAT'S HAPPENED TO ATLANTIS?"

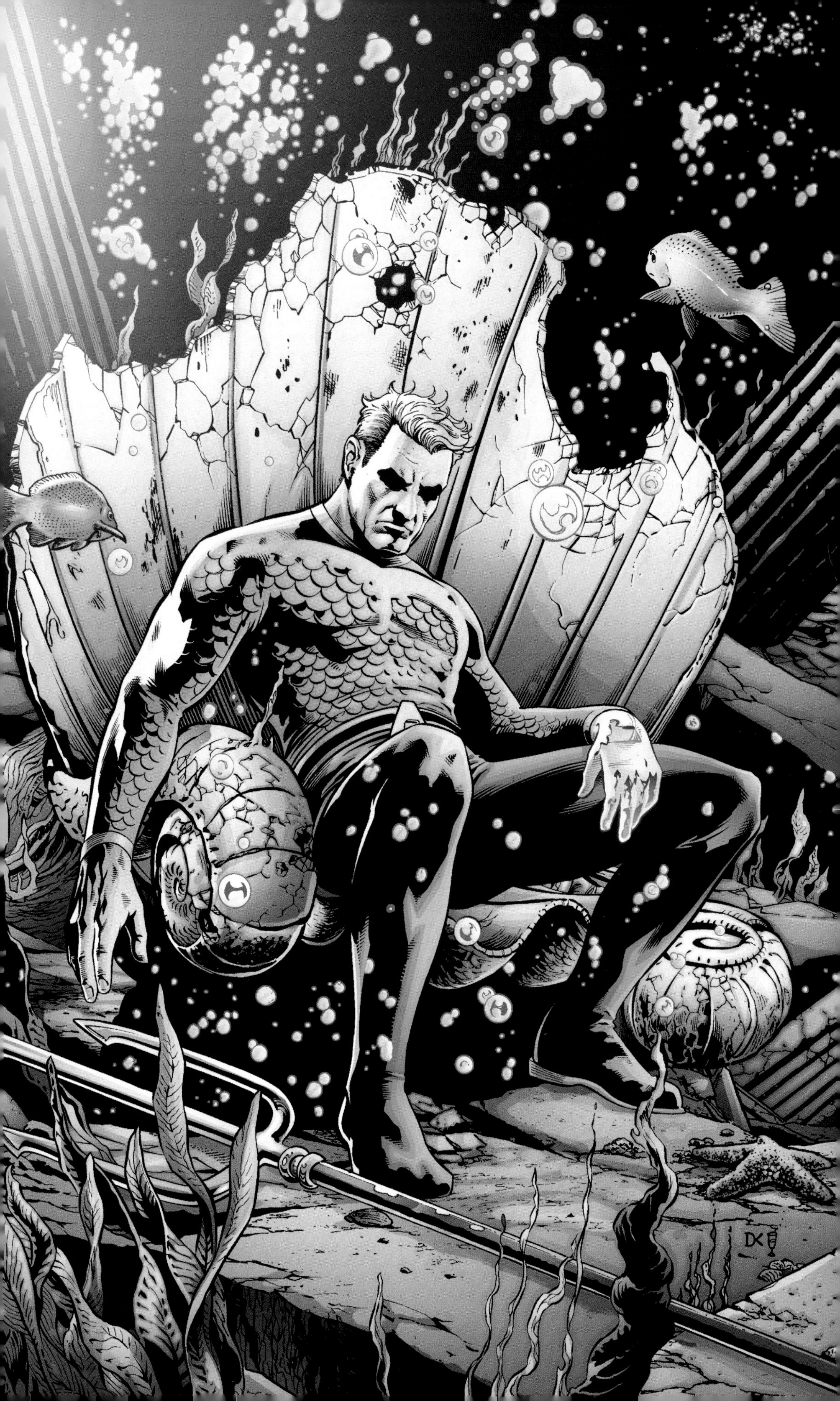

KINGDOM LOST

JOHN ARCUDI
Writer

LEONARD KIRK
Layouts

ANDY CLARKE
Finishes

NATHAN EYRING
Colorist

ROB LEIGH
Letterer

DON KRAMER &
KEITH CHAMPAGNE
Cover

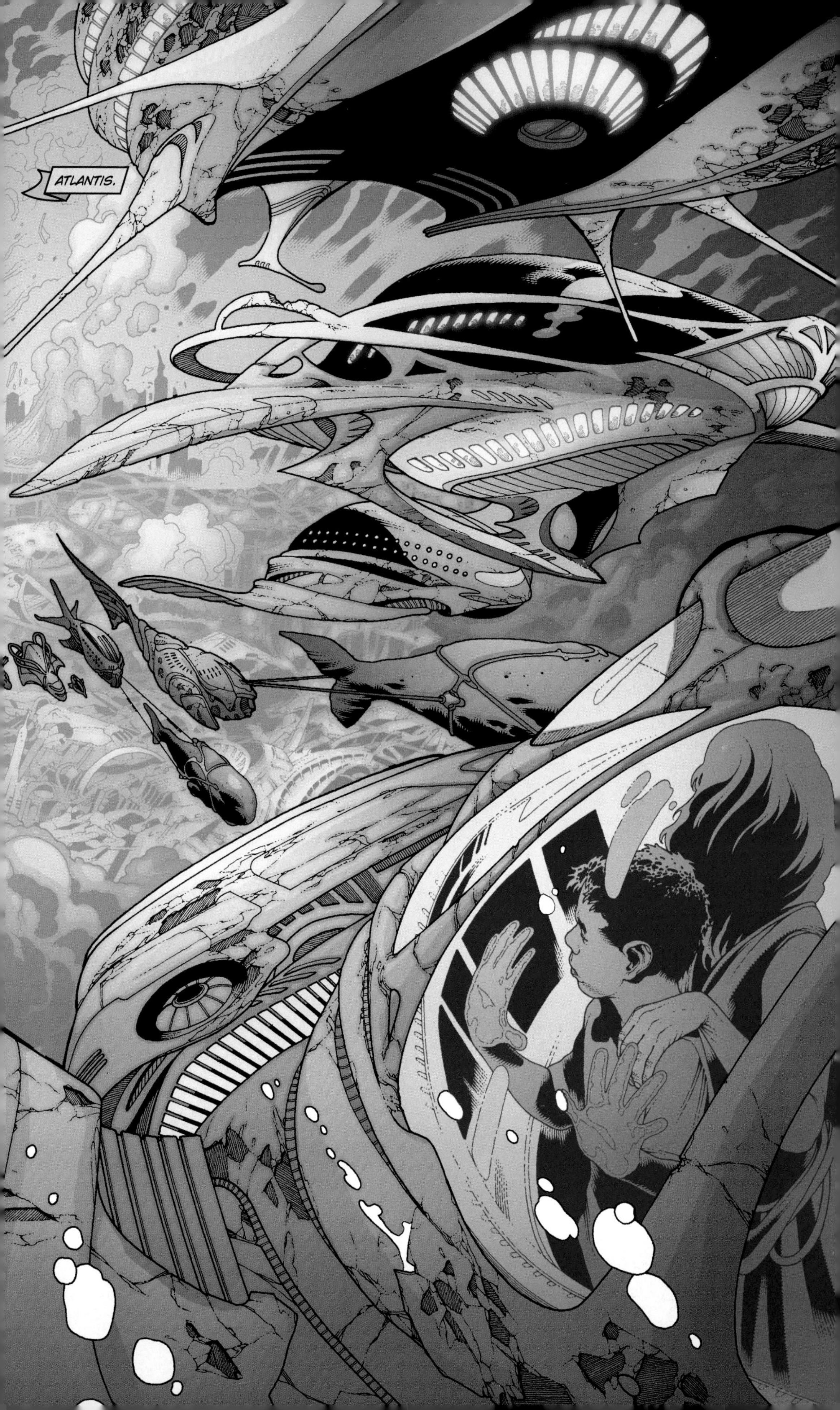
ATLANTIS.

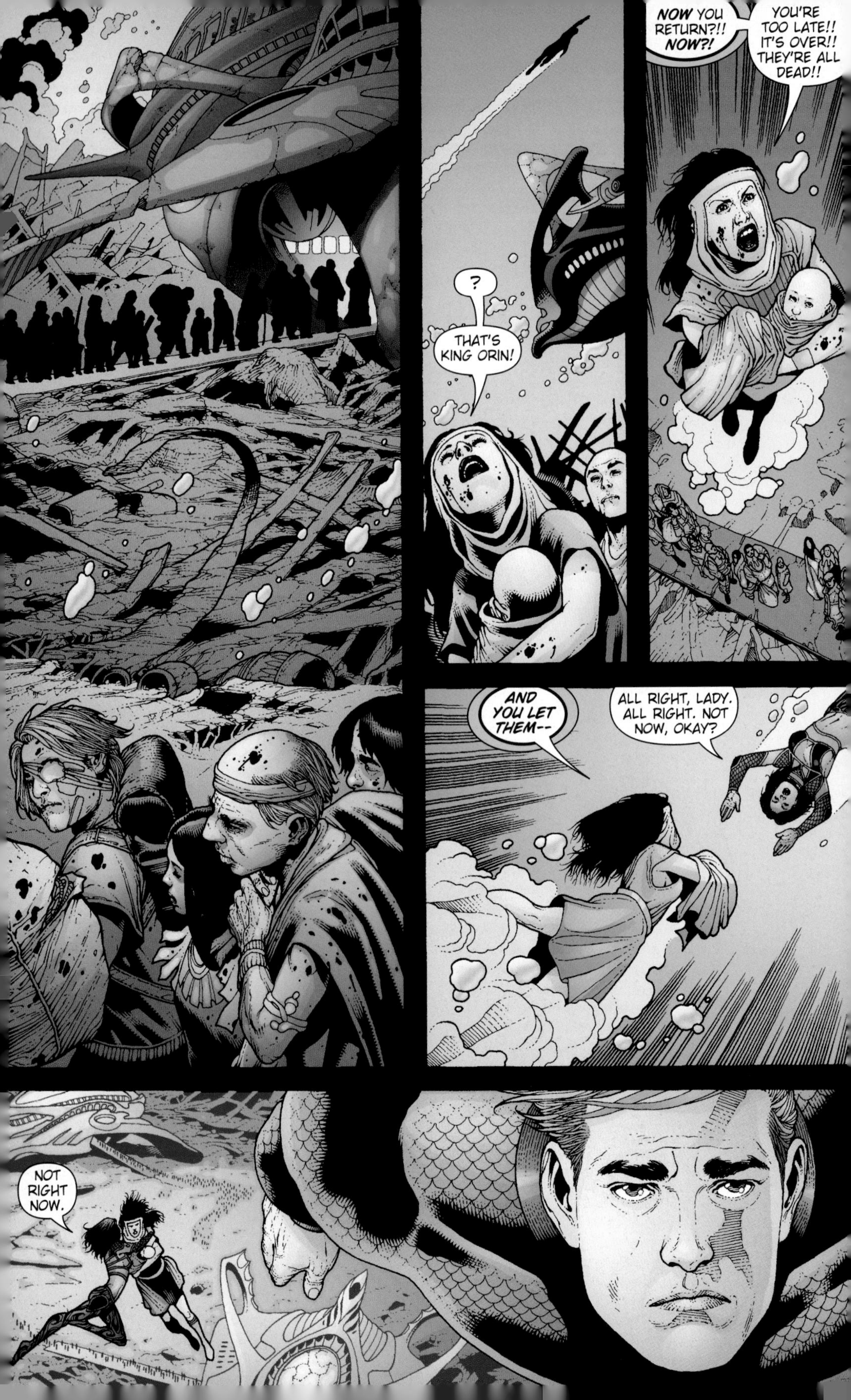
?
THAT'S KING ORIN!
NOW YOU RETURN?!! NOW?!
YOU'RE TOO LATE!! IT'S OVER!! THEY'RE ALL DEAD!!
AND YOU LET THEM--
ALL RIGHT, LADY. ALL RIGHT. NOT NOW, OKAY?
NOT RIGHT NOW.

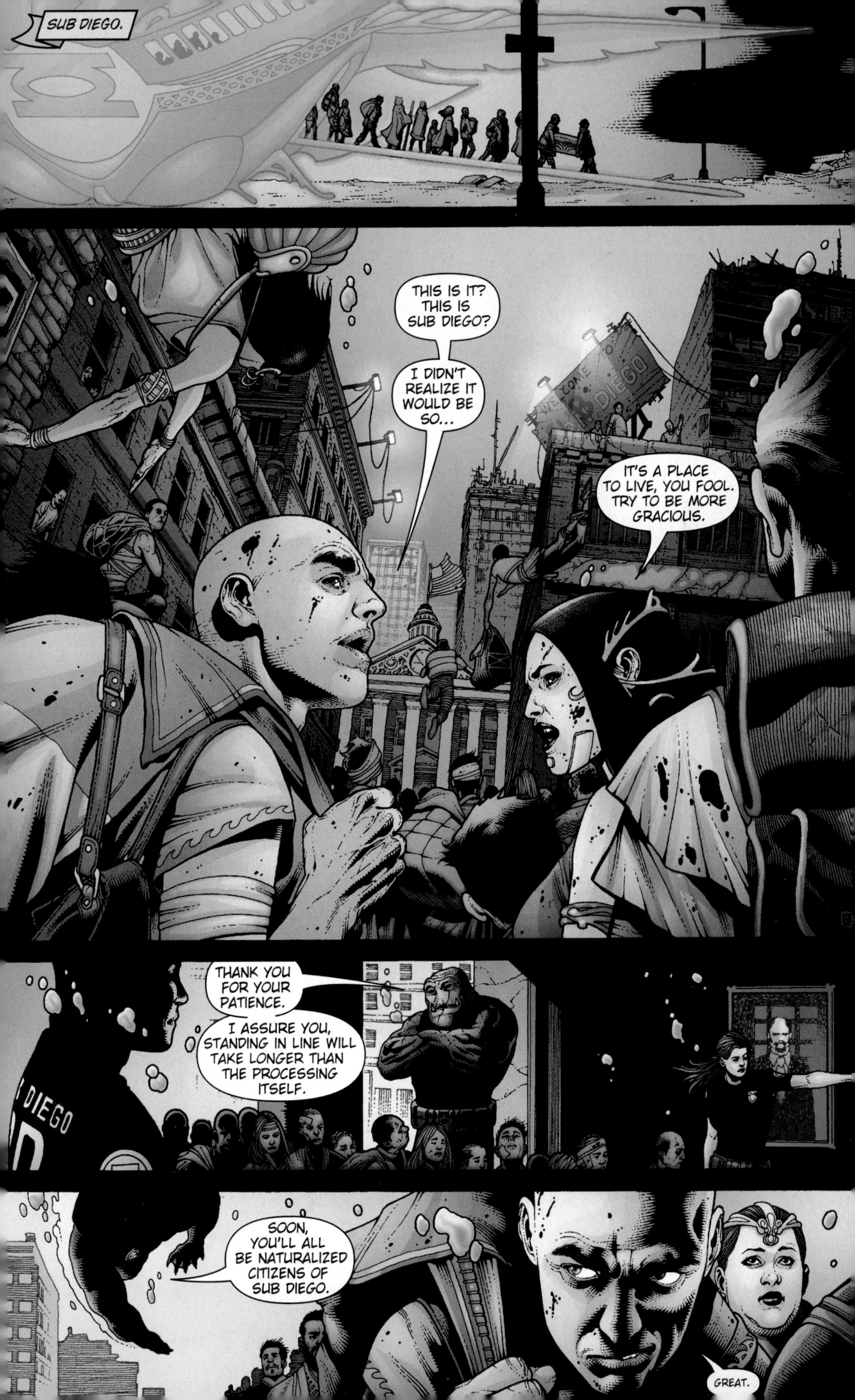
SUB DIEGO.
THIS IS IT? THIS IS SUB DIEGO?
I DIDN'T REALIZE IT WOULD BE SO...
WELCOME TO SUB DIEGO
IT'S A PLACE TO LIVE, YOU FOOL. TRY TO BE MORE GRACIOUS.
THANK YOU FOR YOUR PATIENCE.
I ASSURE YOU, STANDING IN LINE WILL TAKE LONGER THAN THE PROCESSING ITSELF.
SOON, YOU'LL ALL BE NATURALIZED CITIZENS OF SUB DIEGO.
GREAT.

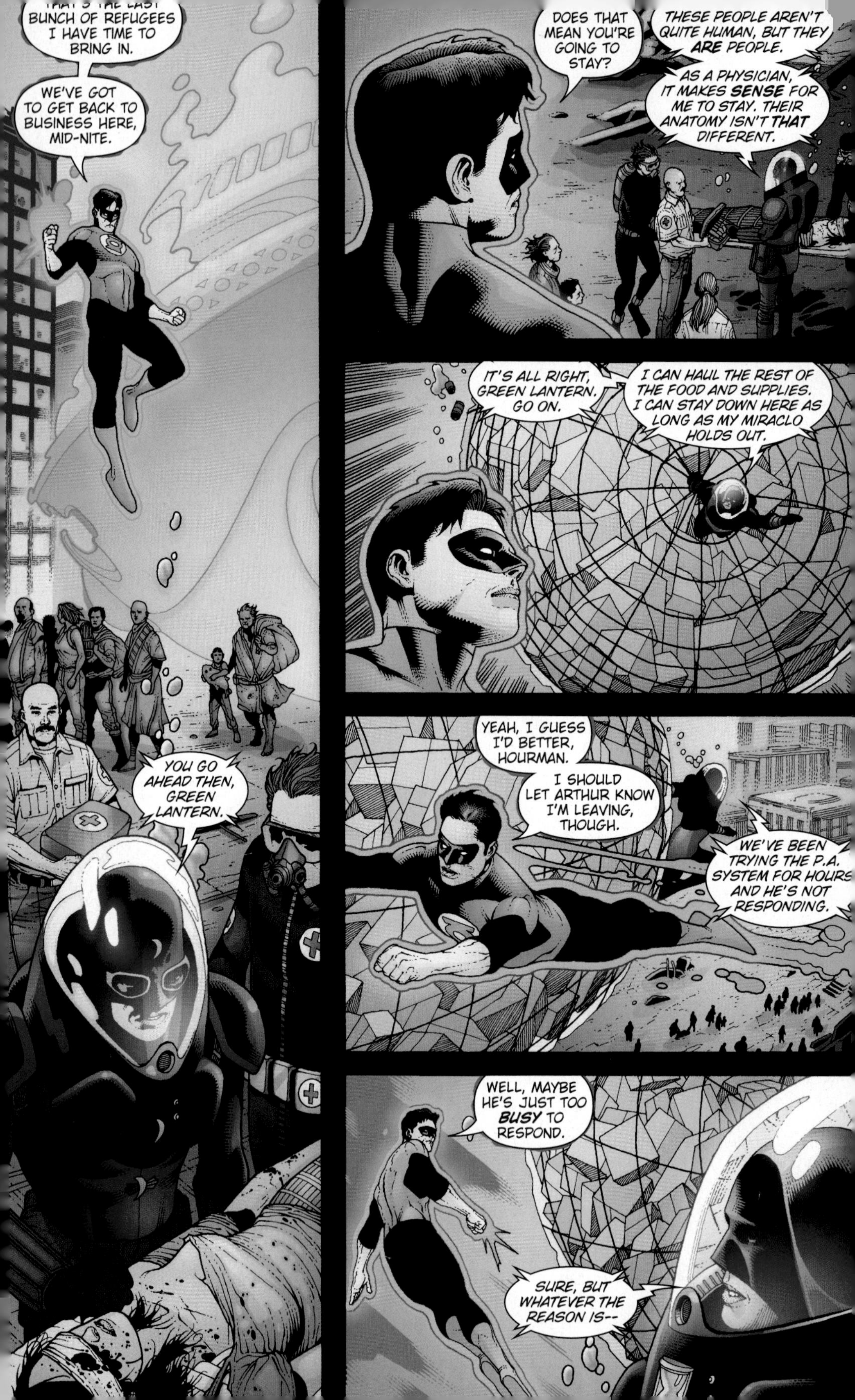

BUNCH OF REFUGEES I HAVE TIME TO BRING IN.
WE'VE GOT TO GET BACK TO BUSINESS HERE, MID-NITE.
YOU GO AHEAD THEN, GREEN LANTERN.
DOES THAT MEAN YOU'RE GOING TO STAY?
THESE PEOPLE AREN'T QUITE HUMAN, BUT THEY **ARE** PEOPLE.
AS A PHYSICIAN, IT MAKES **SENSE** FOR ME TO STAY. THEIR ANATOMY ISN'T **THAT** DIFFERENT.
IT'S ALL RIGHT, GREEN LANTERN. GO ON.
I CAN HAUL THE REST OF THE FOOD AND SUPPLIES. I CAN STAY DOWN HERE AS LONG AS MY MIRACLO HOLDS OUT.
YEAH, I GUESS I'D BETTER, HOURMAN.
I SHOULD LET ARTHUR KNOW I'M LEAVING, THOUGH.
WE'VE BEEN TRYING THE P.A. SYSTEM FOR HOURS AND HE'S NOT RESPONDING.
WELL, MAYBE HE'S JUST TOO **BUSY** TO RESPOND.
SURE, BUT WHATEVER THE REASON IS--

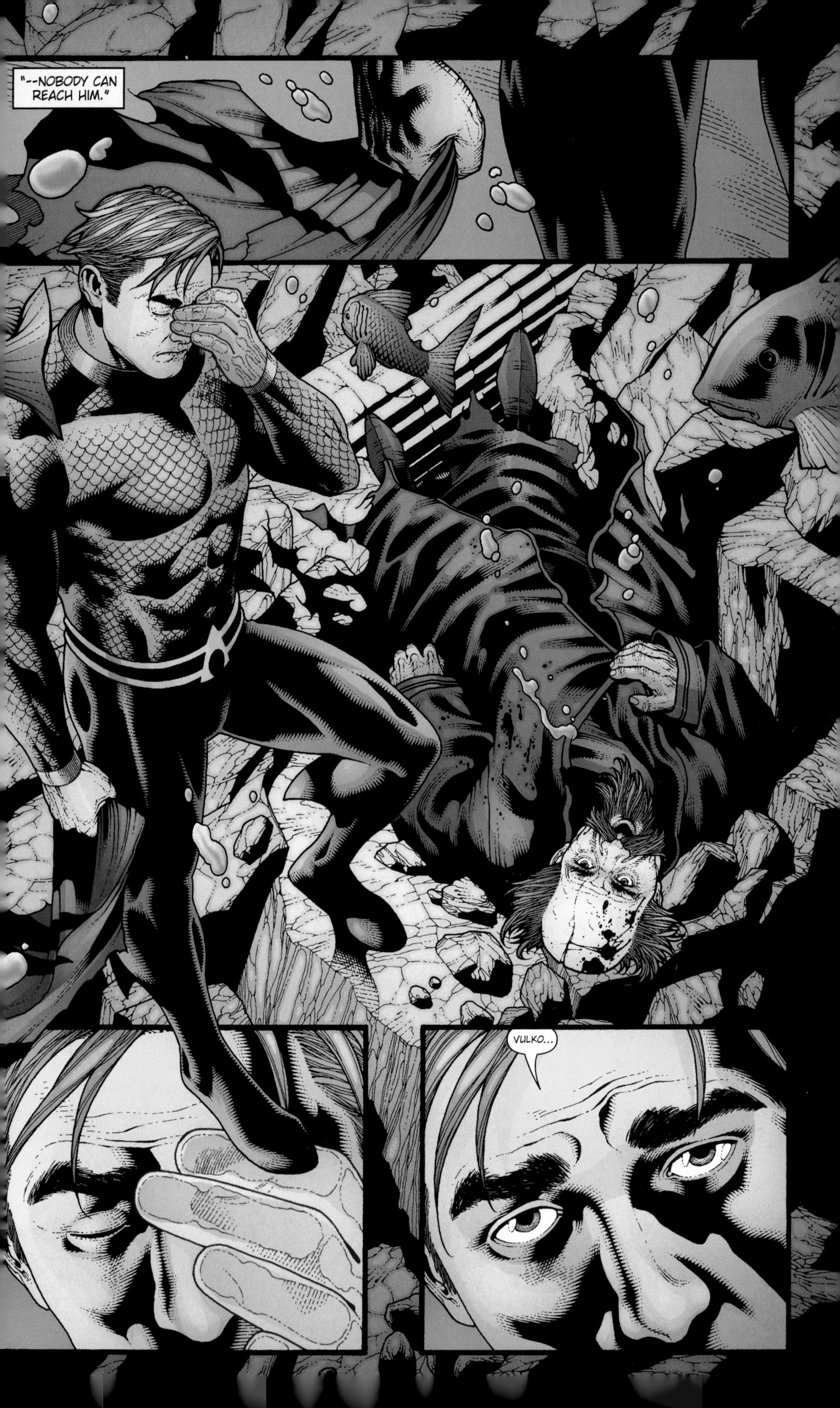
"--NOBODY CAN REACH HIM."
VULKO...

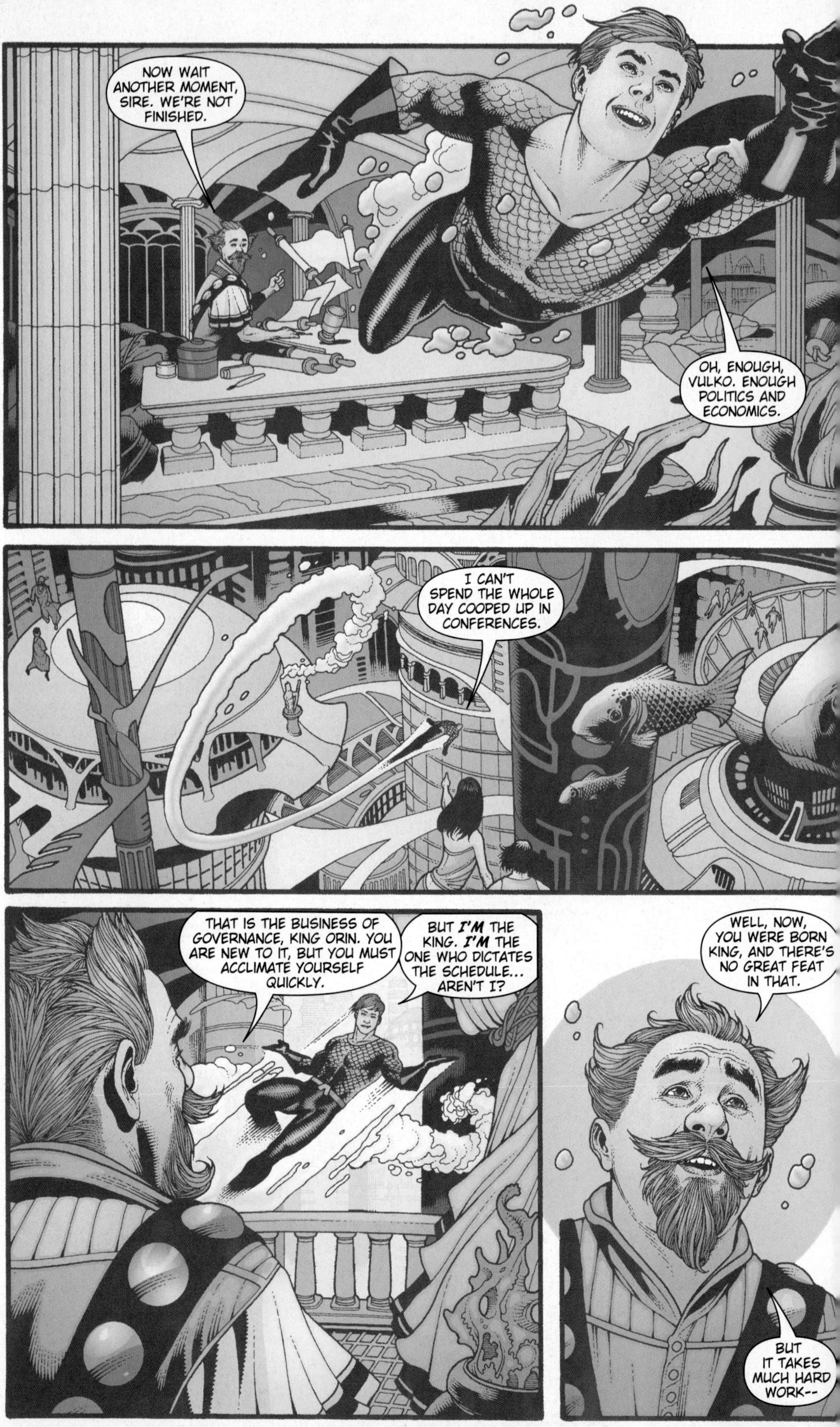

NOW WAIT ANOTHER MOMENT, SIRE. WE'RE NOT FINISHED.
OH, ENOUGH, VULKO. ENOUGH POLITICS AND ECONOMICS.
I CAN'T SPEND THE WHOLE DAY COOPED UP IN CONFERENCES.
THAT IS THE BUSINESS OF GOVERNANCE, KING ORIN. YOU ARE NEW TO IT, BUT YOU MUST ACCLIMATE YOURSELF QUICKLY.
BUT *I'M* THE KING. *I'M* THE ONE WHO DICTATES THE SCHEDULE... AREN'T I?
WELL, NOW, YOU WERE BORN KING, AND THERE'S NO GREAT FEAT IN THAT.
BUT IT TAKES MUCH HARD WORK--

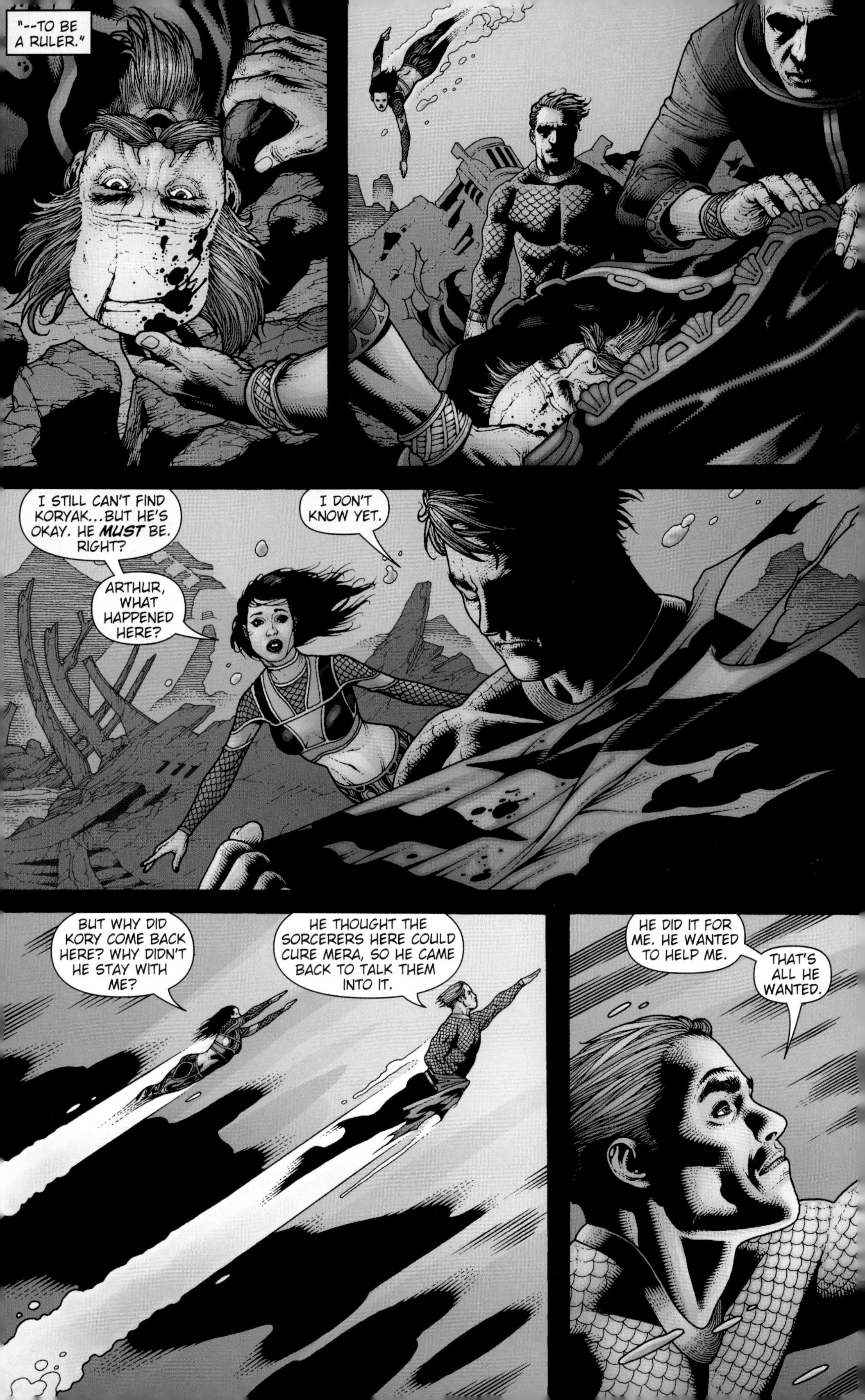
"--TO BE A RULER."
I STILL CAN'T FIND KORYAK...BUT HE'S OKAY. HE MUST BE. RIGHT?
ARTHUR, WHAT HAPPENED HERE?
I DON'T KNOW YET.
BUT WHY DID KORY COME BACK HERE? WHY DIDN'T HE STAY WITH ME?
HE THOUGHT THE SORCERERS HERE COULD CURE MERA, SO HE CAME BACK TO TALK THEM INTO IT.
HE DID IT FOR ME. HE WANTED TO HELP ME.
THAT'S ALL HE WANTED.

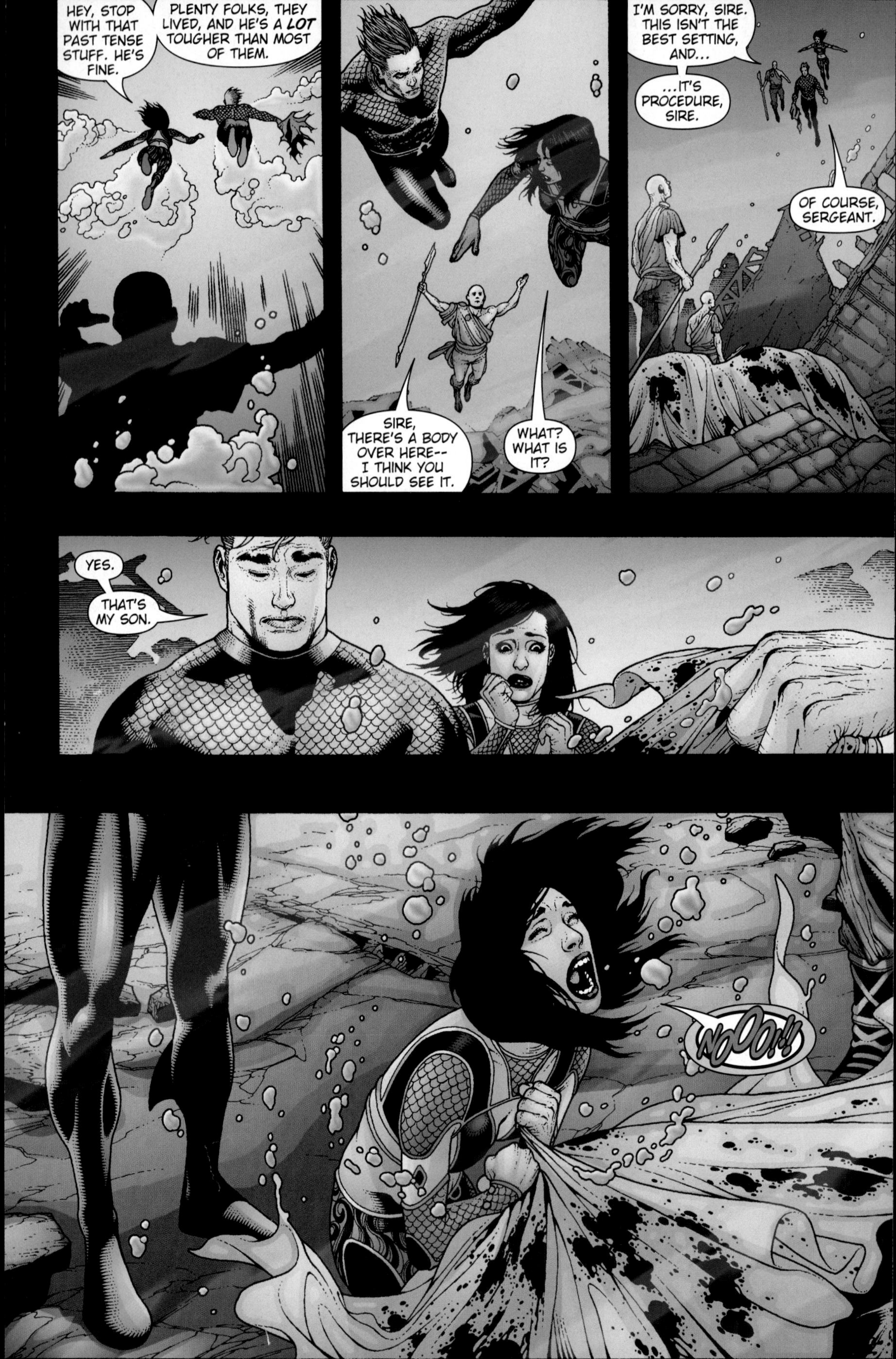
HEY, STOP WITH THAT PAST TENSE STUFF. HE'S FINE.
PLENTY FOLKS, THEY LIVED, AND HE'S A LOT TOUGHER THAN MOST OF THEM.
SIRE, THERE'S A BODY OVER HERE-- I THINK YOU SHOULD SEE IT.
WHAT? WHAT IS IT?
I'M SORRY, SIRE. THIS ISN'T THE BEST SETTING, AND...
...IT'S PROCEDURE, SIRE.
OF COURSE, SERGEANT.
YES.
THAT'S MY SON.
NOOO!!

WE ONLY MEAN TO OFFER YOU THE BEST OF ADVICE, SIRE.

BUT THE BOY DOESN'T SEEM TO BE ABLE TO ADJUST TO LIFE HERE. HE WAS, AFTER ALL, RAISED AS A HUMAN.

SO WAS I.

WELL, *er*, YES, BUT *YOU*, SIRE, YOU ARE KING. LET'S NOT FORGET THAT.

THEN TRY NOT TO FORGET THAT KORYAK IS MY SON.

SIRE, CLEARLY WE MEAN NO DISRESPECT. WE WANT THE BOY TO BE HAPPY, *AND* WE WANT A HARMONIOUS ROYAL COURT.

BUT FROM ALL THAT WE'VE SEEN, NEITHER OF THOSE THINGS IS PRESENTLY TRUE.

WE ONLY WANTED TO BRING IT TO YOUR ATTENTION.

ALL RIGHT. LET ME TALK TO HIM.

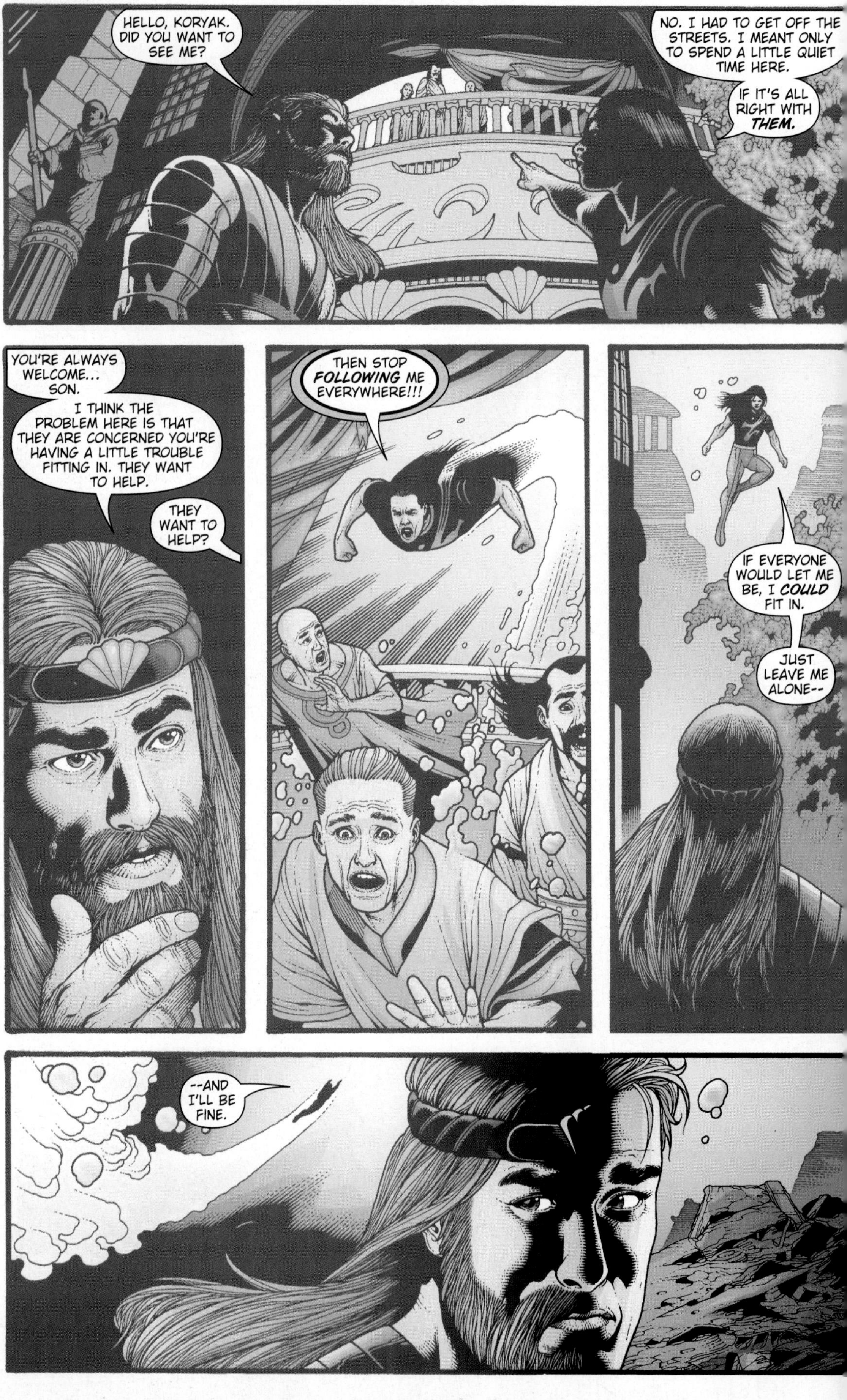
HELLO, KORYAK. DID YOU WANT TO SEE ME?
NO. I HAD TO GET OFF THE STREETS. I MEANT ONLY TO SPEND A LITTLE QUIET TIME HERE.
IF IT'S ALL RIGHT WITH *THEM.*
YOU'RE ALWAYS WELCOME... SON.
I THINK THE PROBLEM HERE IS THAT THEY ARE CONCERNED YOU'RE HAVING A LITTLE TROUBLE FITTING IN. THEY WANT TO HELP.
THEY WANT TO HELP?
THEN STOP ***FOLLOWING*** ME EVERYWHERE!!!
IF EVERYONE WOULD LET ME BE, I ***COULD*** FIT IN.
JUST LEAVE ME ALONE--
--AND I'LL BE FINE.

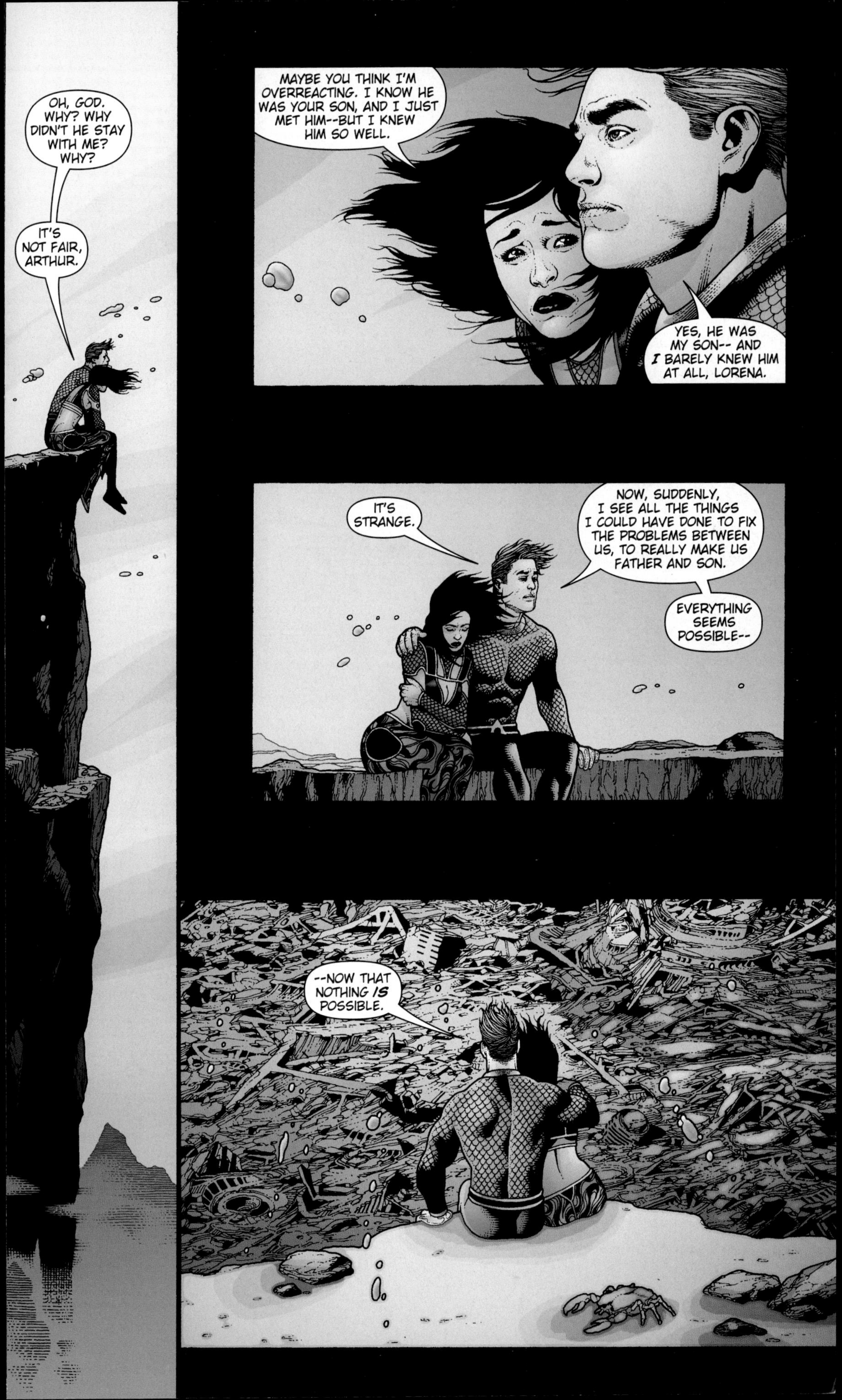
OH, GOD. WHY? WHY DIDN'T HE STAY WITH ME? WHY?
IT'S NOT FAIR, ARTHUR.
MAYBE YOU THINK I'M OVERREACTING. I KNOW HE WAS YOUR SON, AND I JUST MET HIM--BUT I KNEW HIM SO WELL.
YES, HE WAS MY SON-- AND I BARELY KNEW HIM AT ALL, LORENA.
IT'S STRANGE.
NOW, SUDDENLY, I SEE ALL THE THINGS I COULD HAVE DONE TO FIX THE PROBLEMS BETWEEN US, TO REALLY MAKE US FATHER AND SON.
EVERYTHING SEEMS POSSIBLE--
--NOW THAT NOTHING IS POSSIBLE.

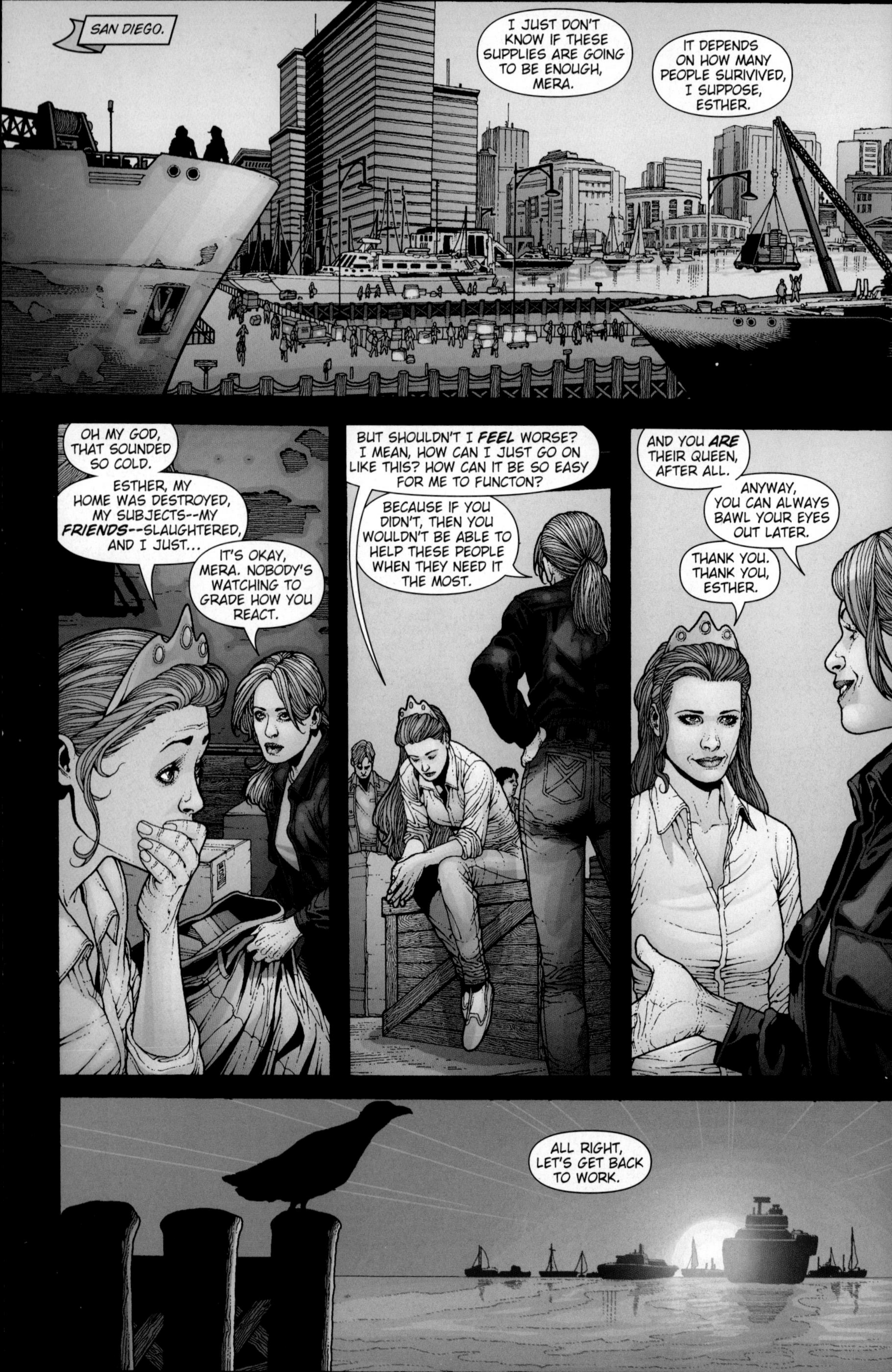
SAN DIEGO.
I JUST DON'T KNOW IF THESE SUPPLIES ARE GOING TO BE ENOUGH, MERA.
IT DEPENDS ON HOW MANY PEOPLE SURIVIVED, I SUPPOSE, ESTHER.
OH MY GOD, THAT SOUNDED SO COLD.
ESTHER, MY HOME WAS DESTROYED, MY SUBJECTS--MY *FRIENDS*--SLAUGHTERED, AND I JUST...
IT'S OKAY, MERA. NOBODY'S WATCHING TO GRADE HOW YOU REACT.
BUT SHOULDN'T I *FEEL* WORSE? I MEAN, HOW CAN I JUST GO ON LIKE THIS? HOW CAN IT BE SO EASY FOR ME TO FUNCTON?
BECAUSE IF YOU DIDN'T, THEN YOU WOULDN'T BE ABLE TO HELP THESE PEOPLE WHEN THEY NEED IT THE MOST.
AND YOU *ARE* THEIR QUEEN, AFTER ALL.
ANYWAY, YOU CAN ALWAYS BAWL YOUR EYES OUT LATER.
THANK YOU. THANK YOU, ESTHER.
ALL RIGHT, LET'S GET BACK TO WORK.

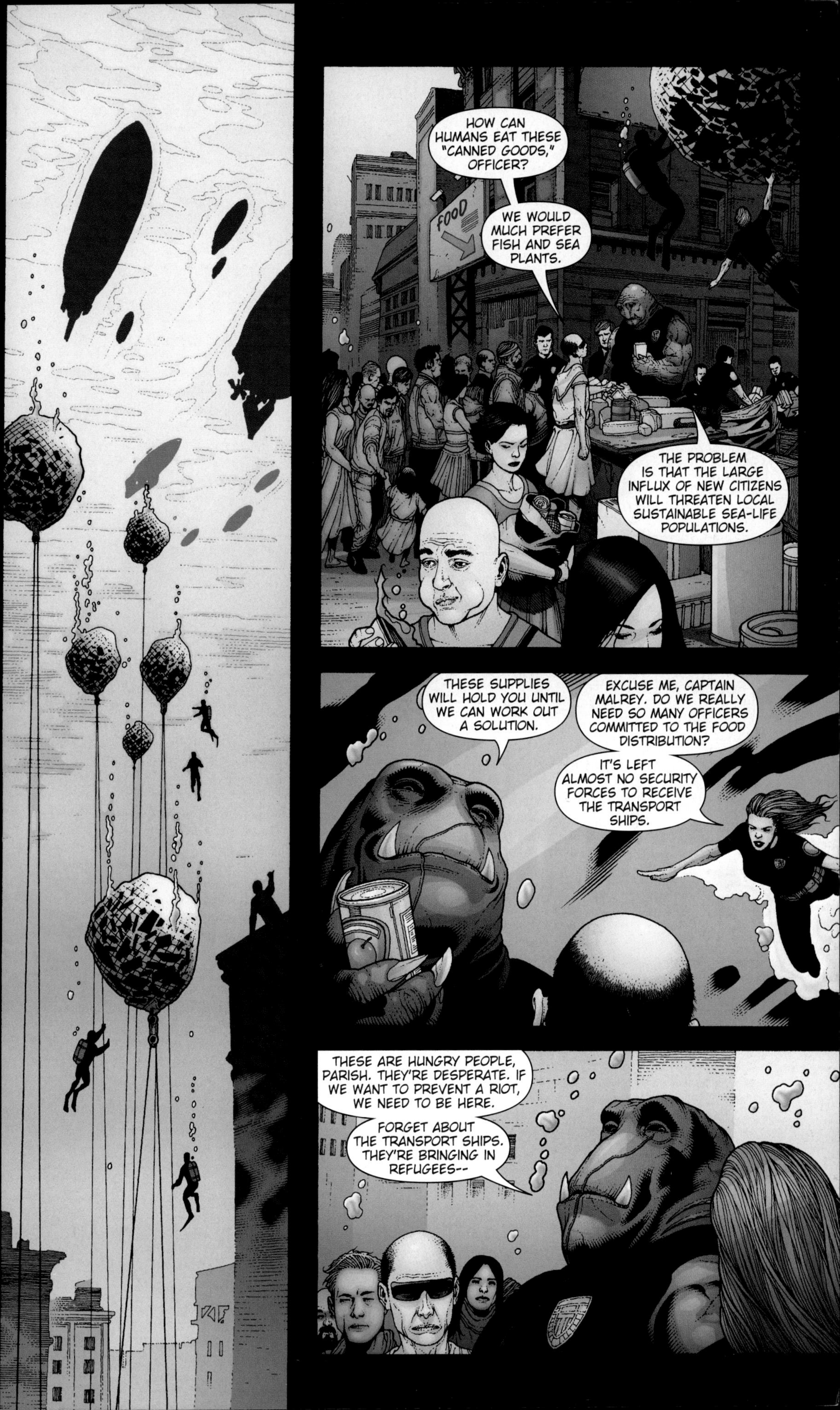

HOW CAN HUMANS EAT THESE "CANNED GOODS," OFFICER?
WE WOULD MUCH PREFER FISH AND SEA PLANTS.
FOOD
THE PROBLEM IS THAT THE LARGE INFLUX OF NEW CITIZENS WILL THREATEN LOCAL SUSTAINABLE SEA-LIFE POPULATIONS.
THESE SUPPLIES WILL HOLD YOU UNTIL WE CAN WORK OUT A SOLUTION.
EXCUSE ME, CAPTAIN MALREY. DO WE REALLY NEED SO MANY OFFICERS COMMITTED TO THE FOOD DISTRIBUTION?
IT'S LEFT ALMOST NO SECURITY FORCES TO RECEIVE THE TRANSPORT SHIPS.
THESE ARE HUNGRY PEOPLE, PARISH. THEY'RE DESPERATE. IF WE WANT TO PREVENT A RIOT, WE NEED TO BE HERE.
FORGET ABOUT THE TRANSPORT SHIPS. THEY'RE BRINGING IN REFUGEES--

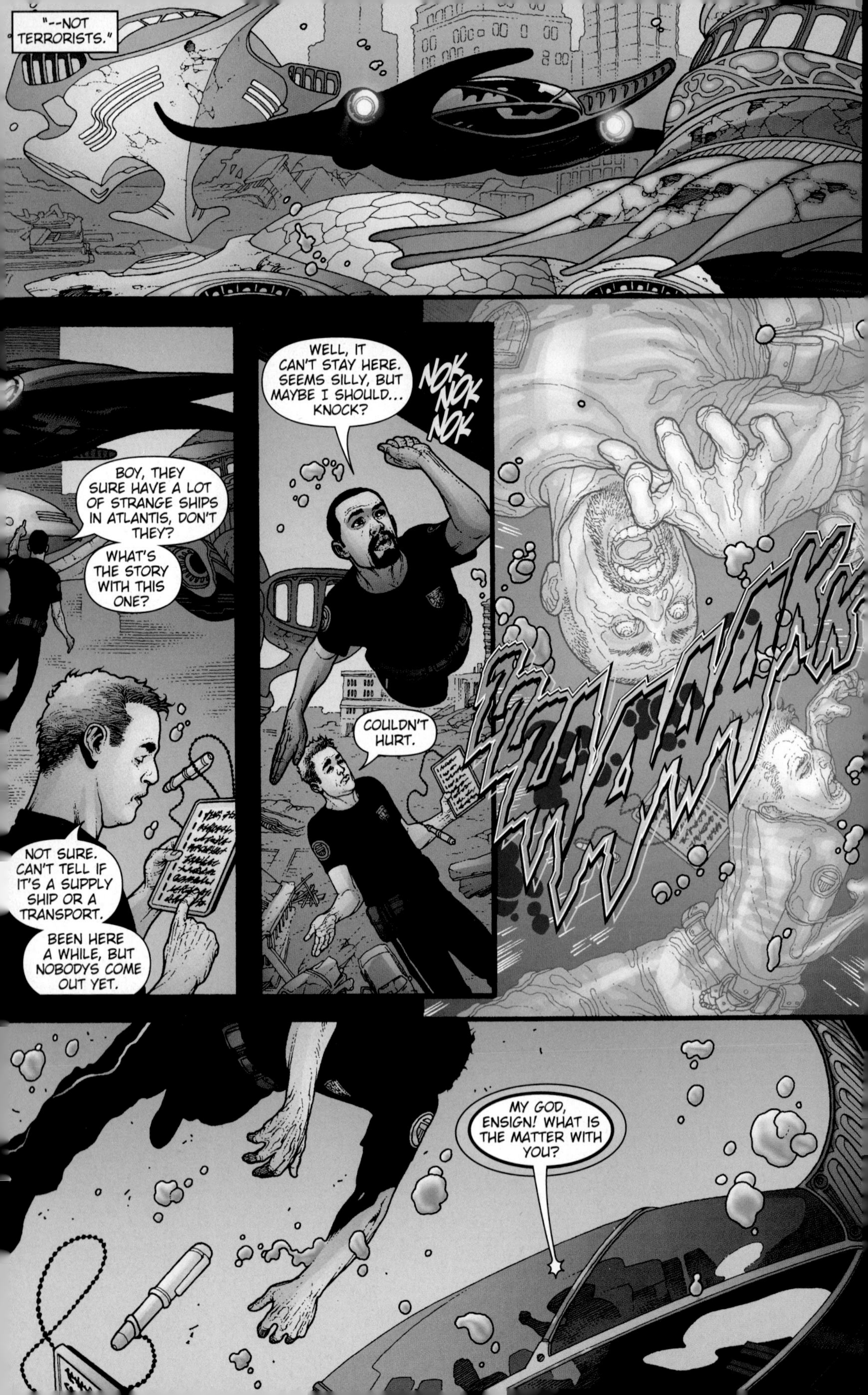
"--NOT TERRORISTS."
BOY, THEY SURE HAVE A LOT OF STRANGE SHIPS IN ATLANTIS, DON'T THEY?
WHAT'S THE STORY WITH THIS ONE?
NOT SURE. CAN'T TELL IF IT'S A SUPPLY SHIP OR A TRANSPORT.
BEEN HERE A WHILE, BUT NOBODYS COME OUT YET.
WELL, IT CAN'T STAY HERE. SEEMS SILLY, BUT MAYBE I SHOULD... KNOCK?
NOK NOK NOK
COULDN'T HURT.
MY GOD, ENSIGN! WHAT IS THE MATTER WITH YOU?

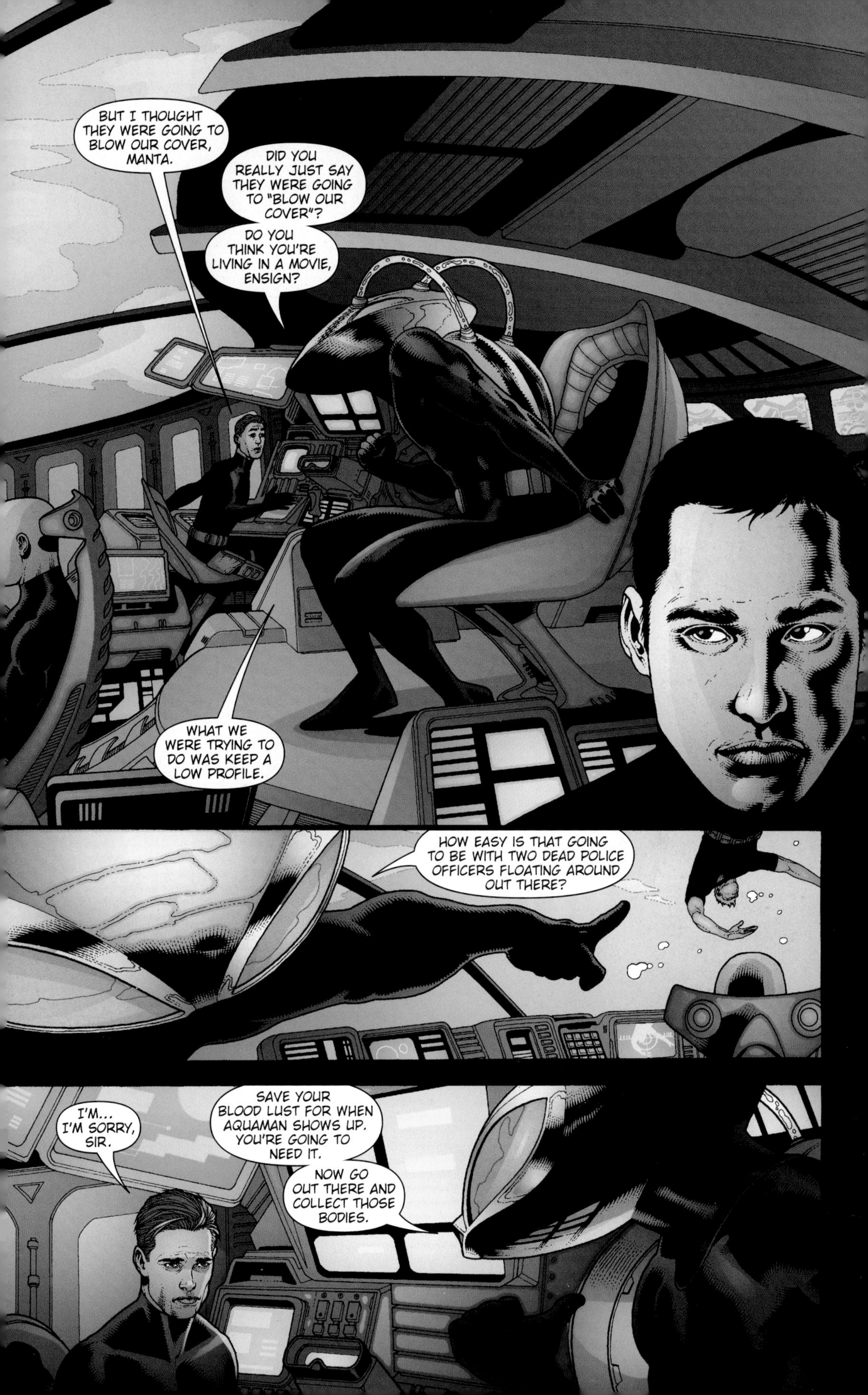
BUT I THOUGHT THEY WERE GOING TO BLOW OUR COVER, MANTA.
DID YOU REALLY JUST SAY THEY WERE GOING TO "BLOW OUR COVER"?
DO YOU THINK YOU'RE LIVING IN A MOVIE, ENSIGN?
WHAT WE WERE TRYING TO DO WAS KEEP A LOW PROFILE.
HOW EASY IS THAT GOING TO BE WITH TWO DEAD POLICE OFFICERS FLOATING AROUND OUT THERE?
I'M... I'M SORRY, SIR.
SAVE YOUR BLOOD LUST FOR WHEN AQUAMAN SHOWS UP. YOU'RE GOING TO NEED IT.
NOW GO OUT THERE AND COLLECT THOSE BODIES.

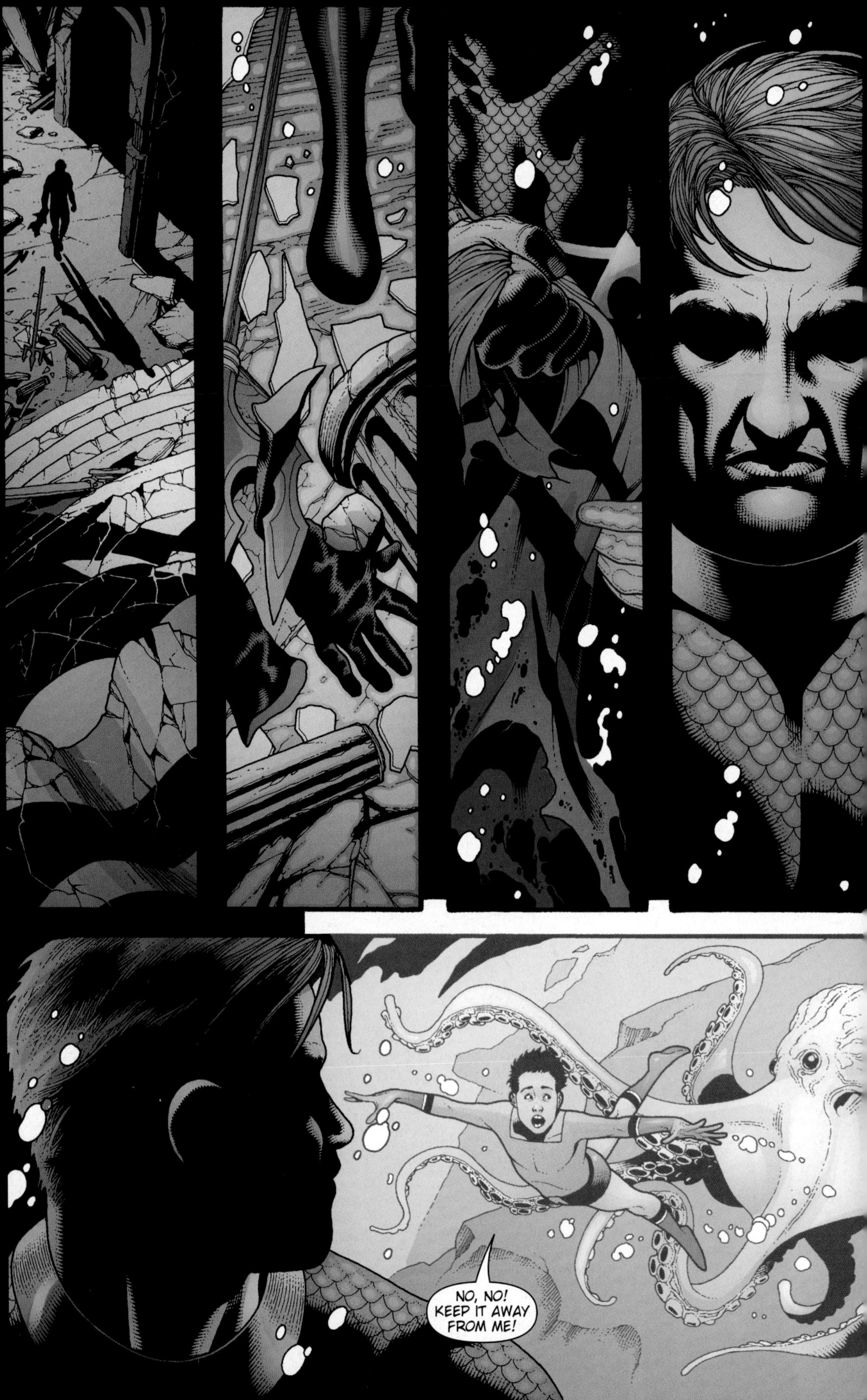
NO, NO! KEEP IT AWAY FROM ME!

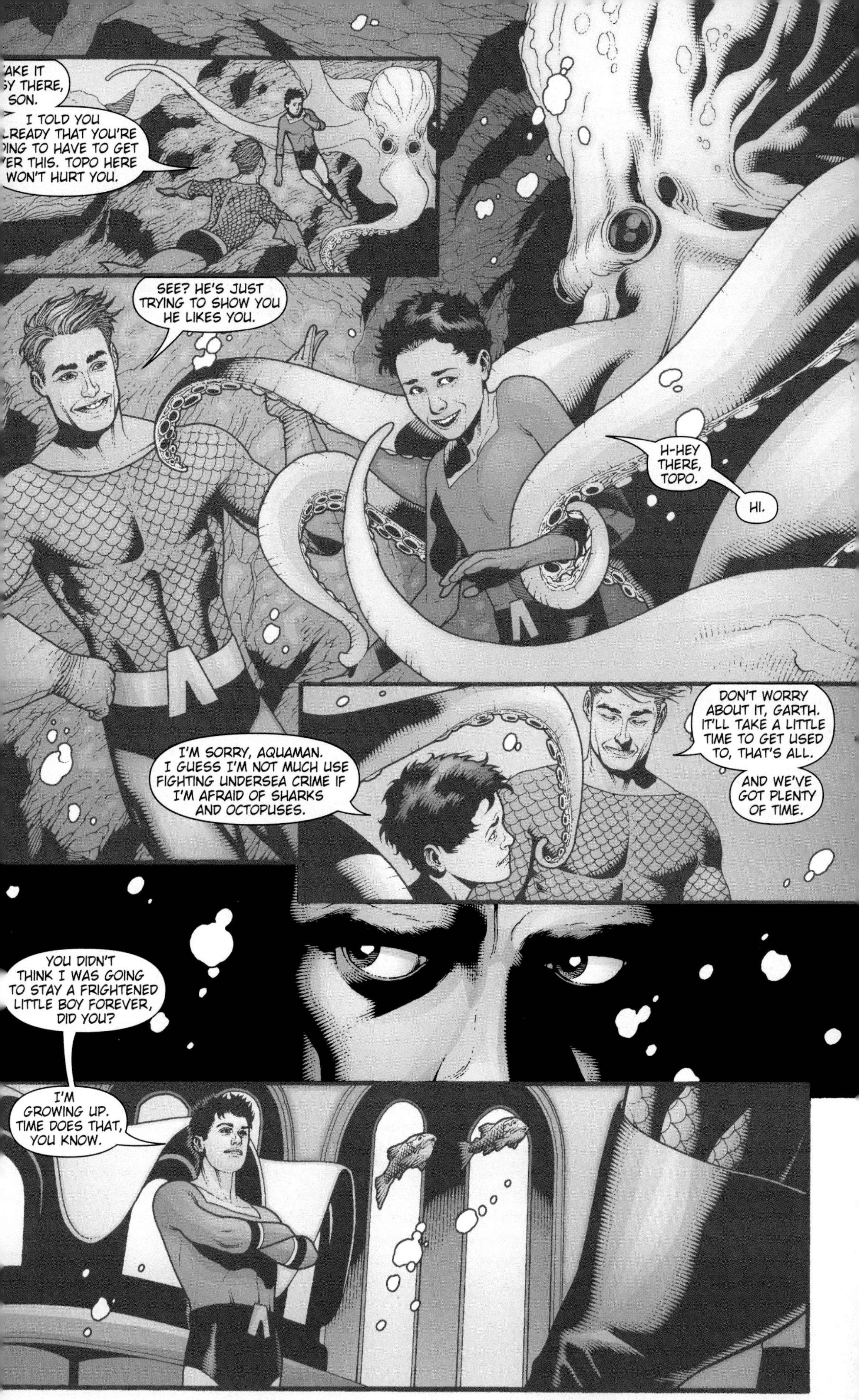
AKE IT SY THERE, SON.
I TOLD YOU LREADY THAT YOU'RE DING TO HAVE TO GET ER THIS. TOPO HERE WON'T HURT YOU.
SEE? HE'S JUST TRYING TO SHOW YOU HE LIKES YOU.
H-HEY THERE, TOPO.
HI.
I'M SORRY, AQUAMAN. I GUESS I'M NOT MUCH USE FIGHTING UNDERSEA CRIME IF I'M AFRAID OF SHARKS AND OCTOPUSES.
DON'T WORRY ABOUT IT, GARTH. IT'LL TAKE A LITTLE TIME TO GET USED TO, THAT'S ALL.
AND WE'VE GOT PLENTY OF TIME.
YOU DIDN'T THINK I WAS GOING TO STAY A FRIGHTENED LITTLE BOY FOREVER, DID YOU?
I'M GROWING UP. TIME DOES THAT, YOU KNOW.

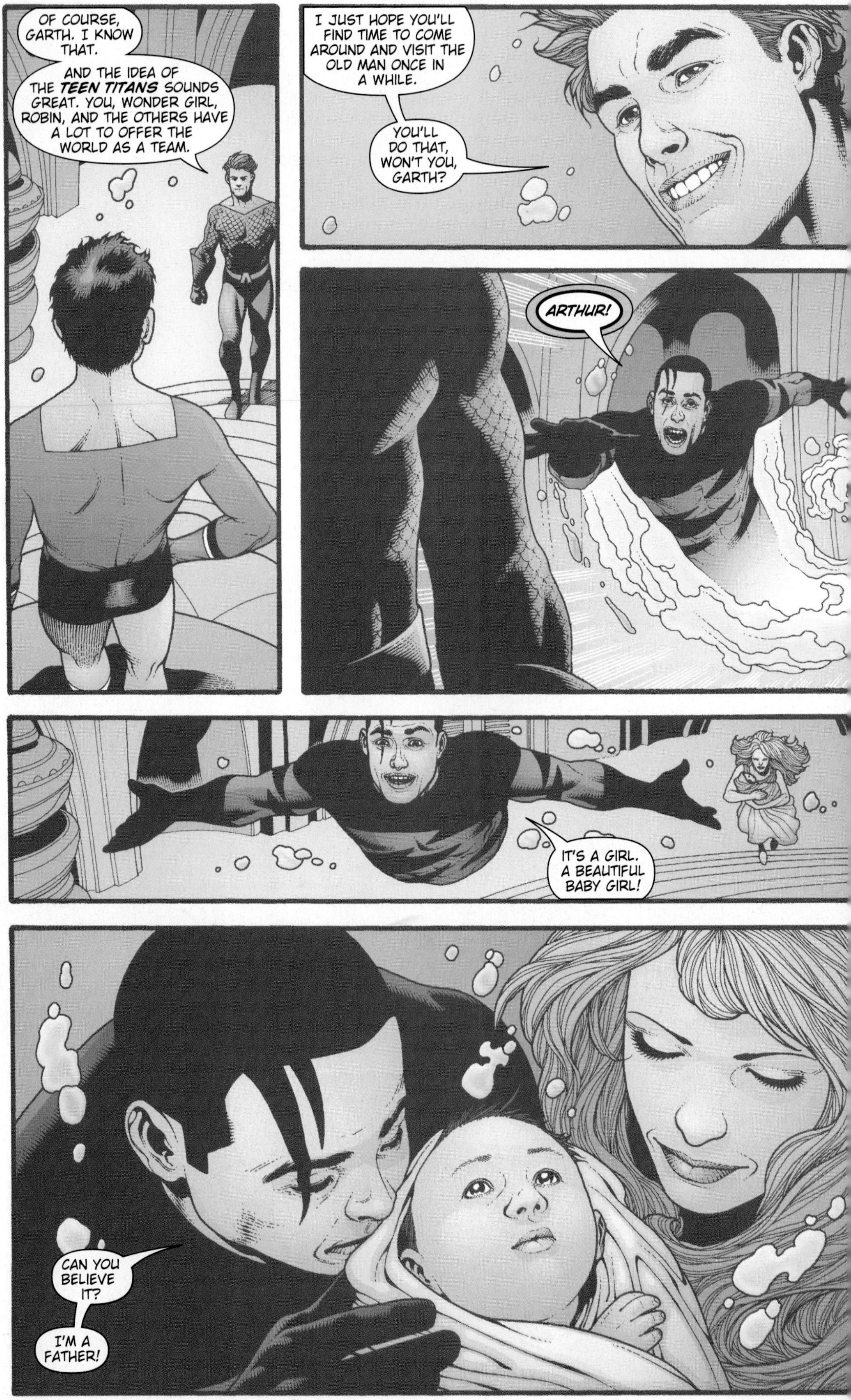
OF COURSE, GARTH. I KNOW THAT.
AND THE IDEA OF THE TEEN TITANS SOUNDS GREAT. YOU, WONDER GIRL, ROBIN, AND THE OTHERS HAVE A LOT TO OFFER THE WORLD AS A TEAM.
I JUST HOPE YOU'LL FIND TIME TO COME AROUND AND VISIT THE OLD MAN ONCE IN A WHILE.
YOU'LL DO THAT, WON'T YOU, GARTH?
ARTHUR!
IT'S A GIRL. A BEAUTIFUL BABY GIRL!
CAN YOU BELIEVE IT?
I'M A FATHER!

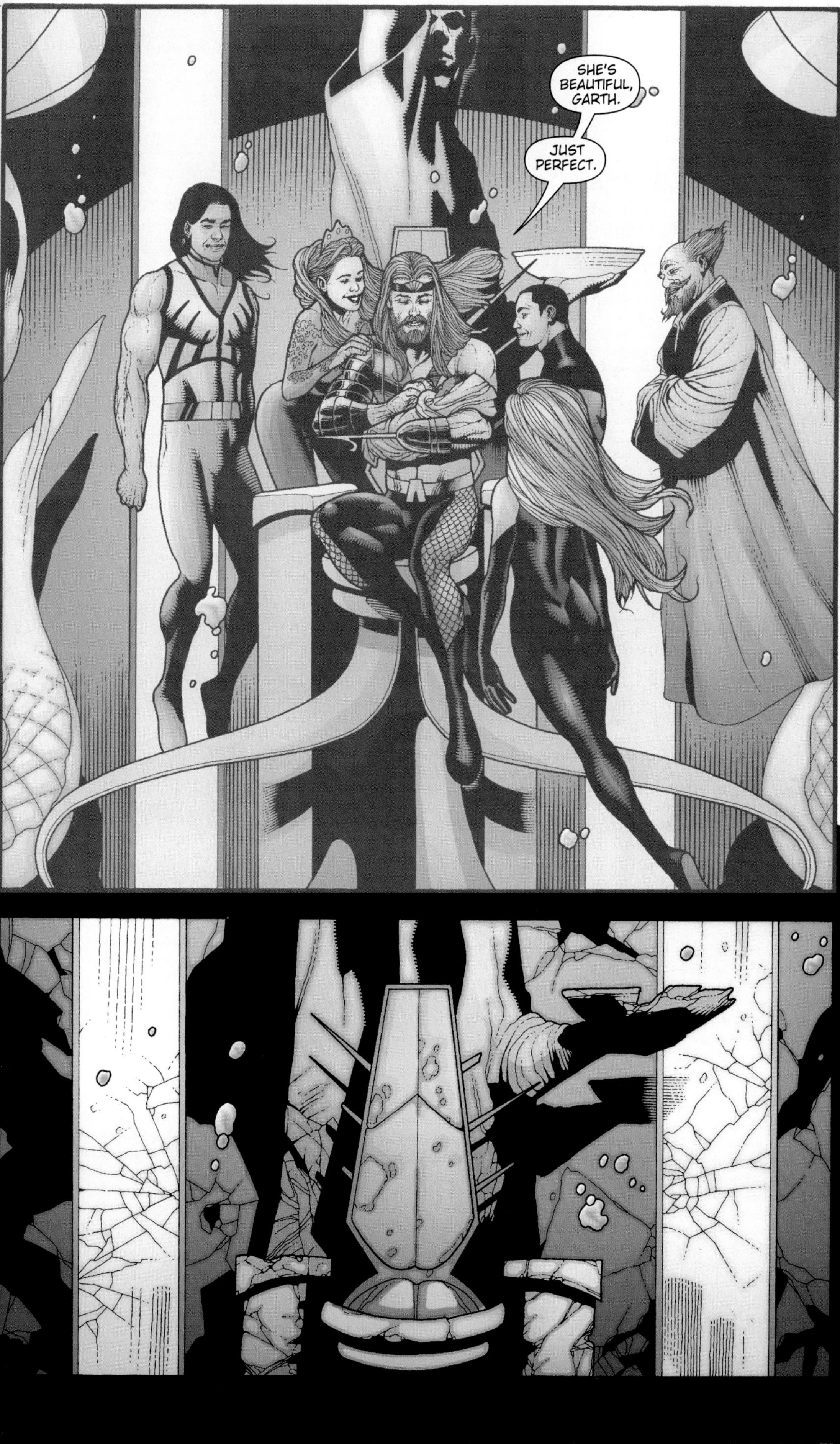
SHE'S BEAUTIFUL, GARTH.
JUST PERFECT.

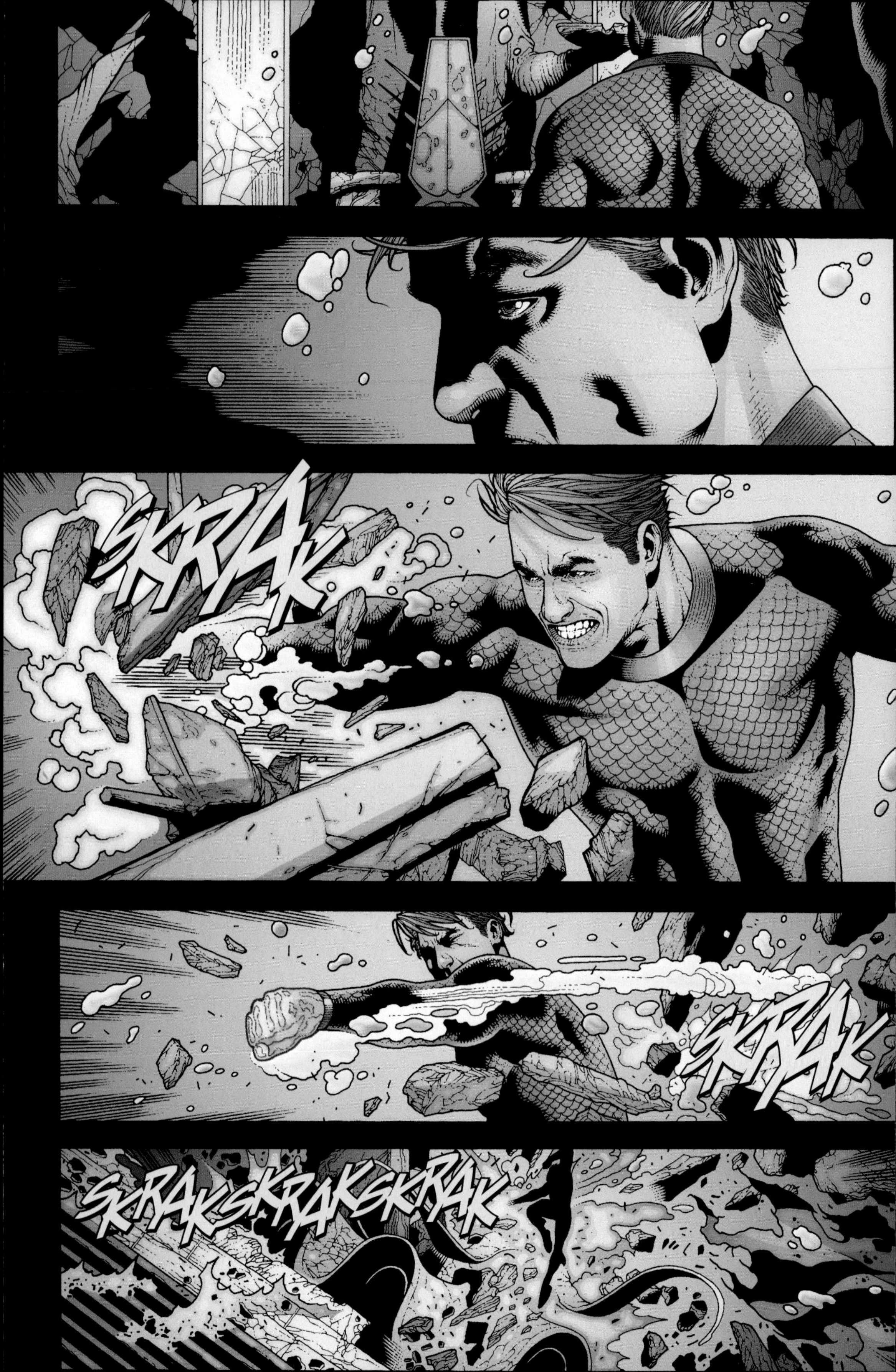
SKRAK
SKRAK
SKRAKSKRAKSKRAK

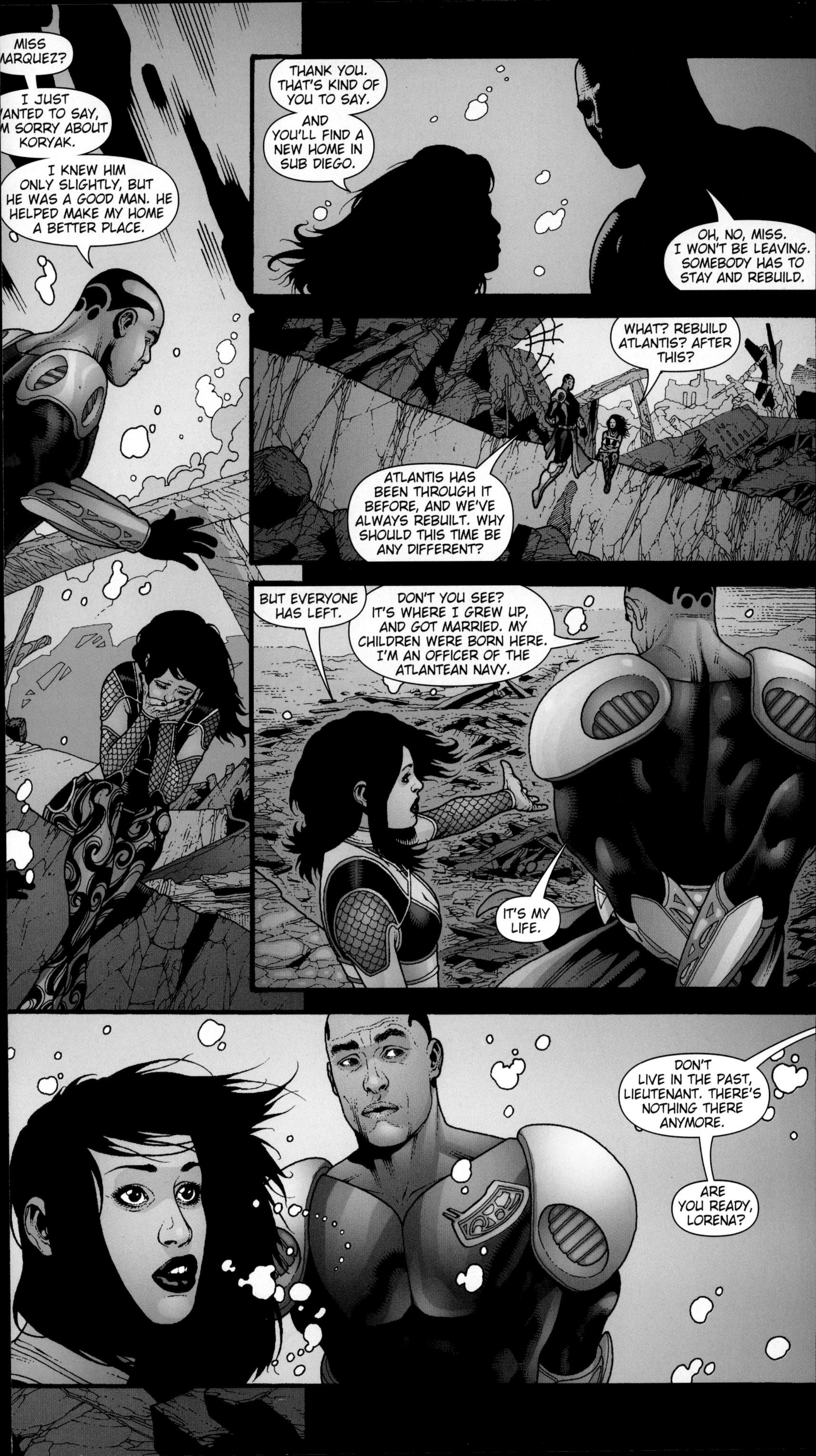
MISS MARQUEZ?
I JUST WANTED TO SAY, I'M SORRY ABOUT KORYAK.
I KNEW HIM ONLY SLIGHTLY, BUT HE WAS A GOOD MAN. HE HELPED MAKE MY HOME A BETTER PLACE.
THANK YOU. THAT'S KIND OF YOU TO SAY.
AND YOU'LL FIND A NEW HOME IN SUB DIEGO.
OH, NO, MISS. I WON'T BE LEAVING. SOMEBODY HAS TO STAY AND REBUILD.
WHAT? REBUILD ATLANTIS? AFTER THIS?
ATLANTIS HAS BEEN THROUGH IT BEFORE, AND WE'VE ALWAYS REBUILT. WHY SHOULD THIS TIME BE ANY DIFFERENT?
BUT EVERYONE HAS LEFT.
DON'T YOU SEE? IT'S WHERE I GREW UP, AND GOT MARRIED. MY CHILDREN WERE BORN HERE. I'M AN OFFICER OF THE ATLANTEAN NAVY.
IT'S MY LIFE.
DON'T LIVE IN THE PAST, LIEUTENANT. THERE'S NOTHING THERE ANYMORE.
ARE YOU READY, LORENA?

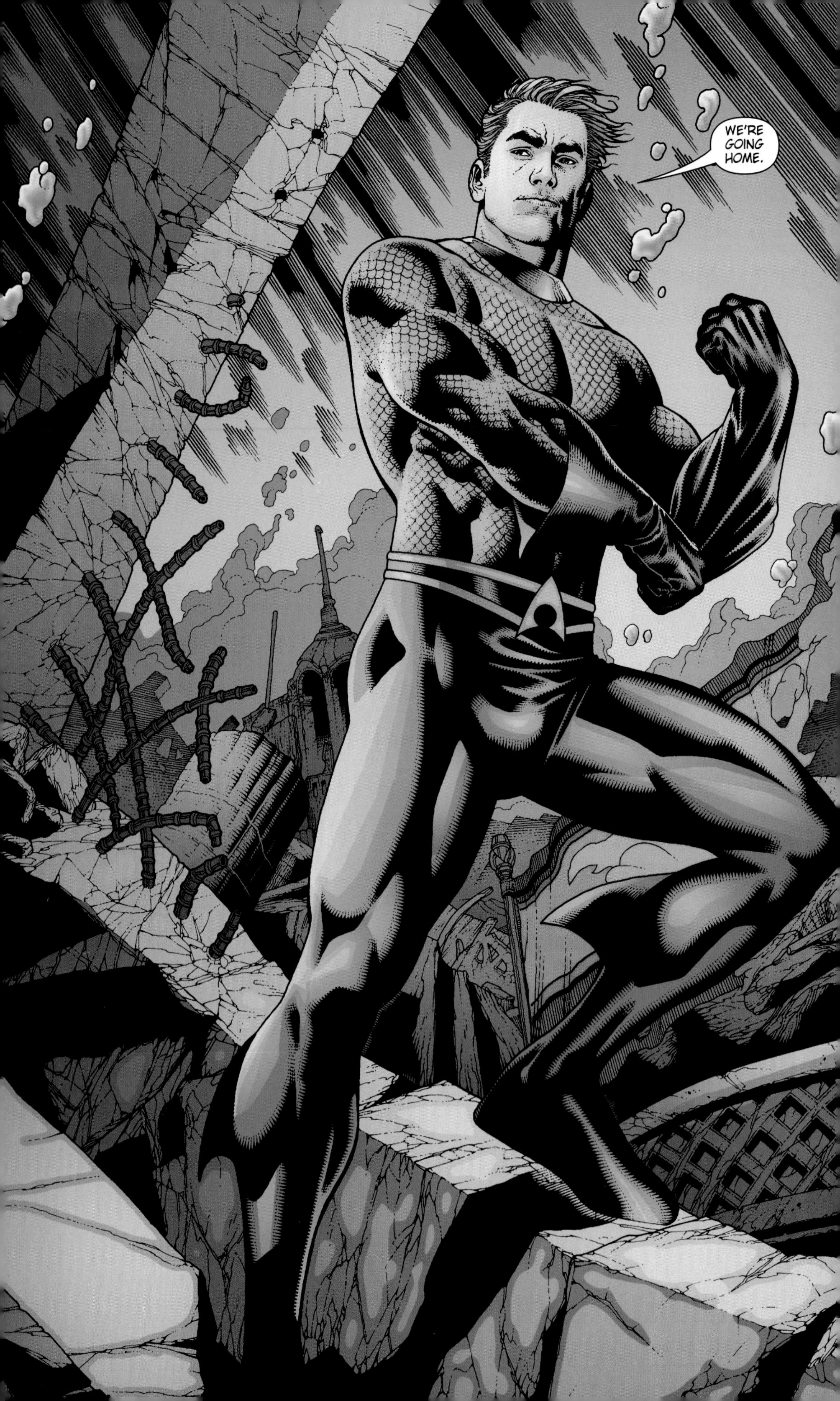
WE'RE GOING HOME.

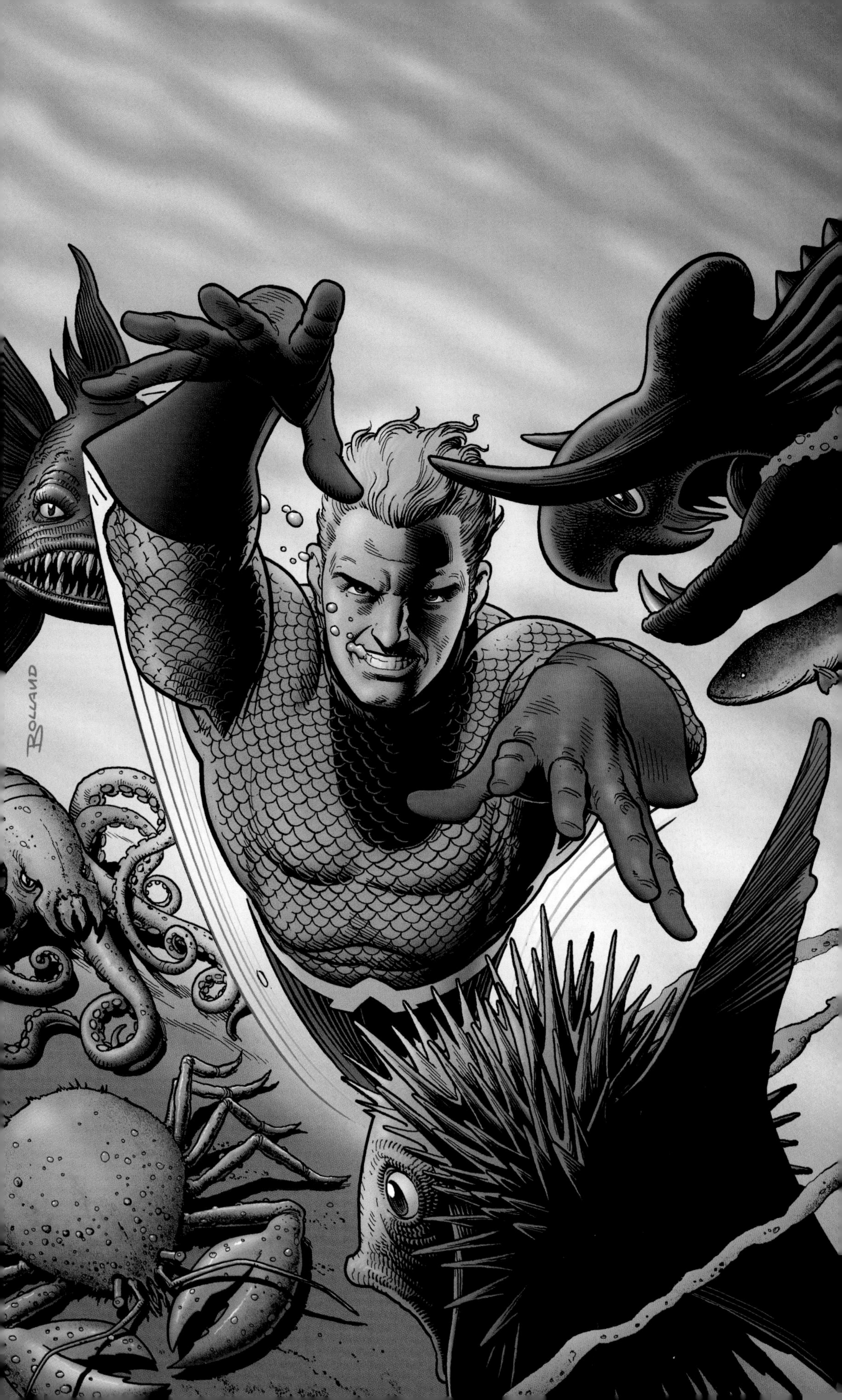
BOLLAND

THE END HAS NO END

JOHN ARCUDI
Writer

FREDDIE WILLIAMS II
Artist

NATHAN EYRING
Colorist

JARED K. FLETCHER
Letterer

BRIAN BOLLAND
Cover

SUB DIEGO

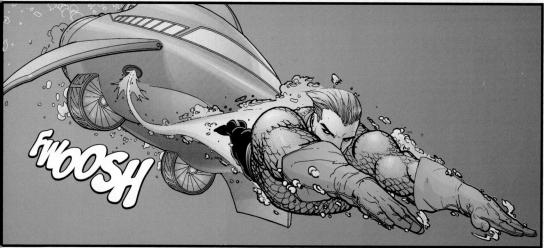

FWOOSH

ISN'T HE COMING INTO THE CITY WITH US?

NOT RIGHT AWAY.

WHY? WHERE IS HE GOING?

HE DIDN'T SAY.

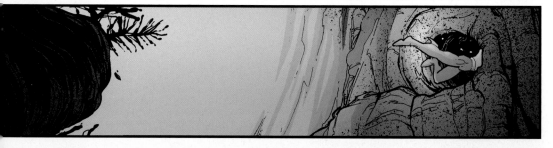

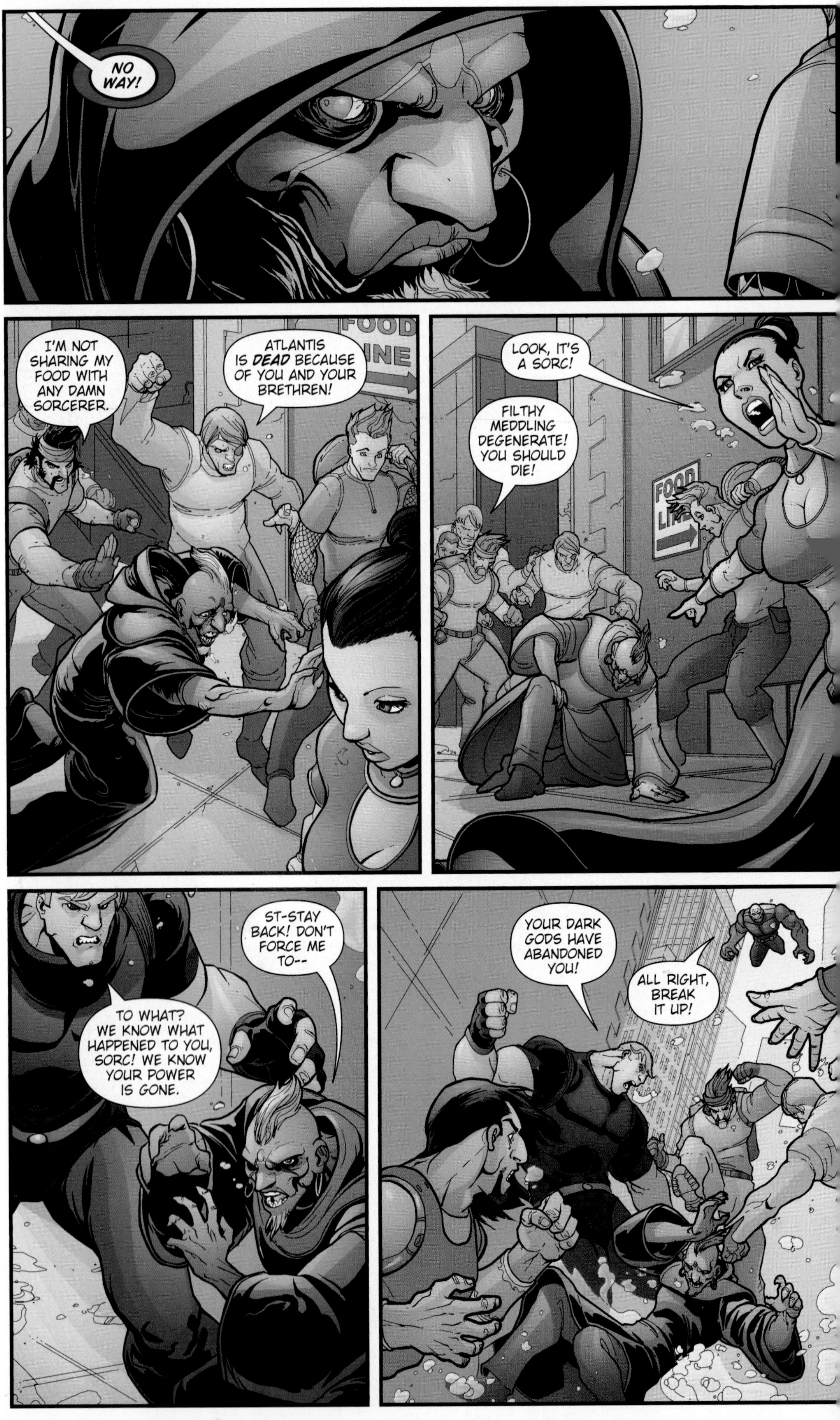
NO WAY!
I'M NOT SHARING MY FOOD WITH ANY DAMN SORCERER.
ATLANTIS IS **DEAD** BECAUSE OF YOU AND YOUR BRETHREN!
FOOD LINE
LOOK, IT'S A SORC!
FILTHY MEDDLING DEGENERATE! YOU SHOULD DIE!
FOOD LINE
ST-STAY BACK! DON'T FORCE ME TO--
TO WHAT? WE KNOW WHAT HAPPENED TO YOU, SORC! WE KNOW YOUR POWER IS GONE.
YOUR DARK GODS HAVE ABANDONED YOU!
ALL RIGHT, BREAK IT UP!

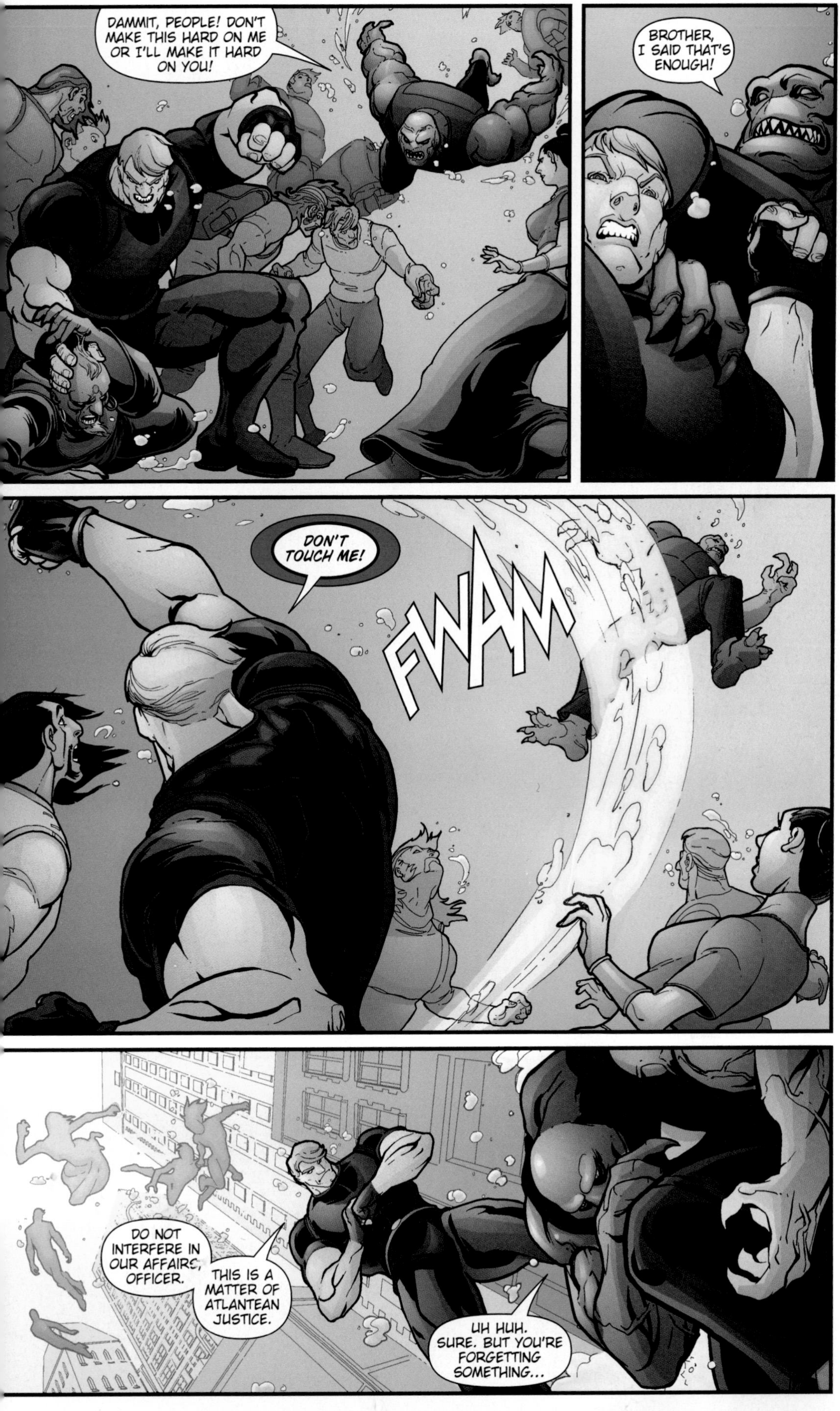
DAMMIT, PEOPLE! DON'T MAKE THIS HARD ON ME OR I'LL MAKE IT HARD ON YOU!
BROTHER, I SAID THAT'S ENOUGH!
DON'T TOUCH ME!
FWAM
DO NOT INTERFERE IN OUR AFFAIRS, OFFICER.
THIS IS A MATTER OF ATLANTEAN JUSTICE.
UH HUH. SURE. BUT YOU'RE FORGETTING SOMETHING...

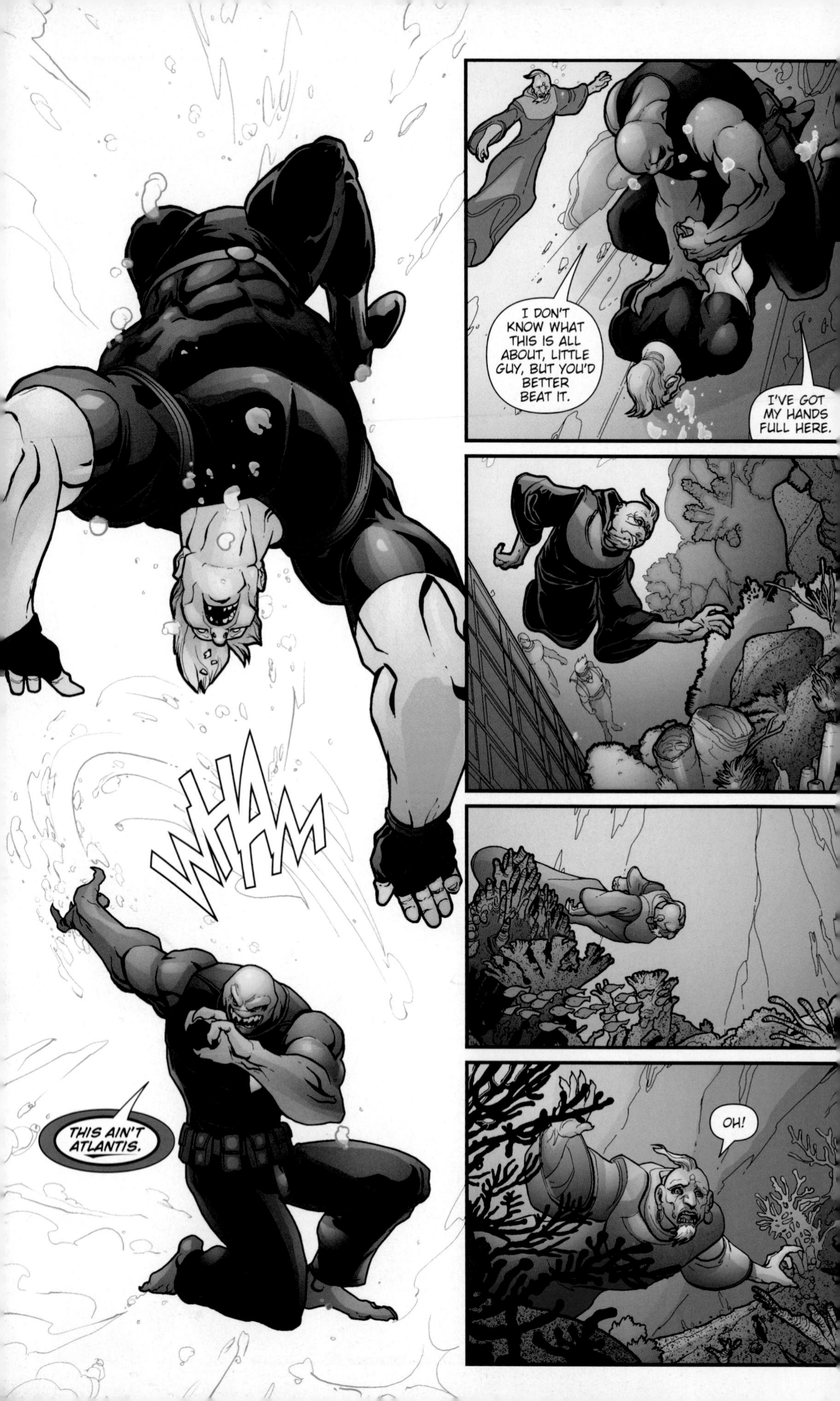
WHAM
THIS AIN'T ATLANTIS.
I DON'T KNOW WHAT THIS IS ALL ABOUT, LITTLE GUY, BUT YOU'D BETTER BEAT IT.
I'VE GOT MY HANDS FULL HERE.
OH!

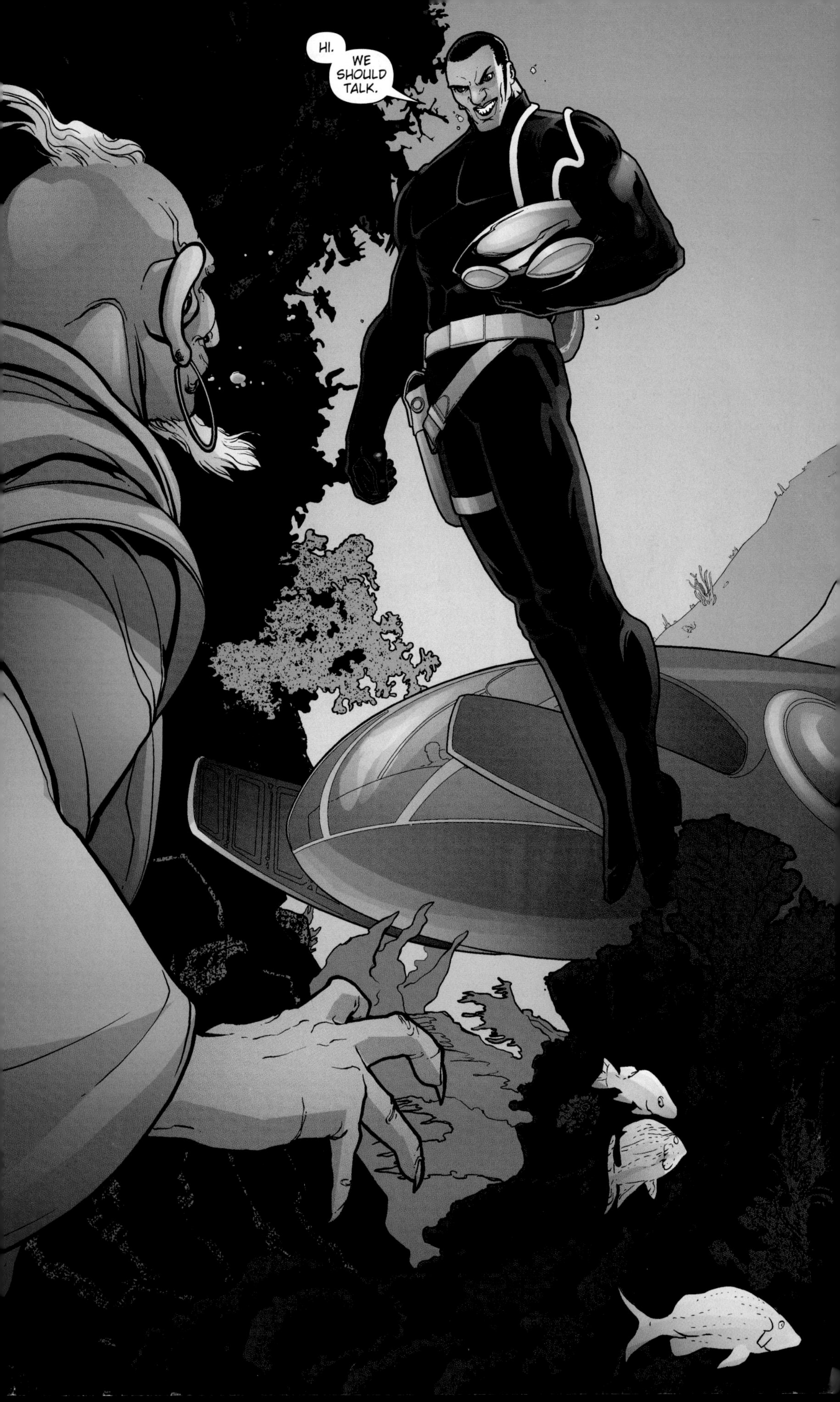
HI.
WE SHOULD TALK.

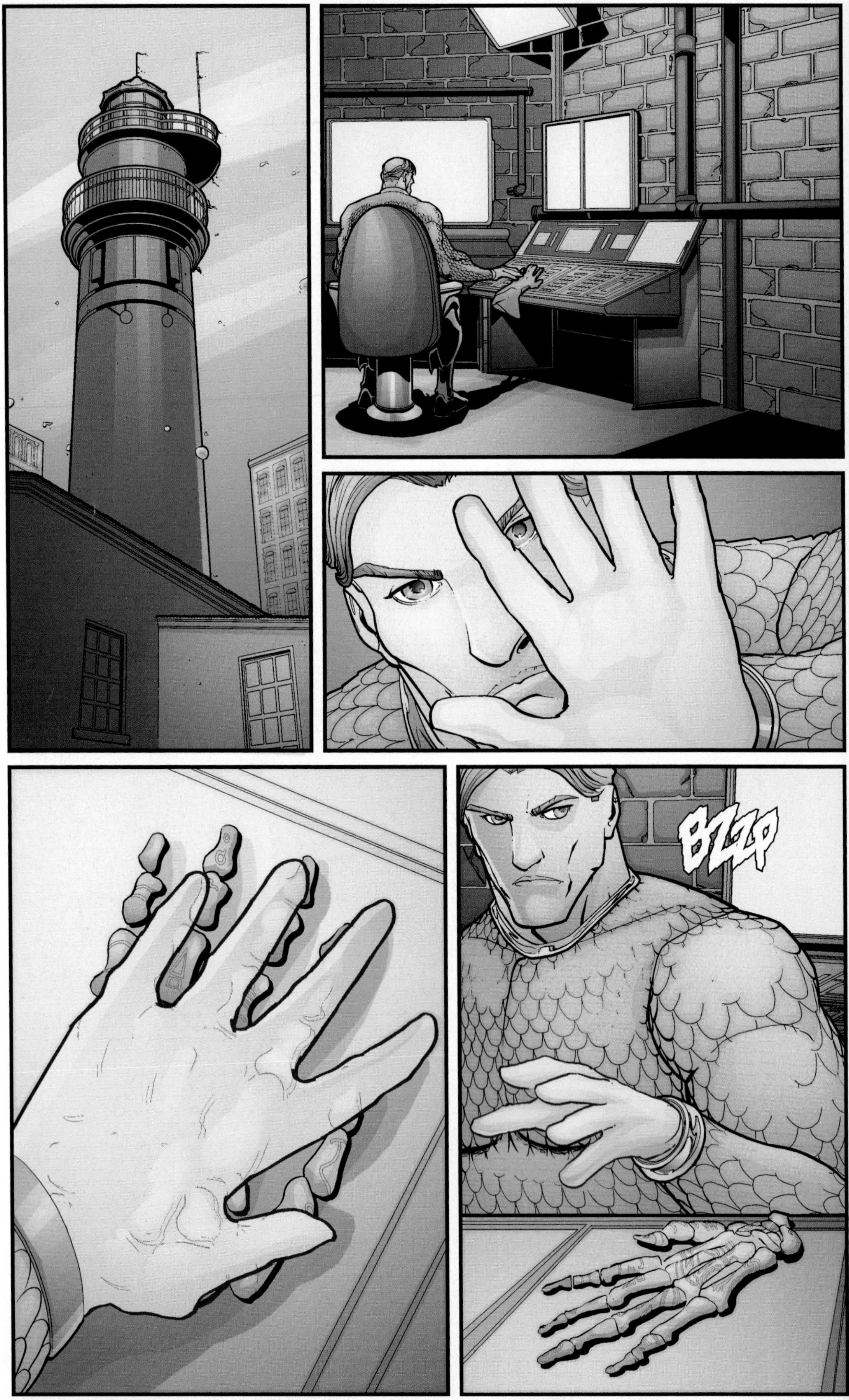
BZZP

HEY, ARTHUR. THOUGHT YOU'D BE HERE.

WHERE DID YOU SWIM OFF TO ANYWAY?

THERE WAS JUST SOMETHING I HAD TO PICK UP. WHAT'S ON YOUR MIND, LORENA?

IT'S NOT ME, REALLY. THERE'S BEEN TROUBLE DOWNTOWN. HAS TO DO WITH YOUR ATLANTEAN PALS.

COPS KINDA HAVE THEIR HANDS FULL, I THINK. THEY CAME TO GET ME... WELL, YOU.

OKAY, I'LL BE RIGHT OUT.

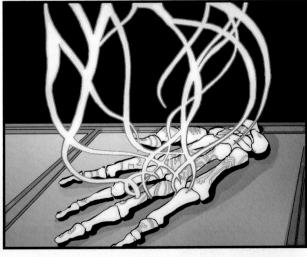

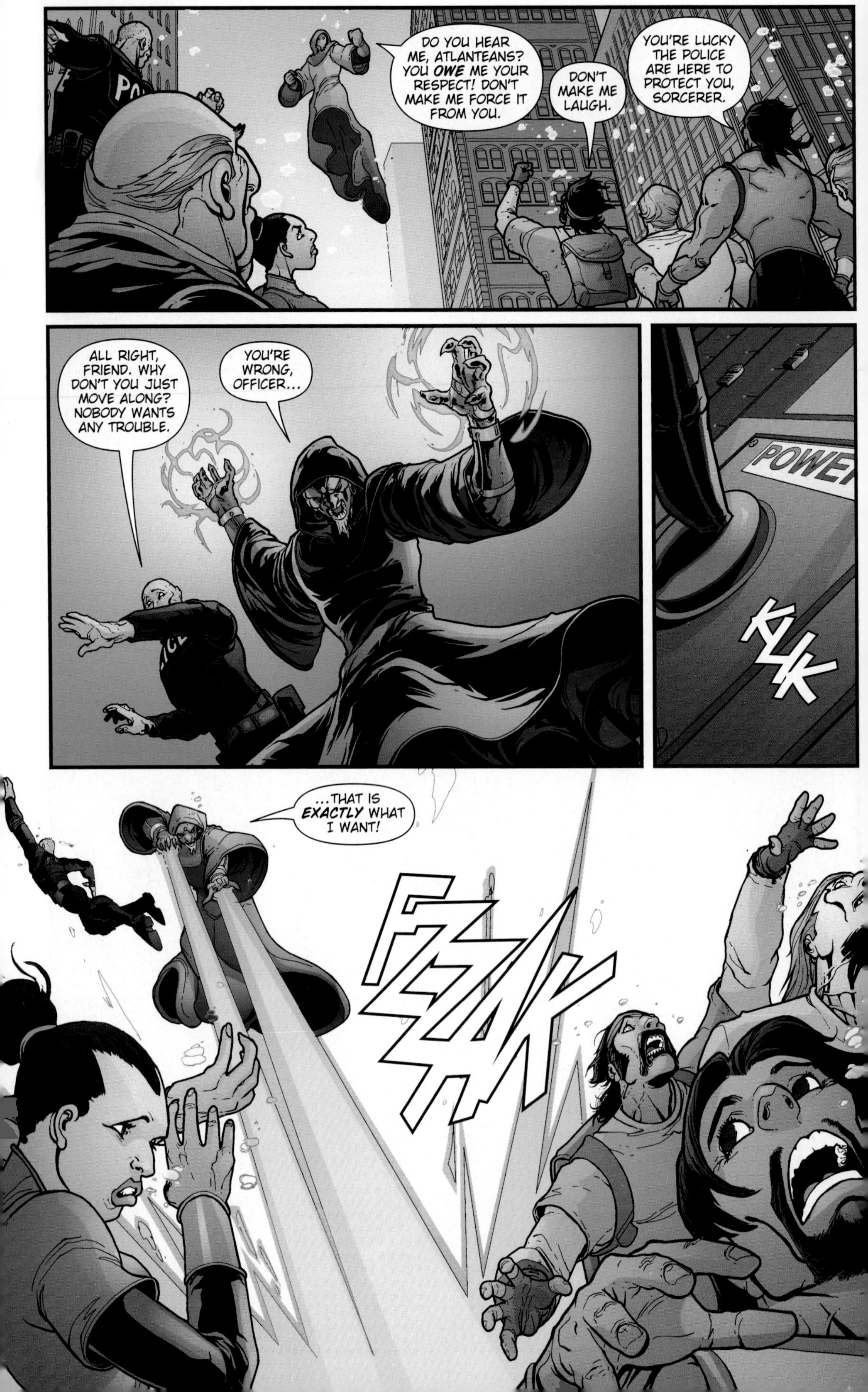
DO YOU HEAR ME, ATLANTEANS? YOU OWE ME YOUR RESPECT! DON'T MAKE ME FORCE IT FROM YOU.
DON'T MAKE ME LAUGH.
YOU'RE LUCKY THE POLICE ARE HERE TO PROTECT YOU, SORCERER.
ALL RIGHT, FRIEND. WHY DON'T YOU JUST MOVE ALONG? NOBODY WANTS ANY TROUBLE.
YOU'RE WRONG, OFFICER...
POWER
KLIK
...THAT IS EXACTLY WHAT I WANT!
FZZAK

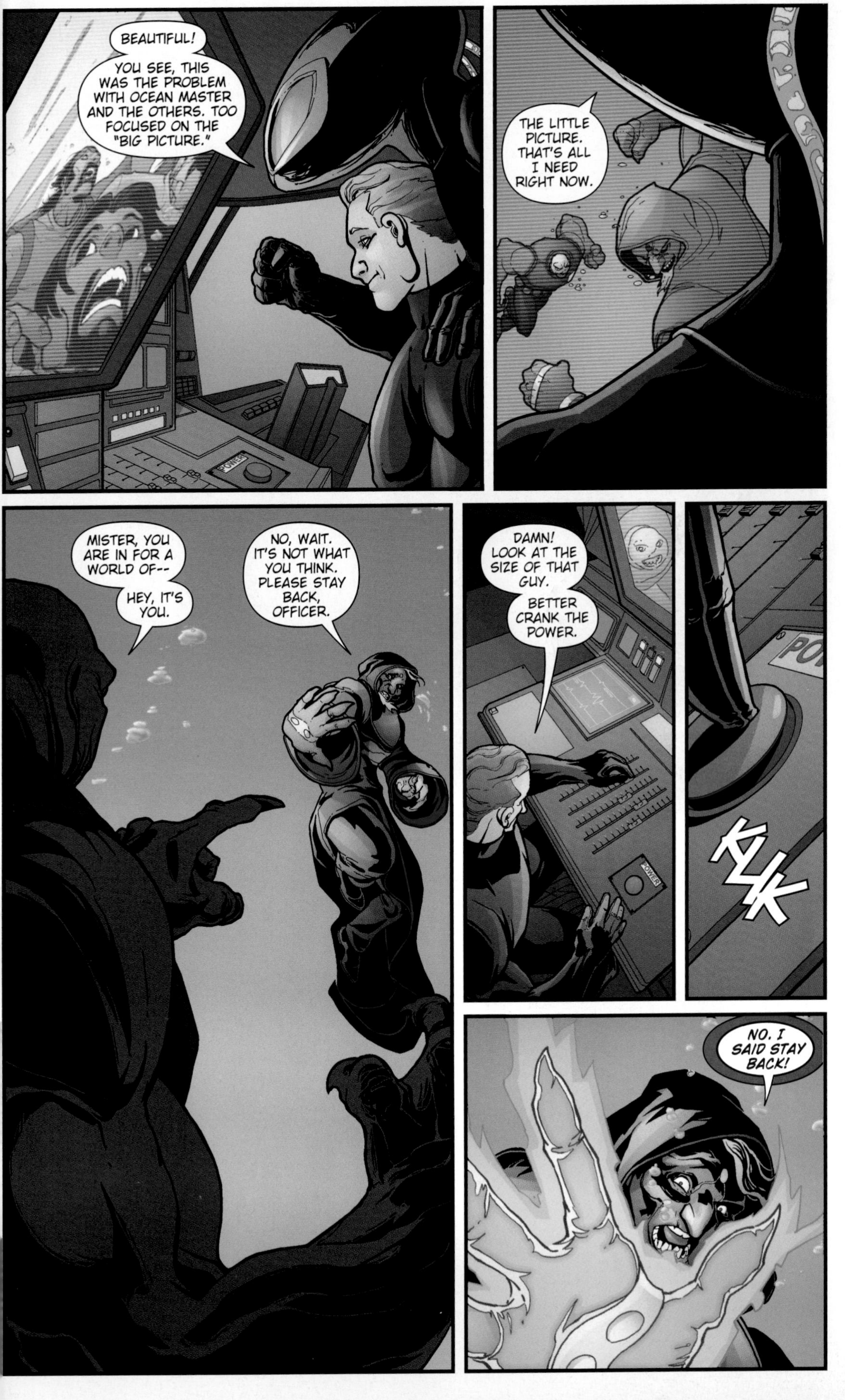
BEAUTIFUL!
YOU SEE, THIS WAS THE PROBLEM WITH OCEAN MASTER AND THE OTHERS. TOO FOCUSED ON THE "BIG PICTURE."
POWER
THE LITTLE PICTURE. THAT'S ALL I NEED RIGHT NOW.
MISTER, YOU ARE IN FOR A WORLD OF--
HEY, IT'S YOU.
NO, WAIT. IT'S NOT WHAT YOU THINK. PLEASE STAY BACK, OFFICER.
DAMN! LOOK AT THE SIZE OF THAT GUY.
BETTER CRANK THE POWER.
POWER
KLIK
NO. I SAID STAY BACK!

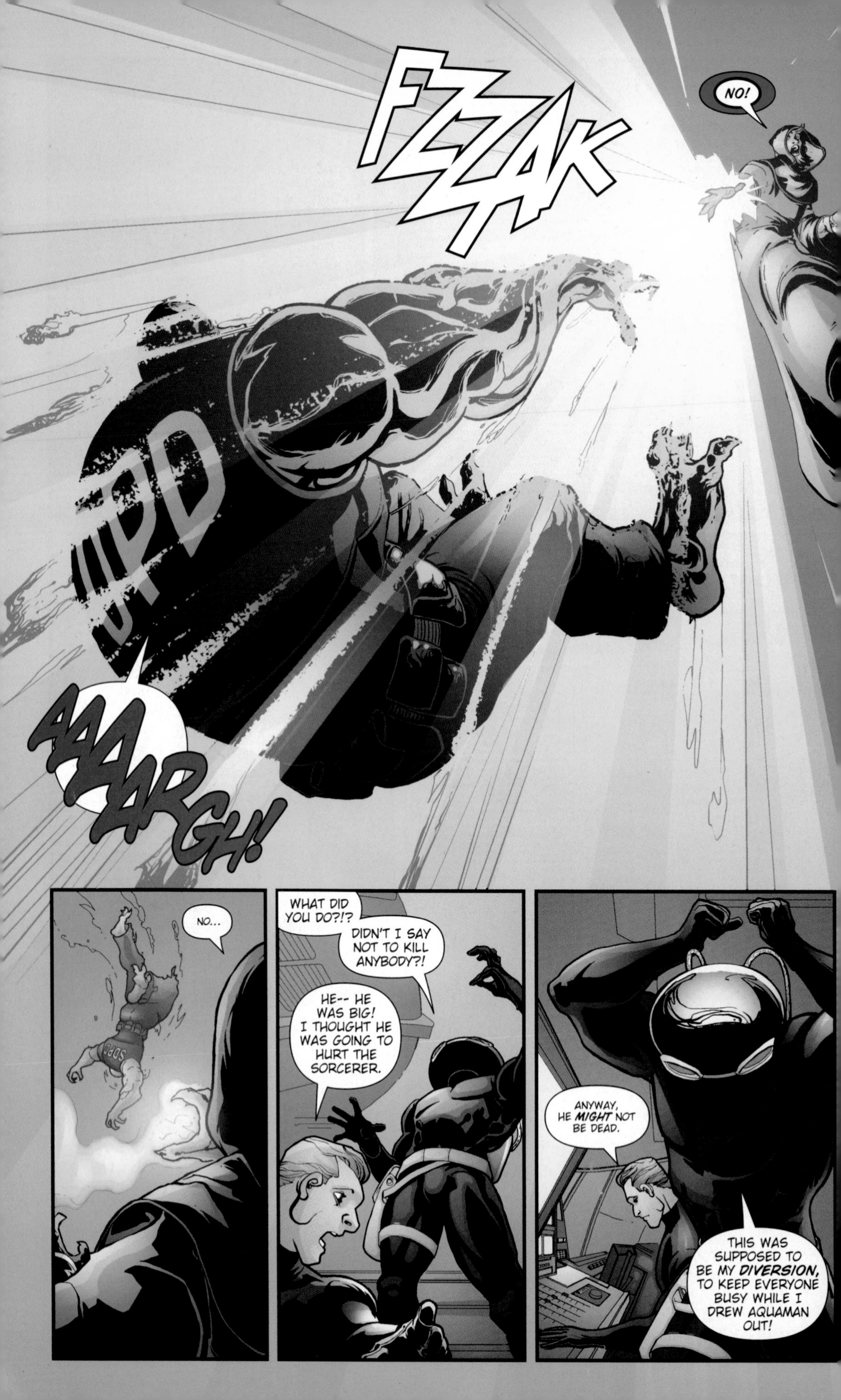
FZZAK
NO!
AAAARGH!
NO...
WHAT DID YOU DO?!?
DIDN'T I SAY NOT TO KILL ANYBODY?!
HE-- HE WAS BIG! I THOUGHT HE WAS GOING TO HURT THE SORCERER.
ANYWAY, HE MIGHT NOT BE DEAD.
THIS WAS SUPPOSED TO BE MY DIVERSION, TO KEEP EVERYONE BUSY WHILE I DREW AQUAMAN OUT!

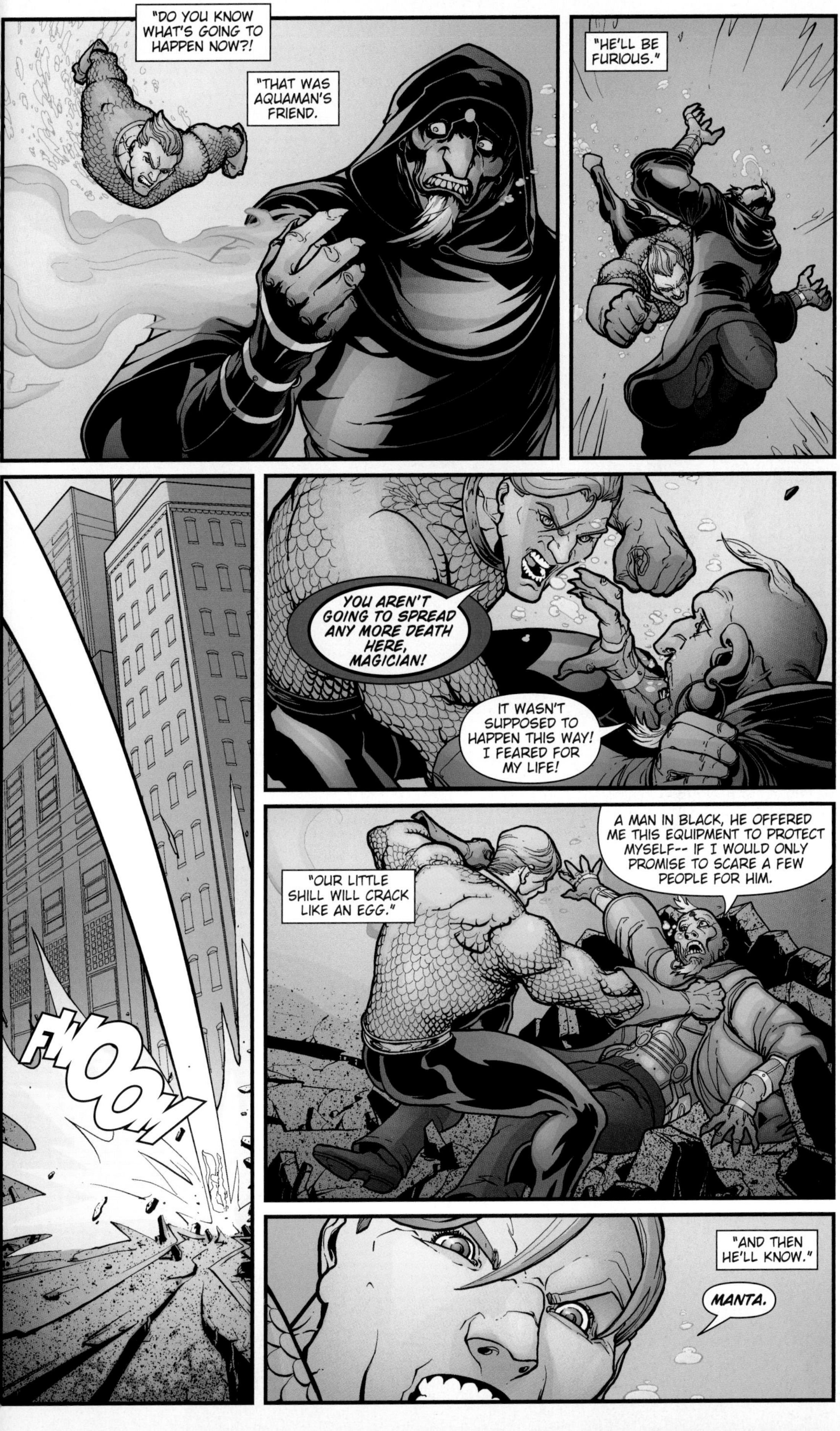
"DO YOU KNOW WHAT'S GOING TO HAPPEN NOW?!
"THAT WAS AQUAMAN'S FRIEND.
"HE'LL BE FURIOUS."
YOU AREN'T GOING TO SPREAD ANY MORE DEATH HERE, MAGICIAN!
IT WASN'T SUPPOSED TO HAPPEN THIS WAY! I FEARED FOR MY LIFE!
FWOOM
"OUR LITTLE SHILL WILL CRACK LIKE AN EGG."
A MAN IN BLACK, HE OFFERED ME THIS EQUIPMENT TO PROTECT MYSELF-- IF I WOULD ONLY PROMISE TO SCARE A FEW PEOPLE FOR HIM.
"AND THEN HE'LL KNOW."
MANTA.

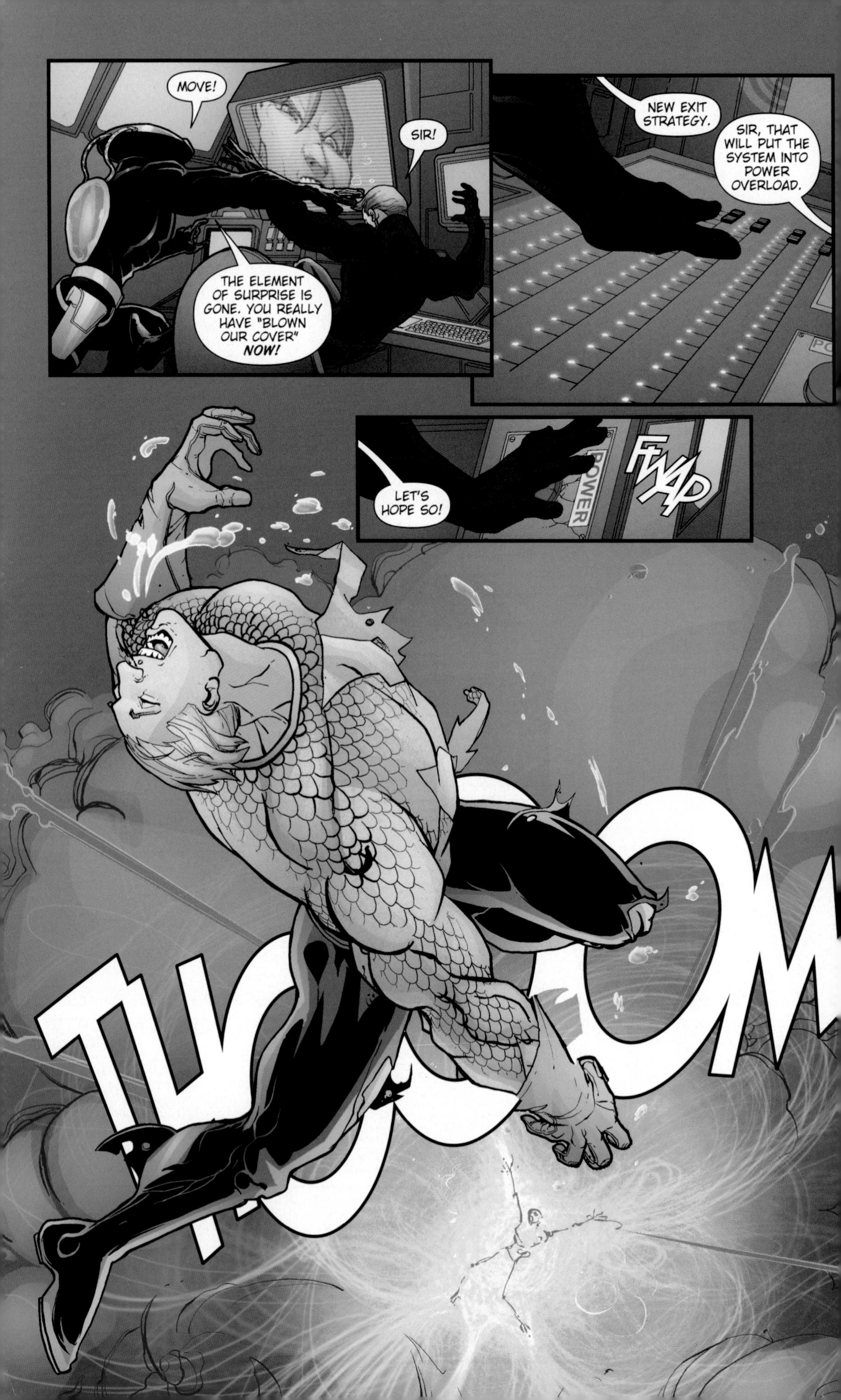
MOVE!
SIR!
THE ELEMENT OF SURPRISE IS GONE. YOU REALLY HAVE "BLOWN OUR COVER" NOW!
NEW EXIT STRATEGY.
SIR, THAT WILL PUT THE SYSTEM INTO POWER OVERLOAD.
POWER
LET'S HOPE SO!
FWAP

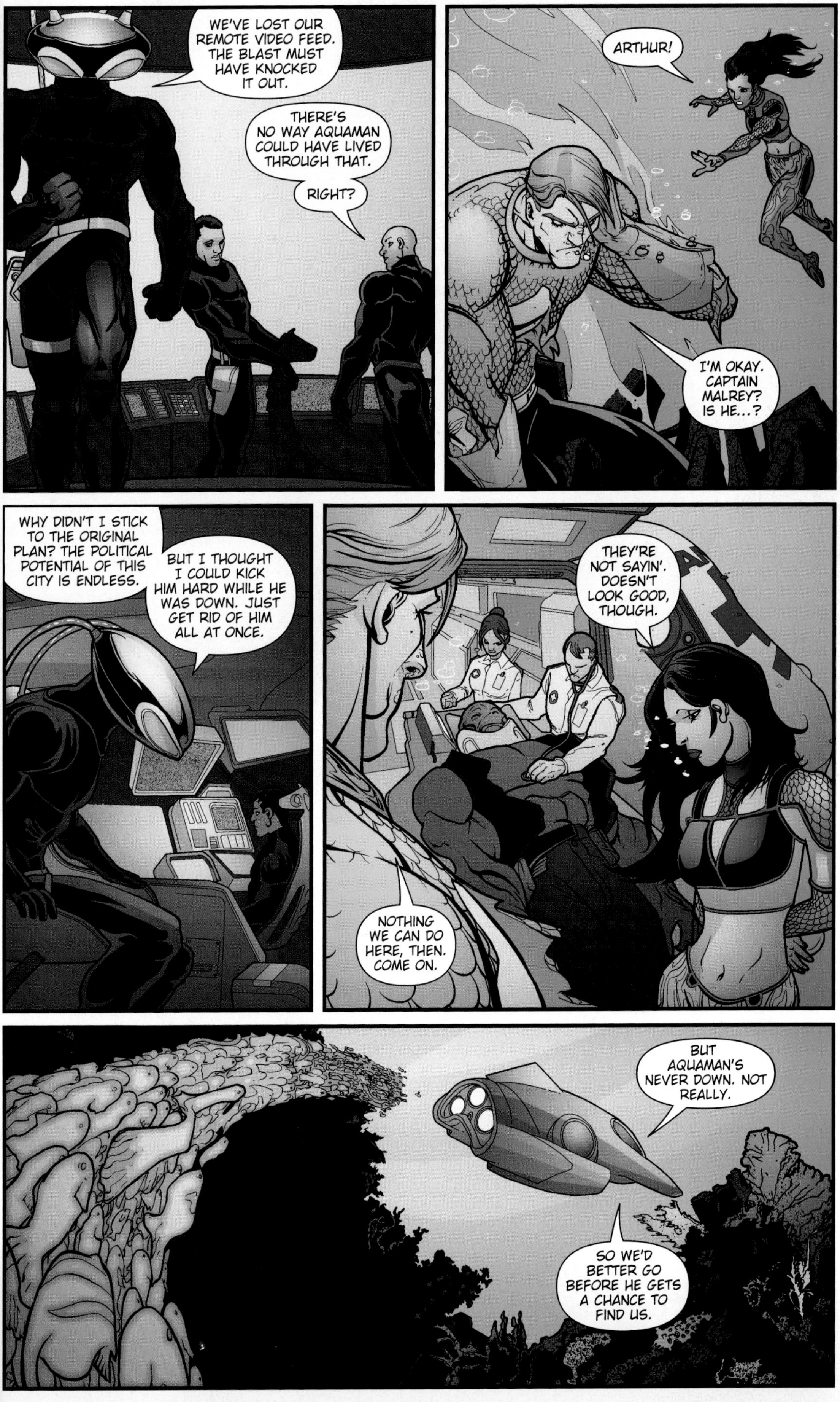
WE'VE LOST OUR REMOTE VIDEO FEED. THE BLAST MUST HAVE KNOCKED IT OUT.
THERE'S NO WAY AQUAMAN COULD HAVE LIVED THROUGH THAT.
RIGHT?
ARTHUR!
I'M OKAY. CAPTAIN MALREY? IS HE...?
WHY DIDN'T I STICK TO THE ORIGINAL PLAN? THE POLITICAL POTENTIAL OF THIS CITY IS ENDLESS.
BUT I THOUGHT I COULD KICK HIM HARD WHILE HE WAS DOWN. JUST GET RID OF HIM ALL AT ONCE.
THEY'RE NOT SAYIN'. DOESN'T LOOK GOOD, THOUGH.
NOTHING WE CAN DO HERE, THEN. COME ON.
BUT AQUAMAN'S NEVER DOWN. NOT REALLY.
SO WE'D BETTER GO BEFORE HE GETS A CHANCE TO FIND US.

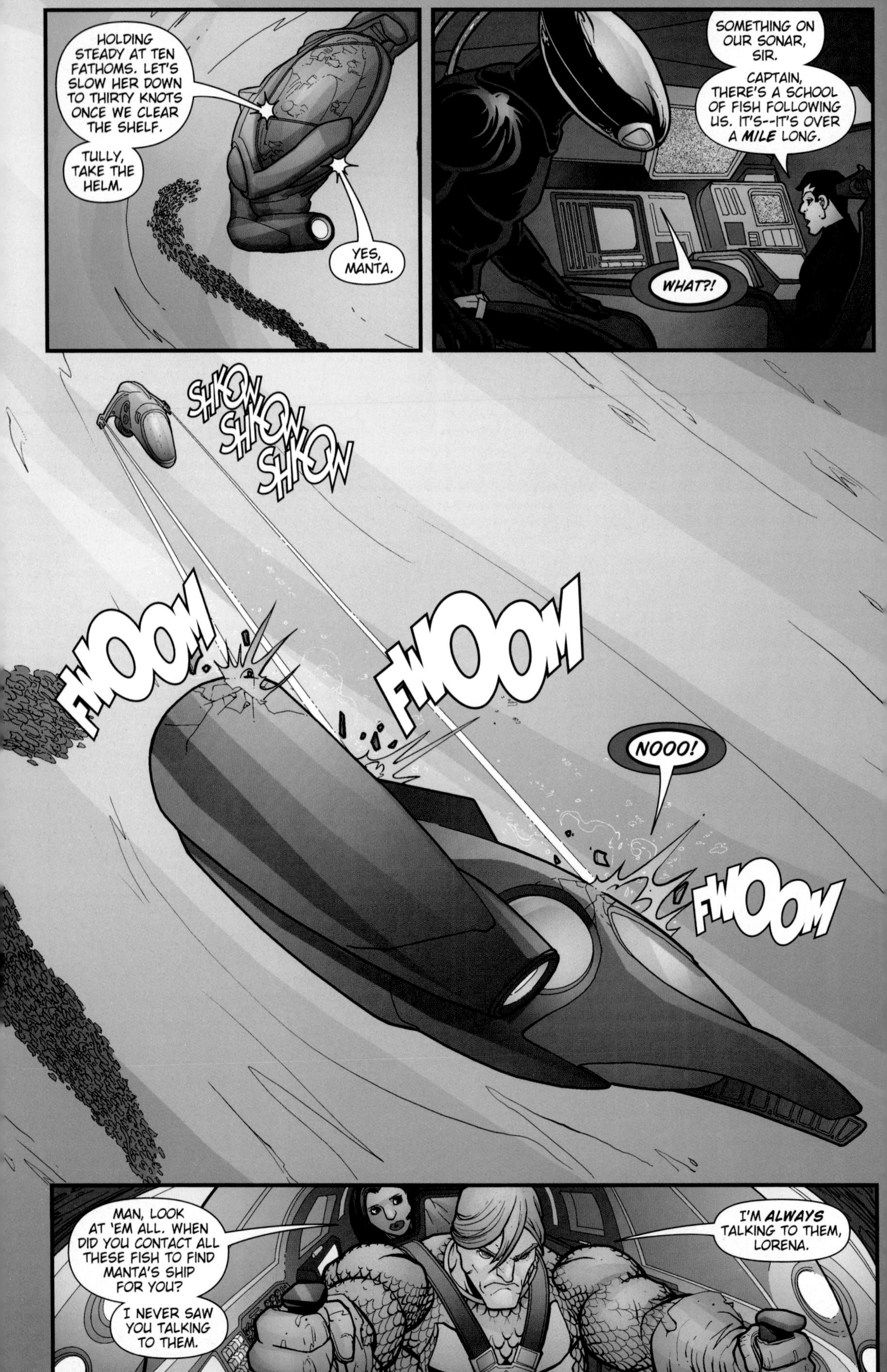
HOLDING STEADY AT TEN FATHOMS. LET'S SLOW HER DOWN TO THIRTY KNOTS ONCE WE CLEAR THE SHELF.
TULLY, TAKE THE HELM.
YES, MANTA.
SOMETHING ON OUR SONAR, SIR.
CAPTAIN, THERE'S A SCHOOL OF FISH FOLLOWING US. IT'S--IT'S OVER A MILE LONG.
WHAT?!
SHKOW SHKOW SHKOW
FWOOM
FWOOM
NOOO!
FWOOM
MAN, LOOK AT 'EM ALL. WHEN DID YOU CONTACT ALL THESE FISH TO FIND MANTA'S SHIP FOR YOU?
I NEVER SAW YOU TALKING TO THEM.
I'M ALWAYS TALKING TO THEM, LORENA.

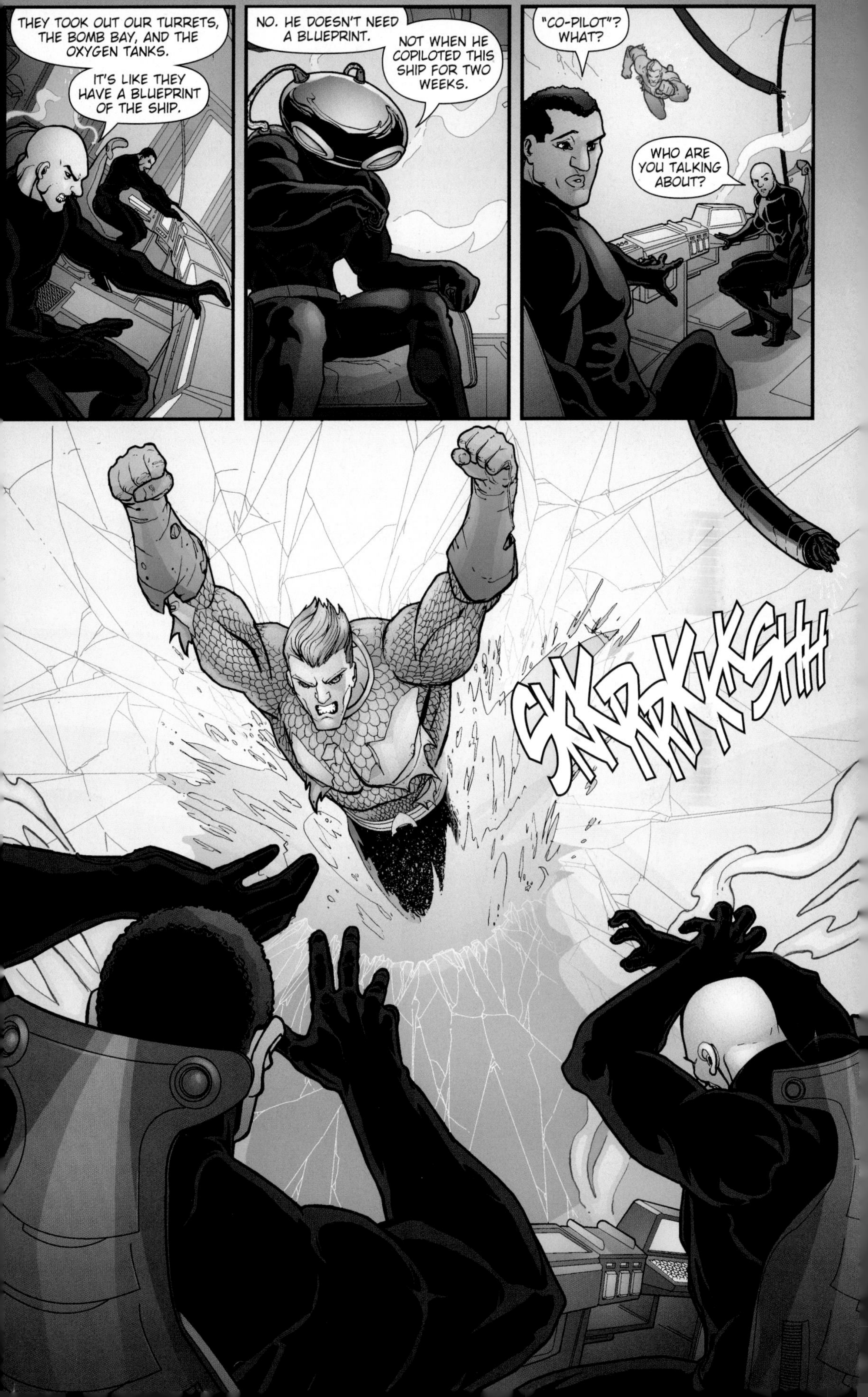
THEY TOOK OUT OUR TURRETS, THE BOMB BAY, AND THE OXYGEN TANKS.
IT'S LIKE THEY HAVE A BLUEPRINT OF THE SHIP.
NO. HE DOESN'T NEED A BLUEPRINT.
NOT WHEN HE COPILOTED THIS SHIP FOR TWO WEEKS.
"CO-PILOT"? WHAT?
WHO ARE YOU TALKING ABOUT?
SKKRRKKKSHH

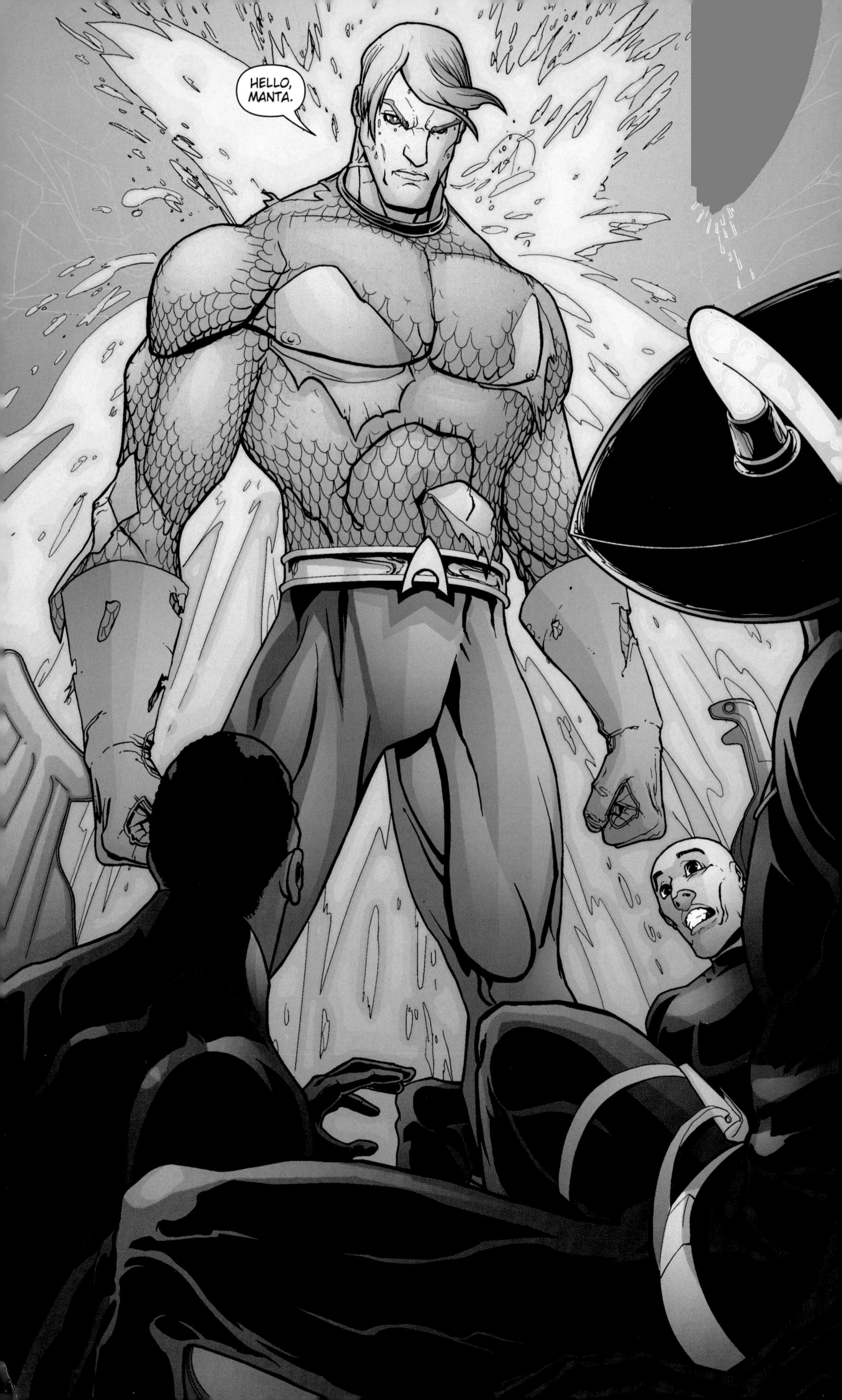
HELLO, MANTA.

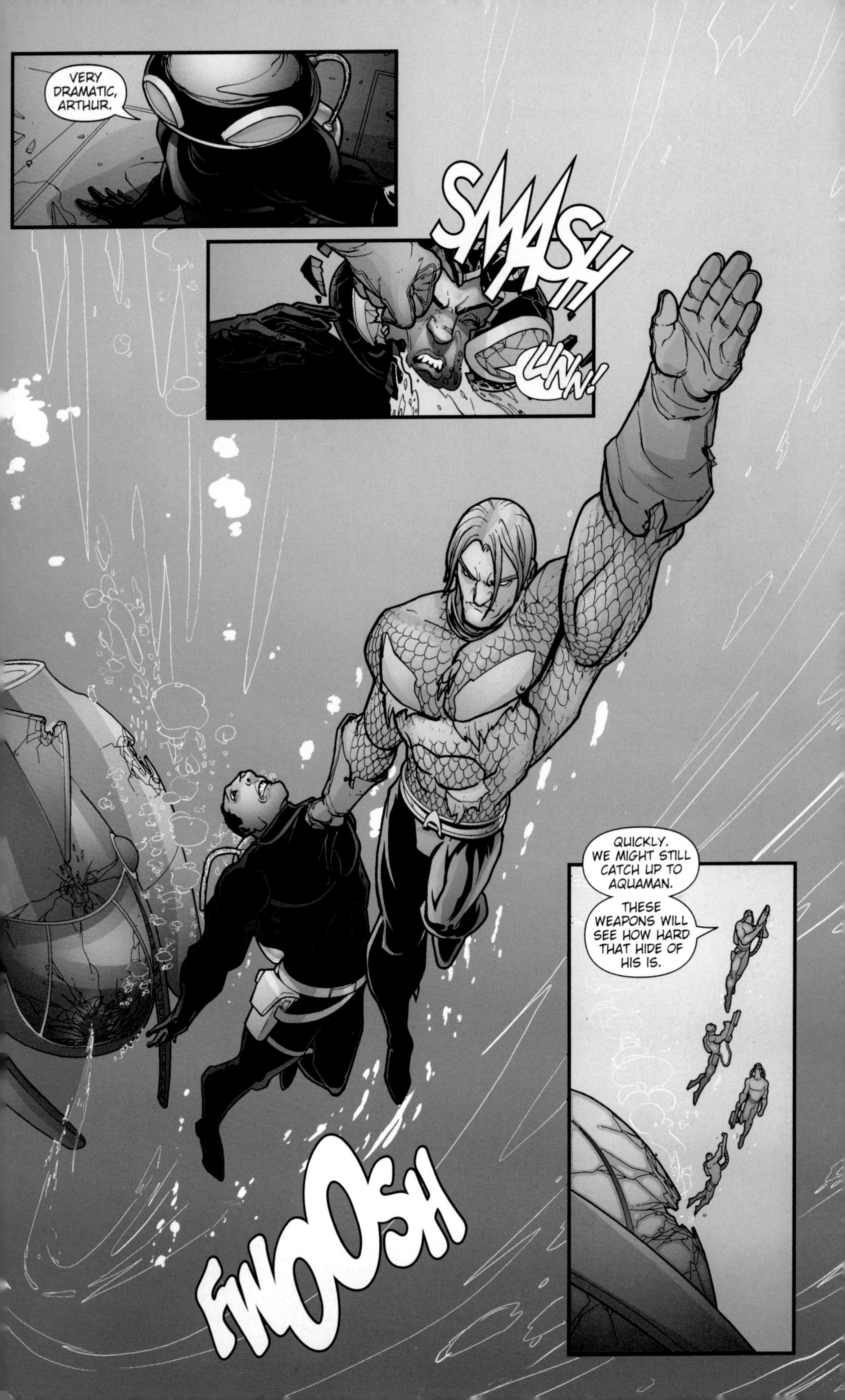
VERY DRAMATIC, ARTHUR.
SMASH
UNN!
FWOOSH
QUICKLY. WE MIGHT STILL CATCH UP TO AQUAMAN.
THESE WEAPONS WILL SEE HOW HARD THAT HIDE OF HIS IS.

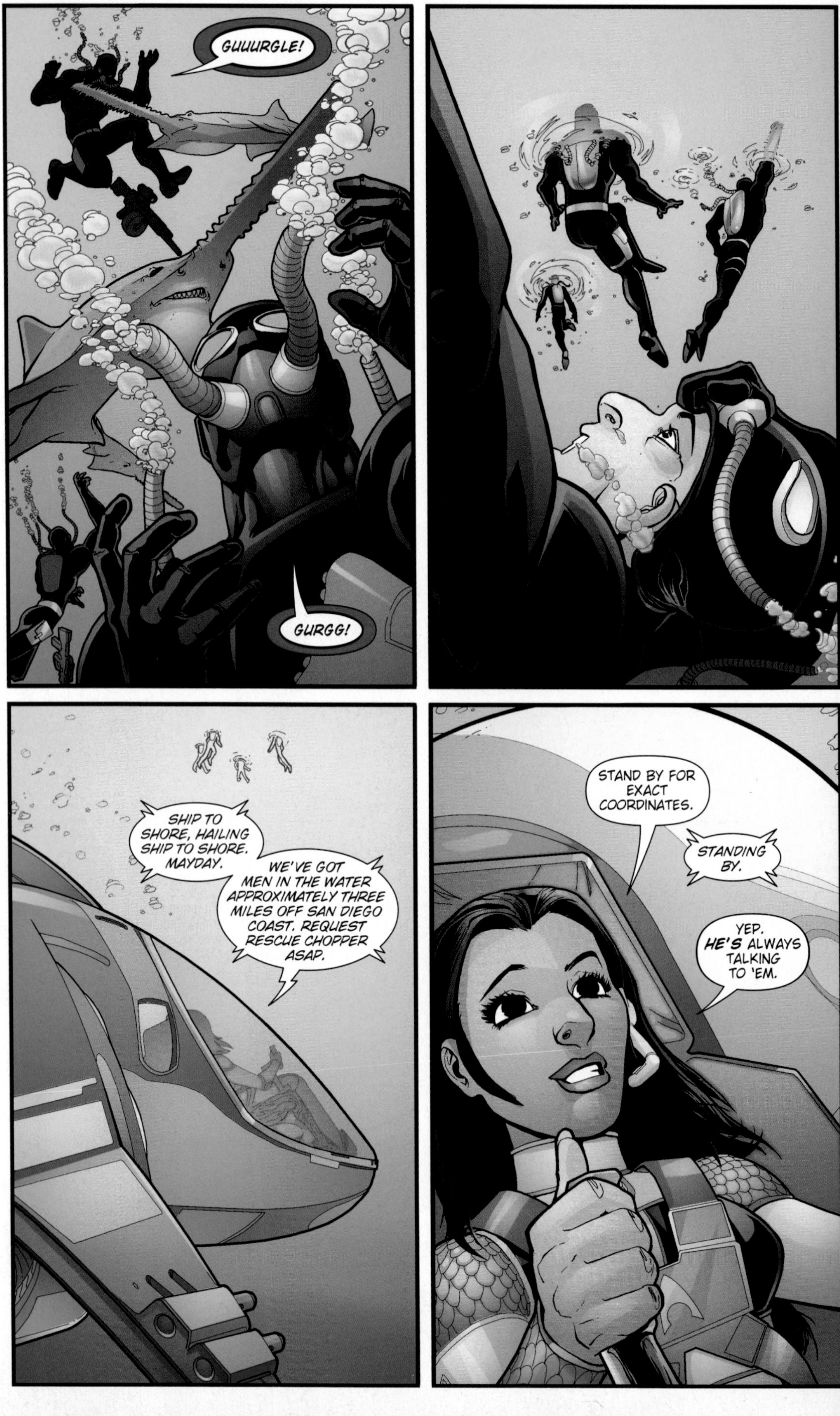
GUUURGLE!
GURGG!
SHIP TO SHORE, HAILING SHIP TO SHORE. MAYDAY.
WE'VE GOT MEN IN THE WATER APPROXIMATELY THREE MILES OFF SAN DIEGO COAST. REQUEST RESCUE CHOPPER ASAP.
STAND BY FOR EXACT COORDINATES.
STANDING BY.
YEP. **HE'S** ALWAYS TALKING TO 'EM.

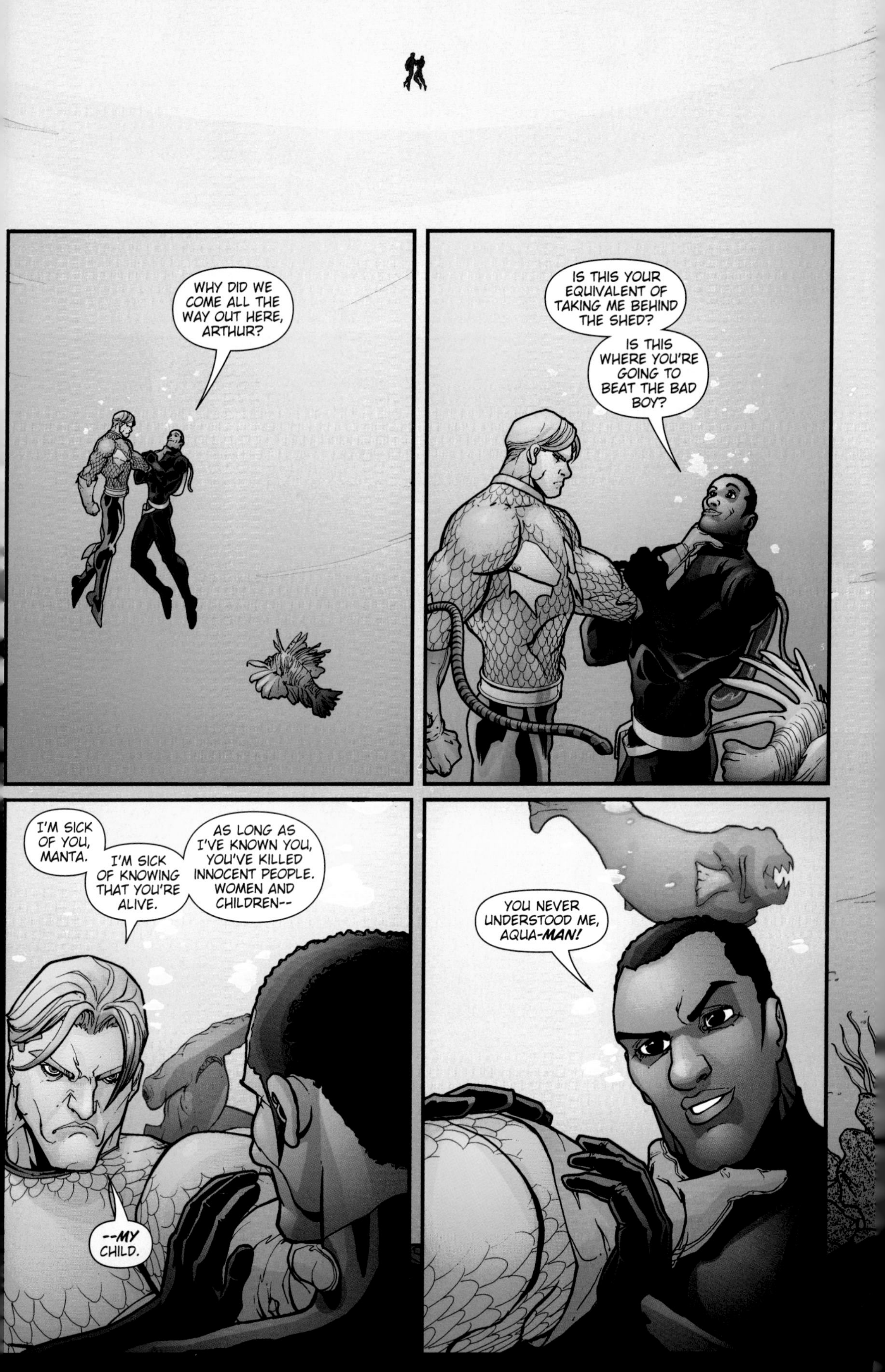

WHY DID WE COME ALL THE WAY OUT HERE, ARTHUR?
IS THIS YOUR EQUIVALENT OF TAKING ME BEHIND THE SHED?
IS THIS WHERE YOU'RE GOING TO BEAT THE BAD BOY?
I'M SICK OF YOU, MANTA.
I'M SICK OF KNOWING THAT YOU'RE ALIVE.
AS LONG AS I'VE KNOWN YOU, YOU'VE KILLED INNOCENT PEOPLE. WOMEN AND CHILDREN--
--*MY* CHILD.
YOU NEVER UNDERSTOOD ME, AQUA-*MAN!*

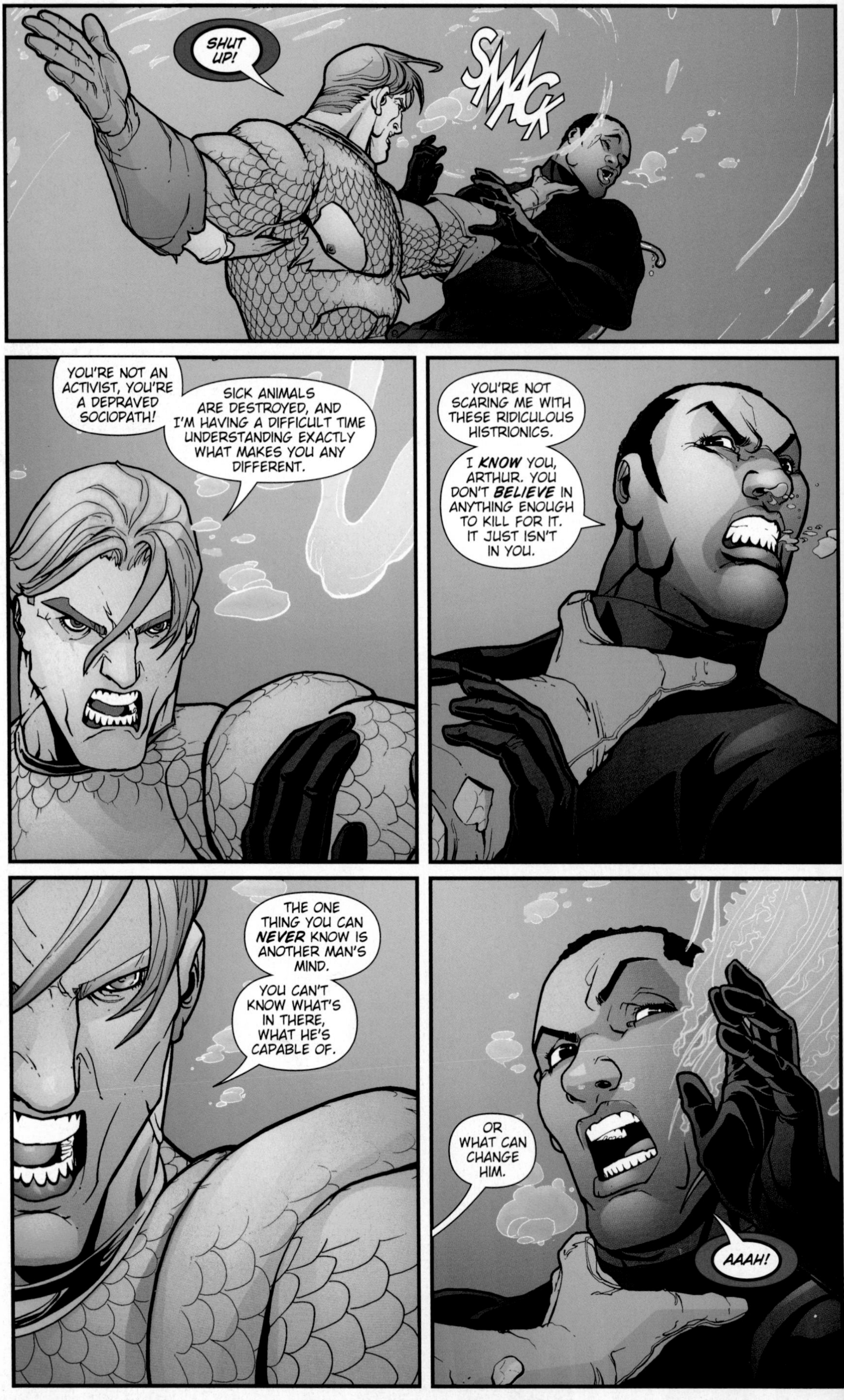
SHUT UP!
SMACK
YOU'RE NOT AN ACTIVIST, YOU'RE A DEPRAVED SOCIOPATH!
SICK ANIMALS ARE DESTROYED, AND I'M HAVING A DIFFICULT TIME UNDERSTANDING EXACTLY WHAT MAKES YOU ANY DIFFERENT.
YOU'RE NOT SCARING ME WITH THESE RIDICULOUS HISTRIONICS.
I KNOW YOU, ARTHUR. YOU DON'T BELIEVE IN ANYTHING ENOUGH TO KILL FOR IT. IT JUST ISN'T IN YOU.
THE ONE THING YOU CAN NEVER KNOW IS ANOTHER MAN'S MIND.
YOU CAN'T KNOW WHAT'S IN THERE, WHAT HE'S CAPABLE OF.
OR WHAT CAN CHANGE HIM.
AAAH!

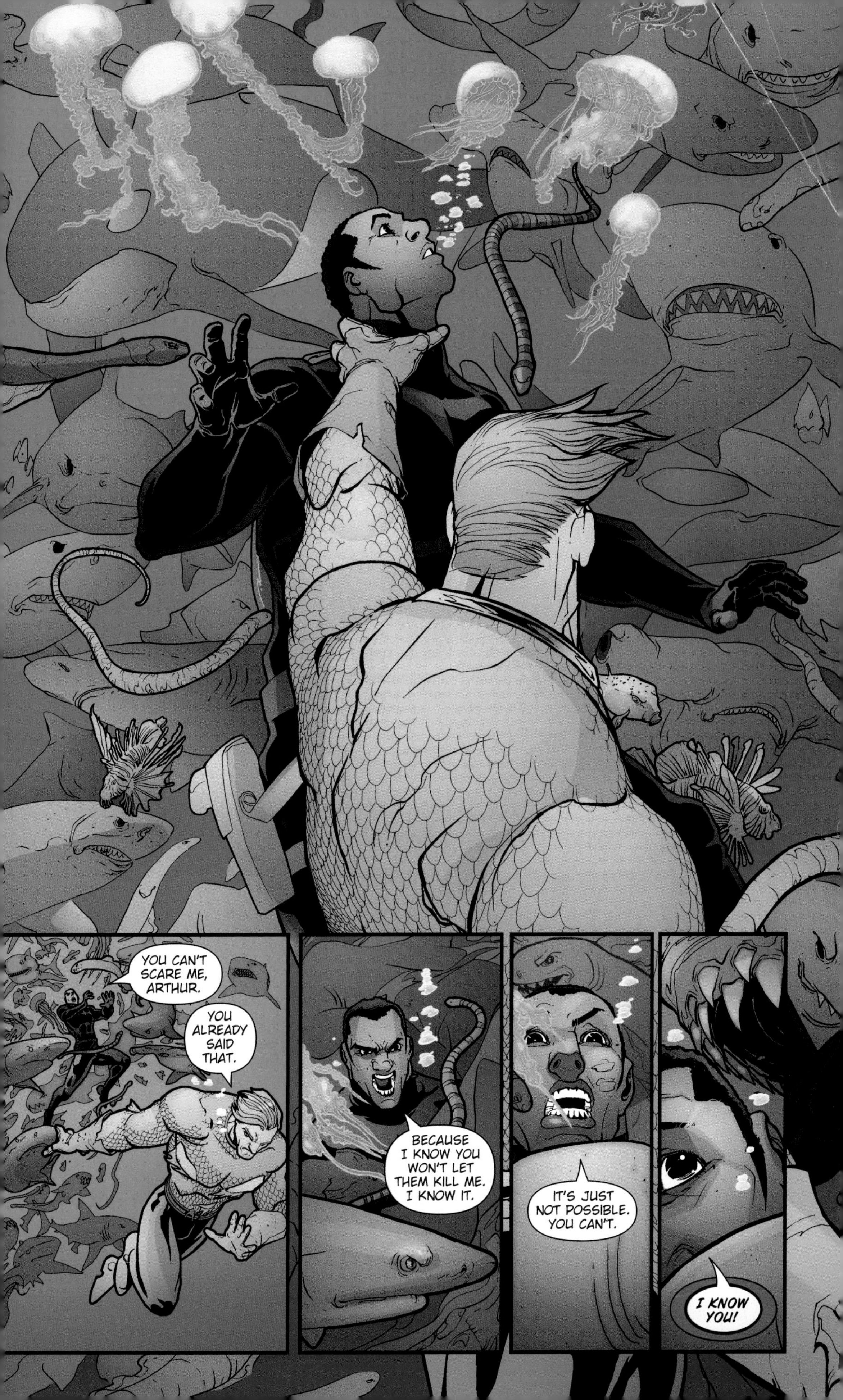

YOU CAN'T SCARE ME, ARTHUR.
YOU ALREADY SAID THAT.
BECAUSE I KNOW YOU WON'T LET THEM KILL ME. I KNOW IT.
IT'S JUST NOT POSSIBLE. YOU CAN'T.
I KNOW YOU!

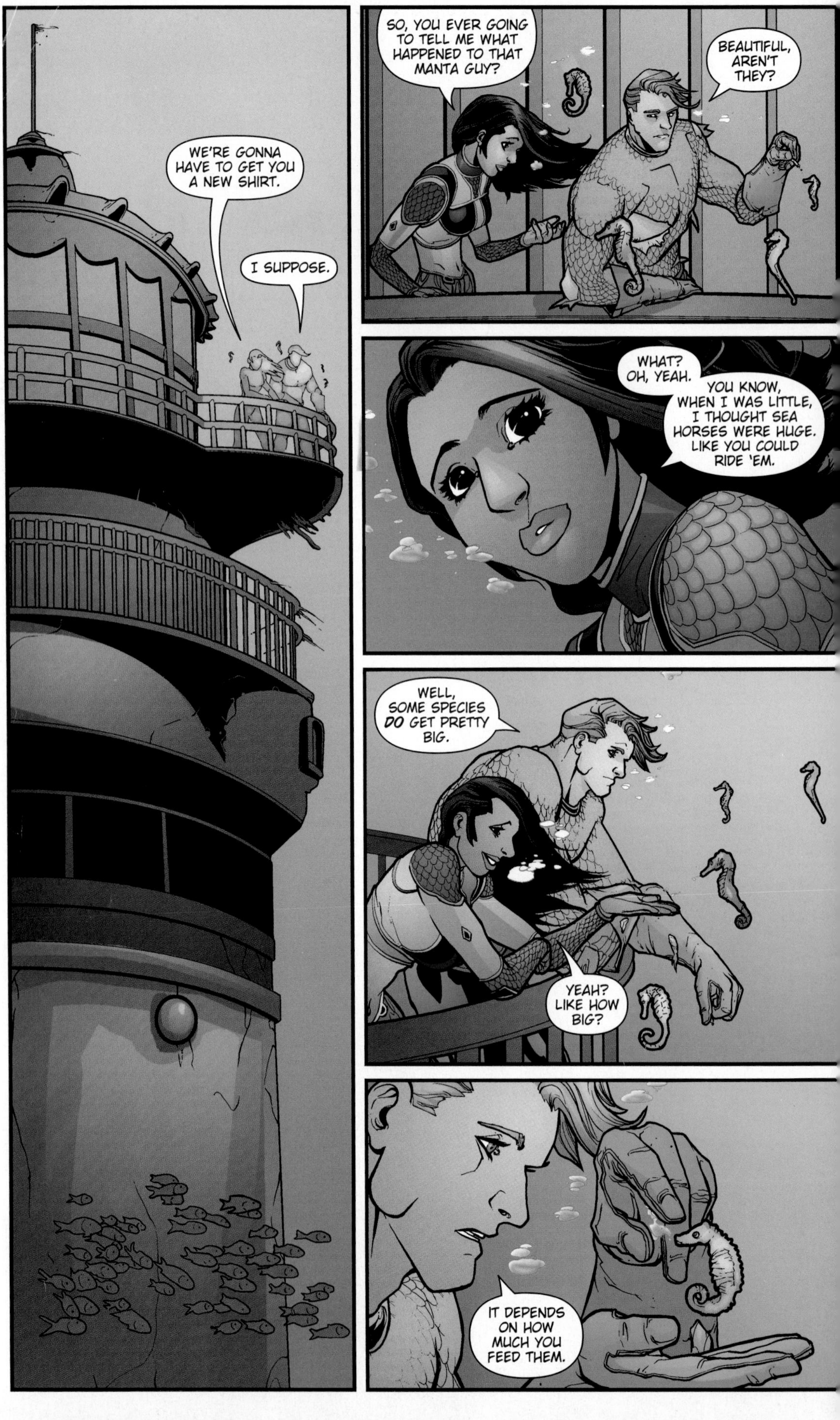
WE'RE GONNA HAVE TO GET YOU A NEW SHIRT.
I SUPPOSE.
SO, YOU EVER GOING TO TELL ME WHAT HAPPENED TO THAT MANTA GUY?
BEAUTIFUL, AREN'T THEY?
WHAT? OH, YEAH.
YOU KNOW, WHEN I WAS LITTLE, I THOUGHT SEA HORSES WERE HUGE. LIKE YOU COULD RIDE 'EM.
WELL, SOME SPECIES DO GET PRETTY BIG.
YEAH? LIKE HOW BIG?
IT DEPENDS ON HOW MUCH YOU FEED THEM.

AQUAMAN #33 *Cover Sketches by* **PATRICK GLEASON**

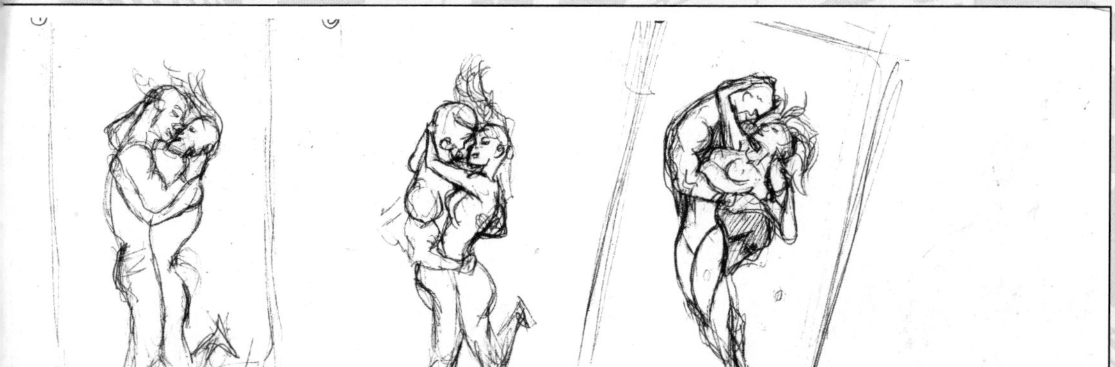

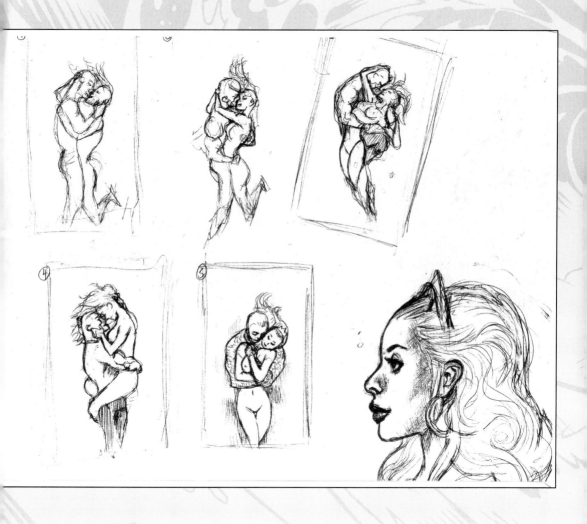

AQUAMAN #34 *Cover Pencils by* **PATRICK GLEASON**

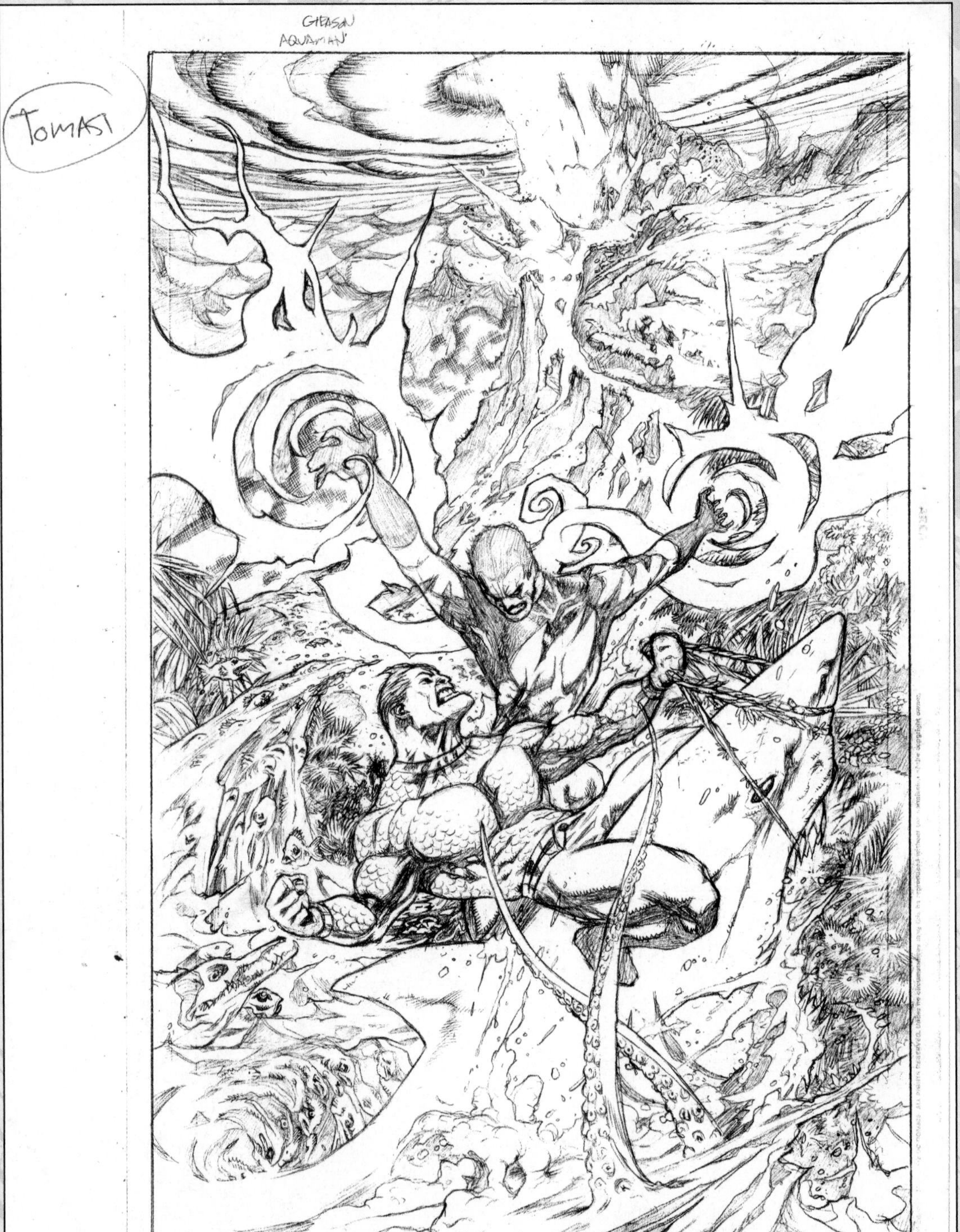
GLEASON
AQUAMAN
TOMASI